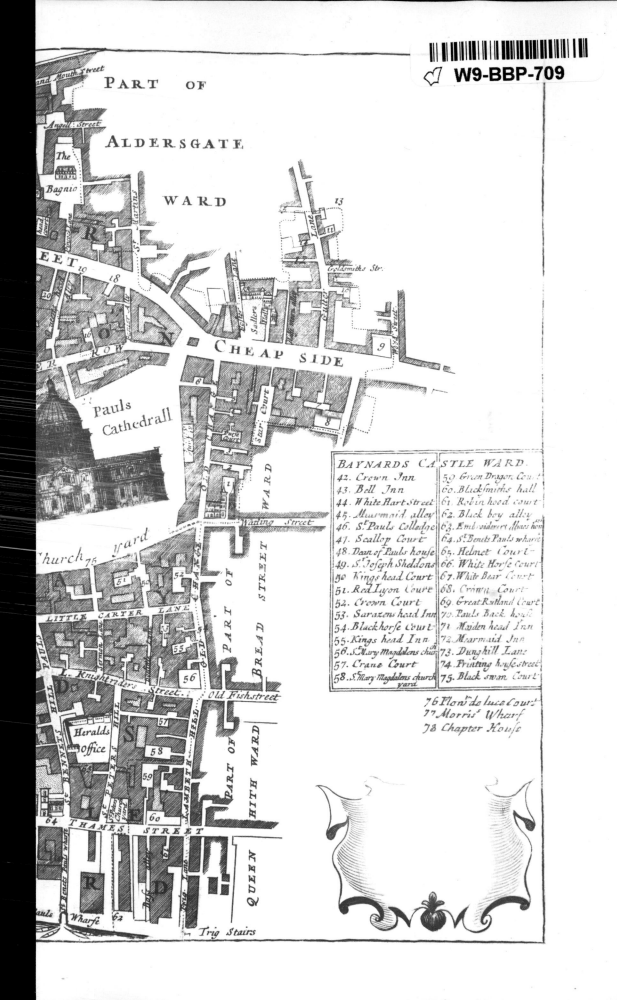

PART OF

ALDERSGATE

WARD

13

Goldsmiths Str.

9

CHEAP SIDE

Pauls
Cathedrall

Church yard

Watling Street

LITTLE CARTER LANE

L. Knightriders Street.

Old Fishstreet

Heralds
office

THAMES STREET

Trig Stairs

BAYNARDS CASTLE WARD.

42. Crown Inn	59. Green Dragon Court
43. Bell Inn	60. Blacksmiths hall
44. White Hart street	61. Robin hood court
45. Muxmaid alley	62. Black boy alley
46. St. Pauls Colledge	63. Embroiderers Almes hou
47. Scallop Court	64. St. Benets Pauls wharf
48. Dean of Pauls house	65. Helmet Court
49. St. Joseph Sheldons	66. White Horse court
50. Kings head Court	67. White Bear Court
51. Red Lyon Court	68. Crown Court
52. Crown Court	69. Great Rutland Court
53. Sarazens head Inn	70. Pauls Back house
54. Blackhorse court	71. Maiden head Inn
55. Kings head Inn	72. Mearmaid Inn
56. St. Mary Magdalens chu	73. Dunghill Lane
57. Crane Court	74. Printing house street
58. St. Mary Magdalens church yard	75. Black swan Court

76 Flour de luce Court
77 Morris Wharf
78 Chapter House

Essays in the history of publishing
in celebration of the 250th anniversary of
the House of Longman 1724–1974

Mark Longman 1916–72, *Chairman of the Longman Group* (1963–72), *by Graham Sutherland,* 1970 (*Longman Group Ltd*)

Essays
in the
history of
publishing

in celebration of
the 250th anniversary of
the House of Longman

1724–1974

Edited by Asa Briggs

Longman

Longman
1724-1974

LONGMAN GROUP LIMITED
London
*Associated companies, branches and
representatives throughout the world*

*Distributed in the United States
of America by Longman Inc. New York*

© Longman Group Limited 1974

ISBN 0 582 36521 X

Library of Congress Catalog Card Number: 74-80025

*Printed in Great Britain by
Spottiswoode, Ballantyne & Co. Ltd.,
London and Colchester*

Contents

Acknowledgements

For permission to reproduce copyright material we wish to thank: the author for the essay 'Mass media in the year 2000', by Leo Bogart from *Gazette*, Vol. 13, No. 3, 1967, pp. 221–35; the Beaconsfield Trustees for extracts from the Disraeli letters; Jonathan Cape Ltd for an extract from *Jonathan Cape: Publisher*, by Michael S. Howard; the Clarendon Press for extracts from *International Copyright Law and the Publisher in the Reign of Queen Victoria*, by Simon Nowell-Smith and an extract from 'Notes on the History of English Copyright', by Sir Frank Mackinnon from *The Oxford Companion to English Literature*, 4th ed.; Sir William Gladstone for an extract from a letter written to Blanchard Jerrold by Mr Gladstone in 1878; Longman Group Ltd for an extract from *Century of Growth in English Education*, by H. C. Dent; John Murray (Publishers) Ltd for extracts from *The Life of Benjamin Disraeli*, by W. F. Monypenny and G. E. Buckle; the National Trust for extracts from the Hughenden Papers; authors' agent, Mrs Sonia Brownell Orwell and Martin Secker & Warburg Ltd for an extract from an article by George Orwell from *New English Weekly*; Penguin Books Ltd for an extract from *Essays*, 1958, by Montaigne translated by J. M. Cohen, copyright © J. M. Cohen, 1958; The Times Ltd for an extract from the article 'Concerning six pennies', by Stanley Unwin from *The Times Literary Supplement*, 19.11.38 and an extract from the article 'Books for the People', by Margaret Cole from *The Times Literary Supplement*, 26.11.38; the proprietors of *The Bookseller* for extracts from articles from *The Bookseller*, and Yale University Press for extracts from Vol. IV of *The George Eliot Letters*, edited by G. Haight.

We are grateful to the following for permission to reproduce illustrations: the Beaconsfield Trustees; the Curators of the Bodleian Library; the John Johnson Collection and the John Carter Collection (Bodleian Library); the Trustees of the British Museum (including material from the Newspaper Library and the Department of Prints and Drawings); Cambridge University Press; the Cameron Machine Company Ltd; Constable & Co. (Publishers) Ltd; the Department of Education and Science; Edinburgh Public Libraries; Farnborough Hill School; the

Geographical Association; the Greater London Council Print Collection and Photographic Library; the Harvard Co-operative Society; the Museum of the History of Education, the University of Leeds; Lady Elizabeth Longman; the Library Association; the London Library; Mary Evans Picture Library; the National Portrait Gallery; the National Trust (Hughenden Manor); the Open University; Penguin Books Ltd; the Radio Times Hulton Picture Library; the Schools Council; the Scottish National Portrait Gallery; the Shakespeare Centre Library, Stratford-upon-Avon; the Victoria and Albert Museum. The illustrations on pp. 144 and 162 are from the Royal Library, Windsor and reproduced by permission of Her Majesty Queen Elizabeth II; those on pp. 33 and 50 are reproduced by kind permission of the Master and Wardens of the Worshipful Company of Stationers and Newspaper Makers. The map used on the end-paper at the beginning of this book is reproduced by permission of the City of London Guildhall Library.

We are grateful to the following people who have kindly lent us material for reproduction: Brian Alderson (pp. 249, 252, 264, 267, 274, 276, 281); R. M. Cooper (pp. 293, 370, 371, 374); Kurt Enoch (p. 307); W. Forster (p. 295); Gillian Rix (p. 402); Tanya Schmoller (pp. 286, 292, 294, 310).

We would particularly like to thank the staff of the National Trust, Hughenden Manor, the Museum of the History of Education (Leeds University), the Shakespeare Birthplace Trust, the University of Sussex Library, and the Victoria and Albert Museum, as well as Mark Cohen, James Mosley of the St. Bride's Printing Library, Michael Turner (curator of the John Johnson Collection), and P. C. B. Wallis, who have all given valuable assistance and advice.

ASA BRIGGS

Introduction:

AT THE SIGN OF THE SHIP

'I was glad to see the old ship again, &
trust it may be auspicious of a good voyage!'
Disraeli to Thomas Norton Longman V, 1880

WHEN Henry Curwen published his *History of Booksellers, the Old and the New* a hundred years ago, he wrote confidently that 'had we possessed all possible leisure for research, every available material, and a space thoroughly unlimited, it is most probable that the result would have been distinguished chiefly for its bulk, tediousness, and monotony'.[1] In fact, though his book ran to nearly five hundred pages and included many fascinating period-piece illustrations, he had carried out very little research and had had little access to the buried documentary material without which the history of publishing can easily become a branch of advertising.

A hundred years later the history of bookselling and publishing, for long directly related activities, remains neglected. With a few distinguished exceptions, 'such commentary as exists on the topic is off-hand and impressionistic'.[2] It seemed appropriate, therefore, that when Longman was contemplating a specially commissioned volume to celebrate two hundred and fifty years of continuous business history – a remarkable span of time which dwarfs jubilees and centenaries – that the essays in the volume should be concerned throughout with aspects of the history of publishing.

The essays include several which are not specifically concerned with the House of Longman: indeed, the very first on copyright is written by a distinguished publisher from a different business.* Yet such has been the scope and the scale of the Longman concern that it would be impossible to write the history of British publishing without bringing in successive generations of the Longman family and their partners – there are at least twenty-eight variations in the imprint since 1724† – at every crucial point in the story.

Though the names have changed, there has usually been continuity in the sign, the sign of the ship, which is even older than 1724. When the first Longman to become a publisher, Thomas (1699–1755) bought for himself a publisher's and bookseller's business in Paternoster Row in 1724, the sign that already hung over the shop was that of a ship in full sail. It had been in use since the reign of Charles I, prominent in a street, which as John Strype put it in 1720, was incomparable 'for handsome signs and uniformly hung'.[3]

* Ian Parsons, 'Copyright and society', pp. 29–60.
† The names are given on p. 28.

There is a magnificent device of a ship on the title-page of John Crook's folio edition of Usher's *Annals*, published in 1654, and it is to John Crook that the beginnings of the history of the business Longman bought in 1724 can be traced. In 1640 he set up a bookseller's and publisher's business in St Paul's Churchyard, at the sign of the ship. The Great Fire in 1666 forced Crook's evacuation to Duck Lane, but Benjamin Tooke, Crook's successor and old apprentice, took the business back to the Churchyard, finally selling it in 1687 to John Taylor who kept the ship as his device. It was John's son William Taylor whose premises, stock and goodwill Thomas Longman I acquired in 1724 after paying £2,282 9s 6d.

Since 1724 there have been many different devices and, later, colophons incorporating the ship: they have reflected changes in taste, however, more than in shipping technology, and the most recent are abstract in design. There have also been swan colophons, introduced long after the ship, but recalling distant days when the sign of the Black Swan hung from an adjacent shop in Paternoster Row also occupied by Taylor.

The ship was a fitting sign for a young, inexperienced but ambitious publisher who had arrived in London from Bristol at the age of seventeen – he had been left an orphan eight years earlier – to become apprenticed to a bookseller named John Osborn, who carried on a business in Lombard Street. It was fitting, too, that the voyage of Woodes Rogers, which inspired Daniel Defoe's *Robinson Crusoe*, a best seller published by William Taylor in 1719, had started from Bristol.4* The Longmans had been soapmakers in Bristol for several generations before Thomas turned eastwards to London when the local soap trade was in decline.5 By contrast the London book trade was a trade of the future. The growth of trade and commerce, the increasing specialisation and adaptability of the financial system and the improvement of printing styles and techniques were changing the economics of the business, and there was justifiable expectation during the 1720s of expanding markets and rising profits. The price of books remained high – more than most sections of the community could afford – but book clubs and circulating libraries were soon to be brought into existence to serve the needs of a small, but increasingly active and self-conscious reading public.

* The name of Longman did not appear on *Robinson Crusoe* until the tenth edition of 1753.

Some of the various devices and colophons used by Longmans, mostly in the nineteenth century.

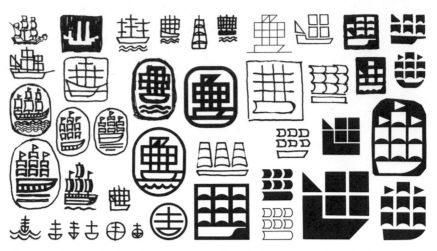

Some of the roughs for the present colophon designed in 1967. *As the company became more international in character it was felt that this aspect of its growth should be reflected in the new design.*

Defoe understood the relevant economic and social processes at a very early stage in their history, just as clearly, indeed, as he understood the mind of Crusoe. There was ample scope for 'a spirit of merchanthood'[6] in publishing, although fifty years after Defoe Dr. Johnson was exaggerating when he observed that 'general literature now pervades the nation through all its ranks.' So, too, at the end of the eighteenth century was James Lackington, shoemaker turned bookseller, who wrote proudly that 'in short all ranks and degrees now READ'.[7] This kind of flourish of exaggeration is familiar to students of the literature of all new 'media' in any age : indeed it is referred to in its current context in one of the last essays in this book.*

    We know very little about the detailed economic calculations which Thomas Longman made during the critical years between 1724 and 1750, although we know a considerable amount about the general terms of the book trade – copyright protection after 1709,[8] raising as many difficult issues for the historian of the publishing industry as the patent system does for the historian of the evolution of eighteenth-century industry; publication not for a completely anonymous market but following the issue of personal subscription lists; risk-sharing by groups of publisher-partners, dealing cooperatively in halves, tenths, twelfths, twenty-fourths or even sixty-fourths of an 'undertaking';[9] publi-

* Tim Rix and Susan Holmes, 'Beyond the book', pp. 319–356.

cation directly linked to general bookselling, sometimes including (as in the case of Longman) the sale of old as well as of new books. Nineteenth-century writing about Thomas I scarcely assists a systematic analysis of the fundamental economics of his business: it has an essentially Smilesian quality about it.*

Between 1725 and 1734 Thomas was in partnership with John Osborn, to whom he had been apprenticed, and in the best manner of a Hogarthian 'industrious apprentice' – he was two years younger than Hogarth – he was for long said to have married his master's daughter who was eight years older than himself. It now seems clear that this is a myth and that his wife was Osborn's sister. One thing not in doubt was Osborn's industry. His choice of book titles reflected his belief in 'the useful and the sure': he left poetry, it has been said, to the Tonsons and the Lintots'[10]† – and Thomas I followed in his footsteps. He took a keen personal interest, for instance, in Ephraim Chambers's improving encyclopaedia which went through five editions between the 1720s and the 1740s. He was a partner also in the first publication of Samuel Johnson's Dictionary and in his prospectus for an edition of Shakespeare in 1756‡ and in new editions of John Locke and, very properly, Isaac Watts. Yet he was never one of Watts's 'timorous mortals' who 'start and shrink to cross the narrow sea'. He fittingly inherited Osborn's *Psalms, Hymns and Spiritual Songs of the Old and New Testament for the edification and comfort of the Saints in Public and Private, more especially in New England.*[11]

One of the few surviving stories about Thomas I concerns that limited branch of publishing history which has always commanded most interest among historians and literary critics – relations between publisher and author. Longman is said to have increased Chambers's remuneration and to have treated him in old age with 'the liberality of a prince and the tenderness of a father':

his house was ever open to receive him, and when he was there nothing could exceed his care and anxiety over him; even his natural absence of mind

* This may be unfair to Smiles, who wrote an excellent study of a nineteenth-century publisher, John Murray – *A Publisher and his Friends* (1891). In his book Henry Curwen depicted Murray reading a newspaper.
† On the very day Thomas I's indentures with Osborn were signed Lintot was advertising in the *Daily Courant* the second edition of Gay's *Trivia*, the fourth edition of Pope's *Rape of the Lock* and the fifth edition of his *Essay on Criticism*.
‡ See David Daiches, 'Presenting Shakespeare', pp. 80–82, 87.

was consulted, and during his illness jellies and other proper refreshments were industriously left for him at those places where it was least likely he should avoid seeing them.[12]

Thomas I may be said to have founded a dynasty – that was certainly how the Victorians looked on him – but he had no children. The family business passed to his nephew Thomas II (1730–97), who had joined him as a partner two years before his death. There was something of a change of horizons after 1756, though less of direction. Thomas II had twelve children and he was married to the sister of one of the patentees of Covent Garden Theatre. Not surprisingly, perhaps, he figured as a joint shareholder in such diverse publishing ventures as the *Arabian Nights*, *Gil Blas* and *Humphry Clinker*: he was also a keen supporter in 1788 of the launching of the 'new periodical' *The Times*.[13] Yet as the share system of publishing began to decline, it is significant that Thomas II's sole publications, like those of his uncle, showed a proper concentration on dictionaries, histories, and Latin and law books. One essay in this volume deals with the place of Latin in the culture of the period.* Less notable in business terms than the multiplication of Longman's titles – as evidenced in his catalogues – was the further development both of provincial and overseas business. The ship was certainly in full sail, as cargoes of books were delivered to America before and after the Declaration of Independence. In all this there was an anticipation of the future pattern of Longman trade.†[14]

Between the death of Thomas II in 1797‡ and the mid-Victorian scene described by Curwen, there was expansion of a different kind which, once again, anticipated the future. Non-Longmans were brought into the business, the first of them, indeed, before Thomas II died. Thomas Norton Longman (1771–1842), usually known as Thomas III, drew in Owen Rees, probably in 1794 – he had been trained as a bookseller in Bristol, and was to serve the firm for forty years – and Rees was followed by Thomas Hurst, Cosmo Orme (the first President of the Booksellers' Provident Institution), Thomas Brown (originally an apprentice), Bevis Green (the first of the Greens in the House, who started as an apprentice to Hurst) and Thomas Roberts (who joined the House in 1826 but waited for thirty years before he

* Robert Ogilvie, 'Latin for yesterday', pp. 219–244.
† See below, pp. 381–388.
‡ He left instructions that there should be no 'pompous' and extravagant funeral.

became a partner). Paternoster Row was now the headquarters of an organisation, and it was doubtless of as much symbolic importance in the history of the firm when the Longmans left the City to live in Hampstead at the end of the eighteenth century as it was later in the nineteenth century when they moved out of London altogether. Sir Walter Scott could write soon afterwards of

> Longman, Brown, Rees, Orme and Co.,
> Our worthy fathers of the Row,[15]

and there was a time when the number of names on the Longman title-pages reached six.

Thomas III was a well-known figure in the literary world, and his Saturday 'Weekly Literary Meetings' were usually well attended. Wordsworth, Coleridge and Southey were all Longman authors. The favourite author, however, was Thomas Moore, who received the then enormous sum of £3,000 for his *Lalla Rookh* in 1814. 'What Scott was to Constable, and Byron to Murray, such was Moore to Longman.'[16] The comparison was not very flattering: indeed, Longman turned down Byron,* but was proud to be given an antique gold ring (if not manuscript) by Scott. The real successes of the firm lay elsewhere. Thomas III took over the *Edinburgh Review* — a story told in one of the essays in this volume† — and was married to a first cousin of Sydney Smith. Bulwer Lytton complained in 1833 that since 'literary works, in the magnificent thought of Bacon, are the Ships of Time', too much precious cargo was being wasted on 'vessels which sunk for ever in a three months voyage'. 'What might Jeffrey and Sydney Smith, in the vigour of their age, have produced as authors, if they had been less industrious as reviewers?'[17] Yet for Thomas III books and reviews were always complementary not competitive. And he liked some of the same kind of staple books as Thomas II. He acquired a major educational best-seller, for example, in Lindley Murray's *English Grammar* in 1799 and a lucrative up-to-date revision of Chambers's *Cyclopaedia* managed by Abraham Rees after whom it was named:

* The criticism of Byron's *Hours of Idleness* in the *Edinburgh Review* goaded him into writing *English Bards and Scotch Reviewers*. He offered it to Longman for publication, but since it attacked several Longman authors it was turned down. Byron retaliated by refusing to offer his *Childe Harold* to Longman. It was published by Murray.
† John Clive, 'The *Edinburgh Review*: the life and death of a periodical', pp. 113–140.

it outshone the *Encyclopaedia Britannica* of its day. Thomas III
decided in 1840 to get rid of the second-hand book trade which
had been a lively branch of the business twenty years before,
when he was advertising 'an unprecedented Collection of the
Rarities and Curiosities of Literature',[18]* but he still thought
of himself as bookseller as well as publisher. Indeed, his first
acquaintance with Wordsworth followed his purchase of Joseph
Cottle's business in Bristol. In 1798 Cottle had published
Lyrical Ballads, but the sale of the book had been so slow that the
copyright was written down by the purchasers as nil. Cottle had
it restored to him and presented it to Wordsworth.

During the 1830s, when yet again the book trade was changing
significantly, Thomas III brought two of his own sons into the
partnership – Thomas IV (1804–79) in 1832 and William
(1813–77) in 1839. These two brothers became the principal
controllers of the firm and guided it through to its mid-Victorian
prosperity. The word 'gigantic' was often used to describe it – by
Curwen, for example – and certainly the number of Longman
publications outstripped those of all competitors in the mid-
Victorian years. In 1851, for example, the year of the Great
Exhibition, Longman produced 216 works as against Murray's
71 and Rivington's 96. (Rivington's firm with its ecclesiastical
and theological preoccupations was to be swallowed up by
Longmans in 1890)†. Among publishing competitors who did
not belong to the Booksellers' Association, over which William
Longman then presided, Chapman produced 61 titles, Bentley
114 and Knight 17.[19] Longman fortunes were almost as impressive as the Longman catalogues. Thomas III had left nearly
£200,000, and when Thomas Brown, the ex-apprentice, died in
1869 after a ten-year retirement he was able to leave more than
£100,000 in legacies and to spread *largesse* among bodies like the
Booksellers' Provident Retreat and Institution, the Royal Literary Fund and the Stationers' Company. Bevis Green, who died
around the same time, left nearly £200,000.

It is no more easy to analyse the relevant nineteenth-century
economics of bookselling and publishing than it is to reconstruct the economic equations of Thomas I. Yet several points

---

* When Keats wished to buy a copy of Chapman's *Homer* to replace Haydon's copy
which he had lost, he wrote 'I must get one at Longmans'.
† Rivingtons also brought the *Annual Register* (first published in 1761) to Longmans.
Another business, that of J. W. Parker, had been acquired in 1862.

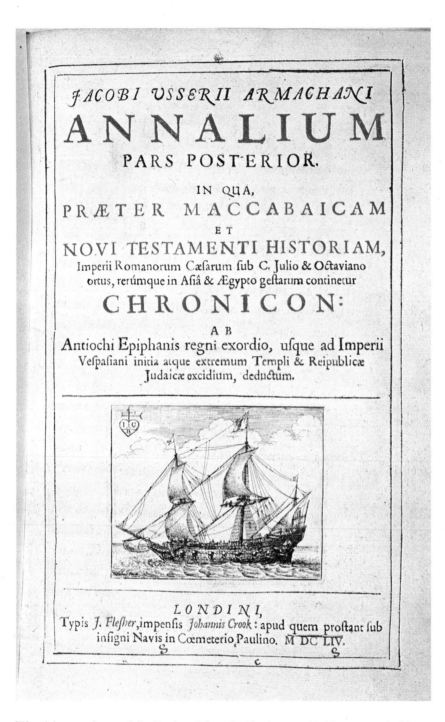

JACOBI USSERII ARMACHANI
ANNALIUM
PARS POSTERIOR.

IN QUA,

PRÆTER MACCABAICAM
ET
NOVI TESTAMENTI HISTORIAM,

Imperii Romanorum Cæfarum fub C. Julio & Octaviano
ortus, rerúmque in Afiâ & Ægypto geftarum continetur

CHRONICON:

A B

Antiochi Epiphanis regni exordio, ufque ad Imperii
Vefpafiani initia atque extremum Templi & Reipublicæ
Judaicæ excidium, deductum.

LONDINI,
Typis *J. Flefher,* impenfis *Johannis Crook* : apud quem proftant fub
infigni Navis in Cœmeterio Paulino. M DC LIV.

The title page from a folio Latin edition of Usher's Annals. (Longman Archives)

Thomas Norton Longman III (1771–1842) *by Thomas Phillips* [c. 1830].
(*Lady Elizabeth Longman*)
Opposite; above: William Longman (1813–77) *by Anthony Salomé* [c. 1848].
(*Longman Group Ltd*)
Below: Thomas Longman IV (1804–79) *by William Reader,* 1879. (*Lady
Elizabeth Longman*)

Thomas Longman IV and his family at Farnborough Hill, 1855. (Lady Elizabeth Longman)

are clear. First, the price of books was falling during the period as compared with prices in the late-eighteenth century and the early decades of the nineteenth. In 1852, when the question of 'free trade in books' suddenly hit the headlines, William Longman reminded his critics – who were many – that before 1825 most books of biography, history, travel and poetry were printed only in quarto editions, whereas by the 1850s these had been replaced by cheaper octavo volumes. Half the works published in 1852 were selling for less than ten shillings.[20] Second, Longmans were not in the vanguard of the cheap publishing movement, although in the wake of Constable's *Miscellany* they had produced their first cheap series in 1828. (They were spending nearly £5,000 on newspaper advertising ten years before that.)[21] It is evident from another essay in this book* that although Longmans were interested in educational books, for use either in the home or in school, and published many children's books during the first half of the nineteenth century, they did not seek to compete in the 'popular' cheap field of children's literature where the SPCK and Cassells held sway. Nor did they exploit the new techniques of book binding and colour printing to capture this growing market for cheap literature.

* Brian Alderson, 'Tracts, rewards and fairies: the Victorian contribution to children's literature', pp. 245–282.

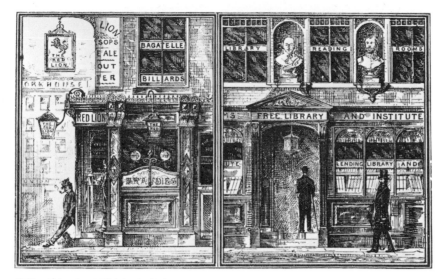

'*The Rivals: Which shall it be?*' *The frontispiece from Thomas Greenwood's* Free Public Libraries, *1886.* (*London Library*)

William Longman believed that the public had no inherent 'right' to cheap books, and that good financial relations with authors might well make cheap production difficult. When Anthony Trollope, a Royal Commissioner on Copyright in 1876–77, asked him whether, for example, he considered that the public was entitled to extremely cheap editions of Macaulay, one of Longman's most impressive and successful authors, he replied no.[22] Macaulay, indeed, found publishing with Longmans a highly lucrative affair, and the famous cheque for £20,000 (reproduced below) covered a payment to him in 1856 on account

The cheque for £20,000 paid to Macaulay by Longman IV. (*Longman Archives*)

of the profits of the third and fourth volumes of his *History*. Volume III sold fifty-six tons in weight on the first day after publication.[23] In 1852, before this third volume appeared, John Murray had told Gladstone that 'if Mr Macaulay's *History* cost 32s – it is because the author had derived from his two volumes at least £12,000.'[24]

William and Thomas's attitudes were consistent. Indeed, they had to be persuaded by John Stuart Mill to issue a cheap People's Edition of his *Works* on condition that Mill forewent a half share of his profits.[25] They may have noted that even Charles Knight's passion for cheaper and cheaper books had dwindled the older he became. 'The general cheapening of books must be gradual to be safe,' he wrote in 1854. 'The soundings of the perilous sea of publishing must be constantly taken. There is no chart for this navigation which exhibits all the sunken rocks and quicksands.'[26] We are back again with the metaphors of ships and voyages.

Longmans' General List for August 1875 ran to 16 pages and listed books under the following 43 categories:

English Reading-Lesson Books
Writing Books
School Poetry Books
English Spelling-Books
Grammar and the English Language
Paraphrasing, Parsing and Analysis
Dictionaries, with Manuals of Etymology
Elocution
Gleig's School Series
Arithmetic
Book-keeping
Mensuration
Algebra
Geometry and Trigonometry
Land Surveying, Drawing and Practical
    Mathematics
Works by John Hullah, Professor of
    Vocal Music in King's College, in
    Queen's College and in Bedford College,
    London
Political and Historical Geography
Physical and Mathematical Geography
School Atlases and Maps
Natural History and Botany
Chemistry and Telegraphy
Natural Philosophy and Natural Science
Textbooks of Science, Mechanical and
    Physical, adopted for the use of
    Artisans, and of Students in Public and
    Science Schools

Mechanics and Mechanism
Engineering, Architecture etc.
Popular Astronomy and Navigation
Animal Physiology and the Preservation
    of Health
Domestic Economy and General Know-
    ledge
Chronology and Historical Genealogy
Mythology and Antiquities
Biography
British History
History, Ancient and Modern
Scripture, History Moral and Religious
    Works
Mental and Moral Philosophy and Civil
    Law
Principles of Teaching etc.
The Greek Language
White's Grammar – School Greek Texts,
    with Vocabularies
White's Grammar – School Latin Texts,
    with Vocabularies
The Latin Language
The French Language
German, Spanish, Hebrew, Hindustani
    and Sanskrit
Knowledge for the Young

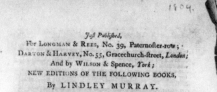

Longmans' advertisements for 1804 and January 1870. (John Johnson Collection)

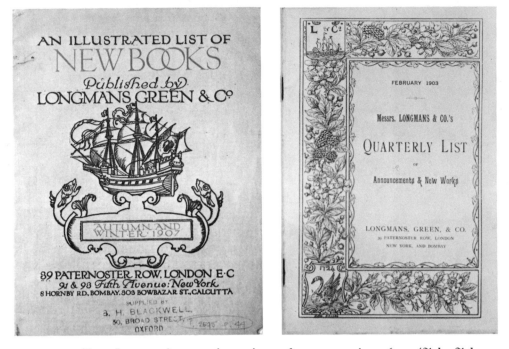

Two Longmans' quarterly catalogues for 1903 *and* 1906–7. (*John Johnson Collection*)

William Longman wrote books as well as published them – one title was *A History of the Life and Times of Edward III* – and Curwen quoted in his chapter on the House of Longman William's comment,

I trust authors will forgive me and not revenge themselves by turning publishers. There is, nevertheless, some advantage in a publisher dabbling in literature, for it shows him the difficulties with which an author has to contend – the labour which is indispensable to produce a work which may be relied upon – and it increases the sympathy which should, and in these days, does exist between author and publisher[27].

He and Thomas enjoyed (even cosseted) their authors while simply noting what was happening to their readers – a further widening of the market; a greater demand for educational books, including the old favourites; the rise and ultimately the decline of Mudie's;* a further growth of free libraries. Not all their successes

* For Mudie's Library and its influence, see below pp. 91, 166–169. Charles Edward Mudie took 2,400 copies of the third and fourth volumes of Macaulay's *History* and had to set aside a special room for handling them.

The wedding at Farnborough Hill on 22 September 1869 of Alice, daughter of Thomas Longman IV, who built the house. (Farnborough Hill School)

are as well remembered as Macaulay's *History of England*. Who now, for example, reads Lady Brassey's *A Voyage in the 'Sunbeam'*, a best-seller of 1877, which was translated into nearly every European language and relatively quickly issued in a cheap sixpenny edition? Even Herbert Spencer's *Principles of Psychology* is now forgotten. Yet there were many remarkable books which have survived – Buckle, Lecky and Froude to set alongside Macaulay; Erskine May, Herschel and Maxwell for the science shelf; Gray's *Anatomy*, first published in 1858; Richard Burton; Newman's *Apologia*.

A journalist spoke of William Longman's combination of 'enterprise and discretion'[28] It is a phrase that sticks. For the exciting immediacies of the period it is irresistibly tempting to go back to the buildings and to events associated with them. In 1863, two years after a great fire in Paternoster Row, a brand new Longmans building was opened (complete with Ship and Swan in the spandrils of the keystone of the new arch). In the best mid-Victorian language it was described as possessing 'features more in common with the Renaissance than with any other period of architecture, but ... treated throughout with that educated freedom which is claimed by the best of our modern architects as necessary to ensure truly representative works of art'.[29] Four years later Thomas IV (blessed with eight children) took up residence in Farnborough Hill (not far from Froude and Kingsley), a building designed 'in the early English domestic style' as conceived by Henry Edward Kendall and later to be occupied by the Empress Eugénie. The pebble-dash on the building was divided from the brickwork by a frieze of stone-coloured terra-cotta panels framed in teak depicting in high relief ships in full sail, swans, and, for good measure, Longman's own initials and groups of angels with musical instruments. Some of the swans were swimming on water surrounded by palm trees, a reference to new Indian ventures of the firm – the Bombay branch was opened in 1895 – which were greatly extended during the last years of the nineteenth century.

Two of the essays in this volume deal with the late-Victorian period after the deaths of Thomas IV and William. One is concerned with the fascinating story of the publication of Disraeli's *Endymion* in 1880*, the other with the launching of a new series of books and a new magazine which dealt, as befitted the times, not with politics or literature but with sport.† Thomas IV had been responsible for accepting Disraeli's *Lothair*, but it was his son Thomas Norton Longman V (1849–1930) who dealt in 1880 with an author who had only just ceased to be prime minister.

Thomas Norton Longman V (1849–1930) [n.d.]. (Longman Archives)

* Annabel Jones, 'Disraeli's *Endymion*: a case study', pp. 141–186.
† Asa Briggs, 'The view from Badminton', pp. 187–218.

The story reveals much about the conditions of publishing on the eve of another great change when the three-decker novel was to disappear — and much with it — and a new generation of publishers was to enter the trade. Yet Paternoster Row was far removed from Gissing's New Grub Street, and the *Badminton* series, like the magazine which followed, had little to do with the new journalism.

In this period of change, when the relations between publishers and authors were beginning to be widely publicised, a new generation of Longmans was in charge. Thomas Norton Longman's brother, George H. Longman (1852–1938), and the two sons of William Longman, Charles J. Longman (1852–1934) and Hubert H. Longman (1856–1940, knighted 1909) were in direct dynastic line. All were alive when Longmans celebrated two hundred years of continuous history in 1924. By then a sixth generation had come in, too, with R. G. Longman (1888–1971) and W. Longman (1888–1967). Harold Cox, the last editor of the *Edinburgh Review*, was as sure of the object lesson of the two hundred years of House history as Smiles would have been.

The example of the firm of Longman . . . shows how, through six generations, a single family has successfully administered an important and constantly expanding business; how it has preserved the traditions on which the original success of the firm was based; and how it has developed those traditions to meet new needs or to seize new opportunities.[30]

In fact, though Charles J. Longman could 'at times roar like a lion' and Thomas Norton Longman (who retired in 1919) had as many interesting literary and social connections as his father before him, the non-Longmans had become increasingly important in the daily operations of the business. The Longman family were sole partners in 1924, but non-Longmans were in a majority at the time of the bi-centenary celebrations. W. A. Kelk, head of the publishing department, made the first speech at the 1924 staff dinner: he had joined the House in 1881 as a youth, and had proved himself 'a first-class trainer of youths himself'.[31] J. W. Allen, an important figure, who was mainly responsible for ensuring that Longmans' reputation as educational publishers was sustained in an age of mass education after the Education Act of 1870, had been in the firm since 1884 and had become a partner in 1918, the year of another landmark, Fisher's Education Act.

C. J. Mills, who had founded the New York House in 1889, had started modestly as a 'Yankee traveller': when he first arrived in New York a few years earlier he had had to auction the shipments of books sent out from England. The moral of all this development was less simple than that drawn by Cox. Longmans were already depending in 1924 on a team of people, not just on a family, and some lines of business were proving far more successful in business terms than others. Non-Longmans were obviously needed when Charles J. Longman, with all his authority, would not allow a telephone on his desk or a woman shorthand typist in his office.[32]

The two-hundredth anniversary celebrations are now as much a period piece as the opening of Farnborough Hill. G. M. Trevelyan, who had not yet written *his* History of England, proposed the toast to 'Literature and Science': other historians present included Tout, Gooch, R. W. Seton-Watson and G. N. Clark, then editor of the *English Historical Review*, which had been published by Longmans since 1886, as it still is today. Sidney and Beatrice Webb, whose *History of Trade Unionism* had been published by Longmans as long ago as 1894, were there also, along with J. L. Hammond, representatives of different traditions, if not dynasties. Also present was the widow of Andrew Lang, who had been a principal literary adviser from 1871 to 1912, and whose 'literary causeries' in *Longman's Magazine* (a new venture of 1882 which lasted until 1905) were headed, like this Introduction, with the title 'At the Sign of the Ship'.[33] Other writers in attendance were Sir Arthur Conan Doyle and Rider Haggard, the latter a friend and collaborator of Lang, as he was of Charles J. Longman. In his speech Haggard anticipated the theme of one of the essays in this book.* In two hundred years, he said, 'probably the publishers of that day will produce picture books again, as the savages did in the beginning. Yes, the circle may meet; it may come to that.'[34] No one mentioned radio or television, but Trevelyan with the nineteenth century behind him warned that 'the danger to literature in the twentieth century is not so much immediate death by starvation as the danger of losing its own soul to the ideals of all-conquering journalism'.[35]

Charles J. Longman himself quoted a Latin verse which he

---

* Susan Holmes and Tim Rix, 'Beyond the book', pp. 319–356.

View of Paternoster Row by Thomas Hosmer Shepherd, 1854. (British Museum [Crace Collection])

translated for his audience in a fashion which would not have been necessary in 1724 or even 1824:

> May green old age and length of days
> Long years attend the Longmans' ways,
> And may the Black Swan never pale
> While still the ship rides out the Gale.[36]
>
> Longa fluat Sociis aetas vireatque senectus
> Neve Olor albescat, dum Ratis urget iter.

There was to be more danger of calm than of gale, however, during the least active of the inter-war years when publishers, old and new, found it difficult to voyage full sail, and even now it is not easy to set the events of the 1920s and 1930s in perspective. On the occasion of the 225th anniversary of the House in 1949, Cyprian Blagden, historian of publishing, felt, indeed, that he had to end his story as early as 1842. 'Those who have controlled the business during the last 107 years', he wrote, 'have provided no *new* answers; the interesting thing is that, in themselves and

Below: the new Longmans' building of 1863 from The Illustrated London News, *6 June 1863. (GLC Print Collection)*
Opposite; above: the 1863 Longmans' building in Paternoster Row after it was bombed, first in December 1940 and subsequently in January 1941. (Longman Archives: photo Sir Cecil Beaton)
Opposite; below: the new Longman building at Harlow designed by Sir Frederick Gibberd, into which the Company moved in 1968.

in their policies, they have provided the old answers over again under new conditions and with changing problems.'[37]

Yet there were new voyages during the inter-war years, some of them towards unknown destinations. Charles Higham and Michael West were to provide just the right books for the Middle East and for India, and the enormous expansion in overseas sales is touched on in one of the essays in this volume, which also tells of the first stages in the story of educational change in Britain.* After the Second World War – with John Newsom – a new approach was to be made to a new generation in British schools, including children who had previously been outside the ranks of Longmans' readers. The approach pointed to even greater educational change, and this story, still unfinished and increasingly controversial, is continued in the last essay.†

In the history of the House itself there were many non-Longmans names, such as Kenneth Potter and Noel Brack, prominent even before the Second World War broke historic continuities by destroying by fire the Victorian building in Paternoster Row. In recent years since 1968 a new Longmans has taken shape in a post-war new town, Harlow.

The building up of the overseas side of the business deserves a volume in itself: it was in its way as revolutionary a development as the 'paper-back revolution' in publishing of the 1930s, discussed in Hans Schmoller's essay. That well-publicised revolution was to have its surprises. No one could have foreseen in 1936 when the Penguin Publishing Company was founded – dedicated to producing cheap books for large numbers of people – that thirty-four years later the newest English publisher – a controversial one at that – and the oldest commercial one would merge. They then had a joint annual turnover of £17 million, more than three-fifths of total sales being accounted for overseas. Ship, Pelican and Puffin were soon to appear side by side as well as Ship and Swan.

Pre-war Longmans became a private limited liability company in 1926 and post-war Longmans a public company in 1947. It changed its name to the Longman Group of Publishing Companies in 1966 and joined up with the Financial and Provincial Publishing Company (now Pearson Longman Limited) in 1968.

---

* Roy Yglesias, 'Education and publishing in transition', pp. 357–388.
† Tony Becher and Brian Young, 'Planning for change', pp. 389–419.

Doubtless the new Longman Penguin Company will have its history written in detail, and the constituent elements in its economic history, at least, will be both more identifiable (and measurable) and more accessible than the antecedent economic elements in the older business history described briefly in this Introduction. Yet the sense of venturing into the unknown continues if only because the social and cultural history of recent years contains, perhaps, more unknowns than it ever has done before. There is as much of a challenge in publishing as there was when Thomas I arrived in London in 1716.

One Longman, Mark Frederic Kerr (1916–72), might have represented continuity at this 250th celebration. He took an immense interest in this book, and his untimely death saddened everyone connected with it. His portrait rightly appears as the frontispiece.

Succession of imprints of the House of Longman 1724–1974

1724	T. LONGMAN
1725	J. OSBORN AND T. LONGMAN
1734	T. LONGMAN
1745	T. LONGMAN AND T. SHEWELL
1747	T. LONGMAN
1753	T. AND T. LONGMAN
1755	M. AND T. LONGMAN
1755	T. LONGMAN
1793	T. N. LONGMAN. ALSO T. LONGMAN
1797	LONGMAN AND REES
1799	T. N. LONGMAN AND O. REES
1800	LONGMAN AND REES
1804	LONGMAN, HURST, REES AND ORME
1811	LONGMAN, HURST, REES, ORME AND BROWN
1823	LONGMAN, HURST, REES, ORME, BROWN AND GREEN
1825	LONGMAN, REES, ORME, BROWN AND GREEN
1832	LONGMAN, REES, ORME, BROWN, GREEN AND LONGMAN
1838	LONGMAN, ORME, BROWN, GREEN AND LONGMANS
1840	LONGMAN, ORME & CO.
1841	LONGMAN, BROWN & CO.
1842	LONGMAN, BROWN, GREEN AND LONGMANS
1856	LONGMAN, BROWN, GREEN, LONGMANS AND ROBERTS
1859	LONGMAN, GREEN, LONGMAN AND ROBERTS
1862	LONGMAN, GREEN, LONGMAN, ROBERTS AND GREEN
1865	LONGMANS, GREEN, READER AND DYER
1889	LONGMANS, GREEN & CO.
1926	LONGMANS, GREEN & CO. LTD.
1959	LONGMANS
1968	LONGMAN

IAN PARSONS

Copyright
and society

COPYRIGHT, IT has often been said, truthfully if somewhat surprisingly, is a right of property. Surprisingly, because at first it is a little difficult to conceive of a property right which not only operates at a distance but affects other people's possessions. As Lord Goodman has put it, 'the idea that a subsidiary legal right reposes in some remote person in relation to an article in one's own household – or on a library shelf – is an alien one'. True enough. Nevertheless the concept of copyright stems from the basic Common Law view that a man is entitled to the fruits of his own labour, and that it does not matter whether that labour is physical or intellectual. In other words, if unaided and not as the servant of another, a man writes a book or a play or composes a symphony, he can regard the result as being just as much his 'property' as if he had built himself a log cabin out of timber that he owned. And in consequence he is entitled to claim protection against any unauthorised use of it. This has not always been so. It is only gradually, and over a period of several centuries, that the idea of copyright as we know it today has evolved. In the process, the Common Law rights of the individual, and what for want of a better term might be called 'the general good of society', have frequently found themselves opposed to one another and sometimes in violent conflict. The history of copyright is to that extent a history of the changing views of society as to where the line should be drawn between the rights of the individual and the interests of the general public.

But let us begin at the beginning. What does the word 'copyright' mean, and what is its origin? According to the *Oxford Dictionary*, the word was first used in 1767, in Blackstone's *Commentaries*, and the *Dictionary*'s definition of it is 'the exclusive right given by law for a certain term of years to an author, composer etc (or his assignee) to print, publish, and sell copies of his original work'. However, the concept of copyright goes back much further than Blackstone, and its origins are now lost in the mists of time. In effect, though, the right only began to assume importance when the invention of printing made the multiplication of 'copies' of a work infinitely quicker and cheaper than the painstaking products of monkish scribes, as well as appreciably more accurate than the compositions of most professional scriveners.

In England it is the year 1476, the year in which Caxton set up his printing press in what is now Tothill Street, Westminster, that for all practical purposes forms our starting point. It was a modest beginning, despite Caxton's energy and hard work, and in the following fifteen years up to his death in 1491, only a hundred or so titles are known to have come from his press. But he had started something momentous and soon had imitators, some of whom did not enjoy the same favour with a succession of monarchs as he did, nor did they accept the responsibilities entailed by royal patronage. It was not long, therefore, before the Crown began to assert prerogative rights in the printing of books and to make a practice of granting monopolies to interested parties in the form of 'the sole privilege' to print certain titles or certain categories of books. As early as 1518, for example, Richard Pynson, the second holder of the office of King's Printer, and John Rastell secured the first grants of this kind, and thereafter the practice spread rapidly. This was not mere venality on the part of the sovereign, just as it was not primarily an attempt to protect the rights of authors or of the printers and booksellers – forerunners of the modern publisher – to whom they had assigned their rights. It was much more an attempt to curb the publication of seditious or blasphemous books by controlling the source of supply; in short, by operating an indirect form of censorship. Indeed, although it would be a gross exaggeration to claim that copyright protection grew out of literary censorship, it is a fact that historically the two notions developed side by side, having a common origin in the growth of printing, and that ordinances and Acts of Parliament designed to protect society against abuses of the press frequently achieved, as a concomitant, the protection of authors and publishers against infringement of their rights. For copyright has a negative as well as a positive side, since by conferring on its owners the exclusive right to *make* copies of a work, it automatically carries with it the right to prevent others from doing so.

As the sixteenth century advanced and the literate population of England grew, so the number of printers increased, and it became impossible to obtain royal protection for each individual item of their multiple and varied output.

Those interested in uninterrupted enjoyment of the profit from an impression of a book were therefore compelled to agree to respect each other's claims on these little monopolies. The Gild of Stationers was the obvious organisation through which such agreement could be worked and the register of claims to 'copies' was the written record to which another claimant could be referred and by which disputes might be settled.[1]

Hence came into being the famous Registers, which have proved of such infinite value to scholars in dating the works of authors – not least those of Shakespeare's plays – from the middle of the sixteenth century up to the passing of the Copyright Act of 1911. Throughout that period the words 'Entered at Stationers' Hall' virtually constituted notice of a claim to copyright.

Copyright entry of Shakespeare's First Folio in the Stationers' Hall. (Stationers' Hall)

For such a claim to have more than theoretical validity some form of sanction was necessary, and this the Stationers secured through the Royal Charter granted by Philip and Mary on 4 May 1557. This provided, *inter alia*, that

no one in the realm should exercise the art of printing, either himself or through an agent, unless he were a freeman of the Stationers' Company of London or unless he had royal permission to do so; and secondly that the

Master and Wardens of the Company were to have the right to search the houses and business premises of all printers, bookbinders and booksellers in the Kingdom for any printed matter, to seize (and treat as they thought fit) anything printed contrary to any statute or proclamation, and to imprison anyone who printed without the proper qualification or resisted their search.

Plenary powers indeed! But one has to look at them in the light of the contemporary situation: a Catholic monarch precariously on the throne again after Henry VIII's abrasive break with Rome. The Charter itself states that it was granted because 'seditious and heretical books, both in rhymes and tracts, were daily printed, renewing and spreading great and detestable heresies against the Catholic doctrines of the Holy Mother Church'.

But the significance of the Charter for our purposes is this, that it enabled the Company, eight years later in 1565, to pass a Resolution whereby a Freeman of the Company could have 'the empression of any Copye, peculiar to him' either by royal grant 'or by the ordenunces of this Companye'. In other words, positive copyright protection could now be secured, either by royal Letters Patent or, if (and only if) you were a Stationer, by virtue of the Company's printing monopoly and powers of suppression. Authors without influence at Court could thus only secure publication by selling their work to a printer or bookseller who was a member of the Company. Not perhaps a very equitable arrangement, though sponsored by government and, it need hardly be said, warmly welcomed and zealously exploited by the Stationers; but out of it grew the whole complex copyright world in which we live.

It was not long, though, before the two sources of protection gave rise to conflict, as the case of the poet George Wither shows. Born in 1588, this colourful character, best remembered today for his lyric:

> Shall I wasting in despair
> Die because a woman's fair?

was imprisoned for writing satires against 'the establishment' (including the Lord Chancellor) before he was thirty. On his release he somehow succeeded in obtaining Letters Patent from James I to publish his *Hymns and Songs of the Church* (1623) and a grant of copyright in them for fifty-one years. All might have been well had not the King 'additionally stipulated that the Hymns should be included in all·bound copies of the Psalms offered for sale by the Stationers'.[2] This was more than the latter could stomach, and having failed to stop publication after successively petitioning Wither, the King, and finally Parliament for the withdrawal of the Patent, the Company 'simply refused to sell the book': 'They let it be known that Wither's translations in it were careless, his versification faulty, and his rendering of the Song of Solomon obscene.' Wither reacted with characteristic spirit, calling the Stationers 'malapert and arrogant . . . peddlers of books, and for the most part ignorant fellows', and putting forward the claim that copyright should properly vest in the author rather than in 'a mere bookseller'.[3] Wither went on to describe booksellers in highly uncomplimentary terms, which did him no good with the Stationers, who continued to boycott his work for the next eleven years. But he had stated a case for the rights of authors that was eventually to win general acceptance.

That it did not do so earlier was due as much to a form of snobbery as to anything else, for almost throughout the seventeenth century authors considered themselves sufficiently rewarded if their works were published, and could be read and discussed by their contemporaries. Writing for financial gain was considered ungentlemanly, and most of the poets and prose writers of the time either had private incomes or earned their living by other means. Donne, Herbert and Herrick were clergymen, Pepys was a civil servant, Sir Thomas Browne a doctor, and so forth. But as the century wore on the climate of opinion changed and Dryden, who only survived a few months into the eighteenth century, was one of the first authors to earn his living entirely by his pen. Only seventy-five years later it was possible for Dr Johnson to assert that 'no man but a blockhead ever wrote except for money'. The assertion was not true, even in his own case, for he had written countless thousands of words in *The Gentleman's Magazine*, *The Rambler*, and other periodicals for which he received little or nothing,[4] but it reflected a radical change in the attitude of authors to their work, and of society to its authors.

Another patent, dating from the time of James I, had infinitely greater importance in the history of copyright than poor George Wither's, and was to lead to a series of controversies stretching over three and a half centuries, culminating in 1963 in the most famous copyright case of modern times. This was the Crown's claim to copyright in the Authorised Version of the Bible. Nobody knows for certain the basis of this claim, though it has been suggested that it may have been that King James paid for the translation himself. Such a gesture would not have been out of character in 'the wisest fool in Christendom'. It is more likely, however, that it stemmed from the Crown's original prerogative in the printing of books, which could be held naturally to apply to the printing of matter of such national importance as the doctrines of the established Church, as later it did to Acts of Parliament and to certain other works 'published by or under the direction or control of the Sovereign or of a Government Department'.

Whatever the original basis of the claim – and so far as the New Testament is concerned it was effective through the King's Printer at least as far back as 1541 – it has survived unbroken from the publication of 'King James's Bible' in 1611 to the present day. With the steady rise in the size of the population the commercial value of the exclusive right to print and publish the Authorised Version increased correspondingly, and by 1770 Dr Johnson's printer, William Strachan, found it good business to purchase a one-third share in the Patent for £5,000. This despite the fact that the cake had by that time been divided into three through the extension, during the seventeenth century, of the privilege of printing Bibles and Prayer Books to the Universities of Oxford and Cambridge. Strachan bought his share of the Patent from a country gentleman named Charles Eyre, whose father had prudently bought the reversion of it some years earlier for £10,000. Strachan lived to the age of seventy, and his daughter Marguerite married John Spottiswoode. The Patent was renewed at regular intervals of thirty years up to 1860, and thereafter 'during her Majestie's Will' – which has only been exercised once, in 1901. Since then it has continued uninterruptedly in the possession of Messrs Eyre and Spottiswoode, the direct descendants of Charles Eyre and William Strachan.

In 1961 the University Presses of Oxford and Cambridge jointly published the New Testament in an entirely fresh translation. This was the first part of the *New English Bible*, a rendering into contemporary idiom commissioned by a Committee of the Churches, who entrusted publication to the University Presses and assigned the copyright to them. Eyre and Spottiswoode, relying on their position as Queen's Printer, claimed the right to participate in the exploitation of this new translation, although they had not in any way contributed to its inception or preparation. To test their claim they published the Gospel According to St John in the *New English Bible*'s version. The Universities responded with a writ for breach of copyright and sought an injunction restraining Eyre and Spottiswoode from printing and publishing any part of the *New English Bible* without their permission. The action came before Mr Justice Plowman in July 1963, who after listening to the arguments of no less than seven learned Counsel, delivered a judgment of such historic importance that the relevant parts of it must be quoted verbatim:

Mr Francis, in an able and interesting argument (as were all the arguments addressed to me), said that this is the first occasion in legal history on which the Court is called upon to decide the precise extent of the prerogative right of printing Bibles. I do not, however, feel myself called on to decide so wide a question. The only matter with which I am concerned is whether the prerogative right of printing extends to the *New English Bible*.

The claim that it does so is at first sight surprising, viewed in the light of the history of Bible printing. For over 300 years the Crown has never claimed the right to print any translation of the Bible or any part of it other than the Authorised Version, and there have been scores of other translations. Never so far as I am aware, has it been decided as a matter of law that the Royal Prerogative extends to any translation other than the Authorised Version. For over 300 years Royal Printers have never themselves printed or published any version of the Bible except the Authorised Version by virtue of their patents. Never in the last 300 years, so far as I am aware have Royal Printers attempted to restrain the publication of any version of the Bible other than the Authorised Version. In particular – and here we approach what I regard as the heart of the matter – never has the Crown claimed, nor until now has it ever been claimed in right of the Crown, that the prerogative can override private copyright.

Private copyright, as we now know it, did not exist in the sixteenth and seventeenth centuries. In those days the Crown claimed the right to control all printing by virtue of the Royal Prerogative and the grant of exclusive rights to print and publish books. It was only if an author were given an exclusive Royal licence to print his own work that he had any protection in the nature of copyright after publication, leaving aside copyright as a domestic matter between members of the Stationers' Company.

Then in the year 1709 the first Copyright Act was passed, the statute, 8 Anne, Chapter 19. That Act is entitled: 'An Act for the encouragement of learning, by vesting the Copies of printed Books in the Authors or Purchasers of such Copies, during the Times therein mentioned'. . .

Copyright is a right of property. It is spoken of as such in Section 3 of the Copyright Act, 1842 and Section 25 of that Act enacts that 'all Copyrights shall be deemed personal property', and transmissible as such. But although the 1709 Act and the 1842 Act each contains a saving of the rights of the Universities and of certain other persons and bodies, neither contains any saving of the rights of the Crown, and what is more important neither Act nor any subsequent Act contains any provision giving the Crown a right to expropriate without compensation the private copyright conferred by the Act in question.

The Defendants' case in this action is that they are entitled in right of the Royal Prerogative to print the *New English Bible* without payment to the owners of the copyright. That is in effect a claim to expropriate the Plaintiffs' property without compensation, and is a claim which, without statutory authority, cannot, in my judgment, succeed. . . .

The absence from the 1709 Act of any saving in favour of the Crown is, I think, explained when one remembers that before 1709 the prerogative right of the Crown to grant exclusive rights to print and publish certain books was not a right to expropriate private copyright for the reason that until 1709 private copyright did not exist. It is true that the Copyright Acts of 1911 and 1956 contain savings in favour of the Crown, but for the reasons I have endeavoured to state no prerogative right to expropriate without compensation, in my judgment, existed when those Acts were passed, and no such right was created by either of them.

The Royal Prerogative does not, therefore, in my judgment, cover the right to print or to authorise others to print any material the printing of which would be a breach of copyright, and in these circumstances the Plaintiffs are, in my judgment, entitled to succeed.

So the Queen's Printer retired discomfited, and the Universities went on their way rejoicing.

We must now return to the year 1709, the year in which, as we have just seen, the first Copyright Act appeared on the Statute Book of this or – I believe I am right in saying – any other country. The Act opens with the following significant words: 'Whereas Printers, Booksellers and other persons have of late frequently taken the liberty of printing, reprinting and publishing, or causing to be printed, reprinted and published, Books and other writings, without the consent of the Authors or Proprietors of such Books and Writings . . .' and goes on to stipulate that, as from 10 April 1710, the author of any book already published, who had not assigned his rights to a printer or bookseller, should have 'the sole Right and Liberty' of printing such books for twenty-one years 'and no longer', and that the author of any unpublished book should have 'the sole liberty of printing and reprinting such books' for a term of fourteen years from the date of first publication. There was an additional proviso that, if the author were still living after the expiration of fourteen years, his exclusive right should continue for a further fourteen years. (In passing it is perhaps worth noting that, multiplied by two, these are precisely the existing terms of domestic copyright protection in the USA.)

The Act of Queen Anne effected a radical change in the law of copyright, creating as it did, for the first time, a statutory right in the author's favour. But it left untouched two long-established conventions: the Crown's power to grant exclusive licences by Letters Patent, and the proprietorial rights of printers and booksellers who had purchased the 'copy' of (i.e. the right to print) an author's work. This soon led to difficulties. For the Crown was apt to grant licences for periods dictated by the royal whim, which might or might not coincide with the statutory periods laid down in Queen Anne's Act, and the booksellers stoutly affirmed that, under Common Law, the authors', and therefore their own, rights of publication were perpetual. The result was that at recurrent intervals throughout the eighteenth century actions were fought in the courts to determine whether or not a given work was out of copyright. Everything turned on whether the claim that Common Law copyright was perpetual survived or was superseded by the Act of 1709. At first, the booksellers carried the day and succeeded in obtaining injunctions, their most signal success being in the case of *Millar v Taylor*. This concerned Thomson's poem *The Seasons*, the copyright of which had expired, under the terms of the 1709 Act, in 1758. The poet had sold all his rights to a man named Millar. Taylor reprinted the book in 1763, and was sued by Millar three years later for breach of copyright. The case was not determined until 1769, when the Court of King's Bench, with Lord Mansfield LCJ presiding, decided by a majority of three to one in favour of Millar.

This was followed, in 1774, by the crucial case of *Donaldson v Beckett*, which again concerned Thomson's *The Seasons*. And here I cannot do better than quote from Sir Frank Mackinnon's admirable précis of that case:

Beckett had bought from Millar's executors the copyright that had been upheld in *Millar v Taylor* in 1769. And Beckett made his claim in the

English Court of Chancery against the Edinburgh 'pirate' Donaldson, who
had reprinted *The Seasons*. Lord Chancellor Bathurst granted a perpetual
injunction against Donaldson, whereupon Donaldson appealed to the House
of Lords. The hearing began on February 4th 1774. The judges, then
twelve in number, being summoned, they all attended with the exception of
Lord Mansfield: it was not the etiquette for him to advise the House; as a
peer himself, if he were present, he would form part of the tribunal. Five
questions were submitted to the judges, to which they gave answers by
varying majorities. But to the most vital question – 'Whether by the Statute
of 1709 an author is precluded from every remedy, except on the foundation
of the said Statute, or on the terms and conditions prescribed therein' – six
answered 'Yes', and five answered 'No'. (Lord Mansfield, who might have
sat, and upheld the view he had taken in *Millar v Taylor* five years before,
did not attend the House.) And on the motion of Lord Camden, on 22nd
February, the House decided in favour of the appellant Donaldson, and
Millar v Taylor was overruled. The English booksellers had found their
Bannockburn.[5]

Thus was Common Law copyright finally abolished. But its
disappearance did not entail, as might have been expected, the
disappearance of perpetual copyright, which survived in three
vestigial forms: in the Crown's prerogative to publish the Authorised Version and the Books of Common Prayer; in the right of the
universities of Oxford and Cambridge, four Scottish universities,
and the colleges of Eton, Westminster and Winchester 'to hold
in perpetuity their copyright in books given or bequeathed to
them for the advancement of useful learning and other purposes
of education';[6] and, subject to certain exceptions, in unpublished
works. The first of these has already been discussed. The second
was enshrined in the Copyright Act of 1775 and was the result of
urgent representations to Parliament, on behalf of the academic
community, following hard on the heels of the decision in
Donaldson v Beckett. The right was to extend only to the nine
named institutions' own books, which had to be printed by their
own presses and for their sole benefit, and could not be delegated.
If such copyrights were leased or sold, or the books printed
elsewhere, the privilege of perpetuity was automatically abro-
gated. This very eccentric piece of legislation is surprisingly still
operative, despite the fact that the Act of 1775 was repealed
long ago. Having survived a succession of Copyright Acts
spanning nearly two hundred years it must surely now constitute
one of the hoariest anachronisms in English law. Understand-

ably, few people are aware of its existence, as was demonstrated a few years ago when a reputable London publisher* was astonished to find himself in trouble with Oxford University Press for printing two of Plato's dialogues in the translation made by Benjamin Jowett. Although Jowett had been dead well over fifty years, he had bequeathed the copyright in his translation to Balliol College, Oxford, and so secured perpetual copyright for it so long as the University observed the conditions laid down in the 1775 Act. The same situation applied to the far more important Clarendon papers, which Lord Clarendon's heirs presented to Oxford University, with the result that for many years they were virtually impounded. It is surely high time that this relic of George III's reign, which has long been a bane to historians, without noticeably benefiting the institutions it was designed to protect, was decently interred.

The third category in which perpetual copyright normally subsists is that of unpublished works. Here the law sensibly takes the view that the term of copyright cannot begin to run until the work itself has been published, and that no limit should be set to the length of time that an author's heirs may retain copyright by refraining from publication. Theoretically, therefore, if a lost play of Shakespeare's suddenly turned up, and could be shown never to have been printed or performed, the copyright would still vest in the dramatist's descendants (if they could be identified) and would be valid for fifty years from the date of its first publication. Within the last twenty years we have actually seen such a case happen, when the greater part of Boswell's extensive private papers, long thought to have been burnt, eventually came to light in an old croquet box at Malahide Castle, near Dublin. They had passed by direct descent to Boswell's great-great-grandson, Lord Talbot de Malahide, who finally agreed to sell them, along with the right to publish them, to Colonel Ralph Isham. A similar situation obtained in the case of Traherne's *Poems* and *Centuries of Meditation*, the manuscript of which came into the possession of the antiquarian bookseller Bertram Dobell, who edited and first published them in 1903 and 1908 respectively. Although Traherne had died in 1674, the copyright was alive in Dobell's hands until the middle of this century, and Traherne's *Felicities*, chosen and edited by 'Q' in 1934, are protected to this day.

* William Kimber.

Since 1956, however, exceptions to this rule have been made, in the public interest, in the case of literary, dramatic or musical works known to exist in libraries, museums or similar institutions open to the public. Subject to certain conditions these may now be published, provided the author has been dead more than fifty years and the work in existence more than one hundred years. This provision superseded an earlier one, also designed to discourage the unreasonable 'freezing' of an author's work by his heirs, which empowered the Judicial Committee of the Privy Council to authorise publication in certain circumstances.

This whole question of the appropriate length of time for which works should be protected is of course central to the notion of copyright, and has been hotly debated ever since Queen Anne's Act of 1709. Initially, as we have seen, statutory copyright ran for twenty-one years from publication in the case of already published writings, and for fourteen years (renewable for a further fourteen if the author was still alive) in the case of unpublished works. But that was sixty-five years before the Lords' decision in *Donaldson v Beckett* put an end to the claim that an *author's* copyright was perpetual. In the interval, controversy raged. Was a term of twenty-one years (or at most twenty-eight) from first publication too short a period of 'exclusive rights' for the author or his estate; was perpetuity too long a one? Dr Johnson had no doubt that it was. Although some of his works were more likely than those of most authors to survive and produce rewards for his heirs, he endorsed the Lords' decision with his usual robust common sense, declaring that 'it is inconvenient to Society that an useful book should become perpetual and exclusive property'. That was in 1774. In 1814 a new Act extended the existing fourteen years to twenty-eight, and if the author was alive at the end of that time, for the rest of his life. This, it was generally felt, was a step in the right direction. Nevertheless, Southey, writing in 1819 in the *Quarterly Review*, deployed his considerable powers of rhetoric in a renewed claim for perpetuity.

The question [he wrote] is simply this: upon what principle, with what justice, or under what pretext of public good, are men of letters deprived of a perpetual property in the produce of their own labours, when all other persons enjoy it as their indefeasible right – a right beyond the power of any earthly authority to take away? Is it because their labour is so light, – the

Robert Southey (1774–1843) by H. Edridge, [c. 1804]. National Portrait Gallery

endowments which it requires so common, – the attainments so cheaply and easily acquired, and the present remuneration so adequate, so ample, and so certain?[7]

He went on to point out that the last descendants of Milton had died in poverty,* coupled with the more doubtful assertion that

* Milton and his widow received £18 in all from *Paradise Lost.*

the descendants of Shakespeare were 'living in poverty and in the lowest rank of life'. He concluded with the following moving peroration:

The decision which time pronounces upon the reputation of authors, and upon the permanent rank which they are to hold, is unerring and final. Restore to them that perpetuity in the copyright of their works, of which the law has deprived them, and the reward of literary labour will ultimately be in just proportion to its deserts.

Southey was warmly supported by Wordsworth, who asked pointedly, 'What reason can be assigned that an Author who dies young [he was thinking of Burns] should have the prospect before him of his Children being left to languish in Poverty and Dependence, while Booksellers are revelling in luxury upon gains derived from Works which are the delight of many Nations?'[8] I cannot help surmising that by 'booksellers' Wordsworth really meant publishers, though the picture he paints would have been almost equally over-optimistic in their case. Ten years later, in 1838, the redoubtable Serjeant Talfourd, egged on by Wordsworth, introduced a Bill to Parliament that sought to provide authors with sixty years' protection after publication; but this was effectively opposed by Peel and Macaulay. The latter proposed forty-two years from publication, or the life of the author, whichever was the longer; and this was in turn amended by Peel to forty-two years or seven years after the author's death, whichever was the longer. This was the term finally adopted in the Act of 1842, the first Copyright Act which seriously set out to clarify and consolidate the whole position. Under it, registration at Stationers' Hall continued to be invaluable to claimants of copyright, and essential to litigants in any dispute involving infringement.

This Act remained in force for nearly seventy years, until superseded by the 1911 Act, which extended the period of copyright still further, in conformity with growing international practice, to fifty years after the author's death. But it also virtually put an end to the importance of the Stationers' Hall Registers by abolishing their legal significance, and contained a number of peculiar provisions relating to the new fifty-year term. Chief of these was the division of the term into two halves, during the first of which ownership of the copyright conferred exclusive rights of publication, but during the second of which anybody was at liberty to publish a book provided he gave statutory notice of his intention and paid a royalty of 10 per cent of the retail price to the copyright owner. Odder still was the proviso that an author could not, except by Will, assign his copyrights, or grant anybody any interest in them, for more than twenty-five years after his death. At the end of that period, in the absence of any testamentary disposal, the copyright automatically reverted to his estate, no matter how comprehensive the terms of the original assignment or how large the sum paid for it.[9] This inevitably led to complications and misunderstandings until the 1956 Act, currently in force, abolished the two-tier term and gave copyright owners a straight fifty years' protection, not (it should be noted) from the date of the author's death but from 31 December following it.

Another clause in successive Copyright Acts that has long proved a bone of contention, and which points up the innate potential conflict between the interests of authors and publishers and those of society, concerns the compulsory presentation of free copies to certain libraries. This provision goes back to the early years of Charles II's reign, when three copies of the best edition of every new book were required to be sent to Stationers' Hall for forwarding to the King's Library and to the University Libraries at Oxford and Cambridge. This was not, one would say, an exorbitant or unreasonable demand in those days. But during the passage of the 1709 Act through the Commons two further libraries were added to the list: those of Sion College and the Advocates' Library in Edinburgh. The Lords then went one better and added the libraries of the four Scottish universities, bringing the total of free copies to nine. Later still, in 1800, the number was increased to eleven by the addition of two Dublin libraries, those of Trinity College and the King's Inn. True, the Act was at first only held to apply to books registered at Stationers' Hall; but this merely had the effect of nullifying the value of the Registers as a record of all books published. Many booksellers and publishers preferred to risk the infringement of their rights rather than have to give away eleven copies of an expensive volume or set of volumes. But in 1805 the University of Cambridge, incited by a certain Professor of Law perhaps inappropriately named Christian, successfully brought an action for the non-delivery of a book *not* registered at Stationers' Hall,

contending that the 1709 Act enjoined the delivery of *all* books,
whether registered or not. This decision called down upon the
luckless Professor the wrath of Southey, who ridiculed him in the
issue of the *Quarterly* already mentioned with a scintillating
mixture of wit, irony and sarcasm. In the course of it Southey
quoted some interesting statistics, such as that 'the delivery of
the eleven copies in four years have cost Messrs Longman's
house £3,000' and that 'Mr Murray's loss, under the operation
of this act, is stated at about £1,275'.* And he listed a whole series
of learned works whose publication had been abandoned, or
indefinitely postponed, on account of the operation of this clause,
including 'a work on the non-descript plants of South America,
by Baron Humboldt', which Longman & Co. 'have declared that,
because of this upset, they have declined to publish'. Southey
also stated that 2,105 books were claimed by the copyright
libraries between June 1815 and March 1817 – a very plausible
figure.

And so the debate continued, with Professor Christian
maintaining that 'it is a great national object that all the Universities should be furnished with a copy of every new publication'
and 'perfectly consistent . . . with sound policy and good government', while his doughty opponent Sir Egerton Brydges asserted
that 'the Copyright Act, as now put into force, is the most perfect
instrument of collecting and disseminating all the mischiefs
flowing out of an abuse of the Liberty of the Press, which human
ingenuity has ever yet contrived'. Each had some justice on his
side. Perhaps the last word was Southey's, who in calmer mood
wrote:

It may be desirable that there should be one library which should receive
every thing; one general receptacle, in which even the rubbish of the press
should be deposited, for the chance that something may be gained by raking
in it hereafter. The British Museum should be the place, as being a national
and metropolitan library. But with regard to the University libraries, it
should be remembered that their original and proper object is the collection
of books which may assist the graver pursuits of the scholar, and which,
because of their cost or scarcity, might otherwise be inaccessible to him. It
cannot be necessary that they should supply the student with Dr Mavor's

---

* It is only fair to point out that Southey's figures were based on the assumption,
not necessarily true even in those days, that every copy given to the statutory libraries would otherwise have been sold.

Catechism for the Use of Children under seven years of age, with the newest editions of Dr Solomon's Guide to Health, nor with treatises upon the theory and practice of gaming, upon the breeding and training of greyhounds, and upon the flavouring of wines and spirituous liquors. It is possible, however, that they may have no other means of ascertaining what is good, than by requiring a general delivery from the booksellers, and by a subsequent selection on the spot. Still the hardship of the general delivery remains.[10]

It remained indeed, and has done so for more than 150 years, although somewhat mitigated by a reduction in the number of privileged libraries to six.* But in the interval the number of books involved has escalated to a peak inconceivable in Southey's day – at a rough estimate, 150,000 volumes every year, worth about £300,000 at retail prices. Is it right that the cost of these, however computed, should fall on the shoulders of those who live by providing them, authors as well as publishers, rather than upon the community at large? Successive governments have held that it was, and have declined to amend this piece of copyright legislation, even though it involved presenting books free to the national library of Eire, a foreign country, some of whose citizens have consistently shown themselves something less than friendly to Great Britain.

*

But the prodigious increase in the number of books published annually is far from being the item that has most radically affected our copyright laws since the middle of the last century. With the advent of photography, the gramophone, the tape recorder, the cinema, wireless and television, the scope of copyright protection has been widened immeasurably, and the law in relation to it elaborated correspondingly. With its elaboration, inevitably, has come increasing infringement of the rights of copyright owners; for the most part unwitting, sometimes disingenuous, occasionally deliberate. Photographs taken by a professional photographer are an example of an activity in which most people are ignorant of the legal position and may

---

* The British Museum, The Bodleian, The Cambridge University Library, The National Libraries of Scotland and Wales (the latter with some limitations), and Trinity College, Dublin. The 1911 Act made it obligatory for the publisher to present a copy of every book to the British Museum within one month of publication; the other five libraries having the right to claim one within a year.

unwittingly commit infringements. In a nutshell, the law is that the person causing the photograph to be taken owns the copyright, unless an agreement is made to the contrary, so that if a society hostess commissions a photographer to do a camera portrait of her she will own the copyright in it unless otherwise agreed. Equally, if a fashionable photographer approaches a well-known actress with a request for a sitting, the resulting photographs will be his copyright, not hers, in default of any agreement to the contrary. That is, unless the photographer is working for a newspaper under a contract of service, in which case the copyright will belong to the newspaper. Broadly speaking, the copyright in all works directly commissioned or carried out during the course of a person's employment will belong to the employer unless otherwise agreed; though the legal definition of a 'contract of service' is more than a little obscure.

Private letters form another area in which much confusion has reigned, though the law here is entirely logical and consistent. If A writes to B, A is just as much the 'author' of his letter as if he had written a book, and therefore the owner of the copyright in it. Accordingly he can prevent B (or anybody else) publishing it without his consent during his lifetime and for fifty years after his death. B, on the other hand, has physical possession of the letter and so can prevent A (or anybody else) from ever printing it if he does not wish its contents to be made public.* That, surely, is entirely right and proper. Moreover B can sell A's letter, either privately or at auction, without reference to anybody. But the purchaser, unless A has been dead more than fifty years, cannot publish it without permission, and he cannot do so even then, if that particular letter has never been published. He has acquired a right of property in the paper and ink, but not in the words on the page. Hence the unwillingness of libraries housing the correspondence of distinguished authors to make such letters available for inspection except under the most stringent conditions.

The same dual property right obtains in the case of pictures and other works of art. The person who creates them and the person who owns them have quite separate and distinct rights in them. And this again is surely fair, for if ownership of a picture automatically constituted ownership of the copyright in it, most

---

* The advent of carbon copies and the invention of photocopying have, of course, greatly reduced this aspect of B's control in recent years.

artists would be materially worse off than they already are. Once
the picture or sculpture is out of copyright, however, the owner is
in complete control and can exploit the work in any way he
chooses. Owners of stately homes with important pictures
hanging on their walls have not been slow to take advantage of
this, by having their treasures photographed and selling the
right to reproduce such photographs, in biographies and similar
publications, for appreciable sums. Erroneously, they almost
invariably claim copyright in the original work of art, though it
may well have been painted in the time of Henry VIII; whereas,
of course, the only subsisting copyright is in the contemporary
photograph. It is for this reason that 'cameras not allowed' notices
appear in so many theatres, museums, and other places of public
interest or entertainment. For if the public could take its own
photographs at will, there would be a much reduced sale for the
owners' own photographs, and for the right to reproduce them
elsewhere. It is probably fair, therefore, that exploitation of the
fact that 'possession is nine tenths of the law' should benefit
private owners in this way, provided that their demands are
reasonable – which is not always the case. Museums and other
public collections are rather different. In most cases their possessions belong to the nation, and are maintained largely out of
government funds to which we have all contributed. That the cost
of upkeep should be partly defrayed by the sale of reproductions,
usually in the form of postcards, is eminently reasonable. It is not
so certain that the additional charge almost invariably levied by
galleries for the right to reproduce them in a book is equally
justified, having regard to the fact that the works in question are
in public ownership, are mostly long out of copyright, and that the
public is now being asked to pay even to be allowed to *see* them.

Disingenuous abuse of copyright, by which I mean the legally
unassailable but morally indefensible use of another's work, is
nowadays far less common than the unwitting infringements to
which I have referred. But it has a long history, studded with
famous names. Samuel Richardson, for example, was an early
sufferer. The second part of *Pamela*, and the whole of *Sir Charles
Grandison*, were virtually 'pirated' in Ireland, where for some
reason English copyright law did not run at the time; this despite
the fact that Richardson had made binding agreements with a
succession of Dublin booksellers under which he was to receive
certain sums in return for exclusive rights. These rights could

Samuel Richardson (1689–1761) by Joseph Highmore, [c. 1754]. Master of the Stationers' Company 1754. (Stationers' Hall)

only be secured to the lawful assignee by ensuring first publication by him, which involved physically preventing the unbound sheets of a new book falling into the hands of other Irish booksellers. For the latter would promptly reprint them locally and sell them, at a cut price, without paying royalty. Richardson, himself a printer in a substantial way of business and one-time Master of the Stationers' Company, took elaborate precautions with the printing of *Sir Charles Grandison* in the summer of 1753, but all to no purpose. Two of his journeymen flagrantly disobeyed his security instructions, purloined sheets of the book as they came from the press, and smuggled them over to Dublin, where some of them arrived ahead of those sent by Richardson himself to the bookseller with whom he had arranged publication. No less than four other booksellers illegally received sheets in this way, and their subsequent machinations caused Richardson much heartburning as well as financial loss. Notwithstanding his eminence both as a writer and a citizen, and the support of powerful friends on both sides of the Irish channel, he obtained little or no redress for his grievances.[11]

Nearly a century later Charles Dickens found himself treated in much the same way by the Americans, who reprinted his books at a quarter of the London price just as soon as they could get hold of them. Tens of thousands of copies, he maintained, had been sold without a penny of reward for the author, owing to the absence of any international copyright agreement. 'Of all men living,' he told a crowded Boston banquet in 1842, 'I am the greatest loser by it.' And he went on to make an impassioned plea, citing Sir Walter Scott as a fellow sufferer, for 'an international arrangement in this respect'.[12] The effect was the opposite of what he anticipated or intended. Fêted and lionised everywhere, not only as a literary celebrity but, somewhat to his surprise, as the high-priest of moral uplift, Dickens was even more surprised to find that his remarks about copyright caused widespread resentment. A later speech in the same vein provoked open hostility in the Press and elsewhere. But a month or so later the *New York Tribune* rallied to his support, asking 'Who shall protest against robbery if those who are robbed may not? Here is a man who writes for a living. Do we look well offering him toasts, compliments and other syllabub while we refuse him naked justice? . . . He has a wife and four children whom his death may possibly leave destitute while publishers, grown rich by his

writings, roll by in their carriages.' Shades of Southey and
Wordsworth! But thirty-six years later Mr Gladstone, writing to
Blanchard Jerrold in 1878, was making the same plea:

I scarcely feel justified in expressing any opinion on the question of copyright in the character of a literary man, as my title to bear that character
might perhaps be questioned.

   I was however a steady and ever zealous coadjutor of Serjeant Talfourd
in his efforts, more than forty years ago, to obtain a just settlement of the
law: and on this ground I may venture to state that I should view with great
satisfaction the adoption of further measures for the development of the
principle of International Copyright.[13]

Blanchard Jerrold subsequently founded the English branch of
the International Association for the Assimilation of Copyright
Laws, but it was not until 1892 that the first International
Copyright Convention was signed. Even then, America declined to join it, so that Scott and Dickens were far from being the
only British victims of this situation. In the first half of the present
century books as famous as Beatrix Potter's *Peter Rabbit*, Helen
Bannerman's *Little Black Sambo* and Norman Douglas's *South
Wind*, to mention only a few, were published in America without
at first any payment to their authors because under American
domestic law they were technically out of copyright. It is only
fair to add that reputable American publishers now invariably
pay royalties on such books, and that the contrary practice has
always been a two-way affair. Washington Irving was among
Dickens's American contemporaries whose books were published
here without payment, and much later Mark Twain's early books
were not only 'pirated' in this sense by John Camden Hotten, the
brilliant rogue-elephant of a publisher who founded my own firm
but had chapters gratuitously added to them by Hotten himself!
   In our own time, the fact that until recently Russia subscribed
to no Copyright Convention led to the bizarre situation under
which royalties on British books published in Russia were sometimes remitted here, more often 'frozen' and only released if the
author went in person to collect them and spent them in the
USSR, or most frequently were not paid at all. Legally there was no
reason why they should be. But on the 27 May 1973 the Soviet
Union became officially party to the Universal Copyright
Convention. This news was not greeted with the applause that
might have been expected. There were even those who chose to

believe that Russia had only joined ucc in order to exercise a stricter control over her domestic authors, and in order further to curtail the publication of underground literature. I think they are wrong, and as a member some while ago of a cultural delegation which discussed the matter at some length with the Russian authorities, I have reason to believe that, before joining ucc, they made some careful calculations which showed them that they had more to gain, both culturally and financially, by joining ucc than by continuing to stay outside any copyright convention. But time will show.

True piracy, by which I mean the deliberate breach of another party's copyright, with malice aforethought and for private gain, is a very different matter. Involving as it usually does an element of forgery (for if a book is worth pirating in this way its physical appearance and editorial details are almost certain to be well known and will therefore need to be imitated) the penalties are correspondingly severe and its occurrence comparatively rare. Nevertheless cases have cropped up fairly regularly, and during the last twenty years have proliferated alarmingly in the Far East. The Portuguese port of Macao, on the Kwangtung coast of China opposite Hong Kong, whose revenue according to *Chambers's Encyclopedia* 'comes largely from licensed gambling houses, lotteries and opium', has long housed a number of back street printing shops producing colourable imitations of popular English and American books. Formosa, South Korea and Hong Kong are other centres of production for forged versions of such saleable items as the complete *Encyclopedia Britannica* or the *Concise Oxford Dictionary*, which have been distributed all over South-East Asia at about a quarter the normal price. According to *The Times* of 16 April 1967, over 50,000 pirated books, valued at more than £10,000, had recently been seized in a raid on Macao, and I regret to say that nearly 25,000 of them were Longman's textbooks. The same article refers to a Formosan catalogue listing approximately 3000 of the world's best-known English-language titles, offered at anything from a quarter to a third the price of a genuine edition. The turnover in this illegal traffic was at the time estimated by the Publishers' Association at over a million pounds a year. So the rewards of this form of piracy can be substantial.

In addition to these hazards, there are many legal limitations on a copyright owner's powers of exploiting his property, and this is perhaps a suitable moment to take a look at some of them.

By and large, society has thought it right that copyright should not be allowed to restrict fair comment, or to impede education, or to discourage healthy competition. Accordingly, under what are known as the 'fair dealing' clauses of the Copyright Act, it is not an infringement to reproduce passages from a copyright work 'for purposes of research or private study', or 'for purposes of criticism or review',[14] or subject to certain conditions 'in the course of instruction whether at a school or elsewhere' provided no use is made of a duplicating process.[15] Each of these acts is therefore permissible, so long as it falls within the scope of the phrase 'any fair dealing'. Unfortunately, the Act omits to define what is to be regarded as 'fair' and what is not. In self-defence, and to forestall vexatious litigation, the Society of Authors and the Publishers' Association jointly agreed some time ago that, for purposes of criticism or review, they would not regard as 'unfair' the quotation of a single extract of 400 words or a series of extracts totalling 800 words in the case of prose works, and 40 lines (provided that this was not more than a quarter of the complete poem) in the case of poetry. On the whole this formula has worked very well. But a few years ago the question of what is permissible by way of quotation in a bona fide work of literary criticism came under review, following a spirited exchange of letters in the correspondence columns of *The Times Literary Supplement* during September–December 1969. This showed that opinions were divided; some critics claiming the right to quote much more than copyright owners thought fair, the authors and publishers wanting to set a limit well inside what the critics considered reasonable. It is a tricky problem, and perhaps one that can only be equitably solved on an *ad hoc* basis. For surely the crucial question is whether the quotations, on balance, illuminate the critic's contentions – are genuinely illustrative of his arguments – or whether they are supererogatory and merely save him the trouble of writing something himself. In which case part at least of the reader's enjoyment will be derived from the writer quoted, not the critic, and the former should be entitled to a fee.

In 1965 the same two bodies that had produced the 'fair-dealing' formula turned their attention to photocopying, and gamely grappled with the series of intricate copyright problems presented by the invention of this simple method of making single or multiple copies of extracts from books and periodicals.

In an attempt both to clarify the legal position in the interests of all concerned, and to curb abuses, they published a 'guide for libraries, teachers and other suppliers and users of photocopies of copyright works.'[16] This set out very clearly the limits to which photocopying may go, in libraries and schools, without infringing the copyright owner's rights. I am not concerned here with the technical details establishing those limits, but the principle behind them is important. Once again it is a question of how far an author's rights should be restricted in the interests of education, research, cultural advantage or public convenience. And though indiscriminate photocopying and tape-recording in schools is sometimes defended in the sacred name of education, I think most people would agree that the authors' and publishers' interpretation of what is 'fair' in this context is very reasonable, and goes as far as is possible to meet the needs of the community without significantly eroding the author's rights. That this is so is indicated by the willing cooperation which the Society and the Association have received from the Library Association, the National Council for Educational Technology, and the Department of Education and Science. In this connection, a controlled experiment is due to be carried out in UK schools during the autumn of 1973 to ascertain how far 'licensed photocopying' would prove an equitable and viable solution to this problem. Abuses occur, of course, and will continue to occur, if only because the unrestricted use of copying machines in railway stations and other public places forms an open invitation to the ignorant and the conscienceless. The much larger question of Reprographic Reproduction is one which has increasingly occupied the attention of the member countries in the Berne Copyright Convention, and one which it is hoped will ultimately be the subject of an International Recommendation promulgated under the auspices of UNESCO in 1974.

Yet another direction in which society has seen fit to limit an author's rights is in the matter of ideas and names. There is thus no copyright in an idea, only in the words in which it is expressed, and none in the title of a book or play. If an author feels that his literary property is being injured by the existence of another book with the same name he cannot sue the rival author for breach of copyright. He can only secure redress under the Passing Off Acts, when he will have to show that there is a genuine risk of a reasonable person buying his rival's book in mistake for his own.

In capitalist countries private property is still largely sacrosanct, and probably for this reason English courts have tended to look hard and closely at any claims to it. They have been reluctant, for example, to listen to pleas of hardship caused by the use of identical names, or to recognise proprietorial rights in them unless the claim was virtually incontrovertible. Thus some years ago the firm of A. and C. Black, publishers and proprietors of *Who's Who*, learning that another publisher proposed to issue a work called *The International Who's Who*, took Counsel's opinion with a view to seeking an injunction restraining them from using that title. They were advised not to, on the grounds that the phrase 'Who's Who' was so generally descriptive, and the qualifying adjective 'international' so specific, that there was no real risk of confusion. More recently the Granada group of companies endeavoured to stop the Ford Motor Company from christening one of their new models 'the Granada', on the grounds that they had spent many hundreds of thousands of pounds building up the name 'Granada' through cinemas, television programmes, publishing interests etc., and why should Ford's be allowed to help themselves to the goodwill thus created in it. But the court turned a deaf ear to their arguments, perhaps concluding that the risks to the public of confusing a car with a book or a bingo hall were sufficiently remote.

Such decisions exemplify the attitude of the courts to these particular aspects of copyright, but do little to indicate the breadth and complexity of other questions which from time to time they have been called upon to decide. One of the most bizarre of these concerned the curious provision in section 19 of the 1911 Act under which gramophone records of a musical work, if such have already been lawfully made, can be made by anybody without infringement provided due notice is given to the copyright owners and a royalty of $6\frac{1}{4}$ per cent of the retail price is paid. The 1956 Act continued this provision, but modified it with the stipulation that the records must be made for retail sale. This seemingly innocent addition led to a famous case, *Chappell & Co. v The Nestlé Co. and Another*, which was fought all the way up to the House of Lords. There, by a majority of three to two, their Lordships decided 'that the supply of records in return for a postal order for 1s 6d, together with three wrappers for Nestlé's 6d milk chocolate bars, was not a "retail sale" within the meaning of Section 8 of the Act'.[17]

I have left till last any discussion of Public Lending Right, partly because it pinpoints most acutely the area of potential conflict between the rights of authors and the interests of society; partly because the matter is currently (1973) *sub judice*. But a brief account of the history of the affair to date, together with a summary of the arguments that have been advanced on both sides and a resumé of the latest proposals, may be useful.

The story begins in the middle of the last century with the Public Libraries Act of 1850. Later in the century a number of individual philanthropists, prominent among whom was Andrew Carnegie, brought together small collections of books in rooms up and down the country which 'the artisans of the towns and the labourers of the villages' could borrow for nothing, and so improve their education. Over the last hundred years or so, the service thus modestly begun has grown to a point where it is true to say that virtually nobody is nowadays out of reach of a public library, and even the inhabitants of remote rural areas are catered for by mobile library vans. The annual number of 'loans' to the public has increased correspondingly, and is now approaching the formidable total of 700 million issues. As a distinguished economist* has graphically expressed it, 'what was once a utilitarian instrument for spreading light and learning in the dark corners of nineteenth-century industrialism – and in the wake of the hungry "forties" – has become increasingly an engine of mass entertainment in the transformed circumstances of the second half of the twentieth century'.[18] In 1951 the Society of Authors accordingly started pressing the claims of their members in respect of public library borrowings, and asked for the creation of a 'Public Lending Right' (PLR) under which authors would receive a small sum each time one of their books was lent, in the same way as composers and song writers receive one, through the Performing Right Society, each time a work of theirs is played or performed. They asked for this as a matter of simple justice. If the government liked to make the massive borrowing of books from public libraries part of the Welfare State, in line with the arrangements under which large sections of the population could obtain 'free' medicines, spectacles or dentures, well and good. But they should not omit to reward the people without whom the libraries would have nothing to lend. They do not

* Ralph Harris, Director of the Institute of Economic Affairs.

forget to reward the doctors, dentists and opticians who work for the National Health Service. Why should authors be treated differently? Later, in 1966 and 1972, the Society conducted surveys which showed that the income of the great majority of authors was less than half the national average, and proved that the phenomenal increase in the use made of public libraries had been accompanied by a steady fall in the domestic sales of hardcover books.

The battle was then joined and under the able leadership of that peerless promoter of good causes, the late A. P. Herbert, a vigorous campaign in support of PLR was conducted. From the outset the suggestion that authors should no longer be expected to subsidise the public libraries met with violent opposition. The Library Association (though, it should be added, not all of its members) took up an entrenched defensive position, declining even to discuss the idea, which they dismissed contemptuously as impractical, inequitable and unnecessary.

They argued that to keep analysable records of copyright books loaned, or stocked, would cost more than the revenue it would yield, and so defeat its own object; that if authors were to be rewarded according to the number of their books purchased or lent, then successful authors would become still richer while their less successful brethren remained virtually as poor as before; and that legislation was in any case unnecessary, for the publishers had only to add a trifling sum to the price of each new book to produce the money required. They supported these arguments with some doubtful analogies, pointing out that the makers of motor cars and washing machines did not expect an additional payment each time a car they had sold to a car-hire firm was rented, or a washing machine was used in a launderette. The supporters of the scheme countered by demonstrating that, using modern statistical sampling methods, the cost of record-keeping could be reduced to acceptable proportions; by pointing out that there was no inherent injustice in a popular author receiving a greater reward than a less popular one; and that to increase the price of books 'across the board' would simply mean that the very people who do support authors, by buying books instead of borrowing them, would be penalised. As for analogies, always a dangerous form of argument, it was pointed out that books are not chattels with which an owner may do as he pleases, for the law of copyright precludes this; and that if taxis and launderettes were ubiquitously available to the public free of charge, we should soon find the manufacturers protesting vehemently against the damaging decline in their sales of cars and washing machines to private customers.

The argument has continued and is still continuing. In the course of it numerous proposals for operating and financing PLR have been put forward, including charging the borrower, defraying the cost out of the rates, and asking the Treasury to finance the whole scheme from Central Government funds; but each of these has now been discarded. Early in 1971 Lord Eccles, as Minister responsible for the Arts, intimated that the government was prepared to consider amending the Copyright Act 1956 by making lending to the public one of the acts restricted by copyright, and set up a working party to consider how this might be implemented. The working party reported in 1972, and as a result a system of 'blanket licensing' under which libraries would pay an annual fee for the right to lend copyright works was favoured. The resulting revenue would be distributed by a central clearing house, similar in constitution to the Performing Right Society, as to 75 per cent to authors and 25 per cent to publishers. More recently, the suggestion has once again been put forward that the normal term of UK copyright should be extended to include a period during which a statutory royalty would be payable to the State, who would use it for 'cultural purposes', possibly including the cost of administering a Public Lending Right scheme. The Gregory Committee, charged to revise the 1911 Act in 1951, considered a similar proposal and rejected it as likely to impose an indirect tax on the public.

This idea apart, the proposals for PLR supported by the Society of Authors and the Publishers' Association did not commend themselves to all authors, and it was not long before a dissident 'Writers' Action Group' emerged which was vehemently opposed to the proposed machinery, as being unjust, and wished to return to the original scheme which involved recording loans. The ensuing controversy has proved almost as bitter as any in the long history of authorship, and aptly illustrates the truth of George Bernard Shaw's assertion that 'when you take the field for the authors you will be safer without a breastplate than without a backplate.'[19] It remains to be seen whether any of these proposals, along with the relevant administrative machinery, will prove acceptable to Parliament, and the necessary legislation find

its way on to the Statute Book. Let me in conclusion quote again
the Director of the Institute of Economic Affairs:

Economists should not be concerned to defend the interest of authors, publishers (or other producers) beyond what is necessary to ensure the interest of
the reading (or consuming) public. . . . Whatever the merits (or proper
limitations) of existing provisions for copyright in Britain, they clearly stand
in the sharpest possible contrast to the unchecked use of library books by
borrowers who comprise the bulk of customers for the output of most
authors but who pay little or nothing towards maintaining its supply.[20]

✱

Finally, what of the future? We live in a technological age, one
which has witnessed the advent of computers, memory banks and
retrieval systems; of tape-recorders, video-tapes and audio-visual
cassettes – radically new methods of storing and disseminating
knowledge. Thus, while not anticipating any marked increase in
the number of distinct rights that will require future copyright
protection, it seems to me certain that the nature and scope of the
protection afforded to existing rights will continue to evolve and
expand. This in turn will make it necessary to create appropriate
systems of control, if we are to prevent the wholesale erosion of
copyright owners' rights.[21] The Writers' Guild is already complaining, with some justification, that legislation has not kept
pace with technical advance, and has expressed concern about
the transmission of television programmes by satellite from one
country to another. This involves International Copyright, which
is outside the scope of this essay; but even control of domestic
copyright is no easy matter when we are dealing with sophisticated communications media, as we have already discovered in
the case of off-shore pirate radio stations. Overseas, where the
claims of education and the free availability of cultural opportunity in the so-called 'developing' countries are vitally important,
it is even harder to draw the line between private interest and
public good. But unless the interests of artists of all kinds – the
creators of literature, music and drama – are suitably protected,
no matter in what way their works may in future be preserved and
disseminated, the fountain is liable to dry up at the source and
the world will be immeasurably the poorer. For without protection there can be no reward, and without some expectation of
reward, however modest, there may be no incentive to create. It
is a formidable problem, but an inescapable challenge.

August 1973

DAVID DAICHES

Presenting
Shakespeare

To SHAKESPEARE, as to most dramatists of his day, a play was something to be performed in the theatre, and its publication in book form was a matter of little or no interest. Indeed, Shakespeare's plays were not his to publish anyway, for they were the property of the acting company to which he belonged and in which he was an important 'sharer'. It was not often in the interests of an acting company to release for publication plays in their repertoire. This explains why certain corrupt and unauthorised texts of individual plays were published by unscrupulous printers. Of course, sometimes the company did release a play for publication, perhaps in time of plague when performances were suspended. But if a company sold a play to a printer, the printing rights belonged henceforth to that printer (or publisher, when these were different persons, as they sometimes were by Shakespeare's time) even if, as often happened, the play had been sold without the author's knowledge or consent. Thus plays were published without being seen through the press and corrected by the author, with the result that the text was often full of errors and sometimes even included emendations and 'improvements' made by the printer. And this gave great scope to editors of a later age, when Shakespeare's works had become regarded as classics to be read as books as well as performed on the stage.

Eighteen of Shakespeare's plays were published individually in sixpenny quarto editions, thus proclaiming themselves cheap popular entertainment and not serious literature. (Sir Thomas Bodley, in founding his great library at Oxford, specified that it should exclude 'such Books, as Almanacks, Plays, and an infinite Number, that are daily Printed, of very unworthy matters and handling, such, as methinks, both the Keeper and Underkeeper should Disdain to seek out, to deliver to any Man'. But he added: 'Haply some Plays may be worthy the Keeping: But hardly one in Forty.') A few of these were what are known as 'bad quartos', with the texts so garbled (as compared with later 'good' quartos of the same play, or with the text in the Folio of 1623) that some special explanation is called for: it seems that these were what the editors of the First Folio called 'stolne, and surreptitious copies' which may have been put together from memory by an actor or actors who knew their own parts but who had pretty hazy recollections of the parts of other characters, particularly of those who were not on stage with them. But even

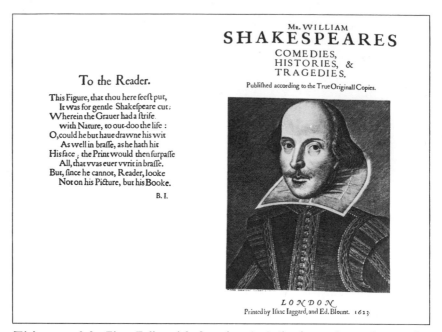

To the Reader.

This Figure, that thou here feeſt put,
It was for gentle Shakeſpeare cut;
Wherein the Grauer had a ſtrife
with Nature, to out-doo the life :
O, could he but haue drawne his wit
As well in braſſe, as he hath hit
His face ; the Print would then ſurpaſſe
All, that vvas euer vvrit in braſſe.
But, ſince he cannot, Reader, looke
Not on his Picture, but his Booke.
B. I.

Mr. WILLIAM
SHAKESPEARES
COMEDIES,
HISTORIES, &
TRAGEDIES.
Publiſhed according to the True Originall Copies.

LONDON
Printed by Iſaac Iaggard, and Ed. Blount. 1623.

Title-page of the First Folio, with the printer's dedication to the reader opposite, much reduced. (Royal Shakespeare Theatre)

with the good quartos there are problems about the text. For the acting company, when they sold the printing rights of one of their plays, would not have been likely to turn over to the printer their own precious prompt-copy, but might well have passed on the author's 'foul papers', that is, his much worked-over manuscript from which a fair copy had been made for acting purposes. This manuscript would contain deletions, additions, alterations, interlineations, often not easy for a printer to make out; further, in such a manuscript there are likely to be inconsistencies in the speech-prefixes and only sporadic stage directions. Evidence of this is, in fact, what we find in many quartos, so that the confusions and mislineations of the printer can sometimes lead us back to the author's workshop. But that was left for the twentieth century to discover.

Unlike Shakespeare, Ben Jonson published a folio edition of his plays during his lifetime, in 1616, and had what was widely regarded as the effrontery to call the volume his *Works*. Plays were not normally regarded as worthy of this treatment at this time. But seven years after Shakespeare's death there appeared a handsome folio volume selling for £1, entitled *Mr. William*

Shakespeares Comedies, Histories, & Tragedies. Published according to the True Originall Copies, with a dedication and an address to

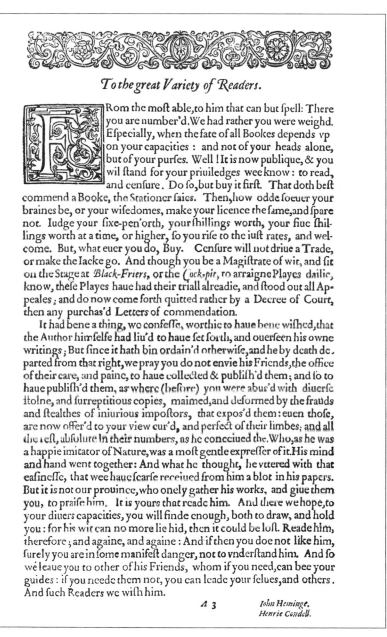

To the great Variety of Readers.

Rom the moſt able, to him that can but ſpell: There you are number'd. We had rather you were weighd. Eſpecially, when the fate of all Bookes depends vp on your capacities : and not of your heads alone, but of your purſes. Well ! It is now publique, & you wil ſtand for your priuiledges wee know : to read, and cenſure. Do ſo, but buy it firſt. That doth beſt commend a Booke, the Stationer ſaies. Then, how odde ſoeuer your braines be, or your wiſedomes, make your licence the ſame, and ſpare not. Iudge your ſixe-pen'orth, your ſhillings worth, your fiue ſhillings worth at a time, or higher, ſo you riſe to the iuſt rates, and welcome. But, what euer you do, Buy. Cenſure will not driue a Trade, or make the Iacke go. And though you be a Magiſtrate of wit, and ſit on the Stage at *Black-Friers,* or the *Cock-pit,* to arraigne Playes dailie, know, theſe Playes haue had their triall alreadie, and ſtood out all Appeales ; and do now come forth quitted rather by a Decree of Court, then any purchas'd Letters of commendation.

It had bene a thing, wo confeſſe, worthie to haue bene wiſhed, that the Author himſelfe had liu'd to haue ſet forth, and ouerſeen his owne writings ; But ſince it hath bin ordain'd otherwiſe, and he by death departed from that right, we pray you do not envie his Friends, the office of their care, and paine, to haue collected & publiſh'd them ; and ſo to haue publiſh'd them, as where (before) you were abuſ'd with diuerſe ſtolne, and ſurreptitious copies, maimed, and deformed by the frauds and ſtealthes of iniurious impoſtors, that expos'd them : euen thoſe, are now offer'd to your view cur'd, and perfect of their limbes ; and all the reſt, abſolute in their numbers, as he conceiued the. Who, as he was a happie imitator of Nature, was a moſt gentle expreſſer of it. His mind and hand went together : And what he thought, he vttered with that eaſineſſe, that wee haue ſcarſe receiued from him a blot in his papers. But it is not our prouince, who onely gather his works, and giue them you, to praiſe him. It is yours that reade him. And there we hope, to your diuers capacities, you will finde enough, both to draw, and hold you : for his wit can no more lie hid, then it could be loſt. Reade him, therefore ; and againe, and againe : And if then you doe not like him, ſurely you are in ſome manifeſt danger, not to vnderſtand him. And ſo wé leaue you to other of his Friends, whom if you need, can bee your guides : if you neede them not, you can leade your ſelues, and others. And ſuch Readers we wiſh him.

A 3   *Iohn Heminge.*
                   Henrie Condell.

First Folio, address to readers by Heminge and Condell. (Royal Shakespeare Theatre)

readers both signed by two of Shakespeare's fellow-actors, John Heminge and Henry Condell. This is the First Folio of 1623. The address to readers includes this interesting sentence:

It had bene a thing, we confesse, worthie to haue bene wished, that the Author himselfe had liu'd to haue set forth, and ouerseen his owne writings; But since it hath bin ordain'd otherwise, and he by death departed from that right, we pray you do not envie his Friends, the office of their care, and paine, to haue collected & published them; and so to haue publish'd them, as where (before) you were abus'd with diuerse stolne, and surreptitious copies, maimed, and deformed by the frauds and stealthes of inurious imposters, that expos'd them: even those, are now offer'd to your view cur'd, and perfect of their limbes; and all the rest, absolute in their numbers, as he conceiued them.

Since only eighteen of the thirty-six plays in the Folio had been previously published as quartos, and of these four in bad quartos only, the Folio is obviously a volume of central importance in the history of the publication of Shakespeare's plays. It is of some concern, therefore, to know whether Heminge and Condell were telling the strict truth in the claims they made for the accuracy of their text. Our knowledge here can only be inferential, for no Shakespearean manuscript is known (except for a passage of three pages in the much revised manuscript play *Sir Thomas More*: this passage is now considered to be by Shakespeare and in his own handwriting). Modern scholarship, with its sophisticated bibliographical techniques and its understanding of Elizabethan and Jacobean printing-house practice, can infer a great deal from an examination of printed texts of the quartos and the Folio. The conclusion now accepted is that the policy of the Folio editors was to make use of a Shakespearean autograph when they could get it, and where they could not to use prompt-copies or transcripts of prompt-copies. If there was a good quarto available, however, they printed from that, which was reasonable enough since the good quartos were themselves printed from authoritative manuscripts. Where there were only bad quartos in print, the Folio used an author's manuscript (except for one case, where a transcription of one was used). Thus for eight plays, where the Folio prints a good quarto, the quarto is our real textual authority; for four plays, which had hitherto appeared only in bad quartos, the Folio provides the only authoritative text; of the eighteen plays first published in the

Folio, six appear to have been printed from prompt-copies, seven directly from the author's 'foul papers', two from somewhat revised author's manuscripts, and three from transcripts of the author's 'foul papers'; for three plays (including *Hamlet*), the relation between the good quarto and the Folio texts is complex, and both texts, though different in some significant respects, have authority; for three plays (including *Othello*) the relation between the quarto and Folio texts is highly complex, both possessing serious deficiencies but the Folio being on the whole the better text. *Pericles, Prince of Tyre* was not included in the Folio at all, and the only text we have is a bad quarto. The Folio was set up by several different compositors, working often simultaneously at different speeds and with differing degrees of skill. This involved fitting each printer's share into a predetermined number of pages, and the process of 'casting off' required for this was not always accurately done, so that omissions or padding were sometimes necessary to join two sections. This, of course, falsified the text, as did the inevitable printers' errors, for though on the whole the printers employed by Jaggard and his fellow publishers of the Folio were reasonably careful and produced their copy fairly accurately, they did make mistakes (some many more than others). Further, it is clear that the proof-reading was extremely careless, generally done without reference to the copy. So the Folio text has its deficiencies. Yet it is a remarkable volume, either our primary or our sole authority for twenty-five of Shakespeare's plays and a valuable secondary authority for five others.

The Second Folio appeared in 1632, it has no independent authority, for it merely reprints the First Folio, with some modernisation of spelling and corrections of stage directions and proper names. Similarly, the Third Folio of 1663 was a reprint of the Second, with some correction of errors but also with the introduction of new errors. The Fourth Folio of 1685 reprints the third, once again with some corrections and with new errors; it includes *Pericles*, which had first appeared in the second issue of the Third Folio in 1664, in the text of the bad Quarto of 1609, and also six non-Shakespearean plays which had also been first introduced in 1664. (The problem of establishing the Shakespearean canon was first faced by eighteenth-century scholars.)

By the end of the seventeenth century Shakespeare's reputation as one of the great English dramatists was firmly established, though not as the absolutely unique genius he became later. Dryden regarded him as 'the man who of all modern, and perhaps ancient poets, had the largest and most comprehensive soul'. Though he criticised some aspects of his language and some of his plots, he admired his 'variety and greatness of characters' and regarded him as one who was 'naturally learned; he needed not the spectacles of books to read Nature' (a view which was to be widely echoed in the eighteenth century). But Dryden could class Shakespeare with Fletcher without sensing that he was comparing great with small and, like many of the educated people of his time, he considered Ben Jonson the more accomplished writer whose work provided 'the perfect pattern of a play'.

The development of neoclassic ideas from France in the late seventeenth century exposed Shakespeare to a variety of attacks on the grounds of his not observing the unities of time, place and action, and of lack of decorum (this having nothing to do with morality, but with what was regarded as the appropriate kind of speech and action for different classes of character). The most famous attack from this quarter was Thomas Rymer's denunciation of *Othello* in his *Short View of Tragedy*, published in 1693. Such attacks did not affect Shakespeare's general popularity, but they did help to determine the way in which Shakespeare was defended in the eighteenth century, which was the first great age of the editing and critical discussion of his plays. It was largely in order to obtain for him exemption from neoclassic laws and categories that Shakespeare was claimed as a unique child of Nature, a very special kind of natural genius, marvellously creative and spontaneous in his understanding and his rendering of the human scene, so that normal rules of composition do not apply to him. Thus, paradoxically, it was the attacks on Shakespeare which provoked the kind of defence that first led him to be regarded as *the* unique genius of English literature. In the seventeenth century he was a much loved dramatist – sometimes regarded as a bit old-fashioned after the Restoration, but still popular, although under attack by pedants and sticklers for the rules. It was during the eighteenth century that Shakespeare was first put into a quite special category and, for varying reasons, he has remained there ever since.

The production of four successive folio editions of Shakespeare's plays between 1623 and 1685 is testimony to their continued popularity. This very popularity contributed to the

Scar. Swallows have built
In *Cleopatra's* Sails their Nests.   The Auguries
Say, they know not——they cannot tell——look grimly,
And dare not speak their Knowledge.   *Antony*
Is valiant, and dejected, and by starts,
His fretted Fortunes give him hope and fear
Of what he has, and has not.   [*Exit.*

  S C E N E **VII.**   Alexandria.

Enter Antony.

  Ant. All is lost!
This foul *Ægyptian* hath betrayed me!
My Fleet hath yielded to the Foe, and yonder,
They cast their Caps up, and Carowse together
Like Friends long lost. Triple-turn'd Whore! 'tis thou *Hit*

Scar. Swallows have built
In *Cleopatra's* Sailes their nests.   The Auguries
Say, they know not, they cannot tell, look grimly,
And dare not speak their knowledge.   *Anthony*
Is valiant, and dejected, and by starts
His fretted Fortunes give him hope and fear
Of what he has, and has not.

Enter Anthony.

  Ant. All is lost:
This foul *Ægyptian* hath betrayed me :
My Fleet hath yielded to the Foe, and yonder,
They cast their Caps up, and Carowse together
Like friends long lost. Triple-turn'd Whore, tis thou

Lines from the Fourth Folio text of Antony and Cleopatra *(right) compared with the same lines from Rowe's edition (left), showing his precise locating of scenes. (Royal Shakespeare Theatre)*

corruption of the text, for printers cheerfully reprinted the preceding edition with casual corrections and some modernisation of spelling and typographical practice; they were catering to a popular demand, not supplying a scholarly or educational need which would have required a carefully authenticated text. By the beginning of the eighteenth century, however, the continued presentation of the plays in the form in which they had been presented in the First Folio was no longer acceptable: Shakespeare's language now seemed old-fashioned. Further, readers now demanded lists of Dramatis Personae, clear stage directions, and the division of acts into scenes with each scene precisely located. This they got (though with no consistency in the division of acts into scenes) in Nicholas Rowe's edition of Shakespeare's plays in 1709, in which we see the first stage of what R. B. McKerrow called 'the transition between the simple reprinting of an author regarded as contemporary and the "editing" of one who has become out of date and somewhat difficult to understand'. Rowe, himself a dramatist, was commissioned to edit Shakespeare by the important London publisher Jacob Tonson, who had some years before bought the rights of the folio text of Shakespeare from the publishers of the Fourth Folio and who may well have wanted to demonstrate his ownership before the new Copyright Act came into force in April 1710.* The massive and expensive folio was no longer considered a suitable form in which to bring out the plays, and Rowe's edition

* See 'Copyright and society', pp. 38–9.

Title-page to Antony and Cleopatra *in the Fourth Folio, and title-page and list of dramatis personae in Rowe's edition of* Antony and Cleopatra, *showing Rowe's introduction of the list of dramatis personae. (Royal Shakespeare Theatre)*

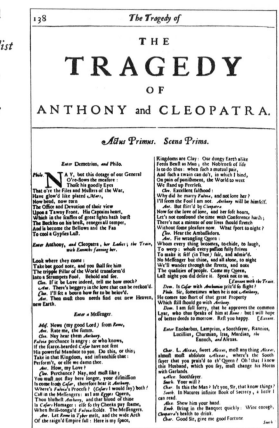

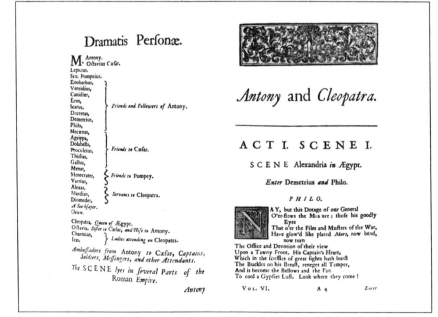

consisted of six octavo volumes which together sold for 30 shillings. (In 1710 a volume of *Shakespeare's Poems*, edited by Charles Gildon and published by Curll, appeared in identical format, so that it would look like a seventh volume of Rowe's edition: this explains why even such a distinguished bibliographer as McKerrow described Rowe's original edition as in seven volumes.) Tonson paid Rowe £36 10s for his editorial labours, of which he may well have considered the prefixed Life of Shakespeare to have been the most important part. This, the first formal biography of Shakespeare, was based on material given to Rowe by the actor Thomas Betterton (*c*. 1635–1710) which included both theatrical traditions Betterton had got from Sir William Davenant (whose Duke's Company of actors he had joined in 1661) and Stratford traditions collected on a special journey to Warwickshire. This remained the standard Life of Shakespeare throughout the eighteenth century.

Rowe's edition was illustrated with forty-five engravings. As for the text, there is some discrepancy between what Rowe claimed to have done and what he actually did. In his Dedication he wrote:

I must not pretend to have restor'd this Work to the Exactness of the Author's Original Manuscripts: Those are lost, or, at least, are gone beyond any Inquiry I could make; so that there was nothing left, but to compare the several Editions, and give the true Reading as well as I could from thence. This I have endeavour'd to do pretty carefully, and render'd very many Places Intelligible, that were not so before.

But, in fact, Rowe based his text on the Fourth Folio, the most corrupt of the folios, and though he seems occasionally to have looked at the First or Second Folio text when trying to solve a difficulty and even used a quarto reading on a few occasions (for some quartos continued to be reprinted, as theatrical play-books, right up to Rowe's time), on the whole it is fair to say that he did not adopt the textual procedure he described in his Dedication. What he produced was a revision of the Fourth Folio (except for *Hamlet*, where he included lines found only in the 'good' quarto text). In matters of lists of Dramatis Personae, stage directions, scene divisions and headings, Rowe gave us the Shakespeare familiar to later generations. And although this made for ease of reading, in some cases it obscured Shakespeare's theatrical intentions. Shakespeare's platform stage did not always require

The frontispiece to Rowe's edition of Antony and Cleopatra. (*Royal Shakespeare Theatre*)

the precisely localised scenes required by the picture-frame stage to which Rowe was accustomed, and certain kinds of fluidity of action intended by Shakespeare and highly effective if presented in the way he intended (such as the battle scenes in Act IV of *Antony and Cleopatra*, divided by editors who followed the Rowe tradition into twelve short scenes, one of only four lines, each set in a different place) disappeared completely with precise localisation. But Rowe's tidying up of the way in which the plays were laid out for the reader remained his most permanent contribution to the presentation of Shakespeare. All subsequent editions up to the present, except for some recent facsimile and old-text editions intended for scholars, have either reproduced or made some use of Rowe's apparatus as later refined by Pope. As for his textual emendations, Rowe adopted what Nichol Smith called the 'armchair method of editing'.[1] If a word puzzled him, more often than not he altered it to what seemed to him plausible without checking any other text. Thus, a reference to 'important' letters in the First Folio text of *The Comedy of Errors* is misprinted as 'im-

The frontispiece to Pope's second edition of Othello, (1728) *designed and engraved by Lud du Guernier. (Royal Shakespeare Theatre)*

poteant' in the Second Folio, changed in the course of printing to 'impotent'. The Third and Fourth Folios take over 'impotent'. Rowe, realising that the sense required the very opposite of 'impotent', changed it to 'all-potent'. An armchair method, indeed, when the correct reading was there for the looking up in the First Folio!

The next edition was that of Alexander Pope, and it says something for the esteem in which Shakespeare was held in the first half of the eighteenth century that the greatest poet of the age was commissioned to produce an edition of his plays. This appeared in six quarto volumes in 1725. In what might be called mechanical matters, Pope took his cue from Rowe and improved on him, retaining Rowe's lists of Dramatis Personae and acting much more consistently than Rowe had done in dividing acts into scenes and indicating the precise locality of each. Although Pope used Rowe's text as the basis of his own, actually sending to the printer heavily corrected pages of Rowe's edition, his method as textual editor was very different. As Nichol Smith put it: 'If

Actus Quartus. Scena Prima.

Enter Prospero, Ferdinand, and Miranda.
Pro. If I haue too austerely punish'd you,
Your compensation makes amends, for I
Haue giuen you here, a third of mine owne life,
Or that for which I liue: who, once againe
I tender to thy hand: All thy vexations
Were but my trials of thy loue, and thou
Hast strangely stood the test: here, afore heauen
I ratifie this my rich guilt: O *Ferdinand*,
Doe not smile at me, that I boast her of,
For thou shalt finde she will out-strip all praise
And make it halt, behinde her.
    Fer. I doe beleeue it
Against an Oracle.
    Pro. Then, as my guest, and thine owne acquisition
Worthily purchas'd, take my daughter: But
If thou do'st breake her Virgin-knot, before
All sanctimonious ceremonies may
With full and holy right, be ministred,
No sweet aspersion shall the heauens let fall
To make this contract grow; but barraine hate,
Sower-ey'd disdaine, and discord shall bestrew
The vnion of your bed, with weedes so loathly
That you shall hate it both: Therefore take heede,
As *Hymens* Lamps shall light you.
    Fer. As I hope
For quiet dayes, faire Issue, and long life,
With such loue, as 'tis now the murkiest den,
The most opportune place, the strongst suggestion,
Our worser *Genius* can, shall neuer melt
Mine honor into lust, to take away
The edge of that dayes celebration,
When I shall thinke, or *Phœbus* Steeds are founderd,
Or Night kept chain'd below.
    Pro. Fairely spoke;
Sit then, and talke with her, she is thine owne;
What *Ariell*; my industrious seruāt *Ariell. Enter Ariell.*
    Ar. What would my potent master? here I am.

Rowe approached his task with the equipment of a dramatist Pope approached it in the spirit of a literary executor.' It is as though Shakespeare, having died without having prepared his plays for the press, left it to Pope to tidy up, alter, improve and rearrange where he thought it necessary. Pope was aware of the textual problem. He knew about the quartos, and possessed quite a number, and he had a copy of the First Folio and probably of the Second also. But his procedure was one quite unacceptable to a modern editor, and this for two reasons. First, he was an 'improving' editor, who felt it his duty to try and smooth out roughnesses, eliminate inconsistencies and even remove anachronisms in Shakespeare's text. (He seems to have been especially upset at Shakespeare's giving hats to his Roman characters, and changed the word to 'caps' whenever he could. But in *Julius*

54   *The* TEMPEST.

'That deep and dreadful organ-pipe, pronounc'd
'The name of *Prosper*: it did bafe my trefpafs.
Therefore my fon i'th' ooze is bedded; and
I'll feek him deeper than e'er plummet founded,
And with him there lye mudded.   [*Exit.*
   Seb. But one fiend at a time,
I'll fight their legions o'er.
   Ant. I'll be thy fecond.   [*Exeunt.*
   Gon. All three of them are defp'rate; their great guilt,
Like poifon giv'n to work a great time after,
Now 'gins to bite the fpirits. I befeech you
That are of fuppler joints, follow them fwiftly,
And hinder them from what this ecftafie
May now provoke them to.
   Adri. Follow, I pray you.   [*Exeunt.*

ACT IV. SCENE I.

Profpero's *Cave.*

Enter Profpero, Ferdinand, *and* Miranda.

PROSPERO.

IF I have too aufterely punifh'd you,
Your compenfation makes amends; for I
Have giv'n you here a third of mine own life,
Or that for which I live; whom once again
I render to thy hand: all thy vexations
Were but my tryals of thy love, and thou
Haft ftrangely ftood the teft. Here afore heav'n
I ratifie this my rich gift: O *Ferdinand,*

Du

The TEMPEST.   55

Do not fmile at me that I boaft her off;
For thou fhalt find fhe will outftrip all praife,
And make it halt behind her.
   Fer. I believe it
Againft an oracle.
   Pro. Then as my gift, and thine own acquifition
Worthily purchas'd, take my daughter.
If thou doft break her virgin-knot before
All fanctimonious ceremonies may
With full and holy right be minifter'd,
No fweet afperfion fhall the heav'ns let fall
To make this contract grow: but barren hate,
Sour-ey'd difdain, and difcord fhall beftrew
The union of your bed with weeds fo loathly,
That you fhall hate it both: therefore take heed,
As *Hymen's* lamps fhall light you.
   Fer. As I hope
For quiet days, fair iffue, and long life,
With fuch love as 'tis now: the murkieft den,
The moft opportune place, the ftrong'ft fuggeftion
Our worfer *Genius* can, fhall never melt
Mine honour into luft, to take away
The edge of that day's celebration,
When I fhall think or *Phœbus'* fteeds are founder'd,
Or night kept chain'd below.
   Pro. Fairly fpoke.
Sit then, and talk with her, fhe is thine own.
What, *Ariel*; my induftrious fervant, *Ariel.*

SCENE II.

Enter Ariel.

   Ari. What would my potent mafter? here I am.   *Pro.*

A page from The Tempest *in the First Folio (opposite) compared with the same lines from Pope's edition. (Royal Shakespeare Theatre and the Shakespeare Birthplace Trust)*

Caesar the conspirators' 'hats are pluck'd about their ears', and Pope realised that you can't pluck a cap about your ears. So he simply cut out the word 'hats' and inserted a dash instead, leaving the reader a prey to the most frightful suggestions.) He had no great knowledge of Elizabethan English, and changed many usages in Shakespeare, which were standard at the time, to conform to usage in his own day. ('This was the most unkindest cut of all' becomes 'This, this was the unkindest cut of all'. Pope could not abide Shakespeare's double comparatives and double superlatives.) He changes words in order to achieve greater metrical regularity. And of course he modernises spelling and punctuation.

The second reason for Pope's deficiencies as an editor applies also to all the other editors of Shakespeare in the first half of the eighteenth century. He did not realise that in editions in the same line of descent only the first has any authority. There is no point whatever in comparing the texts of the different Folio editions of Shakespeare, for the Second is printed from the First, the Third from the Second and the Fourth from the Third. Any different readings between the later Folios and the First must be the product of the printing-house: they will be printers' attempts at emendation, printers' errors, or proof-readers' guesses. Where a different edition is printed from a fresh manuscript, or where the author is himself concerned in seeing it through the press, it is of course another matter. But this was not the case with the Shakespeare Folios. Many of the quartos do represent different lines of descent from the Folio text, but not where a later quarto is a reprint of an earlier, or the Folio text is a simple reprint of the quarto. There is, in short, no point in collating texts in the same line of descent. This simple truth was obscured to earlier editors because they were thinking of the problems of editing classical texts, with which they were much more familiar: in the case of most classical texts the sources are different manuscripts each of which represents a different line of descent, so that each may have independent authority. If Pope's taste suggested to him that a reading to be found in the Second Folio which was not in the First was better than the reading in the First, he considered that he had authority for accepting it, but in fact he had no authority at all. One might add that even if he had realised this point Pope would not have been deterred, for to him taste overrode textual authority anyway. He 'corrected' Shakespeare according to the poetic taste of his own day. It was a hard task and Pope worked at it conscientiously, but the aim was misguided. For the modern reader the most important part of Pope's edition of Shakespeare is his Preface, which gives eloquent expression to the view of Shakespeare prevalent in Britain in the first half of the eighteenth century. 'If ever any Author deserved the name of an *Original*, it was *Shakespear*. *Homer* himself drew not his art so immediately from the fountains of Nature. . . . The Poetry of *Shakespear* was Inspiration indeed: he is not so much an Imitator, as an Instrument, of Nature.' For Pope, Shakespeare has faults, some of them grave, but his greatness as a natural genius who understood human character and the human passions (i.e. emotions) outweighs them all.

Lewis Theobald, classical scholar and dramatist, attacked

Pope's edition in his *Shakespeare Restored: or, a Specimen of the Many Errors, as well Committed, as Unamended, by Mr. Pope in his Late Edition of this Poet. Designed not only to correct the said Edition, but to restore the True Reading of Shakespeare in all the Editions ever yet published*. Theobald found himself cast as the King of Dullness in the first edition of Pope's *Dunciad* for his pains. But as far as critical method goes, Theobald was right and Pope wrong. 'Nothing is altered,' he wrote in the Preface to his own seven-volume edition of 1733, 'but what by the clearest reasoning can be proved a corruption of the true text; and the alteration, a real restoration of the genuine reading.' He did not therefore 'improve' according to his own taste, as Pope so often did, but really tried to restore the original readings. He knew some of Shakespeare's sources, to which he drew attention for the first time, and he had a good knowledge of Elizabethan literature which he drew on in his pioneering explanatory footnotes. In these footnotes he explains Shakespeare's language both by reference to Shakespeare's use of the same word in other contexts and to its use by other Elizabethan writers. But in spite of some brilliant emendations (the most famous of which, only recently called into question, is 'a bab(b)led of green fields' for the unintelligible 'a Table of greene fields' in Mistress Quickly's account of Falstaff's death in *Henry V*) Theobald did not understand the nature of a copy text and, although he collated many more earlier editions than Pope had done and adopted some good readings from some of them which later editors have retained, his collation was far from systematic. Further, in spite of his attack on Pope he actually used Pope's edition as the basis of his own text. Though he made numerous corrections, the basic text remained Pope's, and Theobald unwittingly included very many of Pope's alterations. No matter how much it was corrected with reference to earlier editions, Theobald's text was that of the Fourth Folio (the most corrupt of the Folios) as it had come to him through Rowe and Pope.

Sir Thomas Hanmer's sumptuous edition in six quarto volumes, published in 1744 at three guineas (and costing three times as much in the reprint of 1770), is more interesting as a handsome piece of book-making than as an edition. It had engravings by F. Gravelot after designs by Francis Hayman. Hanmer used Pope's text, corrected by Theobald's, and ignored all earlier editions. His emendations were done entirely on

30   *King* HENRY V,

We doubt not of a fair and lucky war,
Since God fo gracioufly hath brought to light
This dangerous treafon lurking in our way,
To hinder our beginning.   Now we doubt not,
But every rub is fmoothed in our way :
Then forth, dear countrymen ; let us deliver
Our puiffance into the hand of God,
Putting it ftrait in expedition.
Chearly to fea ; the figns of war advance ;
No King of *England*, if not King of *France*.   [*Exeunt.*

SCENE *changes to* Quickly's *houfe in* Eaftcheap.

Enter Piftol, Nim, Bardolph, *Boy, and* Quickly.

Quick. PR'ythee, honey-fweet husband, let me bring
          thee to *Staines*.
Piftol. No, for my manly heart doth yern.
Bardolph, be blith : *Nim,* rouze thy vaunting veins :
Boy, briftle thy courage up ; for *Falftaff* he is dead,
And we muft yern therefore.
     Bard. Would I were with him wherefome'er he is,
either in heaven or in hell.
     Quick. Nay, fure, he's not in hell; he's in *Arthur's*
bofom, if ever man went to *Arthur's* bofom.   He made
a finer end, and went away, an it had been any chriftom
child ; a' parted even juft between twelve and one, even
at the turning o'th' tide : For after I faw him fumble
with the fheets, and play with flowers, and fmile upon
his finger's end, I knew there was but one way ; for
(18) his nofe was as fharp as a pen, and a' babled of
green fields.   How now, Sir *John*? quoth I : what,
man?

(18) *His Nofe was as fharp as a Pen, and a Table of green fields.]*
So the firft Folio. Mr. Pope has obferv'd, that thefe Words, and a Table
of green fields, are not in the old 4to's. This Nonfenfe, (continues He,)
got into all the following Editions by a pleafant Miftake of the Stage-Editors,
who printed from the common peacemeal-written Parts in the Play-houfe. A
Table was here directed to be brought in (it being a Scene in a Tavern where
they drink at parting ;) and this Direction crept into the Text from the
Margin. Greenfield was the Name of the Property-man in that time who
furnifh'd

King HENRY V.   31

man? be of good cheer: fo a' cried out God, God, God,
three or four times.   Now I, to comfort him, bid him,
a' fhou'd not think of God ; I hop'd, there was no need
to trouble himfelf with any fuch thoughts yet : fo a' bad
me lay more clothes on his feet : I put my hand into the
bed and felt them, and they were as cold as a ftone :
then I felt to his knees, and fo upward, and upward, and
all was as cold as any ftone.
     Nim. They fay, he cried out of fack.
     Quick. Ay, that a' did.
     Bard. And of women.
     Quick. Nay, that a' did not.

furnifh'd Implements, &c. *for the Actors. A* Table of Greenfield's.——
As to the Hiftory of *Greenfield* being then Property-man, whether it was
really fo, or it be only a *gratis dictum,* is a Point which I fhall not
contend about.   But were we to allow this marginal Direction, and
fuppofe that a Table of *Greenfield's* was wanting ; yet it never was
cuftomary in the Promptor's Book, (much lefs, in the peacemeal Parts ;)
where any fuch Directions are marginally inferted for Properties or Implements wanted, to add the Property-man's Name, whofe Bufinefs it was
to provide them.   Befides, the furnifhing Chairs and Tables is not the
Province of the Property-man, but of the Scene-keepers.   But there is a
ftronger Objection yet againft this Obfervation advanced by the Editor.
He feems to imagine, that when Implements are wanted in any Scene,
the Direction for them is mark'd in the middle of that Scene, though the
Things are to be got ready againft the Beginning of it.   But the Directions for *Entrances* and *Properties* wanting, ('tis well known,) are always
mark'd in the Book at about a Page in Quantity before the Actors quoted
are to enter, or the Properties to be ufed ; that the Stage may not ftand
ftill.   And therefore, *Greenfield's* Table can be of no Ufe to us for this
Scene.   Nor, indeed, is any Table requifite.   The Scene, 'tis true, is
in a Tavern ; but the Company have no Bufinefs to fit down.   There is
not the leaft Intimation of any Drink going round : It is in *Piftol's* own
Houfe, as he had married *Quickly* : he and his Comerades are on their
Feet, and juft fetting out for *France.*   The Defcription of *Falftaffe's*
Death, and what he talk'd of, is the only Thing that retards them for a
few Minutes: after which they kifs their Hoftefs, and part.   The Con-
jectural Emendation I have given, is fo near to the Traces of the Letters
in the corrupted Text ; that I have ventur'd to infert it as the genuine
Reading.   It has certainly been obferv'd (in particular, by the Super-
ftition of Women ;) of People near Death, when they are delirious by a
Fever, that they talk of *removing* : as it has of Thofe in a Calenture,
that they have their heads run on *green Fields.*——To *bable,* or *babble,* is
to mutter, or fpeak indifcriminately ; like Children, that cannot yet
talk ; or like dying Perfons, when they are lofing the Ufe of Speech.

2   *Boy.*

The famous emendation of 'a table of green fields' in Theobald's edition of 1733.
(Shakespeare Birthplace Trust)

intuition. (Where Iago called Cassio 'a fellow almost damn'd in
a fair wife', Hanmer emended to 'damn'd in a fair phyz', but he
was not always as crass as this.) William Warburton's eight-
volume edition of 1747 is now remembered if at all for the lively
abuse of Theobald and Hanmer to be found in its Preface. He
based his text largely on Theobald's, for all his abuse of him, and
he incorporated into his edition explanatory and critical notes
from Theobald's which he said he had contributed to the earlier
editor. The new work in his edition was, in the words of the later
Shakespearean scholar Edmund Malone, 'his own chimerical
conceits in the place of the author's genuine text'. Warburton
did, however, make one famous and frequently accepted emendation – of the 'good kissing carrion' in the quarto and Folio text

Engraving by F. Gravelot after a design by Francis Hayman for Hanmer's edition of Romeo and Juliet, 1744. (*Royal Shakespeare Theatre*)

Engraving by J. Basire after a design by E. Edwards for Johnson's edition of Measure for Measure, 1765. (*Royal Shakespeare Theatre*)

of *Hamlet*, II, ii, 182, to 'a god kissing carrion', which makes excellent sense and is bibliographically sound.

By now Shakespeare was established not only as a great poet and dramatist but also as an old writer who needed explanation and annotation if he were to be fully intelligible. 'The business of him that republishes an ancient book,' wrote Dr Johnson in his *Proposals for Printing the Dramatic Works of Shakespeare* (1756), 'is, to correct what is corrupt, and to explain what is obscure.' Johnson was well aware of the textual problems. He was well aware that Shakespeare had not seen any of his plays through the press and that 'he sold them, not to be printed, but to be played'.

They were immediately copied for the actors, and multiplied by transcript after transcript, vitiated by the blunders of the penman, or changed by the affectation of the player; perhaps enlarged to introduce a jest, or mutilated to shorten the representation; and printed at last without the concurrence of the author . . . from compilations made by chance or by stealth out of the separate parts written for the theatre: and thus thrust into the world surreptitiously and hastily, they suffered another depravation from the ignorance and negligence of the printers, as every man who knows the state of the press in that age will conceive.

We now know that this is an inaccurate and a far too pessimistic account of the matter. But Johnson was wholly right in his description of editorial method.

The corruptions of the text will be corrected by a careful collation of the oldest copies, by which it is hoped that many restorations may yet be made: at least it will be necessary to collect and note the variations as materials for future criticks; for it very often happens that a wrong reading has affinity to the right.

He proposed to include all the variant reading of the old copies, so that the reader 'may have the means of choosing better for himself' if he disagrees with the editor's reading. He proposed to use Shakespeare's sources to throw light on obscurities in the action of some of the plays. He was aware that 'there is danger lest peculiarities should be mistaken for corruptions, and passages regarded as unintelligible, which a narrow mind happens not to understand', and fully realised the necessity for wide and deep reading of Shakespeare's contemporaries if an editor was to acquire a proper understanding of Elizabethan English. He would make use of the extensive knowledge of the language acquired in the preparation of his *Dictionary*. And 'he hopes that, by comparing the works of *Shakespeare* with those of writers who lived at the same time, immediately preceded, or immediately followed him, he shall be able to ascertain his ambiguities, disentangle his intricacies, and recover the meanings of words now lost in the darkness of antiquity'.

Johnson's edition of Shakespeare finally came out, in eight octavo volumes, in 1765. His actual method as a textual editor was more negligent than his statement of the proper editorial practice would have led one to expect. Johnson was the first editor of Shakespeare who understood about lines of descent. Speaking in the Preface to his edition of the editorial work of Theobald, he says: 'In his enumeration of editions he mentions the two first folios as of high, and the third folio as of middle authority; but the truth is, that the first is equivalent to all others, and that the rest only deviate from it by the printer's negligence. . . . I collated them all at the beginning, but afterwards used only the first.' Yet further on in the Preface he admits his own carelessness: 'I collated such copies as I could procure and wished for more, but have not found the collectors of these rarities very communicative.' He actually used Warburton's edition as his textual base, and inevitably carried over some of Warburton's misprints (which in fact Warburton had carried over from Theobald's second edition). The true glory of Johnson's edition is the Preface, which is the best eighteenth-century critical essay on Shakespeare and a classic of its kind, and the numerous explanatory notes, based on his wide reading and shrewd common sense, are still resorted to by editors.

In his Preface Johnson dismissed once and for all the charge that Shakespeare was culpable for not observing the neoclassic unities of time and place. The only unity that mattered, he asserted, was unity of action. The supposition that a drama was more credible if its action occupied one place and, in the story of the play, took only the actual length of time that passed during the performance, is based on total confusion concerning the nature of dramatic illusion on the stage. To believe that you are in Rome in one act and in Egypt in the next is no greater strain on the imagination of the spectator than to believe you are only in Rome, for the spectator in fact knows that all the time he is really in the theatre and is observing 'successive imitations of successive actions'. This permanently disposed of the unities of time and place, and the matter has never been seriously raised again by English critics of Shakespeare.

It was in the Preface that Johnson made his famous remark: 'Nothing can please many, and please long, but just representations of general nature.' And Shakespeare's long continued and justly earned popularity resulted from the fact that he was 'the poet of nature; the poet that holds up to his readers a faithful mirrour of manners and of life'. His characters are 'the genuine progeny of common humanity, such as the world will always supply, and observation will always find'. He excelled all other authors in 'accommodating his sentiments to real life'. His dialogue 'seems scarcely to claim the merit of fiction, but to have been gleaned by diligent selection out of common conversation, and common occurrences'. Again, '*Shakespeare* always makes nature predominate over accident'. It is useless to attack him, as Dennis and Rymer had done, for making his Romans insufficiently Roman or his kings insufficiently kingly: 'His story requires Romans or kings, but he thinks only on men.' He defends Shakespeare's mixing tragedy and comedy on the same grounds: his plays exhibit

the real state of sublunary nature, which partakes of good and evil, joy and sorrow, mingled with endless variety of proportion and innumerable modes of combination; and expressing the course of the world, in which the loss of one is the gain of another; in which, at the same time, the reveller is hasting to his wine, and the mourner burying his friend; in which the malignity of one is sometimes defeated by the frolick of another; and many mischiefs and benefits are done and hindered without design.

Wherever Shakespeare appears to break the rules of drama, 'there is always an appeal open from criticism to nature'. In spite of Johnson's objections to Shakespeare's neglect of moral instruction, his anachronisms, his occasional 'disproportionate pomp of diction', his quibbles and puns, the critical part of the Preface is basically an eloquent defence, the fullest and best reasoned case for Shakespeare made on the grounds, so dear to eighteenth-century critics, of his 'knowledge of the human heart'.

The next edition was that of Edward Capell, published in ten octavo volumes in 1768. Though this edition was never popular, it was much used by later editors, who owed much to Capell's text. Capell made an eager search for Shakespeare quartos and built up the finest collection of Shakespeare material that had yet been assembled. He collated more old editions than any previous editor. Yet, careful scholar though he was, and pioneer though he was in recognising that the 'good' quartos should where possible be used in determining the text of a play, he had no proper theory of emendation and merely selected those readings that he liked best (rather than those that could be bibliographically defended as most likely to be Shakespeare's). But he did have his text printed from his own transcript and not from an edition of an earlier editor, as all his predecessors had done. He published his notes separately and later, in two large quarto volumes, and he added a third volume, entitled *The School of Shakespeare*, which contained extracts from English books from which Shakespeare's 'several Fables were taken, and some Parcel of his Dialogue: Also, further Extracts, from the same or like Books, which contribute to a due Understanding of his Writings, or give Light to the History of his Life, or to the dramatic History of his Time.' In his notes he included a number of apocryphal stories about Shakespeare which became absorbed in the biographical tradition. Capell left his great collection of Shakespeare quartos to Trinity College, Cambridge, where they proved invaluable to the editors of the important Cambridge edition of 1863–66.

Capell was not the first to publish some of Shakespeare's sources. In 1753–54 Mrs Charlotte Lennox had published her three-volume *Shakespear Illustrated; or the Novels and Histories, on which the Plays are founded, Collected and Translated*. But this is not the place in which to summarise the history of Shakespeare scholarship: suffice it to say that the stream of that scholarship was now flowing ever wider and deeper, until at the end of the century it flowed into the great work of Edmund Malone. More important, as far as the public were concerned, was the continual per-formance of Shakespeare on the stage. The theatrical handling of Shakespeare was admiring but totally irreverent. Already in the previous century Dryden and Davenant had produced a new version of *The Tempest* in which both Caliban and Miranda were given sisters, and a man who had never seen a woman was intro-duced to balance Miranda who had never seen a man (except her father). Nahum Tate adapted *King Lear*, *Richard II* and *Corio-lanus*, the first being immensely popular, holding the stage for a hundred and fifty years from its first production in 1681. In Tate's version Cordelia is in love with Edgar (which is why she won't answer her father in the opening scene: she hopes to put off other suitors) and they eventually marry. The King of France is cut out altogether. Both Cordelia and Lear survive, the former reigning in England with Edgar while the aged Lear retires to

David Garrick as Hamlet, c. 1754, at the Drury Lane Theatre. (Radio Times Hulton Picture Library)

'Mr Garrick reciting the Ode in honor of Shakespeare at the Jubilee at Stratford, with the Musical Performers, etc.' (Radio Times Hulton Picture Library)

live with Kent and Gloucester. The Fool is omitted. David Garrick produced a modified version of Tate's *Lear* in 1756, but though he restored many of Shakespeare's lines, he retained the love scenes between Cordelia and Edgar and kept the happy ending. George Colman brought back even more of Shakespeare into his version of the play in 1768 (though he still left out the Fool and kept the happy ending), but it was not popular. Indeed, between the first performance of Tate's version and Kean's production of 1823 every performance of *Lear* had a happy ending. The fact remains however, as Nichol Smith reminded us, that Shakespeare was regularly acted right through the century:

Not a year passed but several of his plays were produced on the two chief London stages, Drury Lane and Lincoln's Inn Fields or Covent Garden. In the year of *The Beggar's Opera* (1728) the ordinary playgoer could have seen, *Hamlet, Othello, King Lear, Macbeth, Henry IV* (both parts), *The Merry Wives, Richard III, Henry VIII*, and *Julius Caesar*, and about the same time also, *Measure for Measure, Timon of Athens*, and *The Tempest*. In the year of *She Stoops to Conquer* (1773) the list is even longer – *Hamlet, Othello, King Lear, Macbeth, Romeo and Juliet, Richard III, Henry V, Henry VIII, Julius Caesar, The Merchant of Venice, As You Like It, Much Ado, Twelfth Night, The Tempest* and *Cymbeline*.

Shakespeare was thus the great national dramatist not only to readers and scholars but also to actors and playgoers. Every significant eighteenth-century actor made his name by playing Shakespeare. The greatest of them, David Garrick, had a real feeling for Shakespeare's language and introduced more and more of Shakespeare's precise words into his prompt copies. Although, as we have seen, his *Lear* was still partly Tate's, Garrick was responsible for moving away steadily from 'improved' acting versions to the Shakespearean originals. And by organising the Stratford Jubilee of 1769 Garrick virtually founded the Shakespeare tourist industry. This was a three-day festival, beginning with the firing of a cannon in the early morning of 6 September. Fancy dress parades, public feasts, processions, balls, fireworks, illuminations, horse-races, bands, and the recitation of an *Ode to Shakespeare* by Garrick himself in a specially erected wooden theatre, took place in a spirit of high carnival, only slightly damped by almost continuous rain. Shakespeare had now become an institution as well as a popular classic. Garrick had a considerable share in both developments.

✳

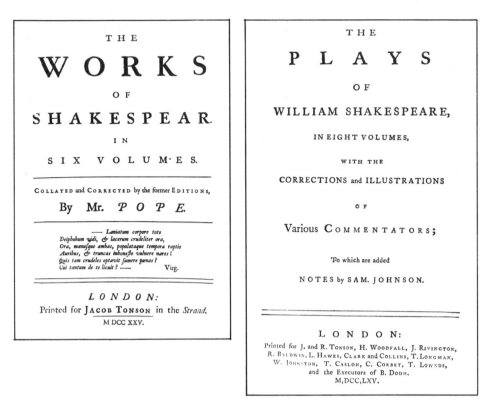

Title-pages of Pope's and Johnson's editions showing the former's single publisher and the consortium of publishers for the latter. (Shakespeare Birthplace Trust and Royal Shakespeare Theatre)

In the early years of the history of printing, printers, publishers and booksellers were the same person, but by Shakespeare's time there were some publishers who employed a printer to print a book and occasionally a bookseller to sell it. The Stationers' Company, an organisation of printers and publishers, was incorporated in 1557 and, except for the university presses of Oxford and Cambridge, had a monopoly of printing throughout England.* Sole rights to print or sell a book were acquired by entering the title (for a fee) in the Stationers' Register. This was the practice in Shakespeare's day. By the end of the seventeenth century, when booksellers were often also publishers, copyright was believed to reside in perpetuity with the bookseller-publisher who had originally acquired it, but the Copyright Act of 1709 limited copyright of books already published to twenty-one years

* See 'Copyright and society', pp. 33 ff.

with a maximum of twenty-eight years for future books. The great bookseller-publishers of the early eighteenth century dominated the book trade. Jacob Tonson opened his bookseller's shop in 1677 and proceeded to buy the copyrights of some of the most celebrated authors of the time, including Dryden and Otway. Tonson's business was carried on after his retirement by his nephew, also Jacob (this was the Tonson who published Pope's Shakespeare) and then by his two great-nephews (one of whom, a third Jacob Tonson, published Warburton's Shakespeare). A rival of Tonson's was Bernard Lintot, who published a considerable amount of Pope's work. A third bookseller-publisher of the period was the 'unspeakable' Edmund Curll, best known now for Pope's attacks on him. In the second half of the eighteenth century there were no single figures comparable to Tonson or Lintot, and bookseller-publishers developed the habit of grouping together to share the risks of a major publication. Dr Johnson's original proposals to edit Shakespeare in 1745 were quashed because Tonson claimed the copyright in Shakespeare's works, but his later proposals of 1756, made when he was now famous, announced that subscriptions were to be taken by 'J. and R. Tonson, in the Strand; J. Knapton, in Ludgate Street; C. Hitch and L. Hawes, and M. and T. Longman in Paternoster-Row'. Under his agreement with these publishers, Johnson was to receive 250 free sets in sheets, for supplying subscribers, with the option of buying additional sets at a guinea each if the list of subscribers exceeded 250. Johnson's *Lives of the Poets* was commissioned jointly by 'about forty of the most respectable booksellers of London'; he asked for, and got, 200 guineas for his labours. (Subscription publishing was common in the later eighteenth century, the author receiving the subscription money less publisher's commission, but much commoner was the sale of rights to the bookseller-publisher for a flat fee.) In the later eighteenth century the firm of Longman was involved in most important cooperative publishing ventures, the original Thomas Longman having been a shareholder in Chambers's *Cyclopedia* and in Johnson's *Dictionary*, both highly valuable properties.

The transition from bookseller-publisher hiring a writer or buying his work outright to publisher acting solely as a publisher and paying the author a royalty on sales took place gradually during the last years of the eighteenth century and the early years of the nineteenth. The history of Sir Walter Scott's relations with his publishers is an important part of this story. But on the whole the publication of Shakespeare followed rather than helped to change contemporary publishing practice.

✳

Before Capell, Shakespeare had been edited by men of letters rather than by expert Shakespeare scholars. George Steevens's *Twenty of the Plays of Shakespeare*, reprinted from original quartos in 1766, marks a further stage in the application of scholarship to the editing of Shakespeare. In 1773 he brought out a complete edition of the plays in ten octavo volumes based on Johnson's edition; this was revised and reprinted in 1778 and further revised by his friend Isaac Reid in 1785. A final edition in fifteen volumes appeared in 1793. Steevens was a quarrelsome scholar with an odd taste for practical jokes – 'the Puck of Commentators' William Gifford called him – and, having quarrelled with two clergymen, Richard Amner and John Collins, he formed the habit of attributing to those wholly innocent characters outrageously indecent notes 'on such passages or expressions [one cannot resist using Nichol Smith's prim phrase here] as are now omitted in school editions'. Steevens was an admirable scholar, but there was more than a touch of malicious irresponsibility about him, and his notes, though learned, are suspect.

Eighteenth-century Shakespeare scholarship comes to its great climax in Edmund Malone. In his edition of 1778 Steevens had included Malone's *Attempt to ascertain the Order in which the Plays of Shakespeare were written*, a pioneer work in the attempt to establish the chronology of the plays. His own ten-volume octavo edition of 1790 (in emulation of which Steevens produced his fifteen-volume edition of 1793) is significantly entitled: *The Plays and Poems of William Shakespeare, collated verbatim with the most Authentick Copies. With the Corrections and Illustrations of Various Commentators, to which are added, an Essay on the Chronological Order of his Plays; an Essay relative to Shakespeare and Jonson; a Dissertation of the Three Parts of King Henry VI; an Historical Account of the English Stage; and Notes by E. Malone.* Malone amassed a great library in the course of his work on Shakespeare, a large part of which went to the Bodleian Library after his death. He was working on a revision of his edition when he died in 1812, and the material he had gathered for this passed to James Boswell (son of the biographer), who made use of it in

360   ANTONY AND CLEOPATRA.   *ACT IV.*

Where their appointment we may best discover,
And look on their endeavour⁴.   [*Exeunt.*

    Enter CÆSAR, *and his Forces, marching.*

  Cæs. But being charg'd, we will be still by land,
Which, as I take't, we shall⁵; for his best force
Is forth to man his gallies.   To the vales,
And hold our best advantage.   [*Exeunt.*

    " Whose whisper o'er the world's diameter,
    " As level as the cannon to his blank," &c.
The words—" So viperous slander," which are necessary both
to the sense and metre, are not in the old copies.   MALONE.
  ⁴ Where their APPOINTMENT we may best discover,
    And look on their ENDEAVOUR.]   i. e. where we may best
discover their *numbers,* and see their *motions.*   WARBURTON.
  ⁵ BUT being charg'd, we will be still by land,
    Which, as I take't, we shall ;]   i. e. unless we be charg'd we
will remain quiet at land, which quiet I suppose we shall keep.
But being charg'd was a phrase of that time, equivalent to *unless
we be.*   WARBURTON.
  " *But* (says Mr. Lambe, in his notes on the ancient metrical
history of The Battle of Floddon,) signifies *without,*" in which
sense it is often used in the North.   "*Boots* but *spurs.*"   Vulg.
Again, in Kelly's Collection of Scots Proverbs :   "— He could eat
me *but* salt."   Again : " He gave me whitings *but* bones."   Again,
in Chaucer's Persones Tale, Mr. Tyrwhitt's edit. : " Ful oft time I
rede, that no man trust in his owen perfection, *but* he be stronger
than Samson, or holier than David, or wiser than Solomon."
But is from the Saxon *Butan.*   Thus *butan leas ;* absque falso,
without a lie.   Again, in The Vintner's Play, in the Chester Collection, British Museum, MS. Harl. 2013, p. 29 :
    " *Abraham.* Oh comely creature, *but* I thee kill,
    " I greeve my God, and that full ill."
See also Ray's North Country Words ; and the MS. version of
an ancient French romance, entitled L'Histoire du noble, preux,
et vaillant Chevalier Guillaume de Palerne, et de la belle Meliur
sa mye, lequel Guill. de Palerne fut fils du Roy de Occille, &c. in
the Library of King's College, Cambridge :
    " I sayle now in the see as schip *boute* mast,
    Boute anker, or ore, or ani semlych sayle."   P. 86.
  In ancient writings this preposition is commonly distinguished
from the adversative conjunction—*but ;* the latter being usually
spelled—*bot.*   STEEVENS.

THE

PLAYS AND POEMS

OF

WILLIAM SHAKSPEARE,

WITH THE

CORRECTIONS AND ILLUSTRATIONS

OF

VARIOUS COMMENTATORS:

COMPREHENDING

𝔄 𝔏𝔦𝔣𝔢 𝔬𝔣 𝔱𝔥𝔢 𝔓𝔬𝔢𝔱,

AND

AN ENLARGED HISTORY OF THE STAGE,

BY

THE LATE EDMOND MALONE.

WITH A NEW GLOSSARIAL INDEX.

ΤΗΣ ΨΥΧΕΩΣ ΓΡΑΜΜΑΤΕΥΣ ΗΝ, ΤΟΝ ΚΑΛΑΜΟΝ
ΑΠΟΒΡΕΧΩΝ ΕΙΣ ΝΟΥΝ.   *Vet. Auct apud. Suidam.*

VOL. I.

LONDON:

PRINTED FOR F. C. AND J. RIVINGTON; T. EGERTON; J. CUTHELL; SCATCHERD
AND LETTERMAN; LONGMAN, HURST, REES, ORME, AND BROWN; CADELL
AND DAVIES; LACKINGTON AND CO.; J. BOOKER; BLACK AND CO.; J. BOOTH;
J. RICHARDSON; J. M. RICHARDSON; J. MURRAY; J. HARDING; R. H. EVANS;
J. MAWMAN; R. SCHOLEY; T. EARLE; J. BOHN; C. BROWN; GRAY AND SON;
R. PHENEY; BALDWIN, CRADOCK, AND JOY; NEWMAN AND CO.; OGLES, DUN-
CAN, AND CO.; T. HAMILTON; W. WOOD; J. SHELDON; E. EDWARDS; WHIT-
MORE AND FENN; W. MASON; G. AND W. B. WHITTAKER; SIMPKIN AND
MARSHALL; R. SAUNDERS; J. DEIGHTON AND SONS, CAMBRIDGE: WILSON
AND SON, YORK: AND STIRLING AND SLADE, FAIRBAIRN AND ANDERSON,
AND D. BROWN, EDINBURGH.

1821.

SC. X.   ANTONY AND CLEOPATRA.   361

    Re-enter ANTONY *and* SCARUS.

  ANT. Yet they're not join'd : Where yonder pine
      does stand,
I shall discover all : I'll bring thee word
Straight, how 'tis like to go.   [*Exit.*
  SCAR.   Swallows have built
In Cleopatra's sails their nests : the augurers⁶
Say, they know not,—they cannot tell ;—look
    grimly,
And dare not speak their knowledge.   Antony
Is valiant, and dejected ; and, by starts,
His fretted fortunes give him hope, and fear,
Of what he has, and has not.

    Alarum afar off, as at a Sea Fight.

    Re-enter ANTONY.

  ANT.   All is lost ;
This foul Egyptian hath betrayed me :
My fleet hath yielded to the foe ; and yonder
They cast their caps up, and carouse together
Like friends long lost.—Triple-turn'd whore⁷! 'tis
    thou

  ⁶ — the AUGURERS—]   The old copy has—*auguries.* This leads
us to what seems most likely to be the true reading—*augurers,*
which word is used in the last Act :
    " You are too sure an *augurer.*"   MALONE.
  ⁷ — TRIPLE-TURN'D whore !]   She was first for Antony, then
was supposed by him to have *turned* to Cæsar, when he found
his messenger kissing her hand; then she *turned* again to Antony ;
and now has *turned* to Cæsar.   Shall I mention what has dropped
into my imagination, that our author perhaps might have written
triple-tongued? Double-tongued is a common term of reproach,
which rage might improve to *triple-tongued.*   But the present
reading may stand.   JOHNSON.
  Cleopatra was first the mistress of Julius Cæsar, then of Cneius
Pompey, and afterwards of Antony.   To this, I think, the epi-
thet *triple-turn'd* alludes.   So, in a former scene :

*Title-page and two pages of text
from the Third Variorum,
'Boswell's Malone', 1821. (Royal
Shakespeare Theatre)*

his twenty-one-volume edition of 1821, known as 'Boswell's Malone' or (for reasons which will become immediately apparent) the Third Variorum.

The Variorum movement sprang from an attempt to provide a scholarly edition of Shakespeare complete with the notes of all commentators who had provided any illumination of the text. (Editions of the classics with explanatory notes of earlier scholars had long been common; these, *cum notis variorum*, 'with the notes of various people', provided the model: the word 'variorum' in this context is a genitive plural and refers to the people whose notes are included, not to variant readings, though in fact the editions did include these.) The First Variorum, Johnson's edition as revised by Steevens and edited by Isaac Reid, appeared in 1803 in twenty-one volumes; the Second Variorum, a reprint of the first, appeared in 1813; and Boswell's Malone was the third. The Third Variorum sums up everything of value that had been achieved in eighteenth-century editions of Shakespeare, and all subsequent editions have been indebted to it. Its three volumes of prefatory matter alone are a marvellous quarry of Shakespeare scholarship and criticism; it includes such important background material as Henslowe's diary and extracts from the Stationers' Register. The Third Variorum is, in fact, the most complete and the most important edition of Shakespeare ever published. The Fourth or New Variorum was begun in 1871 and, with one massive volume to each play, is still incomplete. While it takes years to complete a volume of the New Variorum, which assembles almost everything known and written about and everything possibly relevant to each play as well as presenting the best text that contemporary scholarship can produce, knowledge and understanding of Shakespeare's text has been for many years leaping ahead annually, with the result that in some important respects a New Variorum volume may be out of date as soon as it is published.

✳

By the beginning of the nineteenth century Shakespeare studies had become firmly established as a central part of the high culture of Britain. At the same time, changing notions of decorum – changes which we associate with the Victorian age but which in fact had been developing steadily since the beginning of the century – meant that a great deal in Shakespeare's language and even in his plots was increasingly regarded as unsuitable for presentation to the general public. Thackeray, writing his preface to *Pendennis* in 1850, contrasted the situation in his day with the greater freedom enjoyed by mid-eighteenth-century writers: 'Since the author of Tom Jones was buried, no writer of fiction among us has been permitted to depict to his utmost power a MAN. We must drape him, and give him a certain conventional simper. Society will not tolerate the Natural in our Art.' Most writers and critics, however, rejoiced in what they considered the increase in delicacy and refinement. With the rapid growth of the reading public, and the growing habit of reading aloud by the pater-familias to his assembled family, more and more people asked themselves Mr Podsnap's question: 'Would it bring a blush into the cheek of the young person?' Charles Edward Mudie, whose chain of lending libraries operated on the principle that nothing should be found there that could not be read aloud by a father to his innocent young daughter, exercised an enormous influence, especially on the novel, in the second half of the century; when he began lending books in 1842 the new delicacy was already something absolutely taken for granted. It affected the editing of Shakespeare as early as 1807, a year which saw publication of the first editions of both Lamb's *Tales from Shakespeare* and Bowdler's *Family Shakespeare*.

Though attributed on the title-page to Charles Lamb, the *Tales from Shakespeare* were largely the work of his sister Mary, who did six of the twenty renderings of Shakespeare plays into innocent prose narratives interspersed with some of the gentler and more straightforward verse passages from the original. The book proved immensely popular, although it treated the plays as simple stories rather than as complex verse dramas and provided little or no indication of the nature of Shakespeare's greatness. But at least the Lambs were not guilty of false pretences: they presented their book as 'tales *from* Shakespeare', not as an edition of Shakespeare's plays. Bowdler's *Family Shakespeare* was a very different matter.

Dr Thomas Bowdler was a member of a family both pious and literary. His father, Thomas Bowdler, who died in 1785, used to read aloud to his children in the evening, silently bowdlerising (for we may now use the word which derives from the Bowdler name) as he went along.

'In the perfection of reading few men were equal to my father,' his son Dr Thomas Bowdler wrote in the preface to the fourth edition of the *Family Shakespeare*,

and such were his good taste, his delicacy, and his prompt discretion, that his family listened with delight to Lear, Hamlet, and Othello, without knowing that those matchless tragedies contained words and expressions improper to be pronounced; and without having any reason to suspect that any parts of the plays had been omitted by the circumspect and judicious reader.

His mother, daughter of Sir John Cotton, was a biblical scholar who wrote a commentary on Bishop Percy's Paraphrase of the Song of Solomon in which she proposed expurgations and alterations designed to make the language of the poem more modest. His elder brother John was a great campaigner against indelicacy and indecorum; in his old age he edited an anthology of expurgated poetry, his object being, as he put it, 'not to produce a collection of elegant poetry, but to *do good*'. His sister Harriet appears to have been the real if unacknowledged editor of the *Family Shakespeare*, though the first edition appeared anonymously and the second edition, in 1809, bore Dr Bowdler's name as sole editor. Dr Bowdler, however, did take over the editorship in 1817 and prepared a new, enlarged edition which was published in ten volumes in 1818 by Longmans, Hurst, Rees, Orme, Brown, and Green. Longmans kept it in print until 1925. Dr Bowdler's nephew John (son of his brother John) formed a project when a student to expurgate dirty lines from Latin classics read in schools and always omitted the sixth and ninth satires when reading Juvenal to himself because he had been told they were indecent.

Part of the text from Act II scene 1 of Romeo and Juliet *showing Bowdler's text compared with that of the Penguin edition, edited by T. J. B. Spencer. (Royal Shakespeare Theatre and Penguin Books Ltd.)*

BENVOLIO
30   Come, he hath hid himself among these trees
      To be consorted with the humorous night.
      Blind is his love and best befits the dark.
MERCUTIO
      If love be blind, love cannot hit the mark.
      Now will he sit under a medlar tree
      And wish his mistress were that kind of fruit
      As maids call medlars when they laugh alone.
      O, Romeo, that she were, O that she were
      An open-arse and thou a poppering pear!
      Romeo, good night. I'll to my truckle-bed.
40   This field-bed is too cold for me to sleep.
      Come, shall we go?
BENVOLIO   Go then, for 'tis in vain
      To seek him here that means not to be found.

Ben. Come, he hath hid himself among those trees,
To be consorted with the humorous ' night :
Blind is his love, and best befits the dark.
     Mer. If love be blind, love cannot hit the mark.
Romeo, good night ; — I 'll to my truckle-bed ;
This field-bed is too cold for me to sleep :
Come, shall we go?
     Ben.   Go, then ; for 'tis in vain
To seek him here, that means not to be found.

Shakespeare had been expurgated before, but for political and religious not moral reasons. The Act of 1606 *To Restraine Abuses of Players* was concerned with profanity on the stage and it resulted in the modifying or omission of oaths, as can be seen in the text of many of the plays in the First Folio which were set up from prompt-copies. The Master of the Revels was concerned not only with the suppression of profanity but also with the removal of criticism of the political and religious establishment. Though Shakespeare does not seem to have had much trouble with this kind of censorship – the political implications of his plays were far from subversive – there was difficulty with *Richard II*, and the deposition scene did not appear in print until the fourth quarto in 1608. It was for politico-religious reasons, too, that Oldcastle's name had to be changed to Falstaff in the *Henry IV* plays. But these were all relatively minor matters. The Bowdler aim was more radical both in scope and in method. Profanity was excised and oaths often modified, almost in the spirit of the Act of 1606. The stated aim was to provide a text 'in which nothing is added to the original; but those words and expressions are omitted which cannot with propriety be read in a family'. As Dr Bowdler wrote to the Editor of the *British Critic* in 1823: 'If any word or expression is of such a nature, that the first impression which it excites is an impression of obscenity, that word ought not to be spoken, or written, or printed; and if printed, it ought to be erased.'[2]

Harriet had edited only twenty of the plays, in the anonymous edition published in four volumes in Bath in 1807. Thomas's new edition of 1818 contained thirty-six plays, and in re-editing those which his sister had done he restored some dull passages she had cut on aesthetic grounds only and cut very many others in which his fevered fancy could see obscenity or an invitation to improper thoughts. (But of course he missed innumerable indecent puns which more recent knowledge of Shakespeare's language has taught the modern reader to recognise.) Large parts of the opening scenes of *Romeo and Juliet*, *Othello* and *King Lear* disappear, and, indeed, the meaning of these plays, in each of which sex plays a central part, is attenuated sometimes almost to extinction. Yet they all passed the reading-aloud test; both sexes could read the plays together and they would find them 'unmixed with anything that could raise a blush on the cheek of modesty' (was Dickens thinking of Bowdler's claim when he put the

famous words into the mouth of Podsnap?) and they could be
'read aloud by a gentleman to a company of ladies'. The text
which the Bowdlers bowdlerised was that of George Steevens's
edition, except for the text of *Measure for Measure* (a play which
understandably gave him considerable difficulty), when he used
the acting version prepared in 1789 by John Philip Kemble. But
in the new edition of 1820 Bowdler removed this and substituted
a text in which, in his own words, he 'had recourse to his own pen,
endeavouring to render the comedy as little objectionable as it
can be rendered, without destroying its great beauties, which are
closely interwoven with the numerous defects'.

The word 'bowdlerise' was coined in 1836, and denoted
disapproval of the activity. For not everybody, even in Bowdler's
heyday, approved of bowdlerisation. 'They have purged and
castrated him, and tattoed and beplaistered him, and cauterised
and phlebotomized him,' wrote the *British Critic* in 1822.[3]
Blackwood's attacked Bowdler, and the *Edinburgh Review*,
perhaps in natural opposition to its rival, defended him. Indeed,
it was Jeffrey's eloquent defence of the second Bowdler edition in
the *Edinburgh Review* that assured its position as a bestseller. All
other editions of Shakespeare were now obsolete, he said. 'As
what cannot be pronounced in decent company cannot well
afford much pleasure in the closet, we think it is better, every way,
that what cannot be spoken, and ought not to have been written,
should cease to be printed.'[4] This was written fifteen years before
Victoria's accession to the throne. In his *Studies in Prose and
Poetry*, written towards the end of Victoria's reign, the reformed
and respectabilised Swinburne said of Dr Bowdler that 'no man
ever did better service to Shakespeare'. And a hundred years
after the appearance of the first edition of the *Family Shakespeare*
Robert Bridges, in an essay prefixed to the Stratford Town
edition of Shakespeare edited by A. H. Bullen (Stratford-on-
Avon, 1907) wrote:

Shakespeare should not be put into the hands of the young without the
warning that the foolish things in his plays were written to please the
foolish, the filthy for the filthy, and the brutal for the brutal; and that if, out
of veneration for his genius we are led to admire or even tolerate such things,
we may be thereby not conforming ourselves to him, but only degrading
ourselves to the level of his audience, and learning contamination from those
wretched beings who can never be forgiven their share in preventing the
greatest poet and dramatist of the world from being the best artist.

The Bowdler tradition had a long life.

It was the very fact that Shakespeare had become established as the greatest of all monuments of English literary culture that prompted the activities of the Bowdlers. But there was still a strong evangelical tradition of suspicion of Shakespeare. The *Christian Observer*, reviewing the first edition of the *Family Shakespeare* in 1808, saw that dramatist as a real danger to adolescents, enervating and deranging their minds at a time when 'they ought to be braced and organised'. 'It is scarcely possible for a young person of fervid genius to read Shakespeare without a dangerous elevation of fancy,' the reviewer roundly declared.[5] Early nineteenth-century evangelical writers were often against both the theatre and the novel. That Shakespeare had written for the stage was a fact which some early nineteenth-century Methodist writers found hard to forgive. 'Barefaced obscenities, low vulgarity, and nauseous vice so frequently figure and pollute his pages that we cannot but lament the luckless hour in which he became a writer for the stage,' observed a Methodist preacher in 1806.[6] Edmund Gosse recalled being taken to 'some enormous Evangelical conference' in London in the early 1860s and hearing an elderly man refer to Shakespeare in these words: 'At this very moment there is proceeding, unreproved, a blasphemous celebration of the birth of Shakespeare, a lost soul now suffering for his sins in hell!' But Gosse's father, though an ardent member of the Plymouth Brethren, demurred: 'Before so rashly speaking of Shakespeare as "a lost soul in hell", he should have remembered how little we know of the poet's history. . . . We cannot know that Shakespeare did not accept the atonement of Christ in simple faith before he came to die.'[7]

But these are minority attitudes. Most readers accepted both Shakespeare and the necessity of bowdlerising him to a greater or less degree. The most dogged bowdleriser in the history of English editing, however, the Rev. James Plumptre, was not a popular success. His three volumes of *The English Drama Purified*, published by Cambridge University Press in 1812, never sold well, while his earlier expurgated *Collection of Songs* (where Shakespeare's famous lines appear as 'Under the greenwood tree,/Who loves to *work* with me') is known only to experts, as a curiosity. So far as editions of Shakespeare for family reading went, Bowdler held the field. It was in the publication of Shakespeare for schoolchildren that the next significant wave of expurgation developed. A third wave consisted of selected 'beauties of Shakespeare', which treated the Master as an utterer of great thoughts and made no attempt to show him as a playwright at all. The 'beauties' approach goes well back into the eighteenth century: in his two-volume *Complete Art of Poetry*, published in 1718, Charles Gildon included a collection of 'The Most Beautiful Topics, Descriptions, and Similes that occur throughout Shakespeare's Plays', while in 1752 William Dodd produced *The Beauties of Shakespeare, regularly selected from each Play*, which went into many editions. As an editor of beauties could simply select whatever lines he wanted and present them out of context, he had no problem with indecencies or improprieties.

The development of English literature as an important subject in secondary education resulted in the proliferation of school editions of Shakespeare, all of which were silently expurgated in some degree. 'English literature' as an examination subject was first introduced in the examinations for the Indian Civil service in 1855. The Schools Inquiry Commission, set up in 1864 under Lord Taunton to inquire into the schools not investigated by the Clarendon Commission of 1864 (which looked into the great public schools) or by the Popular Education Commission of 1858, emphasised in its report the importance of English literature in secondary education. The true purpose of such teaching, the report asserted, was not simply to provide examples of English grammar, 'but to kindle a living interest in the learner's mind, to make him feel the force and beauty of which the language is capable, to refine and elevate his taste'. If English literature could be taught to boys in that way, 'the man would probably return to it when the days of boyhood were over, and many who would never look again at Horace or Virgil, would be very likely to continue to read Shakespeare and Milton throughout their lives'. The examiner in English for the Indian Civil Service and for the Royal Military Academy at Woolwich gave interesting evidence of his own examining practice to the Taunton Commission:

I should take forty or fifty passages, selected from what I call fair authors – Shakespeare, Milton, Pope, and some of the later writers, Sir Walter Scott and Tennyson. I have set this question over and over again. 'Here is a passage. State where it comes from, explain any peculiarities of English in it, and state the context as far as you are able to do so'.

Members of the Commission expressed very proper concern lest boys should prepare for such an examination by mere cramming, but the examiner reassured them by saying that clear evidence of cramming (such as every boy repeating from the same manual an identical account of the character of Richard III) would result in loss of marks. But, he added, cramming has its uses. 'I would rather have a boy who is able to learn something by cram, than a boy who is not able to be taught anything by any process at all.' This exchange is interesting, for it shows a conflict between two approaches to the study of English literature at school – that it is a training to read great literature appreciatively in later life, and that it is the acquiring of a body of knowledge – which has not been fully resolved to this day.[8]

The conflict is reflected in the school editions of Shakespeare's plays in the late nineteenth and early twentieth centuries, most of which have critical prefaces which attempt to provide an appreciation of the play and at the same time innumerable notes at the back of the book, glossing, explaining, informing and instructing. The setting of passages to identify, relate to their context, explain and comment on, as described by the Indian Civil Service examiner in 1864, is still a standard practice in both schools and universities (it is known in some universities and on some examination boards as the 'gobbets question'): the identification and relating to context is to show that you have read the play, the explanation is to show that you have understood it, and the invitation to comment is to show that you have read and remembered the notes at the back of the book.

Much nineteenth-century teaching of English literature in schools, however, simply took over the methods of teaching the Greek and Latin classics, as Churton Collins complained in 1887. This was in spite of the good intentions of the Taunton Commission, which resulted in bringing the subject massively into secondary education (with the resulting proliferation of manuals of English literary history). The subject, Collins said, 'has been regarded not as the expression of art and genius, but as mere material for the study of words, as mere pabulum for philology ... Its masterpieces have been resolved into exercise in grammar, syntax and etymology.'[9] The complaint has been perennial. One still hears middle-aged business men complaining that Shakespeare was for ever destroyed for them at school. (Though this remark is at least as often a cover for mental sloth

and a wilful dullness of imagination as a genuine criticism of the
teaching they had received.)

Of course, Shakespeare had come into the schools in some
degree long before the Taunton Commission. The Rev. J. R.
Pitman, impressed by the *Edinburgh Review's* lavish praise of
Bowdler, produced his *School-Shakspere* in 1822: this consisted
of extracts from twenty-six plays – the more famous passages
with 'enough of the general plot' to link them together – with all
improprieties rigorously removed. In 1849 Professor John Hows
of Columbia produced in his *Shaksperian Reader* the first expurgated American *Shakespere*, explaining in his preface that
although as a scholar he preferred 'the pure unmutilated text of
Shakspere', as a presenter of 'Shakspere as a Class Book, or as a
satisfactory Reading Book for Families' he felt he had to 'exercise
a severe revision of his language, beyond that adopted in any
similar undertaking – "Bowdler's Family Shakspeare" not even
excepted'. In England A. W. Verity, the dean of annotated
editors of English literature for school use whose very name has
become the symbol of a type of explanatory note, edited the *Pitt
Press Shakespeare* in thirteen volumes between 1890 and 1895.
The thirteen volumes of the *Warwick Shakespeare* (by various
editors, including Sir E. K. Chambers and C. H. Herford),
published between 1893 and 1898, are still found in schools. Sir
Israel Gollancz's *Temple Shakespeare* in forty neat little volumes
(1894 ff.) provided deftly encapsulated information with an
attractively printed text. Five million copies had been sold by
1934. The famous *Arden Shakespeare* edited by W. J. Craig and
others (1899–1924) provided massively annotated editions of
individual plays, with the notes at the foot of the page rather than
at the back for convenience of reading.

Not all of these editions were expurgated, but those aimed more
specifically at schools (such as the Warwick edition) silently
omitted passages regarded as offensive: the present writer well
remembers studying *Hamlet* at school from E. K. Chambers's
genuinely scholarly Warwick edition and discovering only on
doing textual work on the play at the university that he had all
along been reading an expurgated edition. (Hamlet's remarks to
Ophelia, for example, in the play scene, were severely pruned.)
The Americans proved even more enthusiastic expurgators.
H. N. Hudson's edition of 1872, containing twenty-one plays
in three volumes 'selected and prepared for use in Schools,

Clubs, Classes, and Families', was rigorously bowdlerised: his expanded thirty-eight-volume edition (one volume for each play, the standard practice in school editions on both sides of the Atlantic) sold about nine million copies between 1880 and 1930. Hudson was a fine Shakespeare scholar, who also produced two unexpurgated editions, one in eleven volumes in 1851–56 and one in twenty volumes (the 'Harvard edition') in 1880–81. The so-called *New Hudson Shakespeare*, a revision of Hudson's school edition made by new editors in 1909, professes to follow the First Folio text and to note any variation from it, but in fact it is silently bowdlerised, more severely than the earlier edition. W. J. Rolfe's twenty-volume edition of 1884, published by Harper's, and the much used *Riverside Edition* edited by W. J. White and published by Houghton Mifflin in 1883, are further examples of the enthusiasm of really able American scholars for bowdlerising Shakespeare. According to Noel Perrin, to whose informative and entertaining study *Dr Bowdler's Legacy* these paragraphs are considerably indebted, in the latter part of the nineteenth century 'every major American publisher had a house Shakespeare expurgator . . . just as every major English publisher had one'. In England at least, school expurgating was often less drastic than the bowdlerisation done for public family reading. Longmans showed themselves aware of the difference when they brought out their *School Shakespeare* in 1908, prepared this time not by an amateur moralist like Bowdler but by an editor with proper academic qualifications.

✳

The popularity of Shakespeare in the nineteenth century is borne out not only by bowdlerisation but also by the great variety of editions appealing to different kinds of readers. John Sharpe's series of miniature classics included a Shakespeare in 1800; William Pickering brought out a miniature edition, set in diamond type and issued in thirty-six parts, in 1822–23, while Kent's *Miniature Library of the Poets* also included a *Shakespeare* issued in thirty-six parts, in 1882, with which, for an extra 3s 6d, as Professor Altick has pointed out, 'one could buy a French morocco pocket book, complete with patent clasp, pencil, and compartment into which one could fit either a conventional engagement book or a miniature volume of Shakespeare.'[10] Charles Knight, that earnest worker for popular education,

The Frontispiece for Much Ado About Nothing, *engraved by T. Williams and the frontispiece for* King John, *engraved by J. Thompson, both after designs by William Harvey, for Charles Knight's* Pictorial Shakespeare. (*Royal Shakespeare Theatre*)

publisher for the Society for the Diffusion of Useful Knowledge and publisher of both the *Penny Magazine* and the *Penny Cyclopedia*, issued a number of editions of Shakespeare, of which the most important is his eight-volume *Pictorial Shakespeare* (1843) which enjoyed great popularity, largely because of its lavish illustrations. His *William Shakespeare: A Biography*, produced to go with this edition, was also profusely illustrated. Knight was a considerable Shakespeare scholar as well as a publisher: it was he who first pointed out that the fact that Shakespeare left his wife in his will only his 'second best bed' did not necessarily mean, as even the great Malone had believed, that he cut her off in contempt, for the law entitled a widow to one-third of her husband's estate automatically, and there was no need to specify this in a will. (The bequest, in fact, might well have been a sentimental reminder of conjugal felicity: the best bed would have been in the spare room, for the use of guests.) Knight's *Library Shakspere* appeared in twelve volumes in 1824–44 and his *Stratford Shakspere* in six volumes in 1867. The Pictorial Edition (which incidentally had originally been issued in parts in 1838–41, to make it more easily available to the purchaser of modest means) included notes, variant readings, a glossary, and music to the songs as well as the illustrations and the biography, and was a remarkable combination of popularisation and scholarship.

The enormous popularity of Shakespeare in mid-Victorian England is in considerable degree attributable to the lectures on Shakespeare of Charles Cowden Clarke, John Keats's schoolmaster and friend, delivered between 1834 and 1856. These were received with enthusiasm, and some were later published (*Shakespeare Characters, chiefly those Subordinate,* 1863; *Shakespeare's Characters Contrasted,* 1864). Together with his wife Mary he produced a four-volume edition of Shakespeare in 1864. Mary brought out a *Concordance to Shakespeare* in 1845, and, in 1851–52, in three volumes, *The Girlhood of Shakespeare's Heroines,* an extraordinary example of that species of Shakespeare criticism which concentrates on the characters in the plays and treats them as though they were historical persons with a real life outside the plays which is worth inquiring into. This was the most popular approach to Shakespeare in the nineteenth century. In a highly sophisticated and subtilised form this approach is found in the culminator of 'character criticism' of Shakespeare, A. C. Bradley, whose *Shakespearean Tragedy* (1904) nevertheless transcends this critical mode to investigate larger aesthetic and moral questions. Modern criticism has rejected character criticism, and prefers to concentrate on Shakespeare's use of myth and symbol, his stagecraft, his imagery, or on the plays as dramatic poems.

It was not only among the middle and upper classes that Shakespeare was popular in the nineteenth century. He was a favourite among the self-educated, and there are many stories of working men's groups in which Shakespeare was read and discussed. Thomas Cooper, the Chartist leader, used to lecture on Shakespeare (as well as on Milton and Burns) at Chartist meetings when no immediate political topic required discussion. F. D. Maurice lectured on Shakespeare at his Working Men's College, discussing *King John* as an aid in understanding English history. In 1853 Dickens told a dinner meeting of the Birmingham Society of Artists that 'there are in Birmingham at this moment many working men infinitely better versed in Shakespeare and in Milton than the average of fine gentlemen in the days of bought-

and-sold dedications and dear books'.[11] And we learn from Professor Altick that 'in a mill town in the late 1840s, a group of girl operatives met at five o'clock in the morning to read Shakespeare together for an hour before going to work'.[12] Such interest in Shakespeare was possible among the working classes because publishers such as John Dicks made a deliberate policy of publishing the classics for a few pence. William and Robert Chambers in Edinburgh had pioneered cheap publishing for the people in the 1830s; Charles Knight, as we have seen, was similarly motivated. Thomas Tegg, out of less idealistic motives, produced innumerable cheap reprints of English classics. The movement grew apace from the middle of the century. At the end of the century W. T. Stead brought out his Penny Novelist series, and Stead had educated himself as an office boy in Newcastle by reading Dicks's reprints of Shakespeare's plays in penny numbers.

There was also throughout the nineteenth century a growing Shakespeare industry which attracted scholars and sometimes tempted them into forgery. One of the most impudent of Shakespeare forgers was already at work in the 1790s. This was William Henry Ireland, whose genuine antiquarian knowledge together with his knowledge acquired as a conveyancer's clerk led him to produce his forged *Miscellaneous Papers and Legal Instruments under the Hand and Seal of William Shakespeare* in 1795. (These were, however, speedily exposed as forgeries by Malone.) John Payne Collier, a genuine scholar and a founder of the original Shakespeare Society in 1840, forged some notes and emendations in an allegedly seventeenth-century hand in a copy of the Second Folio and also forged or invented a number of documents relating to Shakespeare's life and contemporaries. In the many books which he wrote on Shakespeare he mingled the results of true research with forgeries and inventions. His eight-volume edition of Shakespeare's works ('The Text formed from an entirely new Collation of the Old Editions. With the Various Readings, Notes, a Life of the Poet, and a History of the Early English Stage'), issued in eight volumes in 1842–44, is a product of real scholarship, but even here there are some suspect notes. Sometimes Shakespeare scholars were tempted into forgery to prove theories they firmly believed to be true but for which they could find no evidence; sometimes they seem rather to have been simply proving to themselves their skill and knowingness in being able to produce what was taken for the genuine article. Shakespeare forgeries are an interesting subject for scholarly and psychological inquiry. Volume II of E. K. Chambers's comprehensive *William Shakespeare: a study of facts and problems* (1930) devotes sixteen and a half pages merely to listing and briefly describing Shakespearean fabrications.

Another nineteenth-century phenomenon affecting the presentation of Shakespeare was the emergence of the rich bibliophile assiduously collecting early editions and other relevant material and producing as a result important new scholarship on Shakespeare. James Halliwell (later Halliwell-Phillips) is the most important of these, and one of the great Shakespeare scholars of the century. He produced a *Life of Shakespeare* in 1840, based on his own researches and using material he had collected, and an elaborate folio edition of Shakespeare in sixteen scholarly volumes (1853–65) with wood engravings by J. W. Fairholt. He also produced lithographed facsimiles of the Shakespeare Quartos in forty-eight volumes (1862–71) and a reduced facsimile of the First Folio in 1876. He then turned his attention to the Stratford archives and extant legal documents connected with Shakespeare. The result, in addition to the publication of several volumes of records and documents, was his *Outlines of the Life of Shakespeare* (1881): its seventh and final edition of 1887 is the

A wood-engraving by J. W. Fairholt to a note for Halliwell's edition.
(Shakespeare Birthplace Trust)

[81] *Why dost thou garter up thy arms o' this fashion?*

The following observations on this line were communicated to me by Mr. Fairholt,—"the long hanging-sleeves appended to the shoulder of the dress, having become entirely useless as portions of apparel, were constantly worn by serving-men of the Shaksperian era; but are alluded to by earlier satirists as indicative of the same class, and worn to swell the ostentatious display of their masters. In the *Dialogus inter Occlyf et mendicam* (Harleian MS. 4826), the servants are noted for having more than enough to do to hold their sleeves out of the mire, and are consequently unable to help their masters, "the side-sleeves of penniless grooms" being able to sweep the streets clean of filth. The annexed engraving, copied from a painting executed at the commencement of the seventeenth century, and depicting a banquetting scene, represents a servant in attendance on the table, distributing fresh plates to the guests. His sleeves are gartered up, and tucked in the girdle, to be out of his way in the hurry and confusion consequent to a great dinner party. Pictorial examples might readily be multiplied of this custom in servants."

basis of all later biographies of Shakespeare. More popular, however, because it satisfied the curiosity felt about Shakespeare by many readers, was Edward Dowden's *Shakspere: A Critical Study of his Mind and Art* (1875). This used the evidence of the plays themselves, as well as external documentary material, to build up a picture of Shakespeare's 'intellect and character from youth to full maturity'. The four periods into which he divided Shakespeare's life – 'In the Workshop', 'In the World', 'In the Depths', and 'On the Heights' – were long accepted as authentic, but Dowden's view that Shakespeare passed through a period of deep trouble and sorrow to emerge serene and happy in the final 'romances' was sharply challenged by C. J. Sisson in his 1934 Annual Shakespeare Lecture of the British Academy, entitled *The Mythical Sorrows of Shakespeare*, and Dowden's picture is now viewed with considerable scepticism.

Another important scholarly edition of the mid-nineteenth century was Alexander Dyce's six-volume edition of 1857, much praised at the time for its readable text and helpful notes. A later edition in nine volumes added an important *Glossary*, and a further

Facsimiles of the same page in different copies of the first edition of King Lear, *1608, showing variations. From Halliwell's facsimiles of the Shakespeare Quartos 1862–71. (Shakespeare Birthplace Trust)*

The Historie of King Lear.

odated man, is no more but such a poore bare forked Animall as thou art, off off you lendings,come on

Foole. Prithe Nunckle be content, this is a naughty night to swim in,now a little fire in a wild field, were like an old leachers heart, a small sparke,all the rest in bodie cold,looke here comes a walking fire.   *Enter Glofter.*

Edg. This is the foule fiend *fliberdegibek*, hee begins at curphew, and walks till the first cocke, he giues the web,& the pin, squemes the eye, and makes the hare lip, mildewes the white wheate,and hurts the poore creature of earth, swithald footed thrice the old,he met the night mare and her nine fold bid her,O light and her troth plight and arint thee, witch arint thee.

Kent. How fares your Grace ?

Lear. Whats hee ?

Kent. Whose there, what i'st you seeke ?

Gloft. What are you there? your names ?

Edg. Poore *Tom,* that eats the swimming frog, the tode,the tod pole, the wall-newt , and the water, that in the furie of his heart,when the foule fiend rages,eats cow-dung for sallets,swallowes the old ratt, and the ditch dogge,drinkes the greene mantle of the standing poole, who is whipt from tithing to tithing, and stock-punisht and imprisoned,who hath had three sutes to his backe, sixe shirts to his bodie, horse to ride, and weapon to weare.

But mise and rats,and such small Deere,

Hath beene *Toms* foode for seuen long yeare-

Beware my follower, peace snulbug, peace thou fiend.

Gloft. What hath your Grace no better company?

Edg. The Prince of darkenes is a Gentleman, *modo* he's caled and ma hu---

Gloft. Our flesh and bloud is growne so vild my Lord, that it doth hate what gets it,

Edg. Poore *Tom* a cold.

Gleft. Go in with me,my dutie canot suffer to obay in all your daughters hard commaunds,though their iniunction be to barre my doores,and let this tyranous night take hold vpon you, yet haue I venter'd to come seeke you out, and bring you where both food and fire is readie.

                                             Lear.

The Historie of King Lear.

odated man, is no more but such a poore bare forked Animall as thou art, off off you leadings;come on bee true.

Foole. Prithe Nunckle be content, this is a naughty night to swim in,now a little fire in a wild field, were like an old leachers heart, a small sparke,all the rest in bodie cold,looke here comes a walking fire.   *Enter Glofter.*

Edg. This is the foule fiend *Sriberdegibus*, hee begins at curphew, and walks till the first cocke, he gins the web, the pinqueues the eye, and makes the harte lip, mildewes the white wheate, and hurts the poore creature of earth, swithald footed thrice the old a nellthu night more and her nine fold bid her, O light and her troth plight and arint thee, with arint thee.

Kent. How fares your Grace ?

Lear. Whats hee ?

Kent. Whose there, what i'st you seeke ?

Gloft. What are you there? your names ?

Edg. Poore *Tom,* that eats the swimming frog, the tode,the tode pold, the wall-wort and the water, that in the furie of his heart;when the foule fiend rages,eats cow-dung for sallets,swallowes the old ratt, and the ditch dogge,drinkes the greene mantle of the standing poole, who is whipt from tithing to tithing, and stock-punisht and imprisoned,who hath had three sutes to his backe, sixe shirts to his bodie, horse to ride, and weapon to weare.

But mise and rats,and such small Deere,

Hath beene *Toms* foode for seuen long yeare-

Beware my follower, peace snulbug, peace thou fiend.

Gloft. What hath your Grace no better company ?

Edg. The Prince of darkenes is a Gentleman, *modo* he's caled and ma hu---

Gloft. Our flesh and bloud is growne so vild my Lord, that it doth hate what gets it,

Edg. Poore *Tom* a cold.

Gloft. Go in with me,my dutie cānot suffer to obay in all your daughters hard commaunds,though their iniunction be to barre my doores,and let this tyranous night take hold vpon you , yet haue I venter'd to come seeke you out , and bring you where both food and fire is readie.

                                             Lear.

revised edition appeared in ten volumes in 1895–1901. But by far the most important and influential critical edition of the nineteenth century was the *Cambridge Shakespeare* edited by W. G. Clark, J. Glover and W. A. Wright (nine volumes, 1863–66). The immensely popular one-volume Globe edition of 1864 used the text of the *Cambridge Shakespeare* and remained the standard one-volume Shakespeare for students until the middle of the present century, its line numbering, for example, being accepted as standard by virtually all critics and scholars. As late as 1949 Professor R. C. Bald complained that in spite of the great advances in the textual study of Shakespeare made in the twentieth century two recent college editions, by the distinguished Shakespeare scholars G. B. Harrison and O. J. Campbell, were content to reproduce the Globe text.

The nineteenth century was the great age of visual illusion in the production of Shakespeare on the stage. J. P. Kemble at Drury Lane (1780–1802) and Covent Garden (1803–17) was an important force here; it was Kemble, too, who began the fashion of dressing the characters in what were considered to be historically accurate costumes, while his brother Charles, together with James Robinson Planché, dramatist, antiquary and authority on the history of costume and heraldry, cooperated in a famous

The Ashbee lithographic facsimiles of Shakespeare Quartos reflect the growing interest in Shakespeare bibliography throughout the nineteenth century. (Shakespeare Birthplace Trust)

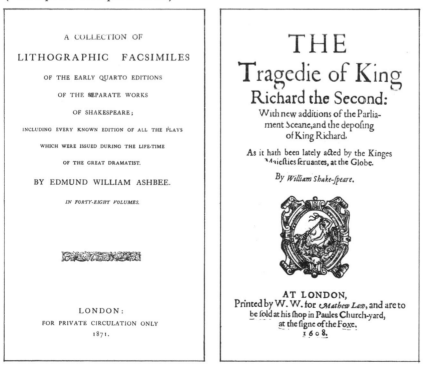

Playbill for Charles Kemble and James Planché's production of King John,
1824. (*Royal Shakespeare Theatre*)

production of *King John* at Covent Garden in 1824, thus beginning the vogue of antiquarian productions that became
immensely popular. 'When the curtain rose', Charles Kemble
recalled many years later, 'and discovered King John dressed as
his effigy appears in Worcester Cathedral, surrounded by his
barons sheathed in mail, with cylindrical helmets and correct
armorial shields, and his courtiers in the long tunics and mantles
of the thirteenth century, there was a roar of approbation,
accompanied by four distinct rounds of applause.'[13] This kind of
spectacular antiquarian production was continued by Charles
Kean, notably in his series of productions at the Princess's
Theatre in the 1850s.

A conflict between those more concerned to present a spectacle
and those more concerned with the speaking of Shakespeare's
language developed during the remainder of the century. At the
end of the century William Poel's campaign to restore Elizabethan conditions of stage production, marked by his founding
in 1894 of the Elizabethan Stage Society and his pioneer production of *Twelfth Night* in 1895, though it did not immediately
discredit the established tradition of 'realistic' sets on a picture-
frame stage, helped to produce a steadily growing awareness of

William Poel's production of Measure for Measure *at the Royalty Theatre,* 1893. (*Royal Shakespeare Theatre*)

J. F. Cathcart as Mowbray in Charles Kean's production of Richard II *at the Princess's Theatre,* 1857. (*Royal Shakespeare Theatre*)

Harley Granville-Barker's productions of Twelfth Night *(above) and* The Winter's Tale *(below) at the Savoy Theatre,* 1912. *(Shakespeare Birthplace Trust)*

the nature of the Elizabethan stage and of Shakespeare's brilliant
theatrical craftsmanship when seen in relation to the kind of
theatre for which he wrote his plays. The reduction of superfluous
spectacle so as to make room for the presentation of Shakespeare's
full text was in a part a result of this movement: in the early years
of the present century Harley Granville-Barker – playwright,
actor, critic and director – concentrated both on Shakespeare's
language and on the rapid flow of the action, always with his eye
on Shakespeare's own kind of stage, and in his brilliant productions of *A Winter's Tale* and *Twelfth Night*, in 1912, created
among the theatre-going public new kinds of expectations about
an Elizabethan play. This has had a permanent effect on subsequent Shakespeare productions and, for all the variety and
experiment and even 'gimmickry' which more recent productions
of Shakespeare's plays have shown, no director has since been
able to ignore the kind of theatre for which Shakespeare wrote
his plays and the Shakespearean stagecraft which the plays
reveal when seen in their proper context. Bizarre interpretations,
modern or some other kind of anachronistic costumes and setting,
the forcing of contemporary kinds of awareness on to Shakespeare's language and action, which can be seen in many modern
productions, may seem to lead away from the Elizabethan
Shakespeare and his stage, but do exhibit the perpetual modernity
of Shakespeare and his continued appeal to different kinds of
minds and temperaments.

✳

The twentieth century saw the continuation and indeed proliferation of annotated editions of individual plays for schools and
universities to which reference has already been made. There
were also many college editions of the complete plays or of a
selection of the plays, especially in the United States. W. A.
Neilson produced his *Complete Plays and Poems of Shakespeare* in
one volume, with introductions and notes, in 1906; the edition
was revised by C. J. Hill in 1942. Neilson also edited, with
A. H. Thorndike and others, the forty-volume *Tudor Shakespeare*,
published in New York in 1911–13. The forty-volume *Yale
Shakespeare*, edited by W. L. Cross, C. F. T. Brooke, and others,
appeared in New Haven in 1918–28. By this time the 'new
bibliography', pioneered by three great English scholars, A. H.
Pollard, W. W. Greg and R. B. McKerrow, was developing new

standards of knowledge and accuracy in the textual criticism of Elizabethan books.

The main problem with which modern critical bibliography and textual criticism concerns itself is the understanding of the processes that take place between the manuscript's leaving the author's hands and the appearance of the printed book. Such understanding permits the reconstruction from the printed text of the text as originally written by the author with as much certainty as possible. The probable relation of the printed 'original' to the author's manuscript is thus the primary topic of investigation; in order to pursue this, an editor requires a detailed understanding of earlier methods of printing and bookmaking, of compositors' and proof-readers' habits, and of all the conditions under which a manuscript text was transferred to type. Examination of a printed text by a scholar with sufficient knowledge of these matters, if done in minute detail and with infinite pains, can tell a surprising amount: for example, it can show that at given points in the setting up of a text a new compositor took over (with his own habits), it can demonstrate the order in which parts of a book were set up, it can reveal through an examination of the variants within a single issue how certain corrections were made in the course of printing and infer the nature and meaning of these corrections.

The first edition of Shakespeare to make continuous use of such of the new bibliography as was by then available was the *New Cambridge Shakespeare* begun in 1921, with a volume for each play, under the joint editorship of John Dover Wilson and Sir Arthur Quiller-Couch and continued after Quiller-Couch's death in 1944 either by Wilson alone or by Wilson with another collaborator. It was Dover Wilson who brought the bibliography and textual criticism into the edition – Quiller-Couch was concerned only with literary and dramatic criticism, of an elegant but somewhat old-fashioned sort – and his notes show him adventuring sometimes rashly but always with infectious enthusiasm into these exciting new realms of bibliographical detection. The sense of pioneering new bibliographical and textual techniques pervades Wilson's notes and gives a special appeal to the New Cambridge edition, which has recently been reissued by Cambridge University Press in paperback.

Peter Alexander's *William Shakespeare: the Complete Works* (1951) has largely replaced the *Globe* as the standard one-volume edition for students, at least in Britain: modern in both spelling and punctuation (as indeed nearly all editions are), Alexander's text is nevertheless based on careful collation and a thorough understanding of the methods of modern textual criticism. 1951 also saw the inauguration of the *New Arden Shakespeare*, conceived originally as a revision of the original *Arden* of 1899, and done in the same style and format with one volume to each play, but soon emerging as in fact a new undertaking. This was first edited by Una Ellis-Fermor and carried on after her death by Harold F. Brooks and Harold Jenkins. (Each volume has in addition its own individual editor.) Similarly, the attractive little *Temple Shakespeare*, originally edited in forty volumes between 1894 and 1896 by Sir Israel Gollancz, was re-edited as the *New Temple Shakespeare* by M. R. Ridley between 1934 and 1936.

The paperback revolution, discussed in another essay, has had a continuous effect on the publication of Shakespeare since the first six Penguin Shakespeare plays of 1937 edited by G. B. Harrison, and later described by a reviewer as 'Avon swans among the Penguins'. Its American counterpart is the *Pelican Shakespeare*, edited by Alfred Harbage in thirty-eight volumes between 1956 and 1967. These, like so many paperback and other editions, devoted a single volume to each play, but in 1969 a revised Pelican text was published in an unusually well-designed single volume by Allen Lane, The Penguin Press. A *New Penguin Shakespeare* is also now in progress. Many other annotated editions, both hardback and paperback but mostly the latter, intended for schools and universities, have recently appeared on both sides of the Atlantic. Among American paperback editions with one volume to each play is the Folger Library

A page from the New Arden paperback edition of King Lear *edited by Kenneth Muir, Methuen & Co. Ltd 1964, showing the layout of text, textual variants and notes, originally devised for the New Arden edition of* 1951 (King Lear, 1952).

General Reader's Shakespeare, edited by Louis B. Wright and Virginia A. LaMar, the *Laurel Shakespeare*, under the general editorship of Francis Fergusson, and the *Signet Classic Shakespeare*, under the general editorship of Sylvan Barnet. Some of these have seemed to be 'gesturing towards an airport news-stand public'. The Americans have also put out a variety of source-books and case-books relating to individual plays, also in paperback, and designed specifically for students.

Editors of these editions – which, needless to say, are no longer in any way expurgated – not only draw on recent Shakespeare scholarship and criticism: they may also make an important contribution of their own. 'The editorial discipline at its fullest,' a Shakespeare scholar has recently written, 'demands close familiarity with all aspects of the text, and some of the soundest critical writing on Shakespeare comes in introductions written no doubt at the end of the editorial agony, such as some of those in the New Cambridge, New Arden, and New Penguin series.' Shakespeare is still the most widely taught English writer in schools and colleges on both sides of the Atlantic. But modern editions designed for academic study are much more lively, much more intellectually exciting, and often more 'relevant' (to use that modish term of students) in the critical discussion they present than their Victorian predecessors.

The position of Shakespeare in our educational institutions as *the* classic of English literature has thus not been challenged. Nor is there any sign of slackening in the search for experimental new ways of interpreting and presenting Shakespeare on the stage. Nevertheless, it is perhaps worth recording that on the occasion of the four-hundredth anniversary of Shakespeare's birth in 1964 a BBC reporter in Southampton, stopping people in the street with a microphone to ask them what they knew about Shakespeare, received answers indicating total ignorance or indifference from everybody except one plumber, who said he loved Shakespeare and read him often, and when asked what was his favourite Shakespeare play replied *Saint Joan*. In his progress from a popular playwright, equally admired by both groundlings and aristocrats, to an established part of our high literary culture richly served by publishers, editors, and interpreters, Shakespeare has become, inevitably, the heritage of a minority of our people. The paradox involved here is far-reaching and concerns much more than the history of publishing.

JOHN CLIVE

The
Edinburgh Review:

THE LIFE AND DEATH OF A PERIODICAL

THE REAL origin of the *Edinburgh Review* must be sought in the numerous clubs and learned societies which carried on the intellectual traditions of Edinburgh's golden age – the period of the Scottish enlightenment of the mid-eighteenth century.[1] Thus the principal names associated with the periodical during its early years – those of Sydney Smith, Francis Jeffrey, Francis Horner, and Henry Brougham – all appear on the membership lists of the Academy of Physics, a society founded in 1797 for the purpose of investigating nature, the laws by which her phenomena were regulated, and the history of opinions concerning those laws. The benevolently stifling despotism of Henry Dundas, 'Harry the Ninth' of Scotland, could not prevent young Whigs from discussing law reform here; though, had he and his cohorts been able to foresee that in the book reports presented to the Academy lay the seeds of the buff-and-blue *Review* which was to herald the resurgence of Scottish Whiggism, they might well have been alarmed. As it was, they were powerful enough to see to it that young Whig lawyers in Edinburgh did not have much legal business coming their way.

And thus, when some time in the late winter of 1801–02 the Reverend Sydney Smith, who had brought his pupil Michael Hicks Beach to the 'Athens of the North' when the Napoleonic wars had made access to Weimar difficult, first suggested the idea of a new review to Jeffrey and Horner, those two found themselves with more than enough leisure to devote to the project. The *Edinburgh Review* was actually founded some weeks later, when Brougham and others were informed of the scheme. It was at this meeting, which took place at Jeffrey's house in Buccleuch Place, that Smith's proposed motto – *tenui musam meditamur avena* ('We cultivate literature upon a little oatmeal') was found too near the truth to be admitted. The motto finally chosen – *judex damnatur cum nocens absolvitur* ('The judge is condemned when the guilty man is absolved') – gave promise, all too richly fulfilled, of severity to come.

The first number, for which the contributors gave their articles *gratis*, duly appeared on 10 October 1802, published by Archibald Constable in an edition of 750 copies at five shillings a copy. It was a roaring success. By 7 November a second edition of 750 was called for, and within another year more than 2,000 copies of the first number had been sold in Edinburgh alone. What mainly attracted the attention of the public was the sharp

Sydney Smith (1771–1845) *by Daniel Maclise.* (*National Portrait Gallery*)

contrast between the old critical reviews, usually monthlies under the control of booksellers containing little more than abstracts of all current publications, and the new quarterly which asked to be distinguished rather for the selection than for the number of its articles. The articles themselves, anonymous from the start, were not so much book reviews as disquisitions on subjects suggested by the books under review. And they were written with an irresistible combination of verve, learning, and acidity. Take, for instance, the first paragraph of Sydney Smith's review of the Rev. Dr Langford's *Anniversary Sermon of the Royal Humane Society*:

An Accident which happened to the gentleman engaged in reviewing this Sermon, proves, in the most striking manner, the importance of this charity for restoring to life persons in whom the vital power is suspended. He was discovered, with Dr Langford's discourse lying open before him, in a state of the most profound sleep; from which he could not, by any means, be awakened for a great length of time. By attending, however, to the rules prescribed by the Humane Society, flinging in the smoke of tobacco, applying hot

Archibald Constable (1774–1827), *first publisher of the* Review, *by Sir Henry Raeburn,* [*c.* 1820]. (*Constable & Co. Ltd*)

flannels, and carefully removing the discourse itself to a great distance, the critic was restored to his disconsolate brothers.[2]

No less than fifteen out of twenty-nine reviews in the first number were negatively critical. Little wonder, then, that the first of the innumerable series of pamphlets provoked by the *Edinburgh Review* should have contained this advice:

> A knack of words you have, some fancy, too;
> But have you judgment, think you, to review?
>
> Treasure this maxim in your thoughts for ever:
> A critic must be just as well as clever.[3]

Just or unjust, critics writing for the *Edinburgh Review* were soon to receive higher remuneration than had ever been paid to members of a profession that had hitherto served as a catch-all for assorted hacks and penny-a-liners. Archibald Constable was wise enough to heed Sydney Smith's counsel that if he gave £200 per annum to his editor and ten guineas a sheet to his contributors he would soon have the best review in Europe. Francis Jeffrey

Francis Jeffrey (1773–1850), *editor of the* Review 1802–29, *cartoon* 25 *in Crombie's* '*Modern Athenians*', [*c.* 1840s]. (*Mary Evans Picture Library*)

accepted the post of editor in May 1803, and noted carefully that he thought he could do so without compromising either his honour or his future interest. The reason for his confidence lay in the assurances he had received from Constable that as editor he was to be totally independent from the booksellers, and in the adoption of an ironclad rule forcing all contributors to accept payment for their contributions. For the first time, book reviewing had become a respectable profession.

As the result of a visit by T. N. Longman to Edinburgh in 1802 his firm became joint publishers of the *Edinburgh Review* with Constable. When, in 1806, Constable proposed to transfer London publication to Murray, Longmans obtained an injunction to restrain any other publisher in London from selling the *Review* without their consent. In the course of the following year, Longmans sold their whole property in the title and future publication of the *Edinburgh* to Constable for £1,000, but seven years later, they repurchased their former rights for four-and-a-half times the price at which they had relinquished them in

1807. The increased price reflected the phenomenal rise in circulation of the *Review*, which totalled 7,000 at the end of 1807, 11,000 in 1809 (when the price was raised to six shillings), and nearly 13,000 five years later. In 1826 came the failure of the house of Constable. It was at this point that Longmans took over, at a valuation, entire interest in the *Edinburgh Review*. From that time on, until it ended publication in 1929, the *Review* was Longmans' exclusive property.[4]

✳

Three misconceptions still continue to exist, in greater or less degree, about the early years of the *Edinburgh Review*: that it was nothing but a tool of the Whig party; that it catered to the aristocracy alone; and that in matters of literary taste it stood forth as the unrelenting foe of the Romantic poets.

Nobody could deny that from the very first the *Edinburgh* 'spread its light wings of Saffron and of Blue', the Foxite colours; least of all Jeffrey, who told Walter Scott (one of the founders of the rival Tory *Quarterly* in 1809) that the *Review* had but two legs to stand on, literature being one, but its right leg politics. Politics meant first of all zeal for reform: opposition to the slave trade, to the Test and Corporation Acts, to the sale of army commissions, to the existing game laws; support for Catholic emancipation, parliamentary, legal, and penal reform, all projects for the diffusion of useful knowledge. It also meant that the *Review* generally sided with the Whig opposition, especially after Brougham began to use the periodical as a means for his own political advancement. Yet one need only examine the Whig reaction to the famous article entitled 'Don Pedro Cevallos on the French Usurpation of Spain', a joint product of Jeffrey and Brougham (1808), which mingled praise of the Spanish patriots who had risen against Napoleon with bitter criticism of the upper classes, British as well as Spanish, and a demand for the reform of the British Constitution, to see that the *Review* did not always truckle to Holland House and Lord Grey.

For the *Edinburgh* reviewers, the Spanish revolt, directed against the common enemy and thus, unlike the French Revolution, posing no potential threat to the safety of Britain, represented a cure for that pathological fear of Jacobinism against which the *Review* had inveighed from the beginning. The 'Cevallos' article envisioned a recurrence of wholesome popular feelings and a state of public opinion that would view radical improvements in the Constitution without horror. It even went so far as to put in a good word for 'the very odious, many-headed beast, the multitude'. Whigs and Tories alike were offended. The Earl of Buchan, who kicked himself into a reasonable form of immortality (in the shape of *The Cambridge History of English Literature*) by booting the 'Cevallos' number into the street, there to be trodden underfoot by man and beast, was no diehard Tory, but a veteran of the radical Whiggism of the early 1790s.[5] There were other occasions on which the *Review* showed itself more aware than the official Whigs of their disastrous alienation from the people, though it must be added that its important function as the party's radicaliser was intermittent rather than consistent.

'There is a set of persons in your city,' the Rev. Dr Folliott remarks to Mr MacQuedy in *Crotchet Castle*, 'who concoct every three or four months a thing which they call a review; a sort of sugar-plum manufacturer to the Whig aristocracy.' The charge that the *Edinburgh Review*, for all its opposition to the (Tory) governments in power, essentially remained an instrument for aristocratic predominance, had been brought forward most devastatingly by James Mill in the first number of the Radical *Westminster Review* (1824). His son John Stuart had helped him do the research for this article. The charge certainly held true to the extent that Jeffrey and his fellow reviewers were Whigs, not democrats. But as one reads through the *Edinburgh* during Jeffrey's tenure as editor (1802–29), one is continually struck by its tone of moral indignation about the indolence, opulence and frivolity of the upper classes, as contrasted with the virtue and industry of 'all those who are below the sphere of what is called fashionable or public life, and who do not aim at distinctions or notoriety beyond the circle of their equals in fortune and situation'.[6] That is how Jeffrey defined what he called the 'middling classes': it was for them that the *Review* reserved its highest praise and its never-ceasing pedagogical efforts. Adam Smith, not Algernon Sidney, headed the hagiology of the *Edinburgh* reviewers.

Perhaps the best-known sentence ever published in the *Edinburgh Review* is that with which Jeffrey opened his review of Wordsworth's *Excursion*: 'This will never do.' Yet before too precipitously castigating the critic as imperceptive, and dismissing him as an eighteenth-century survival unable to recognise the new currents of romanticism, it is well to balance 'This will never do' against some of his other verdicts, such as this concerning Wordsworth, Southey, and Coleridge: 'There is a fertility and a force, a warmth of feeling and exaltation of imagination about them, which classes them, in our estimation, with a much higher order of poets than the followers of Dryden and Addison; and justifies an anxiety for their fame, in all the admirers of Milton and Shakespeare.'[7]

In so far as romanticism represented a breaking away from formalism to feeling, Jeffrey was completely sympathetic to it. But in so far as it meant that pedlars and leech-gatherers were of a sudden endowed with the tongues of philosophers; in so far as it could see a world in the grains of wisdom dispensed by 'the idiot mother of an idiot boy', he felt that it had to be condemned as childish and absurd. For then it played havoc with accepted social gradations, and with the high seriousness of the emotions and morality of the 'middling classes', which he had made it his task to foster and to confirm. Though Leslie Stephen pitied 'poor Jeffrey' for blundering into grievous misapprehensions and surviving chiefly by his worst errors, it must not be forgotten that Stendhal, in 1818, looked on the *Review* as a bulwark of English romanticism; and that one of the influences that prompted John Stuart Mill to abandon his implicit faith in Utilitarianism came from Carlyle's early articles in the *Edinburgh Review*, published by Jeffrey in spite of his innate suspicions of 'German mysticism'.

Jeffrey retired from the *Review* in 1829, after twenty-seven years of what even his literary foes admitted to have been a brilliant period of editorship. He had built what was originally little more than a student prank into the most powerful literary periodical in Europe. The *Edinburgh Review* continued to be fortunate in finding able editors prepared to take on the job for long enough to leave a definite imprint. The two with the longest tenure were Macvey Napier (1829–47), a professor of law at the University of Edinburgh who succeeded Jeffrey, and Henry Reeve (1855–95), who had had previous experience in journalism as foreign editor of *The Times*. Both maintained the high standards Jeffrey had set by preserving the independence of the *Review*, exercising the utmost discrimination in choosing reviewers, and personally overseeing every aspect of editorial procedure. Reeve, for example, not only read all articles in

Macvey Napier (1776–1847) *editor
of the* Review 1829–47, *a pen drawing
by W. F. Watson of a bust by P.
Sclater in Edinburgh University
Library, first exhibited posthumously
in* 1849. (*Scottish National Portrait
Gallery*)

manuscript and revised proof; he seldom decided to publish a
review of a book which he himself had not read.[8] Napier's chief
problem was to keep Brougham in line, and he handled that with
the requisite combination of firmness and tact. Reeve's chief
problem was to maintain the circulation of the *Review* in the face
of ever growing competition.

The greatest contrast between literary London in 1807 and
1875, one reviewer wrote in the course of the latter year, was
the absence early in the century of 'those minor reviews and
ephemeral literary periodicals which now constitute so large an
element in the pabulum of the reading public'. There was then
nothing that corresponded to the *Athenaeum* or the *Academy* or the
literary portions of the *Saturday Review* and the *Spectator*.[9] He
might have added the *Economist*, the *Pall Mall Gazette*, *Blackwood's*, *Fraser's*, the *Nineteenth Century*, and the *Illustrated London
News*. Periodicals of all kinds, often containing some literary
criticism as well as editorial matter, widely and rapidly distributed
once the railroads had become the chief means of communication
within Britain, gradually came to make the life of the old quarterlies more precarious. And there was only one Thomas Babington
Macaulay!

Macaulay had made his *Edinburgh* debut not, as has long been
thought, with an essay on Milton in the autumn of 1825, but
earlier that same year with an article against West Indian
slavery.[10] But it was his 'Milton' that signalled the rise of a new
star on the literary firmament. 'The more I think, the less I can
conceive where you picked up that style', Jeffrey had written to him

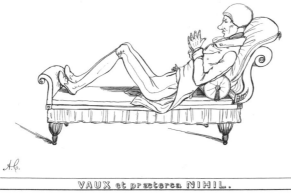

VAUX et praeterea NIHIL.

Published by B.B King, Monument Yard, & T McLean, Haymarket, London.

Henry Peter Brougham, Baron Brougham and Vaux (1778–1868), *cartoon by Alfred Crowquill.* (*Mary Evans Picture Library*)

Thomas Babington Macaulay (1800–59) *by Eden Upton Eddis.* (*Longman Group Ltd*)

on receipt of the manuscript. And for the next two decades that inimitable style, heavily caparisoned with learning and paradox, yet at the same time almost relentlessly clear and vigorous, made its appearance in what were to become some of the most famous essays in the language: 'Machiavelli', the two essays on 'Chatham', 'Bacon', 'Gladstone on Church and State', 'Clive' and 'Hastings'. 'It would be mere affectation in me not to know that my support is of some importance to the *Edinburgh Review*,' Macaulay wrote to Napier in 1833.[11] And that was indeed the case. The essay on Bacon ran to a hundred printed pages, that on Hastings to ninety-six. But to shorten them or to divide them into two parts was out of the question. To cut 'Bacon', Jeffrey advised Napier, 'would be worse than paring down the Pitt diamond to fit the old setting of a dowager's ring'.[12]

Not everyone shared this view of Macaulay's contributions. Some thought they showed too much striving for effect, at the cost of a serious search for the truth. John Stuart Mill held this view. Writing to Bulwer-Lytton in 1836 in order to tell him that his latest article in the *Edinburgh* was filled with a genuine love of the True and the Beautiful – and, therefore, could not possibly be ascribed to Macaulay – he felt bound to add: 'I could not help saying to myself, who would look for these qualities in the *Edinburgh Review*? How the readers of that review must be puzzled and bewildered by a writer who actually takes decided views, who is positively in earnest.'[13]

Macaulay certainly differed from Mill in his view of what a good article in the *Edinburgh* should be like. Above all, he thought, it must be effective when first read. For few people ever read an article in a review more than once. Therefore, 'periodical works like ours, which unless they strike at their first reading, are not likely to strike at all, whose whole life is a month or two, may, I think, be allowed to be sometimes even viciously florid'. It was not by *his* taste, but by that of the fish, that the angler determined his choice of bait. 'A bold, dashing, scene-painting manner, is that which always succeeds best in periodical writing.'[14] And, so far as Macaulay was concerned, earnestness was by no means a necessary ingredient of such a manner. The early *Edinburgh* reviewers had preached it as a virtue to the middle classes, but had not generally practised it as writers. And Macaulay carried on their lighthearted tradition. In recommending Charles Buller to Napier as a potential reviewer, he listed Buller's faults as flippancy and levity, a disposition to make a jest of everything, and went on to say that 'this turn of mind, under some restraint, is, as you well know, by no means ill-suited to the business of reviewing'.[15] Macaulay was not advocating flippancy for its own sake, but as a means of engaging the attention of readers on worthwhile subjects.

It was because Napier was convinced that the reading public had no use for dull books or dull articles that the *Review* under his guidance retained something of the prankish and iconoclastic strain of its early years. James Stephen, no less devoted to seriousness than Mill, though his seriousness stemmed from Evangelical rather than Utilitarian roots, noted in 1842 that there were almost no books that kept hold of the public mind for any length of time, except those with some particular character of style and execution. 'The moral drawn from this,' he wrote to Napier, 'is that the inimitable Sydney Smith, and (though in a different way) the scarcely less inimitable pen of our friend Macaulay, should be employed, if it were possible, as you employ gas in a balloon, to give a long flight to materials of greater inherent weight and value.'[16] But Macaulay was beginning to put his pen to other uses. In 1844 he stopped reviewing for the *Edinburgh*, on the ground that if it had not been for the time spent on his essays he would already have brought out at least two volumes of his *History*.[17]

On Napier's death in 1847 the editorial headquarters of the *Review* were shifted from Edinburgh to London. And perhaps it is hardly a coincidence that those two departures – that of Macaulay, and that from the place that had witnessed the founding and the initial, audacious period of the *Review* – heralded an increase of gravity at the expense of sprightliness. The *enfants terribles* of the early years were turning into those privy councillors to whom, so Bagehot was to write in the mid-1850s, the composition of each number was entrusted. He went on to express surprise at the thought that the *Edinburgh Review* had once been regarded as an incendiary publication, given the fact that the young generation now regarded each of its appearances as a grave constitutional event. Bagehot had a point. After all, when Nassau Senior wrote an article on the Irish Poor Laws (1846), it was revised and modified by Lord Lansdowne and Lord John Russell; and, during the following year, Henry Reeve had the assistance of none other than the Prince Consort in writing his essay on Cracow. With a loss of *brio* and combativeness came a greater diversity of subject matter: less politics, fewer 'causes', more biography, science, fiction, and theology.

But the list of contributors continued to retain its distinction. In the early days it had included names like those of Hazlitt, Scott, and Malthus. Between the 'thirties and the 'fifties were added those of Carlyle, Mill, Bulwer-Lytton, Leigh Hunt, Monckton Milnes, G. H. Lewes, and Herbert Spencer. Some of their articles written for the *Review* are still rightly regarded as landmarks of modern British cultural history. One of these was Carlyle's 'Signs of the Times' (1829) in which he unforgettably limned the mechanical character of the age: 'The shuttle drops from the fingers of the weaver, and falls into iron fingers that ply it faster.' But, more than that, 'men are grown mechanical in head and heart, as well as in hand'. Still, Carlyle did not advocate the destruction of machinery. So far as he was concerned, the very unrest of the age was full of promise, if only the aim to be kept in mind could be that of making mechanisation society's servant rather than its master.[18] Carlyle assured the editor of the *Review* that there could be no more respectable vehicle for any British writer's speculations than his journal. 'Though no Whig in the strict sense,' he continued with a certain amount of understatement, 'I have no disposition to run *amuck* against any set of men or opinions.'[19]

Another famous contributor, no Whig in the strict or in any other sense, was John Stuart Mill. Sixteen years after he had helped his father launch his devastating attack on the *Review* as a prop of the aristocracy, he wrote to Napier offering to establish a connection with the object of that attack; compelled to acknowledge that there was now no room in England for a fourth political party, in addition to Conservatives, Whig Radicals, and Chartists. 'If I can hope to do any good,' he went on, 'it can only be by merging in one of the existing great bodies of opinion; by attempting to gain the ear of the liberal party generally, instead of addressing a mere section of it.'[20] Napier readily accepted his offer, and a few months later printed Mill's brilliant review of the second volume of Tocqueville's *Democracy in America*, in the course of which he contended, along with Tocqueville, that in England as well as elsewhere the power of the upper classes in government and society was diminishing while that of the lower and middle classes was increasing and likely to increase further.

A curious sidelight on this review was that Brougham, who agreed with its anti-aristocratic tone, declared himself disturbed by Mill's assertion that during the past century Britain had owed little innovation to its aristocracy. What about names such as Cavendish, Howard, and Bridgewater, he asked in a letter to Napier. 'Luckily for the *Review*,' he added, 'people now-a-days seem never to think for twenty-four hours about anything they read.'[21]

Perhaps readers thought a bit longer than that, however, about Mill's article on 'The Claims of Labour', one of many social commentaries evoked by the hungry 'forties. In it Mill called Chartism the first open separation of interest, feeling, and opinion between the labouring portion of the community and all above them. The ruling classes had to ask themselves how existing social arrangements could now be justified. Something had to be done to render the multitude more content with the existing state of things. Feudalism was out of date.

The age that produces railways which, for a few shillings, will convey a labourer and his family fifty miles to find work; in which agricultural labourers read newspapers, and make speeches at public meetings called by themselves to discuss low wages – is not an age in which a man can feel loyal and dutiful to another because he has been born on his estate.[22]

For Mill, the answer was cooperation, raising the labourer from being a mere receiver of hire to being a partner in production. Mill called on Parliament to frame a good law of partnership, to help in the accumulation of concentrations of industrial capital by means of an aggregation of small savings. Ten years later another *Edinburgh* contributor, Herbert Spencer, also called on Parliament to play a more active role in social matters, this time to enforce the limits of proprietary contracts entered into by investors in the railroads, in order to put an end to the frauds and dishonesties that continued to occur in this sphere.[23]

Thus economic and social problems and their remedies continued to be expounded in the *Review*. At the same time, its editors continued to be preoccupied with stylistic as well as political concerns. In 1842 Napier had declared himself scandalised by what he called Macaulay's colloquialisms in his essay on Frederick the Great, specifically the historian's use of the terms 'bore', 'awkward squad' and 'shirk'. Macaulay defended himself by pointing out that the first rule of all writing ought to be that words should most fully and precisely convey the writer's

Left: William Empson (1791–1852), *editor of the* Review 1847–52, *by J. Linnell after an engraving by W. Walker.* (*British Museum*)
Right: Sir George Cornewall Lewis (1806–63), *editor of the* Review 1852–55, *by George Richmond.* (*National Portrait Gallery*)

meaning to the great body of his readers. Had not 'shirk' been used by the Duke of Wellington when he reprimanded one of his officers?[24] The offending words remained in the essay. A generation later, Lord Wensleydale complained to Reeve about the *Edinburgh's* lending its high authority to the expression 'firstly'. He had, he wrote, 'a sort of mania' on this subject.[25] Reeve took full responsibility for the 'error'. Longwinded authors presented another constant problem. Sir George Cornewall Lewis took over the editorship of the *Review* in 1852 (William Empson had edited it immediately after Napier's death) and achieved a measure of immortality not as Palmerston's Chancellor of the Exchequer, which he became in 1855, but as the author of the saying that 'life would be tolerable, but for its amusements'. He remarked plaintively: '*Prolixity* is the bête noire of an editor. Every separate contributor has some special reason to write at length on his own subject.'[26]

But if style and length caused perpetual editorial heart-searchings, politics occasionally caused more serious ones. Over the years the *Review* had remained attached to the aims and ideals of the Whig party. That did not mean that it slavishly supported everything the Whigs did or said any more than it had done in its infancy. Brougham recalled complaints from Lord Grey about deviations from the true creed, and his own reply to the effect that the *Edinburgh* would have no authority and would be useless to the party, if it did not at times criticise the Whigs. He remembered the use of phrases like 'merciless aristocracy of the Whigs' and 'as aristocratic as a Whig Peer or a Whig patriot' as proof that the journal's party allegiance had been constant, but not total. 'A Liberal, a Whig, it has always been, and always must be,' he wrote to Napier, 'but the mere organ of a lot of men it assuredly never was, excepting for a few years.'[27]

When Napier became editor, Jeffrey advised him to make one of his criteria for the acceptance or rejection of an article his own view as to the safety or danger of doctrines contained in it, 'and its tendency either to promote or retard the practical adoption of those liberal principles to which, *and their practical advancement* you must always consider the journal as devoted'.[28] Those principles remained, in part, identical with the major doctrines of the classical economists. Thus when, in 1830, J. R. M'Culloch upbraided him for accepting an article on economics by Spring-Rice, since he felt that topic belonged to *him*, Napier defended his editorial prerogative. But, he went on, had he been asked to insert an article hostile to 'the great doctrines you have so long and strenuously advocated', he would not have agreed to do so. 'I should *then* have a reasonable and intelligent ground of refusal, – that of the propriety of preserving something like consistency on great questions.'[29]

On the whole, 'liberal principles' or 'just views', as they were sometimes called by Macaulay and others, tended to be in accordance both with Whig precepts and policies, and with what the editors felt or imagined to be the moderately reformist opinions of the bulk of the *Review's* readers. 'Moderate' is the key word here. Thus Jeffrey, in 1837, advised Napier against a decided advocacy of franchise extension or an attack on the government of the day, since 'either of these topics would be generally distasteful to that class of readers who have hitherto been most influenced by the opinions and reasonings of the *Edinburgh Review*'. And, shortly after becoming editor, Reeve wrote to Tocqueville that it was the height of his ambition to make the *Review* an organ of liberal and moderate opinions.[30] Reeve had

Henry Reeve (1813–95), *editor of the* Review 1855–95, *by A. D'Orsay,* 1839. (*National Portrait Gallery*)

no doubt that those opinions coincided with loyalty to the Whig party. In 1857 he published an article on 'The Past Session' by Robert Lowe, denouncing those members of the government – Gladstone and Lord John Russell, in particular – who, in 1855, had deserted Lord Palmerston and had made common cause with the opposition. Like everything else Lowe ever undertook, it was a brilliant performance.

He began by pointing out that the Liberal party had suffered as a result of the triumph of its own principles. The avowal of civil and religious liberty, reform, retrenchment and free trade (as good a summary as any, by the way, of Reeve's 'liberal and moderate opinions') now cost and meant so little that it was no surprise to find it often made with little sincerity, and acted on with little consistency. General content and prosperity had half superseded the vocation of reformer. The fuel that had fed the flame of discontent was gone, and with it the cravings for major reforms. Meanwhile, the vastly increased influence of public opinion and the press had brought with it the decline of party. No party leaders in the House of Commons were bold enough to make a resolute stand. Thus Lord John Russell, who had left the Aberdeen government early in 1855 'under the influence of an unhappy delusion which has led him of late years to suppose that no liberal Government can be formed without his headship', had subsequently seceded from Lord Palmerston's first cabinet. Gladstone had previously deserted, leaving Palmerston to conduct the Crimean War. 'Like the elephant given by some eastern prince to the man he intends to ruin, Mr Gladstone is an inmate too costly for any party to afford to keep long.'[31]

Lord John Russell was so shocked by this piece that he wrote to Thomas Longman, condemning the present conduct of the *Edinburgh Review* as tending to plunge the Whig party into the swamp of political immorality. Longman himself was convinced that the attack on Russell had been a mistake; and, in the end, Reeve gave way. Lord John Russell received a promise that the offensive number would not be republished.

Politics, then, led to an occasional crisis. But it would be a mistake to think of the *Edinburgh Review* during the nineteenth century as wholly, or even primarily, a political journal. The great majority of the articles it published dealt with other subjects – religion, education, science, and, of course, literature. In matters of religion, as might be expected from a Whig periodical, the *Review's* attitude was solidly Broad Church. It was in the columns of the *Review* that Thomas Arnold, in 1836, delivered his frontal attack against Newman and his associates, for whose fanaticism, 'a fanaticism of mere foolery', he found the sole analogue in those malignant fanatics who had plotted to assassinate St Paul. After its publication, the trustees of Rugby asked Arnold to acknowledge the article, and contemplated his dismissal. But he stood his ground.[32]

In the early 1850s the *Edinburgh* published a series of articles on church matters both amusingly and incisively written by the Rev. W. J. Conybeare. His well-known essay on 'Church Parties' is still indispensable for any student of Victorian religion.[33] But his other reviews are also well worth re-reading, if only for their style. Here he is on Bishop Phillpotts, whom he tried to depict, 'not as he is pictured by the enthusiastic dreams of the Anglo-Catholic young ladies, who oscillate between the ballet and the Opera House and the morning service at S. Barnabas, nor yet as he is represented in the darker visions of their aunts or grandmothers, who derive their theology from the columns of the *Record*'. And this is what he had to say about the condition of certain Welsh churches: 'The precincts of the sacred building are used by the parishioners for purposes quite incompatible with the spirit of sanitary reform, for the Persian imprecation, "May the groves of your ancestors be defiled," would hold no superstitious terror for the villagers of Wales.'[34]

A certain amount of social awareness as well as a real concern for freedom of inquiry were characteristic of the Broad Church; and evidence of both is to be found in the *Edinburgh*. In 1856, in the course of his review of a three-decker enticingly entitled *Perversion*, Richard Monckton Milnes expressed the hope that within a large and liberal school of Christianity the Gospel could be made a reality 'to the masses of the people now sufficiently educated to be no longer credulous, but far from unwilling to become credent of holiness and Christian truth when offered to them with the sympathy and single-mindedness of the first disciples of the Founder'.[35] Five years later, in his article on *Essays and Reviews*, Arthur Stanley stressed the dangers of stifling free discussion and research on theological subjects. He was not uncritical toward the volume, but his conclusion was that the future lay with *Essays and Reviews*, and not with its adversaries.[36] It was thought by Stanley and his mother that this article prevented him from ever becoming a bishop. The reception of Renan's *Life* of Jesus showed the limits of the *Edinburgh's* tolerance. Certainly, it was better to become acquainted with the life of Christ through the pages of Renan than not at all. But the immediate effects of the book were likely to be deplorable. However, English readers were safe: 'They have an obstinate faith in the existence of an outer world, wherein God works.'[37]

Had some of them obtained this faith by virtue of a public school education? One of the causes the *Review* had taken up in the early 1830s was that of opposition to the fagging system prevalent at Eton and elsewhere. Sir George Cornewall Lewis called it 'the only regular institution of slave-labour, enforced by brute violence, which now exists in these islands'. In the same article he unfavourably compared an Eton education, with its totally classical emphasis, with the more advanced and liberal system prevalent in Scotland.[38] A generation later James Fitzjames Stephen gave higher marks to Arnold's Rugby. In a characteristically vigorous review of *Tom Brown's Schooldays*, he attributed the (to him) welcome absence of 'dreams' and 'visions' among the English to the influence of a public school education. It was a system that 'dispels illusions, calms the imagination, and sobers the whole moral and intellectual constitution as effectually as it hardens the muscles and braces the nerves'. It was the great glory of the English public schools, Stephen wrote, that they taught so many of their pupils to acknowledge the laws and submit to the evils of life, not with pain and grief, but with a hearty assent which invigorated human nature. Still, he had to admit that under Dr Arnold the atmosphere at Rugby had become excessively moral. Only a Rugbeian 'finds as many morals in a boxing match as Mr Ruskin does in the twist of a gargoyle's tail, or the shape of a wall-flower's root'.[39]

What of women's education? In 1869 Margaret Oliphant, reviewing Mill's *Subjection of Women*, rejected what she called the author's hypothesis that woman was man in petticoats: 'It is not so; it never was so; and devoutly we trust never will be.' But it was not long before another reviewer was able to document the fact that women were now becoming doctors, scholars, even post office employees. The number in which this particular article appeared (July 1887) carried a special footnote inserted by the editor which reported that a Miss Ramsay had that year been alone in being placed in the first class of the Cambridge Classical Tripos.[40] Things had changed since Adam Sedgwick confided to Napier that he believed a woman was the author of *Vestiges of Creation*, partly from its fair dress and agreeable exterior; 'and partly from the utter ignorance the book displays of all sound physical logic'.[41] By the time he reviewed the book, he had discovered that his hypothesis was false, and he apologised. 'But we know by long experience,' he still went on, 'that the ascent up the hill of science is rugged and thorny, and ill-fated for the drapery of a petticoat.'[12]

By mid century the reading public for books like the *Vestiges* had come to include not merely naturalists by profession or avocation, but 'that far wider intellectual class which now takes interest in the higher generalizations of all the sciences'. The phrase comes from a review of *The Origin of Species*.[43] The reviewer expressed his lack of sympathy with the 'Biblical' objectors to that work, but concluded that natural selection was 'not proven'. Some years later W. Boyd-Dawkins, the reviewer of *The Descent of Man*, was respectful enough, but could not bring himself to sympathise with Darwin's 'Lucretian' doctrine that a mysterious force of reproduction was the dominant fact of life: 'In a heathen poet such doctrines appear gross and degrading, if not vicious. We know not how to characterise them in an English naturalist, well known for the purity and elevation of his own life and character.'[44]

Religion and science, then, constituted a good deal of the subject matter in the *Edinburgh Review* during the middle decades of the nineteenth century. But it goes without saying that literature also continued to attract the attention of the reviewers. In 1838, on the basis of *Boz*, *Pickwick*, *Nicholas Nickleby*, and *Oliver Twist*, Dickens was welcomed as the truest and most spirited delineator since Smollett and Fielding of English life amongst the middle and lower classes. But his merits were not thought of as merely literary. The tendency of his writings was to make readers 'benevolent'. His humanity was plain, practical, and manly.[45] Three times during the 1840s Dickens promised to write articles himself for the *Edinburgh Review* – and failed.[46] In 1843, the *Review* applauded Tennyson's *Poems*, but expressed the hope that he would soon find a large enough subject to take the entire impress of his mind and energy. By the time Coventry Patmore came to review 'Maud' and 'Simon Stylites', he had found such a subject and had become Poet Laureate. But Patmore expressed the view that those two poems possessed the serious defect 'of leaving the mind of the reader in a painful state of confusion as to the limits of the sane and the insane'.[47]

Ever since Jeffrey, in 1821, had congratulated Bowdler for seeing to it that youth even in reading Shakespeare ran no risk of corruption in the pursuit of innocent amusement or valuable instruction,[48]* the *Review* had tended to emphasise the moral aspect of the literary works on which it pronounced judgment. Thus Monckton Milnes praised *Middlemarch* for its healthy tone and honest purpose as well as its admirable interior action, and welcomed it as another volume acceptable to both sexes. And a few years later Rowland Prothero tempered his laudatory comments about Rudyard Kipling with an injunction that bade him abandon his 'mistaken mission' of convincing the British public that literal coarseness of treatment and a gratuitously rough tone were required in order to emancipate art from pedantry.[49]

Literary immortality, so Arthur Balfour put it in an *Edinburgh* article on George Frederick Handel, 'is an unsubstantial fiction

* See above, pp. 91–95.

devised by living artists for their own especial consolation'.[50] The very number in which his essay appeared proved that the *Review* did not merely concern itself with immortals, actual or potential. In 1881 Archbishop Tait wrote to Reeve that it seemed to him that the *Edinburgh Review* would do much good if it published an article on 'the pernicious periodical literature which spreads low Radicalism and second-hand scraps of infidelity amongst the labouring classes, both of town and country'.[51] Presumably as a result of this letter such an article duly appeared, pointing out the trashy nature of much of the cheap literature in circulation. The author, B. G. Johns, reported his pleasure at finding *Faust* among the Penny Dreadfuls – well printed, on good paper, and not badly translated. But at the bottom of each page, in 'staring capitals', was imprinted the legend of somebody's incomparable pills, 'words that seem to haunt and desecrate every scene in the mighty drama'.[52]

It should be pointed out that throughout the century the great works of foreign literature received more than such casual mention in the *Review*. In 1844 Mill brought Michelet to the notice of the readers of the *Review*; twelve years later, Monckton Milnes praised Heine's poems, though with the painful admission that they could not be judged by Christian standards; and in 1862 Goldwin Smith hailed Mommsen's *Roemische Geschichte* as the best history thus far of the Roman Republic.

In a country whose statesmen wrote novels as well as commentaries on the classics, literature and politics were necessarily connected. In 1847 Monckton Milnes had contributed to the *Review* what Robert Blake has called to this day the best statement for the prosecution of Disraeli's novels.[53] It was by no means the only attack on Disraeli in the *Edinburgh*. In 1853 Abraham Hayward concluded his character sketch of Disraeli in the following terms: 'Far from regarding this Caucasian luminary as having shed a wholesome light over our political firmament, we saw little but what augured evil in its lurid and fitful coruscations, and felt neither regret nor astonishment in its eclipse.'[54] The eclipse was shortlived, of course; and before too long Gladstone himself fulminated in the pages of the *Review* against Disraeli's Reform Act of 1867, dubbing it a piece of plagiarism and tergiversation. Once again, as in 1829 and 1846, 'resistless destiny' had decreed that the Conservative Party 'must become itself the instrument of strangling the idol it had adored'.[55]

When Longmans became the publishers of a Disraeli novel, *Endymion,* the reviewer in the *Edinburgh* was more friendly, but remained unimpressed.*[56]

While Gladstone was prime minister for the first time, he contributed to the *Review* an article about the Franco-Prussian war, in which, having castigated France for her role in the events leading up to that conflict, he ended by rejoicing that Britain by the bounty of Providence had been given a place of vantage in effecting the new rule of public right that was gradually taking hold in the world. He also took pride, in words that must have proved hard for him to re-read within a very short space of time, in the fact that 'Ireland, our ancient reproach, can no longer fling her grievances in the face of Great Britain'.[57] That article represented Gladstone's finest hour in the pages of the *Edinburgh*. Four years later Reeve attacked him on behalf of the journal and the Whig party for having lost the general election because he had deviated to too great an extent from moderate towards extreme liberal principles. Appropriate lines of verse were reserved for both sides. Disraeli's cabinet, which included a Lancashire banker, a Cambridgeshire farmer, and a Westminster tradesman, was compared to Sydney Smith's salad:

> Some onion atoms lurk within the bowl,
> And scarce suspected animate the whole.

For the Liberal opposition, on the other hand, suddenly surrounded by gloom and darkness, only Milton's fallen cherub would do:

> See'st thou yon dreary plain, forlorn and wild,
> The seat of desolation, void of light.[58]

Reeve's fear of radicalism, and what it might do to the Whig traditions of the Liberal party, became increasingly pronounced. In reviewing Mill's *Autobiography* – he called it a far more destructive work than Rousseau's *Confessions*, since Mill would deny man the rights of property in this world and the hopes of existence thereafter – Reeve proudly accepted the old charge that the *Edinburgh Review* favoured the aristocracy. After all, the Whig theory of aristocracy was not that of a closed nobility, but of an aristocracy open to the whole intelligence of the country by way of the civil and military services, the Bar, and the Church. Mill and his friends would not have effected the slightest good,

* See below, pp. 175, 178 ff.

if they had not had the main body of the Whig party behind them. Mill's own latent gifts had been crushed by 'a cruel education, a false philosophy, and an evil fate'.[59]

In 1880, in an article entitled 'Plain Whig Principles', Reeve attacked Joseph Chamberlain's electoral caucus as 'a democratic artifice to make the will of the few appear the choice of the many', and reiterated as true Whig principles the defence of life and property as the foundations of society, and the support of a church as inclusive as possible. The Whigs – and the *Review* – stood, not for what was popular, but for what was sound, just and right. And among those things were freedom of trade and the Union with Ireland.[60] When 'the skilful plagiarist', who had presided over the last Parliament, fell from power a few weeks later, the *Review* expressed hopes that 'plain Whig principles' would become part of the Liberals' creed.[61]

Those hopes were disappointed. In 1886 Reeve attacked Chamberlain as the *enfant terrible* of the Liberal party's 'phantas-magoria of a false Jacobinism', excoriated Home Rule, and noted that 'plain Whig Principles' were now in the possession of Conservatism, which did not essentially differ from the Whig-gism of the past half century.[62] But Chamberlain came to uphold the Empire, and to gain the *Review's* plaudits for so doing, and it was Gladstone who through his advocacy of Home Rule became the real villain of the *Edinburgh*. The great names of yesteryear – Sydney Smith, Macaulay – were invoked in support of the Union; and Gladstone was compared to Napoleon, with whom he was said to share a belief in popular enthusiasm accompanied by contempt for the educated classes of society.[63] By 1887 it was clear that so far as the *Edinburgh Review* was concerned, the Liberal party could not be reunited under Gladstone: 'He is the great irreconcilable and the great obstacle in the way of recon-ciliation.' His views on Ireland showed his affinity to the Jacobin spirit of the French Revolution. He had betrayed the Liberal party; and thanks were due to dissentient Liberals such as Hartington and Goschen for their efforts on behalf of saving the Union.[64]

It was quite appropriate therefore, that when Reeve died in harness in 1895 he should have been succeeded as editor of the *Review* by Arthur Elliot, the second son of the Earl of Minto, one of the first Liberal MPs to have declared for the Union in 1886. In 1903 Elliot was appointed Financial Secretary to the Treasury

The Honourable Arthur Elliot M.P. (1846–1923) editor of the Review
*1895–1912, reproduction of a drawing by Miss Leighton by the Autotype
Company. (British Museum)*

in Balfour's government, but as a free trader he resigned over the
tariff issue. He was known to some as 'the last of the Whigs', and
his views were reflected in the *Edinburgh's* increasingly alarmist
attitude toward the socialist danger. In an article entitled 'Socialism in the House of Commons', published after the Liberal
landslide of 1906, the *Review* noted that the spirit of socialism
pervaded the whole of the House to a greater degree than in any
previous Parliament. Free meals, old age pensions, unemploy-
ment insurance – those were the topics of the day. But social
reformers must control themselves. For example, 'the assumption
that because a child looks hungry he necessarily is hungry is

quite unwarrantable'. In fact, so the reviewer opined, there was very little want of food among the poor. The plan for free meals he called quite the most 'pernicious' of all socialist and semi-socialist proposals. As for old age pensions, they would merely create new hardships. Individuals, not the state, should make provision for old age. The fact was that the classes were far closer together now than in the past. Bicycles and cricket flannels were owned by village lads whose grandfathers walked about in rags. There were seaside holidays for mill hands, and theatres and music halls for all. Some of the general improvement in conditions was due to the efforts of the trade unions. But, let it be remembered, state socialism was the natural foe of trade unionism. For if men were taught that the state would provide for them in any event, why should they join a union?[65]

It seems as if suddenly the issues are no longer Victorian, but 'modern', and one is not surprised to find, in the same number with the article just cited, an essay on 'Some Tendencies in Modern Music', praising Debussy's string quartet for having 'blurred with irridescent rays the severe contours of Chamber composition' and taking Richard Strauss to task for having transferred music's centre of gravity from the end to the means.[66]

In 1912 Harold Cox became the last editor of the *Edinburgh Review* which, in the course of that same year, dropped its long-established policy of anonymity. In his youth Cox had been influenced by Edward Carpenter, and had spent nearly a year working as an agricultural labourer in Kent and Sussex in order to gain insight into the lives led by ordinary Englishmen. Later he collaborated with Sidney Webb on a book dealing with the eight-hour day. Nevertheless (some might say as a consequence), he ended his life as a free-trade Liberal and an uncompromising opponent of socialism. When the first world war broke out, he editorialised in the *Review* against the 'socialist newspaper' and the 'socialist politician' who had accused Lord Grey of duplicity and hypocrisy.[67] In 1925 he called on the Conservatives to re-establish the power of the House of Lords, make income tax universal, raise the minimum age of voters to at least twenty-five, make public relief worse than self-help, and set up fee-paying elementary schools again. Were these ideas reactionary? His answer was proudly affirmative: 'They represent the healthy spirit of reaction which inspires a swimmer who, finding himself in the trough of a wave, makes an effort to rise to the crest.'[68]

Harold Cox (1859–1936), *editor of the* Review 1912–29, *by William Strang.*
(*British Museum*)

Here was a fitting epitaph for the *Edinburgh Review*. The
journal which had started out to do battle with Eldonian Toryism,
which had stood for so many years under the Liberal banner when
that banner had written on it progress and reform, now ended up
a defender of reaction. But it was not so much that its ideas had
changed as that they had not. Events had overtaken them.
Perhaps the real epitaph of the *Edinburgh* had, in fact, appeared
seven years before, at the end of the first world war, when
Edmund Gosse, concluding his critique of his fellow reviewer's
Eminent Victorians, had declared: 'The time has doubtless come
when aged mourners must prepare themselves to attend the
obsequies of the Victorian Age with as much decency as they can
muster.'[69]

The *Edinburgh Review* had contributed greatly to the intellectual vitality of that age. But twentieth-century readers required new ideas and a different approach. In 1929 it published
its last number.

ANNABEL JONES

Disraeli's *Endymion*

A CASE STUDY

BENJAMIN DISRAELI's *Endymion* was published by Longmans in 1880, one year before his death. It was very widely reviewed, and, whatever their opinions on its merits, reviewers were sure that it would be read avidly. 'Never was public curiosity more excited,' declared the *Edinburgh Review*, which Disraeli himself told Thomas Norton Longman V he preferred to all other quarterlies:[1] *Fraser's* felt that it could safely predict for Disraeli's new novel 'a notoriety excelling that even of his previous works'. It was 'a book which will soon be in all hands, and eagerly studied, not only by the *clientele* of the circulating libraries but by the world at large'.[2]

It is possible to reconstruct in detail, largely from unpublished letters, the circumstances in which Disraeli wrote his last novel and Longmans published it. The story is not only of intrinsic interest – Longman paid for the copyright the highest sum that had hitherto been given by any publisher for the copyright in a work of fiction – but because of the light that it throws both on the relationships between author and publisher and the changing organisation of the publishing world. Thomas Norton Longman himself in what must have been one of the understatements of the year called the book 'a very interesting publication'.[3]

The correspondence between Longman and Disraeli covers many basic themes in publishing history – the drafting of an agreement; the processes involved in book production; the publishing schedule; and the proof-reading, binding, printing, advertising and the sending out of review copies. It shows too the main concerns of a publisher who is bringing out what he expects to be a best-seller: the importance of publicising the feature of the book that he knows will help to increase sales (in this case, the *roman à clef* aspect of the novel); the significance of the libraries' (and particularly Mudie's) subscription orders; the exact timing of publication and the possible adverse effect on sales that any crisis in public affairs could have; and, last but not least, the anxiety that all the newspapers and weeklies should receive their copies for review on the same day, the reason being then (as now) that the book stood in danger of not being reviewed in those papers which received their copies late, thus causing possible damage to sales.

Finally, it is interesting to note that the same kind of detail which Thomas Norton Longman brought to Disraeli's attention, and certain decisions which he made regarding publishing

Benjamin Disraeli, Earl of Beaconsfield (1804–81); *a photograph taken by Downey towards the end of Disraeli's life. (Reproduced by gracious permission of Her Majesty the Queen)*

strategy, were very similar to those with which his father, Thomas Longman, was also concerned when he published Disraeli's previous novel, *Lothair*, ten years earlier. It was then that Disraeli first established a cordial relationship with the Longmans, a relationship which was further strengthened in 1877 when Disraeli accepted an offer from the firm to acquire the copyright of all his novels for two thousand guineas.[4] The success of *Lothair* must have persuaded Thomas Norton Longman that a new Disraeli novel would be an excellent investment. It had been translated into every European language, and in America, where for a time there had been outbreaks of 'Lothairmania',[5] its sales had been even greater than those in Britain. Meanwhile, however, between 1870 and 1880 Disraeli had established his international reputation as a statesman and was prime minister from 1874 to 1880. A prime minister-novelist was a unique phenomenon.

✳

Montague William Corry, Lord Rowton (1838–1903). *'The pattern private secretary'*, Vanity Fair, 3 *March* 1877. (*Longman Archives*)

Disraeli had actually started to write *Endymion* during the summer of 1870 soon after the publication of *Lothair*. Robert Blake has suggested that between then and the autumn of 1872 Disraeli wrote the first sixty chapters (over half the book), that chapters 61 to 78 were written when he was again prime minister, probably in 1878, and that he finished the final chapters in May, June and July of 1880, when he was seventy-six years old. Montague Corry (created 1st Baron Rowton in 1880), who had been Disraeli's private and extremely efficient secretary since 1866, did not learn of the manuscript's existence until 1878, and did not actually read any of it until August 1880.[6]

The period dealt with in the novel starts with that of Disraeli's youth: it begins with the death of Canning in 1827 and covers the next thirty years of political life. During these years Disraeli himself had entered Parliament, become leader of the Young England group, written *Coningsby*, *Sybil* and *Tancred* and held his first cabinet post in Derby's first ministry in 1852. The period ends with the Crimean War and the defeat of the Coalition government in 1855. The characters and plot of the book reflect many features of Disraeli's own life, his own experiences, people he had known and places he knew.

During the months covered by his correspondence with Thomas Norton Longman relating to *Endymion*, that from July 1880 to March 1881, Disraeli spent most of his time at Hughenden Manor. (He had been defeated at the general election of April.) The negotiations having been carried out by Lord Rowton during August 1880, Longman went to stay the weekend at Hughenden in the middle of that month, and returned again in September, when he stayed overnight and collected the manuscript. During September the manuscript was set, and by 7 October the proofs had all been read. In the middle of October Disraeli suffered from a severe attack of gout which lasted for about a month; on 12 November he went up to London in order to visit his doctor. While there, he stayed with Lord Alfred de Rothschild, and on one occasion was visited by Longman. He returned to Hughenden on the 18th a few days before publication day. Only ten weeks had elapsed, therefore, between the handing over of the manuscript and its publication.

Events were to move even faster for Disraeli in 1881. At the beginning of March, his health began to fail, unhelped by the peculiarly cold weather. He wrote to Lord Rowton, who had spent much of the previous few months abroad: 'My health has been very bad, and I have really been fit for nothing but perhaps the spring which commences in a week may help me.'[7] On 22 March he caught a chill which was to develop into bronchitis, and it was at the beginning of this illness that he received his last letter from Longman. Lord Rowton returned to England on 7 April, and a few days later saw Disraeli, who was by now extremely ill. He died on 19 April 1881.

✳

Such was the time framework. What was the agreement between Disraeli and Longman which set out their business understanding?

Simon Nowell-Smith has pointed out that by the middle of the nineteenth century there were five basic methods used by

publishers to pay their authors.[8] First, there was that of publishing on commission: this meant that the author kept his
copyright, paid both the cost of production and advertising, stood
any loss incurred by the publisher if the book did not pay for
itself, and was able to claim the profit when it did. The publisher
was paid a commission, normally an agreed percentage of the
production costs. It was a method which, on the whole, was only
chosen by the publisher when he doubted the potential success of
the work. Second, there was the half or three-quarters profit
system whereby all production and advertising costs were met
initially by the publisher, but charged against the book: when
these costs had been met by sales, author and publisher shared
the profit equally or on an agreed ratio. Third, where the copyright in a work was sold outright to a publisher, an agreed sum
was paid by him to the author. The publisher could lose or make
a profit which – if the book was a success – could be such as to
make an author, who often forgot the risks taken by the publisher,
feel hard done by. Fourth, where the publisher bought a short
lease on the copyright he bought the right to publish a certain
number of copies or editions for a specified number of years.
When this period expired, the copyright reverted to the author
to do with it as he wished. This second transaction could involve,
for instance, an outright sale to the publisher or its transference
to another publisher on another lease or outright sale.

Finally, there was the royalty system, generally used nowadays,
but which had developed only slowly in the nineteenth century.
The publisher took the whole risk, and in return the author
received a stated sum, usually, not always, a percentage of the
list price, which might increase after a certain specified number of
copies had been sold. By the late nineteenth century the system
was fairly widely used, contracts tending to be specific in defining the percentage given for different editions of a title; for
example, 25 per cent might be given for a three-volume edition,
15 per cent for a cheap London edition and threepence or
fourpence per copy for a cheap colonial edition.[9]

For all his novels written before *Lothair*, Disraeli had had
arrangements with his publishers whereby he had either leased
them his copyrights or had had his work published on a shared-
profits basis. For *Lothair* he was paid a royalty by Longmans. In
1877, as we have seen, he finally sold them the copyright in all
his novels.

The agreement for *Endymion* was negotiated by Lord Rowton. Disraeli had always managed his own financial affairs badly and he paid tribute to Rowton's handling of the agreement when he referred to it as a result of 'Monty's diplomacy'. It has been pointed out that he probably had his own relationship with his secretary in mind when he wrote the following passage in *Endymion*:

The relations between a minister and his secretary are, or at least should be among the finest that can subsist between two individuals. Except the married state, there is none in which so great a degree of confidence is involved, in which more forbearance ought to be exercised, or more sympathy ought to exist. There is usually in the relation an identity of interest, and that of the highest kind; and the perpetual difficulties, the alternations of triumph and defeat, develop devotion.

Certainly Rowton managed the negotiations with as much identity of interest as Disraeli could have wished.

Rowton was determined to obtain as large a sum of money as he possibly could for Disraeli. Talks between himself and Longman probably began in July 1880. At the first two interviews agreement was not reached since Rowton was able to demonstrate that the figures Longman produced for *Lothair* did not represent a true picture of that book's earnings. He was able to do this since he had previously requested Disraeli to let him have his figures for the book. On 17 July Rowton thanked Disraeli for letting him have these, adding that they would give him 'a powerful weapon for my next interview with Longman. I anticipate that he will seek one soon, and that he will come with a mind opened by his dip into his Father's books'.[10] Longman saw Rowton on 20 July, and the following day Rowton told Disraeli what had transpired and the good use that he had been able to make of his figures:

Longman called on me yesterday.

He showed me the figures which he and his partner had taken out of their books as your share of "Lothair" – making a total of only £6,056!

I was able, at once to show him that they had at least omitted America – all the annual payments between 72 and 77 – and the Copyright.

I then gave him our figures, when he, at once, acknowledged that theirs must be regarded as worthless as a basis for estimate, and with some shame, undertook to review the whole matter, at once. I am to see him very soon again.

Before leaving me, he told me that he had come prepared to make an offer – on the basis of the figures which your memo: enabled me to prove so fallacious – and that was the sum of £7,500 down for all rights.

He took back his offer, with his miscalculations!

Our next interview will be interesting! [11]

Blake estimates that the American sales of *Lothair* probably amounted to around £1,500;[12] Longman was probably unconvinced that the same results could be expected from *Endymion*, the American market having become increasingly prone to piracy.

By 3 August Longman had made up his mind to reconsider his offer. He wrote asking Rowton if it would be possible to see him that day at the House of Lords; he assured him that 'two minutes will be sufficient for all I have to say'.[13] In fact, Longman must have seen him the following day. On 4 August during a debate in the House of Lords, Disraeli (who had by then become Lord Beaconsfield) was given a note by Rowton informing him of Rowton's success:

There are things too big to impart in whispers! so I leave your side, just to write these words – Longman has today offered *Ten Thousand Pounds* for *Endymion*.

I have accepted it! I cannot tell you what a pleasure it is to me to see my ardent ambition for you gratified!

And you have an added honor [sic] which may for ever remain without precedent.[14]

On the same day Longman made his formal offer: it was a carefully worded letter, in which he put the responsibility for assessing the value of the work squarely in Disraeli's court:

Private   39 Paternoster Row, London E.C.
                                                      August 4 1880

Dear Lord Rowton,

I have thought over carefully the various conversations that have lately taken place between us and you will I hope allow me to bring before [you] in writing our decision on what cannot but be considered a large and important matter of business.

It has become clear to me that you are decidedly of opinion that the copyright of the work in question is worth the large sum you have constantly named to me, and I know you are aware that I have considered a smaller sum might represent its commercial value. The matter however

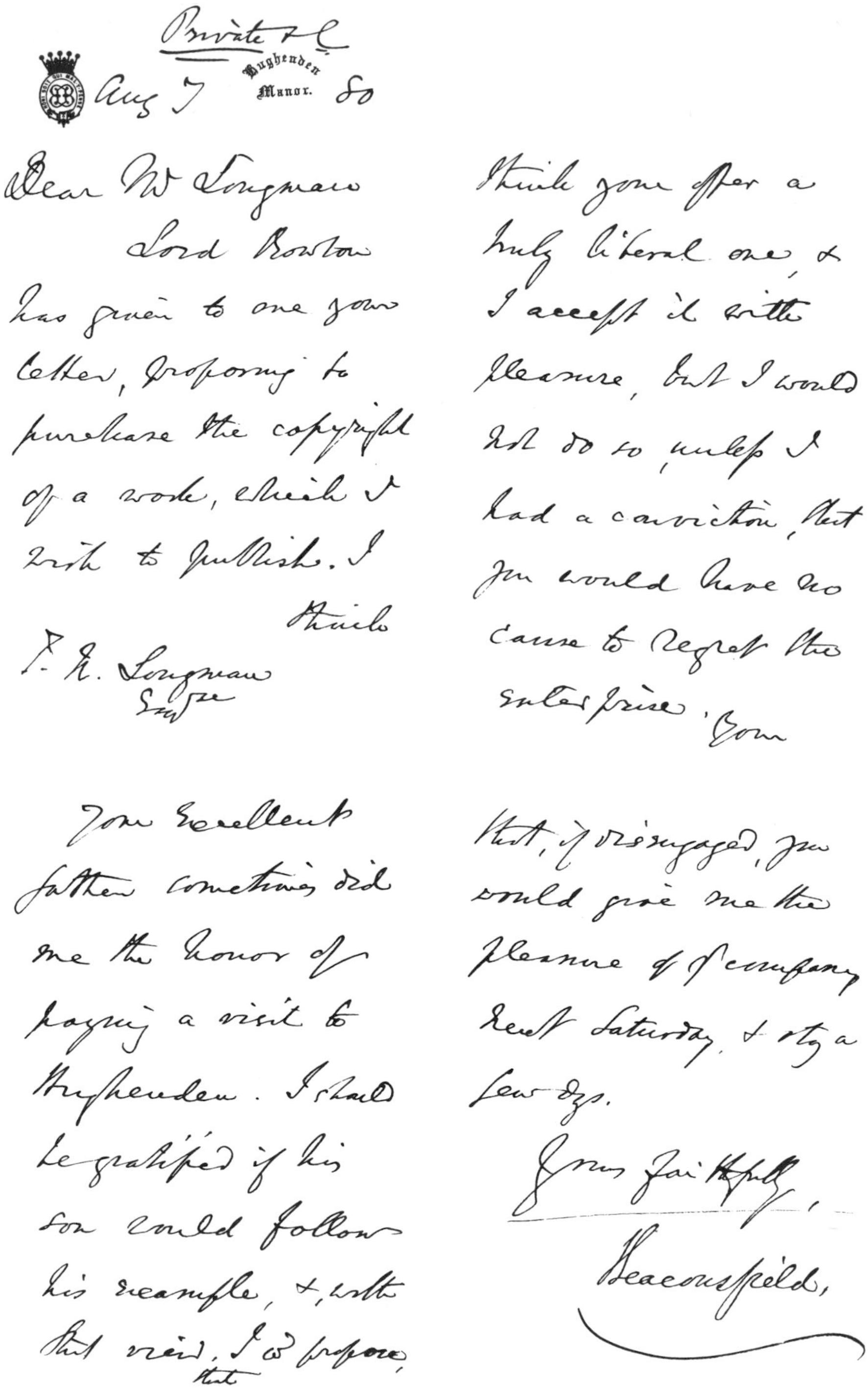

Private & C.

Hughenden Manor.

Aug 7 80

Dear Mr Longman

Lord Rowton has given to me your letter, proposing to purchase the copyright of a work, which I wish to publish. I think your offer a truly liberal one, & I accept it with pleasure, but I would not do so, unless I had a conviction, that you would have no cause to regret the enterprise. Your excellent father sometimes did me the honor of paying a visit to Hughenden. I shall be gratified if his son would follow his example, &, with that view, I wd propose that, if disengaged, you would give me the pleasure of yr company next Saturday, & stay a few days.

Yours faithfully,

Beaconsfield.

T. N. Longman Esqre

Disraeli's letter of 7 August 1880 to Thomas Norton Longman, accepting Longman's offer of £10,000 for the copyright in Endymion. (*Longman Archives*)

rests entirely with Lord Beaconsfield and I am content to let it be so. Indeed
it is but equitable and right that his Lordship should endeavor to receive
what he, not without practical evidence, considers the value of a work of
fiction from his pen, and he has done me the honour of giving me the first
offer of this valuable property. I have repeatedly told you that I have a
strong desire to be the publisher of "Lothair's Brother" and I am anxious
Lord Beaconsfield should consider not only that I have determined to view
the matter in a liberal spirit, but that I prefer bringing the business arrangements before him in such a shape as I think most agreeable to his Lordship
and perhaps still more so to yourself.

It is therefore with considerable satisfaction and I may add with some
pride I now write on behalf of my firm to make the same offer to Lord
Beaconsfield as was made to Mr Disraeli some time ago. We are willing to
pay Lord Beaconsfield the sum £10,000 for the copyright of the work of
fiction now nearly complete provided the following arrangements meet with
his Lordship's approval.

1st that the said M.S. is to form a work in three volumes similar to Lothair
and that it will be placed in our hands in sufficient time to enable us to
publish on 1st of December next.

2ndly that the agreed sum of Ten Thousand Pounds be made in two payments,
the first of £2,500 on delivery of the M.S. and the balance £7,500 on
April 1, 1881.

In conclusion I have only [to] express the hope that Lord Beaconsfield
will accept this proposal and thus allow me the privilege of stating that I have
paid the distinguished author of Coningsby what I believe to be the largest
sum ever paid for of [sic] work of fiction, and that in the business arrangements of this publication, I may prove myself a worthy successor of one for
whom I know his Lordship had so much regard.

> I remain
> Yours very truly
> T. Norton Longman[15]

Disraeli accepted the offer on 7 August, at the same time inviting
Longman to stay with him:

Dear Mr Longman,

Lord Rowton has given to me your letter, proposing to purchase the
copyright of a work, which I wish to publish. I think your offer a truly
liberal one & I accept it with pleasure, but I would not do so, unless I had a
conviction, that you would have no cause to regret the enterprise.

Your excellent father sometimes did me the honor of paying a visit to
Hughenden. I should be gratified if his son could follow his example, &,

with that view, I w^d propose, that, if disengaged, you would give me the pleasure of yr company next Saturday, & stay a few days.

Yours faithfully,
Beaconsfield[16]

Rowton also replied to Longman's letter, thanking him for the offer and letting him know the state of the manuscript. Both men, in replying to Longman's letter, took the trouble to reassure him that they were confident he would not be the loser:

I, last night, was able to put into Lord Beaconsfield's hands your letter, in which you recapitulate what you said during our very brief interview on Tuesday. I must apologise for my hurry on that occasion! What I hope I made clear to you was due to my being, then, in the middle of a not simple Mining Arbitration in which I had no Assessor.

I was anxious that Lord Beaconsfield should with his own hand acknowledge your letter, whence comes my silence for these two days. I am aware that he has today expressed to you his sense of the large spirit in which you and your Firm have acted, and his readiness to accept and meet your proposals in your letter of the 4th, which I need not rewrite.

I shall be here all this week – and, together with Lord Beaconsfield, I am counting on the pleasure of seeing you under this roof at the end thereof.

You will, I am glad to say, find a *complete* M.S., which you will look into with interest, I doubt not!

I am pleased to be able to say '*complete*', as I had no certainty on the subject when we last met.

I cannot help feeling that you are taking a step upon which *you* and the *author* are to be equally congratulated. It is one, I believe, which you will never regret – and such, as you say you perceived, has been my honest conviction (quantum raleat!) for some time.

I heartily rejoice that your famous firm have adopted 'Endymion' – 'Lothair's Brother'![17]

Accepting Disraeli's invitation – 'one I shall remember for ever' – Longman told Lord Rowton:

It is a great satisfaction to feel this matter has been brought to a satisfactory conclusion and I cannot refrain from asking you to accept my sincere thanks for the *personal* kindliness and consideration I have met with.

He also enquired whether the manuscript would be ready for him to take away.[18] Rowton doubted whether the manuscript was

quite ready to leave Hughenden.[19] He did not read the manuscript himself until after he had concluded the agreement in
August. It was arranged, however, that Longman should return
at the beginning of September to collect the manuscript. He went
to Hughenden therefore on 14 September, having been invited
to stay until the following day.

Both men left accounts of what Longman called 'the solemn
and complicated task of the formal delivery of the manuscript'.
Longman, indeed, left a very detailed and vivid account in his
diary, struck as he was by the combination of secrecy and cere-
mony that accompanied the incident.[20] Disraeli wrote to Lord
Rowton, telling him about Longman's visit; if it had not been for
the cheque which was handed to him, he said, he would have
believed it all a dream the following morning: 'I know no magic
of the Middle Ages equal to it!'[21]

One of the unusual features about the acceptance of the
manuscript was the fact that neither of the two men negotiating
the agreement had seen it. This would not appear to have been
normal practice, for the publisher at least. John Blackwood, for
instance, had refused to accept *Felix Holt* without having first
seen the manuscript, despite the fact that he was extremely
anxious to secure the next work of so eminent an author as
George Eliot (her previous work having gone to Smith, Elder[22]).
It was not that he doubted her talent, but rather, as he put it, that
'it would be against the principle upon which I really enter into
and take a pleasure in my own business were I to decide finally
on such a matter without having some opportunity of forming an
opinion of the book by seeing a volume or so'.[23]

The other unusual characteristic of the agreement between
Disraeli and Longman, not only unusual, indeed but unique, was
the actual sum paid to the author. Robert Blake says it was
'believed to be the largest sum ever paid for a work of fiction'.[24]
Disraeli himself wrote to Lady Bradford that he accepted the
amount 'with a scruple, such a sum never having before been
given for a work of fiction, or indeed any other work'.[25] Certainly
other large offers had been made. Disraeli himself had received
an offer from a publisher for £10,000 for a novel after his resigna-
tion from office in 1868,[26] and George Eliot had been offered
£10,000 for *Romola* (1863) by Smith, Elder for the entire
copyright – though she turned this down in favour of an offer of
£7,000 under which the copyright reverted to her after six

The house at 19 *Curzon Street, on which Disraeli was able to buy a lease with the proceeds from* Endymion *in January* 1881. (*Bodleian Library*)

Hughenden Manor, High Wycombe, 1881. (*National Trust, Hughenden Manor, photo: Clarence Sweetland*)

years.[27] G. H. Lewes had commented that the figure of £10,000 was 'the most magnificent offer yet made for a novel'.[28] Although Trollope had earned nearly £70,000 from his works when he wrote his autobiography, the highest sum he was actually paid for a novel was £3,525 for *Can You Forgive Her?* (1864).[29]

This was not to imply that a novel could not *earn* for its author sums equal to and more than this. In twenty months, for example, *Dombey and Son*, published in monthly parts between 1846–48, had earned Dickens over £9,000. His agreement with the publishers, Bradbury & Evans, provided that after deduction by them of all expenses, agents' allowances and 10 per cent commission on gross sales, Dickens should receive three-quarters of the profits.[30] Published first in serial form, Part I of which had appeared in December 1871, *Middlemarch* had brought in over £8,000 for George Eliot by 1879 on a sale of about 33,000 copies (including foreign editions), and she earned over £9,000 from *Daniel Deronda* between 1876 and 1879. Both titles were published under royalty agreements.[31]

A royalty agreement for a successful author could therefore be extremely advantageous, as Disraeli had discovered with *Lothair*; for the first time he knew what it was to make a substantial amount of money from writing; he had earned over £7,500 by 1876.[32] Why therefore did he not choose a similar arrangement for *Endymion* four years later? There was, probably, a particular reason why he wanted to sell the copyright of *Endymion* outright. He must have known that he had not a very long time to live (he had, after all, made provision in 1878 for the finishing of *Endymion* should he die before its completion, leaving a note on how the plot should end so that Corry, as he was then, could complete the book if he saw fit). He probably thought it doubtful, therefore, that he would live to feel the real benefit of a royalty agreement, which would of course only really start to accrue in anything like the amount he wanted after the cheap edition was published. Future income would then depend on its success. Moreover, left without a London house after the death of his wife, he now needed a house of his own there. Froude certainly saw this need for money as a compelling reason for Disraeli to finish the book after he left office, and he did in fact secure a seven-year lease on 19 Curzon Street in January 1881 with the proceeds from *Endymion*.

✳

The production and publication of *Endymion* followed the pattern of most novels published between 1850 (and in some cases before) and 1890, and the correspondence between the publisher and author deals with many aspects of the details which were involved. The production schedule was tight, but Longman felt it was imperative to publish the book well before the beginning of the Parliamentary session at the beginning of the following January if he was to obtain the maximum amount of publicity, and Disraeli, appreciating this, worked with some speed as far as his own part in the production was concerned.

Although he probably planned to issue the novel in a cheaper form soon after the publication of the first edition, as his father had done with *Lothair*, Longman expected the manuscript 'to form a work in three volumes' when he received it.[33] On his first visit to Hughenden in August he made the following notes on a proposed schedule:

M.S. to be delivered on Monday September 13.
First Proof to be sent out on Monday September 20.
The whole M.S. to be in type (in a fortnight) by Monday October 4.
Sheets to be returned for press regularly and the whole to be in printers hands for press by Wednesday October 27.
This will allow five weeks and two days for reading and correcting the proof sheets of the whole book, say about 196 pages a week.
If sheets are returned regularly the following would be the result.
Vol   I for Press on Oct 2
Vol II   Do   Oct 14
Vol III   Do   Oct 27
Which would enable us to carry out any American arrangement we might make.[34]

On 18 September Longman wrote to Disraeli commenting on the length of the book in terms of its production in three volumes:

On estimating your M.S. I find it is rather a larger work than "Lothair", but by having one more line on a page and one letter broader "Endymion" will make altogether as near as possible the same sized work as "Lothair". According to the printer's estimate the Volumes, printed as I have described above, will run as follows.

Vol   I about 320 pages
Vol II Do   314   Do
Vol III Do   318   Do

This is quite satisfactory to us and I hope you will agree with me that the appearance of the page has not been damaged.[35]

This was, in fact, the standard length of a three-volume novel. George Bentley described such a novel to one of his authors as being '920 pages long, with twenty-one and a half lines on each page and nine and a half words in each line'. Bentley's own contracts were often nearly as specific; the contract drawn up for *Barnaby Rudge*, for instance, provided for 'three volumes, Post Octavo, of similar pages to those of *Oliver Twist*, each volume to contain at least three hundred and ten pages'.[36] Various manuals prepared for authors described the requirements for three-volume novels in similarly precise terms of pages and words per line.

In the same letter of 18 September Longman outlined the arrangements he had made for *Endymion*:

In order to avoid any risk of the printers devil letting the 'cat out of the bag' I have arranged to have the proofs sent to Paternoster Row* and will forward them to you. This plan will make no difference at all in our arrangements but will I think be prudent. You will of course return the proofs to the printers direct in the envelopes as agreed.

The first proof will be sent out on Monday and will no doubt reach you on Tuesday by the first post.[37]

Disraeli received proofs for the first volume on 21 September, as Longman had promised, and wrote to tell Longman that he had sent half of them back to the printers that same day. He added: 'As the errors only arise from my imperfect Ms they are merely verbal & I have not asked for revises = only the greatest care must be taken in the correction, as any neglect would necessarily ensure, from their very verbal nature, terrible blunders. All that is required is attention'.[38] Disraeli also assured Longman that 'the rest of the 1st Volume will reach the printers tomorrow', and sent off the second half of the first volume on the 22nd.[39] He was worried, however, about an error he had overlooked regarding the spelling of the name of one of the characters, Jawett (spelt 'Jowett' in the uncorrected proofs). This he was afraid would in all probability, if not corrected, be seen as a slur on the 'celebrated Oxford Don';[40] Longman reassured him that its correction would cause no difficulty and offered revises if he wished for them, since he knew they would only be in Disraeli's hands 'a few hours'. The speed with which Disraeli had completed the proof-reading was not lost upon his publisher, for he commented: 'The energy

* From Messrs Spottiswoode, the printers.

and promptness you have kindly shewn in correcting the proofs, I feel sure will be by no means the least remarkable feature connected with this important publication.'[41] On 26 and 27 September Disraeli wrote to Longman, concerned about two further errors he had missed, and on the 27th added: 'I shall be in better discipline for the other volumes: remember I had not seen a proof for ten years.'[42] The following day Longman told Disraeli that he had decided to have revises from Spottiswoode after all: 'I have therefore this morning gone over revises of Vol I up to page 224 and am in a position to say that your corrections have all been carefully carried out. With your permission I shall continue to watch the printers in this way. The delay of an hour or two is nothing.'[43]

Disraeli received the proofs of the whole of the second volume on 28 September and returned them to go to press on the 29th, commenting that he had 'taken pains with them, but it is a comfort to me that your eye also will re-examine them'.[44] On 6 October he sent back the proofs of the third volume. The manuscript had been set and passed for press in just over a fortnight. Longman had allowed five weeks and two days for reading and correcting, planning to have the whole passed for press by 27 October. He wrote to Disraeli:

I am much obliged to you for letting me know you had finished correcting all the proofs of "Endymion". You have therefore completed the correction of the whole work in about a fortnight! This, I consider, a literary feat of interest and importance; a feat of which the author may well feel proud and the publisher should offer his congratulations and thanks.[45]

Although Longman's tone here may be thought rather fulsome, it should be remembered that Disraeli at the time was seventy-six years old, his sight was not good (he described himself to a correspondent in March 1881 as 'blind and deaf'), and he also suffered from bronchitis, asthma and gout. The next day he sent a note to Longman of some further mistakes in the proofs which he had missed on 7 October, but these caused no bother.[46]

In the meantime, the secret, so carefully guarded, had escaped, although the leak was not to prove as serious as Longman feared at the time: 'I am sorry to see by the Journal called "Truth" that the cat is out, Endymion is announced as in preparation. I am quite unable to explain how the cat escaped.'[47] Disraeli replied:

I never see "Truth" or any "society" papers; very few others indeed. Am I to understand, that the very title of the work is announced? If not, it may only be a shot. I am sure nothing has leaked here, and the communications with the Printer have been so much less than we contemplated, that I hardly think th$_y$ w^d have attracted the attention of the P.O. here.[48]

Longman wrote back immediately:

I am much obliged to you for your kind note of the 8th inst. I found the paragraph in one of the Daily papers here so I send it to you at once. I fear it has been the round of all the London Journals. My private opinion is that it must have got out through the printing office. I was told by the manager that the compositor recognized your handwriting. However it is wonderful to me we have kept the secret so long, indeed it is far from out yet. I hope and believe people pay little attention to a paragraph in Truth![49]

The newspaper cutting he attached from *Truth* read as follows:

Lord Beaconsfield – Although it has been asserted that the Earl of Beacons-field is only revising his former literary productions, and is not writing a new novel, I believe he is doing both. The title of the new novel is, I hear, "Endymion". An *edition de luxe* of his former works is to be published next year, and will include, for the first time, the famous "Letters of Runnymede".[50]

Thomas Longman IV had obviously been afraid of the same danger of the news of *Lothair's* publication being leaked through such a source: he had written in 1870 to Disraeli that 'at present the cat is well in the bag, and . . . the printers have not been tampered with'.[51] It is interesting to note the use of the same metaphor by father and son.

When Disraeli had returned the last of the proofs on 6 October he mentioned to Longman that nothing now remained 'but the title page', and he added: 'You must remember the motto. Your good father used to think the motto of "Lothair" had something to do with the success of the work'.[52] Longman promised that he would not forget, and the proof title-page, including the motto '*Quicquid agunt homines*', was subsequently set and sent to Disraeli. Longman requested that the proof should be sent back by return of post. This speed was probably necessary in order to comply with American copyright regulations whereby the American publisher would have to deposit the title-page in

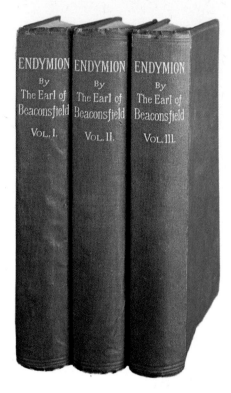

Bound in red cloth with silver lettering, Longman considered that Endymion *had 'a rather bright coat'. (Longman Archives)*

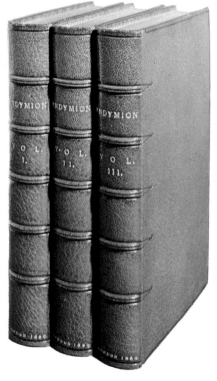

Disraeli's own copy of Endymion. *Longman had three copies bound in dark green morocco – for the Queen, Disraeli and himself. (National Trust, Hughenden Manor)*

America prior to publication in order to register the book there.*

Disraeli returned the proof of the title-page on 28 October, saying that he required no preface or dedication, but that he would want a few copies for his own use, which were to be placed to his account, and he particularly wished that the Queen should receive her copy before publication.

By 5 November the sheets were at the binders, Riviere, one of the largest fine binderies of the period. The first edition was bound in red cloth with silver lettering. This, Longman told Disraeli, was 'a rather bright coat' and he did not 'consider the cover to be quite my own taste', but the salesman in him attached 'importance to the public being able to recognise the book at a glance.'[53] Longman, who intended to send out presentation and press copies on the 23rd, arranged also for the Queen's copy to be bound in dark green morocco. Disraeli said that he would send her the copy himself so that

it will reach her royal hands instantly; . . . if sent otherwise, what between equerries, secretaries & Ladies in Waiting, a week may elapse before it reaches the Queen, & even then she would not know exactly whence it came —

You are extremely loyal in binding the volumes for Her Majesty — "Lothair" went to court in his ordinary dress. But I dare say the Queen will be pleased to receive Endymion in a more stately garb. I shall let H. Majesty know he owes the distinction to the loyalty of my publisher.[54]

✳

As well as looking after every stage in the production of the book, Longman also had to turn his attention to the American and Canadian markets. America, in particular, had proved a good market for *Lothair*. A brief look at the situation in America and Canada regarding copyright law and the consequent increase in piracy helps to explain Longman's probable doubt as to whether he could expect the same success for *Endymion*.† The situation did not however prevent him from making arrangements for publication of the novel in both Canada and America.

In his memorandum of 13 August Longman had noted that the dates he had calculated 'would enable us to carry out any American arrangement we might make'. American copyright

* See below.
† See above, p. 149, and also 'Copyright and society', pp. 51–52.

ENDYMION

BY THE AUTHOR OF

"LOTHAIR"

"Quicquid agunt homines"

IN THREE VOLUMES

VOL. I.

LONDON
LONGMANS, GREEN, AND CO.
1880

Title-page to the first edition. (Longman Archives)

The inscription by Longman in Disraeli's copy of Endymion. *In a letter to Disraeli of* 18 *November, Longman wrote 'I have taken the liberty of writing your name in the copy I present you with and request the favour of its finding a corner in your library not too far from his brother Lothair.' (National Trust, Hughenden Manor)*

Disraeli's inscription to the Queen on the title-page of her copy. (Reproduced by gracious permission of Her Majesty the Queen)

ENDYMION

VOL. I.

law before 1891 required that in order to secure American copyright the book had to be registered by deposit of the title-page before publication, and a copy of the book had to be deposited within a stated period after publication (between 1870 and 1891 within ten days after publication). However, in order to secure British copyright, first publication had to be in Britain, so that a publisher wishing to secure both British copyright for the English author, and American copyright for the American publisher to whom he had sold the rights, had to plan according to an extremely tight schedule.

American copyright law did not secure for the American publisher freedom from the reprinter. Indeed, before 1891 there was a positive encouragement in American law to reprinters, or pirates. In 1870 the United States Congress had passed an act which secured copyright to authors who were citizens or residents in the United States; one section 'expressly allowed the importation, vending, reprinting and publishing in the states of any book written or published abroad by any person not being a citizen'.[55]

In common with other English publishing houses, Longmans had for a long time been concerned at the situation which existed in America with regard to the copyright of English authors. Some American publishers however, facing increasingly fierce competition at home, welcomed the idea of an international copyright convention of some form, and began to organise a system among themselves whereby the right of republication in a work by an English author was given to the publisher who first secured the copy. An English publisher would arrange to sell either an edition in sheets or a set of early sheets or stereo plates from which the American edition could be printed: the American publisher could thus gain a start over his local competitors. A well-known English author, therefore, could bargain for the sale of his American rights, even though there was no legal protection and piracy was inevitable.[56]

By 1880 the situation in America had become worse than it had been when Disraeli wrote *Lothair*, a book with a large American sale. Thomas Norton Longman told Disraeli on 15 October 1880 that he had mentioned to Lord Rowton that 'the present state of things in America would damage the market there'.[57] For about ten years after 1860 high production costs in the United States had ensured good American sales for English books, but this period had ended at the beginning of the 1870s when numerous cheap American reprints started to appear which also found a market in Canada. *Lothair* had probably benefited from the earlier situation, and Longman was aware that the changed situation would not produce the same results for *Endymion*. On 26 October he wrote: 'We are doing our utmost to defeat the re-printers, the battle will be a desperate one. This to me is one of the most interesting features of this very interesting publication.'[58]

By 9 November the American arrangements had been made:

We have heard today from our agent in America, with final arranged [sic] as to publication. We publish here on the morning of the 26th, they are to publish in America & Canada at 2 O'clock on the same day.[59]

Yet Longman's battle to defeat the pirates was, as he had feared, lost to some extent. On 14 December he wrote to Disraeli:

I hear that Mess[rs]. Appleton; the publishers of Endymion in the book form sold 5000 copies in a few hours, but the reprinters, or more properly speaking the pirates, did not give them peace and quiet very long, as the "Seaside Library" had their edition out on the 30 of November, only four days after the publication of Appleton's edition. I have the pleasure of sending you by this post a specimen of this charming form of high class literature!! They are simply newspapers and nothing else. Of course we get nothing from Mr George Munro the enterprising publisher of the "Seaside . . . Robbery".[60]

Unauthorised copies they may have been, but they presented a potential slump in possible American royalties that Longman might otherwise have been able to expect from Appleton.

The Canadian situation was equally tricky. Among the colonies, from the point of view of copyright law, Canada was the most important country – 'anything Canada got away with other oversea territories would be sure to copy'.[61] In 1875 a distinct Canadian copyright was established whereby United Kingdom and other authors could secure Canadian copyright even if their books had previously been published elsewhere in the Empire, and they were protected against the import into Canada of American or other unauthorised editions. The Canadian firm with whom Longmans arranged Canadian publication, Danson Brothers, claimed themselves that the publication of *Endymion* in Canada 'precipitated the first thorough attempt' to work this new Canadian law:[62]

It is the Detroit frontier which bothers me most. We have gone to the expense of a Detective of our own at Windsor and the Minister of Customs has waked up the Collector there. I am anxious to have a suit for this is the first thorough attempt to work our law and I want to find out where the weak spots are.[63]

✳

The timing of the publication of books is important: today it is usually geared towards a particular time of year – the spring and autumn lists, or towards a particular event. *Endymion*'s publication however was probably governed by the reassembly of Parliament. It was not uncommon for the publication of a book to make prominent news in the press, if it did not have to compete with the business of Parliament.[64] Longman's tight production schedule meant that *Endymion* would be published before the meeting of Parliament in January 1881. Any hint of an early meeting gave Longman cause for anxiety. This seemed possible during November when there was continual speculation as to whether an immediate session of Parliament would be called for the purpose of passing the Irish Coercion Bill. Had this occurred, it would have overshadowed the event of the publication of a novel which, with no competition for the headlines, was sure to create a stir in the newspapers. On 18 November Longman mentioned to Disraeli that he most sincerely hoped there would be no early meeting of Parliament.[65] There was another scare a few days later around the 22nd, and the Cabinet met again on 25 November. When it was announced a day later that there was to be no December session of Parliament, Longman breathed again; Disraeli wrote to him, 'You are relieved about the meeting of Parlt. I had a good nose in that matter, & never credited it.'[66]

In December, Longman was still anxiously watching public affairs with regard to sales: he told Disraeli that the 'awful condition of Irish affairs is absorbing more of public attention than the publisher of Endymion cares about. I fear it will affect the sale.'[67]

As far as advertising the book was concerned, Longman told Disraeli that 'Our present intention is to fix Friday the 26th of November as the day of publication, but not to issue any advertisements before Friday the 19th. I think it is necessary to advertise in the Saturday Review, Atheneum [sic] and other weekly papers the week before publication.'[68]

In the Longman Impression Account for June 1882 there is a figure of £171–8–0 for advertising for *Endymion*.[69] This figure can probably be assumed to refer to the first edition. It compares reasonably with amounts spent on advertising by other publishers on those books that they hoped would be best-sellers. According to R. A. Gettman's calculation, £171 for a book was quite a high figure to spend (although he points out that some publishers spent £200 or even £300 on a title): Bentley, for example, spent £168–12–3 on Rhoda Broughton's *Nancy* (1873), printing a first edition of 2,250.[70] Longman's first printing was 7,000 and his advertising figure cannot therefore be thought excessive.

In addition Longmans advertised the book in their own publication *Notes on Books*. This was a periodical issued by the firm each quarter to bookbuyers, containing an analysis of those works due to be published in the coming four months. Longman sent the notice they intended to insert to Disraeli:

I have the pleasure of sending you the enclosed proof of the little notice we propose to put in our book circular called "Notes on Books". I dare say you will remember we did something of the same kind with 'Lothair'. Please make any alteration you may think desirable. It may interest you to know the article is written by my cousin and partner Charles Longman. I hope it will meet with your approval.[71]

This notice Disraeli thought 'judicious and ingenious'.[72] It referred to the span of years covered by Disraeli's own career as a novelist and the period covered in *Endymion* itself. It drew attention to Disraeli's own fascination with the energy of youth, which was revealed once again in *Endymion*, and made a careful reference to what Longman knew would be a selling point – the appearance in the book of characters many of whom were based on people in public life whom Disraeli had known.

✳

Spending money on advertising, however, was only a small part of the process by which a publisher could try and make his book a success. Probably the most important factor of all in the latter half of the nineteenth century was the opinion of it held by the circulating libraries, and, in particular, of Mudie's Circulating Library.

These libraries had not been the originators of the three-volume edition, but the development of their system on that form had the effect of strengthening it to such an extent that between 1850 and 1870 it had become a generally accepted form of publication for the first edition of a novel for an author intent on success, if his work was not published in a serial form or in monthly parts – a form which the libraries also stocked.[73] The first editions of many books published between about 1850 and 1885 were therefore, in effect, library editions, published in three volumes at 31s 6d. The larger libraries demanded high discounts on a three-volume novel, paying 15s a copy and demanding a free copy for every 100 ordered.[74] For a subscription of one guinea a year, Mudie's subscribers could have one exchangeable volume at a time: 'To be able for twenty-one shillings to have for a quarter of a year ten volumes of excellent literature,' wrote one contented publisher, 'seems to me a real privilege and a capital return for one's money'.[75]

Subscribers who paid two guineas a year could take out as many volumes as they could read. Thus, with three-decker novels Mudie could circulate the three different parts of one title to three separate subscribers and, with the discounts thus obtained, double or triple his profit on a single-decker. Since Mudie's whole method of distribution and success was based on the three-decker form, he was reluctant to stock or advertise a one- or two volume edition.

During the hey-day of the three-decker, the attraction of the libraries to the publisher was the minimum market he was guaranteed, and, *ipso facto*, a minimum profit on the first edition. Not unreasonably the publisher preferred a reliable customer in this form to a general sale to the public of a one-volume novel, which, at 12s 6d, would at best be unreliable, beyond the means of many of Mudie's estimated 25,000 subscribers. Guinevere Griest points out that a publisher would reassure an author with details of Mudie's order, since the size of that order would indicate the potential success of the book;[76] according to Mrs Oliphant, Mudie's announcement that he intended to take a large number of copies of any title was its best advertisement, 'a sort of recognition from heaven'.[77] Not surprisingly, therefore, Longman was elated when he was able to tell Disraeli on 16 November:

Good news cannot be received too quickly. I feel sure you will be as glad to learn as I have pleasure in telling you that "Endymion" is subscribing well.

The bright coloured young gentleman was introduced to Mr Mudie yesterday and he put his name down for three thousand copies! I believe this to be quite unprecedented. I cannot refrain from sending you this intelligence by early post. The rest of the London trade appear to be taking considerable numbers but of course the subscription is not yet finished.

The first edition of Endymion's brother "Lothair" was only 3 or 4000 at the most.[78]

Other books for which Mudie subscribed in large numbers were, for example, *The Mill on the Floss* (1860: 2,000 copies) and *Enoch Arden* (1864: 2,500), the largest order ever known to have been placed for a book of poems.[79] For non-fiction, however, Mudie had sometimes gone above 3,000 – he subscribed for 3,250 copies of Livingstone's *Missionary Travels in South Africa* (1857) – so that Longman's belief that the subscription was 'unprecedented' probably was based on a comparison with subscriptions for works of fiction only.

Mudie's rivals were smaller circulating libraries, such as Cawthorn & Hutt of Cockspur Street, Day's of Mount Street, Miles of Islington and the Grosvenor Gallery;[80] on the size of their orders depended the success of a first edition of most novels. The public – the richer section of it – did not normally buy books. It was the subject of several comments between George Eliot and her publisher. G. H. Lewes, for instance, remarked to John Blackwood, in connection with *Middlemarch*, that the public had got out of the habit of buying books, relying on the libraries instead.[81]

There was a certain amount of rivalry between the libraries, and Disraeli, curious to know what sort of success the book might expect, enquired of Longman about both library and trade subscriptions. He was told that 'the "London Trade" had subscribed altogether about 5,500 copies' and that 'orders were coming in fast from all parts of the kingdom'.[82] On 24 November Longman wrote to Disraeli that he had '. . . printed 7,000 copies to begin with and I doubt whether we shall have *very* many left by tomorrow night, *the day before publication*! We are of course printing more.'[83] Later in November another 2,000 were printed. Four days after publication Longman noted that '. . . the *great* rush is subsiding but the demand for the book continues briskly'.[84] On 3 December he was able to inform Disraeli that 'the first edition will really be 10,500 copies, which

is simply gigantic! & we still have between two and three thous-
and left. The fact is the rush of orders just before publication was
so great that we extended, or rather enlarged our first impression
to this tremendous size'.[85]

By 10 December Longman doubted whether they would
require to go to press again 'just yet',[86] and on the 22nd he wrote
that 'the demand for the book now is not very large but it continues steadily'.[87] Why the demand slowed down is not clear;
Longman had earlier feared the effect of the early leak in the
press, but this does not seem to have had an adverse effect on
sales at the time of publication.

By February 1881 Longman had decided to go ahead and
print a cheap 6s edition. He wrote to Rowton on 9 February:

I think I should let you know that we are making our arrangements for the
popular edition of 'Endymion', indeed the printers are actually at work.

Under these circumstances my suggestion as to a Preface is more urgent
than I anticipated. If Lord Beaconsfield is so good as to think favorably of the
matter the M.S. should be in the printers hands next week, say by the 17th.
I am sure you must know that I did not ask Lord Beaconsfield to consider
this matter without much hesitation but the great importance to us of having
if possible a few Prefactory remarks to the new edition induced me to take so
bold a step. Nothing I think would contribute more effectually to increase
the popularity of the work than the author pointing out the purpose he had
in writing the book. Many of the critics and many of his readers have failed
completely to apprehend the real object of the work. Some I think have
remarked the author's object was to portray some of the chief insidents [sic]
of political history and to trace under the veil of fiction incidents [sic] and
characters which have already passed from the scene. Might I go so far as to
say that these reminiscences constitute the charm of the work and if Lord
Beaconsfield could see his way to state that it was from them he drew the
inspiration of his tale it would be adding a fresh interest of considerable
importance to the cause of 'Endymion'.

Please observe I have written *private* at the head of this letter.

[At the head of this letter, there is a note in Lord Rowton's hand which
reads as follows: Saw Mr Longman Feb 14][88]

It must have been decided not to include such a preface, since the
cheap edition does not contain one.

✻

Although the library sale was an important factor in deciding the
success or failure of a novel, a publisher obviously hoped for the

maximum amount of publicity in the press. With this in view, Longman sent out copies for review to newspapers ensuring that they all arrived on the same day. He was anxious to avoid any favouritism towards any one member of the press, some of whom, as soon as the book was advertised, pressed Longman for advance copies or sheets; he was particularly shocked at the suggestion that he might do so for any kind of monetary consideration:

The impatience of the reviewers is really quite troublesome. I have three fresh applications before me at this moment to say nothing of the gentlemen who call asking for early sheets.

I have declined all such applications. I intend to favor none. The presentation copies will be sent out on Tuesday the 23rd, all at the same time. One gentleman told me this morning that if we would supply his paper, a daily, with one copy of the work before any other journal he would pay – well, I *believe* a very considerable sum, but of course I did not entertain the proposition for a moment.[89]

Disraeli replied:

Much obliged for your letter & enclosure – but I must not ride a willing horse to death.

I have therefore ordered all the morning papers (six) to be sent here from next Monday till further orders.

I also always see S$^{t.}$ James' Gazette.

For literary papers, I take in the 'Athenaeum', I've no other.

This will lighten your friendly labours: & for any notices in other quarters, I shall be most grateful to you.[90]

Such was the organisation of his publishers, however, that it was easier for all reviews to be sent to the author. This, and possibly Rowton's request that all the reviews should be kept for him to see on his return from abroad, has resulted in the fact that there are no less than 110 British and Irish reviews and notices of *Endymion* among Disraeli's papers at Hughenden. The following extract from a letter of Longman's to Disraeli gives some idea of the excitement that could build up prior to the publication of a novel written by a famous man; Longman obviously found it infectious:

I send you herewith some preliminary expressions of the press. Nothing can exceed the excitement with the reviews. I am answering today no less than 16 applications for early copies. One comes from St. Petersburg by telegram. At this very instant my clerk brings me in an application from the Manchester Guardian with a cheque in payment for two copies (*full* price) to be sent with the one presentation copy. They are clearly not satisfied with one copy they must have *three*!! Applications are coming in at every moment and some of these distinguished gentlemen of the press will not take 'no' for an answer – Again, I am interrupted – I think think [sic] I must put up a notice outside informing our friends who failed in literature & art[91] that their services are not required any further.[92]

On 23 November, however, a bombshell fell. The *Standard* had managed to get hold of an early copy of the book and gave a complete summary of the plot. The account also made references to the identity of the characters and in the last paragraph commented ominously that '. . . it will probably be thought [that the political narrative] has less of plot and dramatic interest than almost any of the novels even of Lord Beaconsfield.'[93] Longman was furious: he saw all his carefully laid plans for publication in ruins. He wrote to Disraeli on 23 November:

The notice in the Standard this morning is most troublesome and vexatious.

Could anything be more annoying than to have one's sole object of being perfectly straight forward and anxious to place all the Reviews on the same footing defeated in this sort of way. How the Standard became possessed of the copy their reviewer had to work upon is a mystery. We took special care to send *all* the copies out at the same time. I mean we had taken steps to let the London press copies reach their destination on the same day viz this day the 23rd. There is some trick at the bottom of this and I am determined to find it out.[94]

Longman's annoyance stemmed from the fact that the system of reviewing by the daily and weekly press rested, as it still does today, on the adherence by the publisher and the press to a date named by the publisher, before which the book should not be reviewed. If for any reason a paper managed to get hold of an early copy and reviewed it before this date, it could happen that no other paper would review it, thus putting sales seriously at risk: hence, a remark of Disraeli to Longman that he feared the *Standard* incident might affect 'the disposition of the other journals'. (In the event Longman was fortunate, and although he nevertheless seemed to think that the incident *did* affect sales, the reason for this is not clear.)

I was going to sympathise with you today about the Standard escapade, fearful it might influence the disposition of the other journals, but before I cd.

write, I (rec'd) received all the London Morning papers, by wh: I observed, that thy had not misapprehended the incident.

. I think the journals have floated you well, & that there is nothing to complain of. Strange the hostile one is the "Post", &, I think, the most friendly intelligence (t) [sic] is the "Daily News".[95]

On the same day Longman wrote to Disraeli, saying he doubted that there had ever been such a rush of reviewers; 'the sensation grows and rapidly'. He noted too the lack of political bias in the reviews: 'It is I think most satisfactory to see that Conservative and Liberal, Whig and Tory and even Radical Organs have treated the work without party spirit. Indeed the leading article in the Daily News is really quite striking in this respect.'[96] He remained worried, however, about the *Standard*:

Private
Dear Lord Beaconsfield

I find it quite impossible to begin this letter without attending to the fact that this is the advertised date of the birth of "Endymion". It is my privilege to issue to the world of letters today a new work by the author of 'Lothair'. I confess this is an event in which I feel much pride and thus wish to record it in the correspondence of my firm. This desire is the more strengthened by the striking fact that on the day of publication no less than 7000 copies are distributed throughout the Kingdom. This great rush for the work, the numerous and many complimentary reviews, are facts which I think and hope it may not be unbecoming on my part to offer you my warm congratulations. The 26th of November 1880 is a red letter day in my life and I have stamped it in my own home by presenting my wife with a pair of diamond earrings worthy I hope of the admiration of even "Endymion" himself.

I have the pleasure of sending you a further supply of press notices.

This affair with the Standard is the subject I wish particularly to bring before you in this communication. It is a matter of serious importance from many points of view, and perhaps none more so than that of removing the cloud now hanging over my clerks, to say nothing of the printers and binders. There can be no doubt of the fact that some person did get possession of a copy of the book by unfair means. I feel convinced in my own mind that a bribe was given. I say this because an individual from the Standard office did attempt to bribe me for an extra early copy. The Editor of the Standard declines to give any explanation whatsoever. Have you any suggestion to offer me? Do you happen to know anything about the writers in the Standard? All sorts of stories are going about. I was told the other day that it had been stated openly in society that the first notice was to appear in a daily paper and that £1000 had been paid it [sic]. I feel much hesitation in

troubling you with the details but I hope you will excuse me but independently of the importance of finding out the culprit I have reason to believe the
book has decidedly *suffered* and this must be my excuse for bringing the
matter before the author.[97]

Disraeli was most sympathetic and explained the situation as
best he could:

And now with regard to that most vexatious affair of the "Standard", &
which has proved, as I feared, some check upon your otherwise most
energetic and ably-devised, tactics in the publication of our book.

The editor, Manager, & virtually proprietor, of the "Standard" is a Mr
Mudford,* who under the will of the late proprietor of the paper succeeded
to a great & peculiar interest in it.

Mr Mudford, I believe, is not a trained journalist – Mr Johnson, the late
proprietor, left him under the will the post of perpetual Editor & Manager of
the paper, with a permanent charge of £5,000 p^r ann^m. on it, &, I believe,
an almost uncontrolled power of disposition over the capital fund of the
journal, – which is very large. When I was Minister, Mr Mudford expressed
a wish to become a member of the Carlton Club, & those in authority, by a
great effort, induced the Committee to admit him at once as a selected
member. I doubt whether he ever visits the Carlton now, but I am assured he
does visit Sir Charles Dilke every day, & Mr Chamberlain! It is supposed,
from the tone of his paper, & other [?circumstances], that he wishes to
supersede the "Times" (supposed, tho' I doubt it, to be in a declining state)
in its position of complete independence of party: at least avowed independence for in reality all the journals are more or less in commiseration with
existing governments.

Lord Rowton, who knows much about the press, told me all this, & much
more, & I agree with you, that Ld Rowton's absence at this moment is a
calamity:† but were he here, I hardly think he w^d. be able to penetrate the
mystery wh: has baffled you. It is too dark a business ever to discover. There
can be no doubt, that the book was obtained by a bribe, & one probably of no
ordinary amount. Mudford is quite reckless as to expenditure where the
interests of his paper are concerned, & he may be said to have [? illimitable]
pecuniary resources at his command. He is still obliged to affect a general
conservative tone, or he might otherwise seriously diminish his circulation &
that tone makes his assistance more effective to his secret liberal allies.

* W. H. Mudford was born in 1839, the son of the proprietor of the *Kentish
Observer* and *Canterbury Journal*. He was editor and manager of the *Standard*
from 1876, resigning the editorship in 1900. He belonged to the Carlton and the
Junior Carlton. He died on 18 October 1916. See *Who Was Who, 1916–1928*,
p. 757; *Annual Register*, 1916, p. 192.
† Lord Rowton had had to take his invalid sister to Algiers in the middle of November: see above, pp. 146, 170.

I hope that "Endymion", as it gets read, & more known, may to a certain, if not a complete, degree counteract the check, wh: you may have experienced. It is some consolation that you have escaped a meeting of Parliament.[98]

Disraeli's account of the *Standard* and its proprietor would appear to be fairly accurate. Bought by James Johnson in 1857, the paper became a direct rival to the *Telegraph*, which in 1880 had a circulation of more than a quarter of a million. The *Standard*, including morning and evening issues, followed closely with about 180,000. (*The Times*'s circulation was then about 100,000.)[99] Between 1870 and 1874 it became one of the three main penny daily papers (the other two being the *Daily Telegraph* and the *Daily News*). In Fox Bourne's opinion Johnson had made a new paper of the *Standard*, giving it a moderate but progressive Conservative opinion; he died in 1876, leaving as Disraeli rightly said, W. H. Mudford in sole control.[100] Under Mudford, the paper supported Disraeli while he was in office, and continued to be Conservative, at the same time taking a more independent line. Fox Bourne's tone in his account of Mudford's editorship is one of general approbation, and the *Annual Register* commented that Mudford was a good judge of men who had built up an efficient staff: 'The *Standard* during his editorship was a real power in the land and represented the views of the propertied and mercantile classes.'[101] Disraeli's opinion of Mudford seems to imply that he was devious: this may well have been so, but contemporary accounts stress his unwillingness to follow what he saw as a subservient Tory line. There is no indication that the paper habitually concentrated on paying large sums of money in order to procure a 'scoop'.

Longman was grateful for the information Disraeli gave him and wondered whether it would be desirable to take any steps to 'make the trick public'. He added, 'When a man has been imposed upon he does not feel inclined to sit down and do nothing. However, I do not intend to do anything hastily.' Longman had in fact consulted his solicitors about the matter on the same day that the *Standard*'s review had appeared. He invited Mudford to see him on 24 November, but Mudford declined the invitation.[102] On 30 November Disraeli told Longman he thought 'that it w^d not be wise to stir in any way, unless with a very fair chance of detection.'[103] Longman would appear to have taken his advice, and probably his solicitor's, and not followed the matter further, but from what Disraeli wrote to Lord Rowton on 6 December he certainly appeared to have thought that the leak damaged his potential sales fairly substantially:

... As for private affairs, I can't give you the definite information I could wish. His [Longman's] original plan of the campaign turned out to be a right one. The response was enormous, but something happened about the Standard, which according to his view, has played the devil. I can't attempt to go into the story.

Disraeli continued:

As for literary verdict, very generally in favor.

But as for society, I can say nothing. I am a hermit and see nobody. Those, the very few, to whom it was given, send of course mechanical applause.[104]

Although the reviews were quite favourable, he thought generally that the speed with which they had to get the reviews out 'prevented any real approximation to real criticism'.[105] He thought the *Spectator*'s 'poor stuff' (and perhaps felt cheated since he had 'expected a diatribe');[106] the *Observer* criticism struck him as 'adequate to the occasion' and 'writ by a wise hand';[107] the one that seems to have pleased him most was that of M. Cucheval-Clarigny[108], who had reviewed the book in the *Revue des Deux Mondes*—'that capital periodical'—Disraeli thought it 'the only notice, out of the hundreds whi we have received in which the critic has read the book he reviewed'.[109]

Longman himself had fixed up what he thought was 'a

The account of Longman's solicitor, Sharon G. Turner for advice he gave to Longman regarding the Standard *review. (Longman Archives)* satisfactory arrangement for Review of the work in the Edinburgh'.[110] When it appeared in January, Longman wrote to Disraeli, comparing it with the *Quarterly*'s review:

> I am a little curious to know your candid opinion on the Edinburgh review of Endymion, but I cannot refrain from remarking, whether it is considered good or bad, that it is worthy of a higher rank than the 'article' in the Conservative organ. I say *article* because it cannot be named a review of Endymion.[111]

The *Quarterly*, despite its being the 'Conservative organ', had long been antagonistic towards Disraeli, ever since the start of his literary career, when he had lampooned Murray, Croker and Lockhart in *Vivian Grey* (published in 1824). Lockhart, who had edited the *Quarterly* for forty-eight years, more or less consistently ignored Disraeli and even when the *Quarterly* did mention him, it was hostile. The long tradition of animosity towards him would not have led him to expect kindly treatment at their critic's hands. Disraeli admitted that he preferred the *Edinburgh* to any of the other quarterlies, but even then he didn't think the writer had 'exactly hit the nail on the head'.[112]

Punch viewed the publication of the novel more light-heartedly, marking the event with the following verses:

ENDYMION

THE shades of night were falling fast
Round Hughenden,—for some time past
A Statesman, working day and night,
A flowery fiction did indite—
   Endymion.

His hair was dark, and you could trace
A *soupçon* of an ancient race;
And still, in quite his early way,
He wrote of Lords and Ladies gay—
   Endymion.

"Tempt not the Press," Lord ROWTON said,
"Of critics have a timely dread:
They skinned you when you wrote *Lothair*."
He answered, with his nose in air,
   "*Endymion!*"

"Oh stay," the Tory said, "and make
That wicked GLADSTONE writhe and quake."
A twinkle flash'd from out his eye:
"I'll give him rope," he said, "and try
   Endymion!"

"Beware the day they may begin
To break the Treaty of Berlin!"
This was the Tory's last appeal.
He only said, "I will reveal
          Endymion!"

And so, when Ireland was aflame,
The Eastern Question just the same,
Conservatives beheld with doubt
Their Leader bring his novel out—
          Endymion.

And all who waded through the book,
Met Titles, Tailor, Prince and Dook:
What wonder it is all the rage?
For epigram adorns thy page,
          Endymion!

There, in the twilight, cold and grey,
Serene in Curzon Street he lay.
"This cheque from LONGMANS' will go far,"
A voice said. "Now for a cigar!"
          Endymion![113]

The cartoonists were not slow to miss an opportunity, and Disraeli, always a favourite target in the political field, was lampooned with equal enthusiasm as a novelist.

There were four main aspects of the novel which the reviewers seized on. Some looked for the autobiographical element. Many pointed to comments from the author on major political events over the previous fifty years, which form the background to the book. Some deplored what they saw as the lack of morality (this struck others differently). But all drew attention, however, to what the *Saturday Review* called the author's 'favourite reproduction of real personages in a more or less transparent mask'; in its opinion, 'in none of his former works had he indulged so largely and with so little disguise' as in this exercise.[114]

The autobiographical element was considered to be slight, and the *Standard* declared that any who expected much in this direction would be 'disappointed'.[115] The *Daily Telegraph* began its review by observing that 'everybody who reads these three volumes – and everybody sooner or later will read them – must prepare for a deep disappointment if they expected political revelations, official confessions, or the still more exciting confessions, or the still more exciting material of personal polemics'.[116] The *Edinburgh Review* thought it was a tale without a plot and decided for the main part of its review to pick out 'the more important crises' dealt with in the novel, since to the reviewer it seemed that the novel could be seen as Disraeli's retrospect of chief political events he had witnessed. Both the *Daily Chronicle*[117] and Lord Houghton in the *Fortnightly Review* compared events in the novel which were taken from actual events in which Disraeli was known to have played some part, Houghton taking the opportunity to discuss Disraeli's individual part at some length.[118]

The *St James's Gazette* noted that 'nothing which can be called "views" are to be extracted from these sparkling pages'.[119] The *Morning Post* warned that those who were looking forward 'to the perusal of its pages with an eye to gathering some inkling of the author's political views . . . may at once be informed that their

Left . . . ' "And the Minister flattered himself that both the literary and the graphic representations of himself in Scaramouch *might possibly for the future be mitigated." Vol. i, p. 312.*
Ahem! He did flatter himself!'
Cartoon in Punch, 4 *December* 1880 (Punch *was portrayed as a magazine called* Scaramouch *in the novel*).

Right: 'John Bull – "Why Ben! Got to the books again?"
Ben – "Yes, I couldn't be idle; and when I lost my situation, I thought I'd go back to my old trade. I've something here quite in my best style, and I hope you'll give me a good big order."'
Cartoon in Funny Folks, 4 *December* 1880 (*British Museum*)

ENDYMION.

—"AND THE MINISTER FLATTERED HIMSELF THAT BOTH THE LITERARY AND THE GRAPHIC REPRESENTATIONS OF HIMSELF IN *SCARAMOUCH* MIGHT POSSIBLY FOR THE FUTURE BE MITIGATED."—Vol. I, p. 312.
[*Ahem! He did flatter himself!*

BENDYMION.

expectations will be disappointed'. It continued:

Seeing that the action deals with the last fifty years of British life and takes place in the upper circles of society it would be impossible but that political topics should be treated at some length – indeed they are so, with much acuteness and vivacity; but nothing occurs in the course of this narrative of the career of Endymion Ferrars which could furnish any idea of the author's private views – it is essentially a romance.[120]

It was this element of 'romance' which caused enthusiasm on the part of some reviewers and infuriated others. To the *Spectator* there was 'hardly a touch of genuinely moral reflection in all his many novels'. The book taught only the value of ambition and, in the *Spectator*'s view, Disraeli's own 'only very humble stock of worldly wisdom'.[121] The *Saturday Review* complained of a lack of any trace of 'the enthusiasm of humanity, or of deep interest in social progress'.[122] The *Standard*, without deploring this lack of moral content, commented:

Everyone in "Endymion" is well born, well bred, and wealthy, or marvellously lucky, or beautiful, or brilliant, or irresistably attractive. The moral, of the work, so far as it can be said to have any, is that all who deserve prosperity may secure it, and that want and obscurity are only the heritage of defective ability and feeble will . . .[123]

Neither did the *Edinburgh Review* feel that the book should be taken with any real seriousness:

To take such a book *au grand serieux* . . . would be a mistake; but as a satirical picture of life, with the transformations of a Christmas pantomime, it has the merit of entertaining an enormous number of readers. . . . There are but the coloured shadows from the magic-lantern of life: the lamp within shines, we trust with a purer and a steadier light.[124]

The style of the work was generally agreed to be up to the standard set by Disraeli in his previous novels, although some compared it unfavourably with *Lothair*. Again, the *Standard* reflected the opinion of many reviewers:

The pages of "Endymion" literally sparkle with the splendour of prosperity, and some of the descriptions of the jewels and diamonds of his fine ladies are unusually gorgeous, even for Lord Beaconsfield. The novel is not a work of art; but it is a book which could only have come from one who to a large knowledge of the world adds a perfect mastery over the arts of satire and epigram.[125]

Given the fact that Disraeli's new novel fell short of many expectations on several counts, where did the main interest lie? What was really going to engage the attention of the 'world at large'? The *Athenaeum* provided the answer:

The interest of the book . . . does not consist in any revolutions or discoveries but rather in the successive sketches of the various characters introduced in the reflections put in their mouths or given more rarely as the author's own, and in the adumbration of not a few important historical figures and incidents.[126]

The *Observer* confirmed this impression:

It is the portraiture of personages and of society that confers yet more interest [than the story] on these pages; though readers will vainly look for absolute portraits. Here and there one thinks to catch a feature of the face of some public bore or blockhead. But suddenly his aspect changes, and the cap seems to fit some other head. . . . Myra . . . marries Lord Roehampton, in whom some people have chosen to see a portrait of Lord Palmerston, which only shows what bad judges they are of likenesses.[127]

From the start of Disraeli's literary career he had satirised contemporary events and people, often doing himself much harm.[128] *Endymion* was no exception, and among the correspondence in the Longman archives there is a note in Longman's hand as follows:

Names of persons given to me (August 1980 [sic]) by Lord Rowton as being represented in "Endymion"
Lord Lyndhurst
Lord Rothschild
George Smyth
Lady Jersey
Lord Cockburn
Himself
Lord Hertford.[129]

Longman was quick to recognise that this was to be one of the selling points of the book, pointing it out to Lord Rowton when he suggested a preface by Disraeli to the cheap edition,[130] and referring to it in the notice he had inserted in *Notes on Books*. Lord Houghton in the *Fortnightly* was in a minority in criticising 'the frequent combination of portraiture and fiction' which in his view 'acted as a check on genius, which if left free to work out its own imaginings would have left works more permanent and real than those which must depend for their repute and sympathy in a great degree on the accidents and figures of the day'.[131] For the most part reviewers all mentioned the attraction to readers of guessing who was who, and indulged in the pastime themselves. The *Standard* for instance, contained the following paragraph:

The daughter is taken into the palace of Mr Neuchatel, the banker, at Hainault House – *alias* Rothschild and Gunnersbury – as companion to his child Adriana; and here she meets many distinguished and opulent person-ages: Colonel Albert, the Count of Otranto, the Comte de Ferroll, and Prince Florestan – in whom there may be recognized respectively the linea-ments of Louis Napoleon and one of the Orleanist princes – and Lord Roehampton, who immediately suggests Lord Palmerston.[132]

Disraeli was contemptuous of such suggestions. Of the *Observer* critic he commented to Longman that he was 'not such a fool as to believe Ld Roehampton was intended for Lord Palmerston',[133] and he said of the *Post* and *Daily News*, 'at least they don't make Ld Montfort Prime Minister, & the Count of Ferroll Monsieur de Morny'.[134] Yet many 'keys' were quickly produced, as *Fraser's* had predicted they would be, and Longman sent one to Disraeli on 20 December which he called the most elaborate he had ever come across.[135] (He might have been referring to the key which appeared in *Notes and Queries* on 18 December which listed twenty five characters and their originals.[136]) The magazine *Harper's*, of New York, also printed a key for trans-Atlantic readers, listing the originals of no less than twenty-nine of the characters.[137]

Perhaps the two following extracts indicate the contrast between the general good nature that was evident in some reviews, and the view of those who, while only too ready to acknowledge Disraeli's own stature as a statesman and politician (and these estimates obviously varied with the political bias of the paper), were reluctant to admit literary talent where they found little evidence of it:

Whether liked or disliked, condemned or approved, it will be read uni-versally, and there is no class of readers who will not find in it something to instruct or amuse them. Were it less attractive than it appears to us as a novel of manners, and of the stirring incidents which preceded and followed the Reform movement, it would yet fascinate as an indirect revelation of one who has left the impress of his genius and ambition upon the age, and has long been a significant, if still veiled figure in that mingled drama of social and political excitement which he so well describes.[138]

On the whole, the book, like most of Mr Disraeli's works, is a poor and flashy one, with plenty of cleverness in it, though not nearly so much as the three stories which preceded his official career, – *Coningsby, Sybil* and *Tancred*. None of these works will live for their own sakes, nor at all, except as illustrating the career of one of the most unique of the men of genius of our day. For though there are distinct traces of the genius which made Mr Disraeli Prime Minister of England, in his novels there are only traces even in the best of them. Lord Beaconsfield the politician is . . . much more able than these rubbishy and incoherent stories. . . . Audacity can only be effectually shown in real life. In literature, it is a very ambiguous sort of quality, being very apt to bring rubbish to the surface, and pass it off as gold.[139]

✳

In the history of publishing, *Endymion* was significant much more for its impact than for its content. In 1884 193 three-volume novels were published: in 1897 only four. Already by 1880 the end of the three-decker was in sight, and *Endymion* can perhaps be seen as marking the beginning of the end of an era in publishing, in which the circulating libraries played a fairly large part in influencing the publishing policy of some publishing houses. But perhaps too, the novel can be seen as heralding a new era in which it has gradually become the practice of some publishers to pay large sums of money in order to secure the contract to publish the work of a public figure whose work may or may not have literary merit.

Protests against the form and price of the three-decker had been heard every so often in the columns of the newspapers and periodicals since about 1860.[140] *Endymion* appeared late in the life of the three-decker, when publishers and authors were becoming increasingly dissatisfied with the demands made on them by the form, and the publishers themselves were coming under attack. Its publication in 1880 provoked a storm of controversy. In a letter to *The Times* on 17 December of that year James Griffin, a publisher (though hardly worthy of the name according to Longman), attacked the system.[141] He estimated that if *Endymion* had been issued at 2s 6d, 500,000 copies might have sold in England alone. The profit to the publisher, of one shilling a copy of such an edition, he estimated at £25,000, and he declared that American and Colonial markets were also open to such an enterprise. *The Times* concentrated on the subject in its leader in the same issue. And while taking a balanced attitude, it noted that the situation was 'aggravated by the authorship of an ex-Prime Minister' and drew attention to the bitterness of many who were unable to afford his new novel. It pointed out that a guaranteed market was provided by the libraries, and that, uninfluenced by any reviewer's criticism, this enabled the publisher to gauge the market for a cheap edition of the book with no loss to themselves. It went on to argue that if the book were to have a much larger sale, for example of 500,000, as suggested by Griffin, then the copyright fee would have to be proportionately larger, thus eating into the potential net profit of £25,000. Indeed, the whole premise on which the calculations were based seemed far-fetched: 'To attribute to half a million of people, even in a country so fond of its aristocracy as this, a craving to hob nob with Lord Beaconsfield's latest creations in politics and the peerage seems a somewhat extravagant reckoning.' As far as the American situation was concerned, the paper commented: 'Until the improbable event of an international copyright treaty the mass of book buyers of the United States will hardly be inclined to pay 2s 6d for our novels any more than 31s 6d. At the present moment, it is said, "Endymion" is being sold in the United States for fifteen cents.'[142]

Griffin's letter, in particular, caught Longman on the raw: he was so incensed that he felt impelled to comment on it at some length to Disraeli:

You are not much of a reader of newspapers I know, and for fear it might escape your notice allow me to draw your attention to Mr Griffin's letter & the article upon it in today's Times.

I feel sure you will agree with me in thinking the letter quite foolish and unworthy of the attention the Times has given it. There is far more sense in the article and I certainly agree that the present Library system is a curse to genuine bookselling.

Mr Griffin does not know what he is writing about as his remark about America clearly proves. We know but too well that the United States in its present very deplorable state is almost a blank.

Does Mr Griffin suppose we are not alive to our own interests and know nothing of the circulation of cheap books? Does any sensible man suppose the question of form, price etc of "Endymion" was never considered at No 39? Why the very point he brings forward of issuing a cheap edition *at once* was carefully considered. Indeed, the matter will not bear investigation but I cannot refrain from making one more remark, or rather one more query, who is likely to know best how to manage, from a commercial point of view, the publication of a great work like "Endymion"? a small publisher – or I should better describe him as a retail bookseller in the provinces – or a firm of at least a hundred and fifty years experience in large matters of business of this kind!

This nonsense however will all help to sell the book.[143]

Disraeli appeared more pragmatic in his attitude. After all, he had been subjected to criticism all his life: 'I read Griffin's letter & perceived he did not understand the subject he was writing about. The "Times" only half understood it. If the book sells never mind anything that is said.'[144]

The letter was followed up, however, on 20 December by a letter to *The Times*, which was signed 'A Novel Publisher'. Longman approved of this correspondent's argument and told Disraeli that 'the "Novel Publisher" who writes to the Times this morning is not your humble servant, but he is a very sensible man'.[145] The writer of the letter looked at the situation, he remarked, from a more realistic point of view than Griffin:

If they [Messrs Longman] had issued it [*Endymion*] at half a crown, and if they had sold 500,000 copies (as Mr Griffin imagines) and had made 1s. profit on each copy, unquestionably a net profit of £25,000 would have been the result. But let me put it another way. Suppose Messrs. Longmans start with a load of £10,000 paid to Lord Beaconsfield and suppose their sales only reached the enormous total, say, of 200,000, and suppose further, that their net profits amounted only to, say, 10d. a copy (which is, I fancy, nearer the mark than 1s.), they would receive about £8,300 over and above the outlay for production, and would thus make a dead loss of £1,660 by their investment. I cannot imagine that any sane publisher would lay down £10,000 for authorship and £5,000 (for production of 200,000 copies) with such a possibility before him; for you will observe that the sole chance of making any profit at all lies in the copies sold beyond, say, the first 230,000.

If such experiments are to be tried, the whole burden must not be thrown on the publisher, the author must share it with him. On such a footing I would willingly publish Lord Beaconsfield's next novel at 2s 6d., and hand his Lordship £20,000 out of the £25,000 when the book had earned that comfortable sum.

The whole truth of the matter lies in a nutshell. The great novel-reading public infinitely prefers (in 99 cases out of 100) borrowing a three-volume novel for 6d. to buying it in one volume for 2s 6d.; the hundredth case is "Endymion". I heartily wish it were otherwise; but the attempt has frequently been made and has as frequently failed.[146]

In this case, moreover, it was the library, the real villain of the piece in many people's eyes, which was the loser. Mudie had ordered 3,000 copies, but this proved far too many, and he unsuccessfully offered the books for sale; he subsequently claimed that his premises were taken up for years with stacks of the 9,000 volumes.[147] Indeed, he suffered such a loss on this book that he reduced his orders of Bentley's novels to keep his accounts 'in trim'; at the same time he added another request: 'I wish to ask you to hold what books you can *back* for the next $\frac{1}{2}$ year.'[148]

Mudie was also hit in another way. One of the restrictions often placed on publishers was a pledge demanded by libraries that no cheap edition of a novel should be published for a certain length of time after the publication of the first edition: this allowed the libraries to make a maximum profit from their stock both from lending to subscribers and, eventually, selling off stock second-hand. The appearance of a cheap edition soon after the publication of a first edition cut at both sources of the libraries' profit. Yet Thomas Longman had produced such a cheap edition of *Lothair*, and his son repeated the strategy with *Endymion*, leaving Mudie on both occasions with surplus stock and therefore – it is safe to surmise – poor returns on his investment. Longman was not alone in refusing to wait for a year before the issue of a cheap edition. William Blackwood, for example, had decided against giving such a pledge to Mudie in connection with *The Mill on the Floss*, though he admitted that it would be unwise to issue a cheaper edition 'until the three volume one has had it's [sic] full swing'.[149] It is probable that Longman was following the same policy in 1881, hoping to obtain maximum publicity and interest with the 'library' edition, making as much as he could from the luxury trade, and then, having saturated the market, to bring out a cheap 6s edition, thus getting the best out of both forms of publication.

The cheap edition of *Endymion* was published at the beginning of March 1881 as a one volume cabinet edition, at 6s. By 12 March Longman had been able to inform the sick Disraeli that it was 'making a good start'.[150] By 24 March, he went on, they had sold 'over 8,000 copies'. 'I feel sure,' he added, that 'it will be as satisfactory to you to know, as it is to me to inform you, that the sale, up to the present time, compares favourably with the popular edition of "Lothair".'[151]

Throughout 1881, before and after Disraeli's death, Longmans brought out Disraeli's other novels in a cabinet edition and continued to publish them as part of their *Modern Novelists Library* series, printing 20,000 copies of *Endymion* for this latter edition in December 1881, and a further 5,000 in March 1882. In July 1881 they also published the Hughenden edition of his works in eleven volumes. The focus was on the outstanding public figure.

With the letter of 24 March the correspondence between the two men ends. There is, however, a sequel. Disraeli himself had been rather less than sanguine regarding the potential success of the deal as far as Longman was concerned, despite his reassurances to Longman when the agreement was drawn up. On the day of publication he had told Lady Bradford that he thought the transaction would 'prove rather the skill of Monty's diplomacy than Mr Longman's business acumen'. If this were the case, he added, 'my conscience will force me to disgorge'.[152]

In March Disraeli was afraid that his worst fears had been justified, and, through Lord Rowton, offered to 'disgorge', proposing to cancel the existing agreement and accept one whereby *Endymion* was published on the same terms as *Lothair* — i.e. the publisher would pay a royalty of 10*s* on all copies sold. Longman saw this as Disraeli virtually offering £3,000 to the firm. He replied, however, in the same spirit as his father had shown some sixteen years earlier when he refused to be indemnified for unsold stocks of *The Revolutionary Epick*. In Buckle's words:

Mr Longman at once replied that it was true that the three-volume edition of *Endymion* had not been the commercial success that the three-volume edition of *Lothair* was; but that the firm had made their offer with their eyes open and the result had quite answered their expectations; and that they could not think of availing themselves of Beaconsfield's liberal and considerate suggestion.[153]

Lord Rowton recorded the final instalment of the venture:

Mr Longman visited me, at 19 Curzon St, a few days before Lord Beaconsfield's death, and authorized me to inform Lord B. – who heard the intelligence with extreme satisfaction – that his firm had just turned the corner, & was beginning to make a profit out of the bargain.

I believe this was the last piece of business on wh: he and I ever spoke together.

After so many! and such![154]

ASA BRIGGS

The view from Badminton

THE WORD 'badminton' is best known to most late-twentieth-century sportsmen as the name of a game which was first played 'only at Bath, Cheltenham and other places where retired Indians congregate' and which eventually made its way round many countries of the world. During the last years of the nineteenth century, however, and on into the early twentieth, the name was widely associated with a highly successful and far-ranging series of books on 'sports and pastimes', beginning with hunting, the subject of the first volume, published in 1885, and including 'motors and motor driving', the subject of a volume which appeared in 1902 soon after the beginning of a century when automobiles were to transform not only sport but society.

In his preface to the series, the general editor, the Duke of Beaufort, who lived at Badminton and named the series after his great country house, justified its publication with the words, 'there is no modern encyclopaedia to which the inexperienced man, who seeks guidance in the practice of the various British sports and pastimes, can turn for information'. Many editions of Blaine's *Encyclopaedia of Rural Sports*, which first appeared in 1840, had been published during the following thirty years, but when Longmans discussed the possibility of bringing the encyclopaedia up to date in 1882 they very quickly decided that the task was impossible. This was one of the many critical occasions in the history of publishing when account had to be taken of a huge national shift in attitudes and tastes. The word 'rural' in the older title was far too restrictive once large parts of

Britain, including parts where organised sports were most popular, were urbanised and industrialised. Moreover, a contents page of any encyclopaedia of sports and pastimes which included badger baiting and left out football was clearly in need of more than revision.

Charles James Longman (who also edited *Longman's Magazine*, first published in 1882) suggested that instead of producing one great new work in the tradition not only of Blaine but of Joseph Strutt's *Sports and Pastimes of the People of England* (1801) several little books on sport should be published, each written by a specialist and designed to appeal to a particular set of devotees. The idea was subsequently to be taken up by many publishers. Perhaps, Longman argued, seven or eight volumes might eventually appear. In fact, thirty volumes were to appear, and the member of the Longman family most interested in the project as it took shape was Thomas Norton Longman V, who was responsible for all the illustrations.[1] Since the books were produced at a time when the place of sport in society was changing rapidly and when sports news and features were becoming staple ingredients in newspapers and magazines, there was no doubt about the commercial viability of the venture.

What is most interesting about the Badminton series is that the different volumes make few concessions to some of the main social changes of the time – the rise of spectator sports for mass entertainment; the development of professionalism; the emergence of new forms of business organisation in both local and national sport; and the increasing 'nationalisation' of what had hitherto been mainly local sporting activities. Alfred E. T. Watson, sub-editor of the series and after 1895 the editor of the *Badminton Magazine* which derived from it, was out of sympathy with much that was happening: when his career was summed up in 1923, after his death, he was described as 'a good sportsman, a true gentleman' who had 'drifted into journalism, like so many noted journalists'.[2] His first love was racing, and for years he was Turf Correspondent of *The Times*. He was also a friend of the Duke of Beaufort, who was invited by Thomas Norton Longman to become editor of the new sports series 'without fee or reward'.[3] It was Watson who selected the names of authors and submitted them to the Duke for approval. It was he, too, who examined the 'schemes' they proposed and struck out passages of which he did not approve before sending corrected proofs to the Duke.

The choice of the eighth Duke of Beaufort (born in 1824) was a shrewd one. Badminton, his great house, not only gave its name to the series but was illustrated on the first page of the preface to each volume as it would have been on the Duke's own private notepaper. Given that the Badminton series was meant to appeal to 'good sportsmen and true gentlemen', the Duke had imposing qualifications to sit in the editorial chair. He was hereditary Master of one of the most famous packs of hounds in England,* and he not only chose hunting as the subject of the first Badminton volume but contributed an essay himself on 'Hunt Servants and their Duties'.[4] He was also a prominent member of the Jockey Club and at the time of accepting the general editorship of the series was in possession of both the Cup and the Whip at Newmarket. He was a coachman of unequalled skill and experience who took particular interest in the volume on 'driving' which appeared in 1889: indeed, he wrote a chapter in it on 'the road', recalling nostalgically his boyhood days in Brighton and the West Country.[5] Finally, he was an expert fisherman, and fishing enjoyed the special privilege of two volumes to itself, as did both shooting and yachting.

The Duke was introduced to Longmans by Tom Paine, a member of Tattersalls and a friend of Thomas Norton Longman. Although Beaufort depended as general editor on Alfred Watson, whom he always addressed in that 'affectionately conventional

Alfred E. T. Watson (1849–1922)
Badminton Magazine, *Vol. viii.*
(*Bodleian Library*)

* In 1853 he had hunted on 103 days out of the year. His children were rationed to three days a week until they were five years old (see F. M. L. Thompson, *English Landed Society in the Nineteenth Century* (1913) p. 146).

form of address' of the age of Sherlock Holmes, 'My dear
Watson', he had ideas of his own. Something of the flavour of his
authority is conveyed in a passage in his chapter on hunt servants
written in 1885:

A huntsman, whether he be a gentleman or a professional, should impress on
his whippers-in certain things that they should or should not do. This is
better done by quietly talking to them in the kennels or elsewhere than by
blowing them up or swearing at them in the hunting field, though it is
necessary at times to speak out there.[6]

The Duke hated slang or what he thought to be slang, which
accounts for his use of the term 'whipper-in' rather than 'whip':
a whip, he said, was an implement and not a man. The men
themselves must often have irritated him. 'I have known several
whippers-in – good men in their own way,' he writes, 'I should
like to have taken out with the muzzles on.'[7]

Watson always took care to interpret the Duke's wishes. After
explaining, for example, why he had suggested a book on cycling,
which could be a plebeian, even a socialist, sport, he contrived to
make even cycling sound aristocratic:

Shooting and *Hunting* had appealed chiefly to the 'classes' perhaps but we
wished to appeal to the 'masses' also – to adopt Mr. Gladstone's distinction –
and at the time never supposed that multitudes outside this latter category
would be attracted by a book on such a subject. Still some persons *did* ride,

The Duke of Beaufort (1824–99) *by
G. D. Giles,* Driving: *frontispiece.
(Bodleian Library)*

Title-page of Hunting. *(Bodleian
Library)*

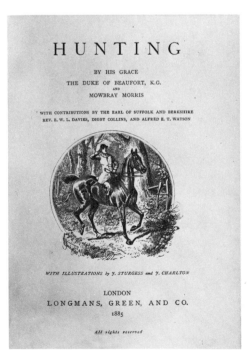

the then Lord Bury among them, and he consented to write in conjunction with Mr. Lacy Hillier, who was one of the few who had adopted 'the wheel' with distinction.[8]

Cycling was a special case given that it was related to 'the business of life' as well as to sport. It was 'fast becoming the custom', as the Badminton volume put it, 'for workmen to go home on their bicycles during the dinner hour', while 'the number of clergymen who use the tricycle in the discharge of their parish duties, and find in the silent carriage, always ready at a moment's notice, the most useful and convenient of vehicles for their work is very large'.[9] Not even the publication of a Badminton volume on cycling – which noted that the Khedive of Egypt kept three tricycles* – could keep it aristocratic, and as late as 1939, when a writer proposed to a leading London publishing firm – not Longmans – a book based on a bicycle tour of England he was told politely that 'the best booksellers would not be interested'.[10] G. Lacy Hillier, however, was a special kind of author as well as a special kind of cyclist. A stockbroker by profession, he was the predecessor of Alfred Harmsworth (later Lord Northcliffe) as editor of *Bicycling News* which had first appeared in 1876. Hillier disapproved of Northcliffe's journalistic methods, including his cutting of his 'serious' articles into short, readable paragraphs.[11] The contrasting styles of the two men reflect the opposing tendencies of the period in journalism as much as in sport.

'In the Badminton Country' by John Sturgess, Hunting: frontispiece. (Bodleian Library)

* *Cycling* (1887), p. 10. 'One in particular, which I have had the honour of inspecting, is so covered with silver plating, that one can hardly see the black enamel it is supposed to adorn.'

In most sports of the 1890s – even if football must be excluded* – the aristocracy (not the journalists or the business-men) still called the tune, and Watson set out to mobilise the best aristocrats among them. The Duke of Somerset was invited to discuss 'old coaching days'; Lord Walsingham, who enjoyed 'the deserved credit of being an unsurpassed authority on all matters concerned with shooting' wrote the main chapters in the volume on that subject; the Earl of Suffolk knew more about Newmarket than any one else in the country, and his chapter on the subject was thought by Watson to be among the 'best work' in all the Badminton volumes; Gerald Lascelles wrote on fal-conry, while Lord Pembroke, described by Watson as 'one of the most quietly humorous and picturesque of all the Badminton authors', was given chapters in *Yachting* (1894), 'a branch of the subject to discuss which had specially appealed to him – the pleasure that might be enjoyed by the employment of sailing boats'.[12] No one liked a lord more than Watson, and though he survived most of his aristocratic contributors, among the peers who sang his praises at the time of his obituary notices in 1923 were the Duke of Rutland, Lord Lonsdale, who confessed him-self a great admirer of the *Badminton Magazine*, Lord Dunraven and Lord Coventry.[13]

There had long been a close relationship in sports like racing and boxing between the peer and the working man, a traditional relationship which was carried forward into the age of urbanis-ation and industrialisation by men like Lord Lonsdale who 'lived every minute of his life' and was known to all 'sporting sections of the population'.† It is interesting to note, with these traditions in mind, that when William Heinemann decided in 1901 to launch a new *Encyclopaedia of Sports and Games* he selected as editor the Earl of Suffolk, one of Watson's favourites. The aristocracy was still setting the pace. Throughout the Badminton

* Although A. F. Kinnaird, later Lord Kinnaird, an old Etonian and a 'Wanderer', had appeared in nine Cup Finals before 1884: he once stood on his head for joy in front of the pavilion at the Oval after Old Etonians had defeated Blackburn Rovers.

† Lord Coventry was equally well known. A young nephew once walked with him to Epsom Station after the Derby and 'was immensely struck by the fact that every one we met in the crowd seemed to recognise him'. This fine old English gentleman said to me 'How is it that everybody knows me?' See E. Cadogan, *Beyond the Deluge* (1961), p. 219.

'*A bad man on a good horse*' Hunting, *p.* 188. (*Bodleian Library*)

volumes, therefore, whatever sport or pastime was being discussed
(with a very few exceptions) the view we obtain is the view from
Badminton, often a very direct view.

It was through the influence of the Duke of Beaufort that the
series as a whole was dedicated to the Prince of Wales, his
'friend', whom he described generously as 'one of the best and
keenest sportsmen of our time'.[14] We are left in no doubt about
the privileged angle of vision when we read in the ducal preface
this sentence: 'When the wind had been blowing hard, often have
I seen His Royal Highness knocking over driven grouse and
partridges and high rocketing pheasants in first-rate workmanlike style.' The use of the word 'workmanlike' catches the feel of
the peer group,[15] and in a further sentence the Duke somewhat
extends its span. The Prince's 'encouragement of racing is well
known,' he goes on, 'and his attendance at the University, Public
School and other important Matches testifies to his being, like
most English gentlemen, fond of all manly sports.'

We are reminded in the use of the term 'manly sports' that it
was not only the crowds who were turning increasingly to sport
during the last decade of the nineteenth century and the first
decade of the twentieth, but the élites in public schools and
universities. There had been a great change after 1850. Speaking
of 'our Universities' in the Badminton volume on *Athletics and
Football* Montague Shearman wrote that he had 'seen the foundation of the present prosperous clubs at both Cambridge and
Oxford, and with the exception of the crick-run at Rugby and
the steeplechase at Eton, prior to 1850 no public school had any
established athletic contest'. 'Thirty years ago, it was the exception for a senior wrangler or a senior classic to figure in the
University boat or the eleven.'[16] A new edition of J. Wells's

Oxford Life, published in 1899, included a chapter on 'the social life' which had been completely rewritten since the first edition appeared in 1887. It had something to say about football as well as about rowing and beagling:

Whereas football fifty years ago was practically unknown at Oxford; and regarded as a schoolboy's game, to be cast off like a schoolboy's discipline by the University man . . . it now excites much interest as well in the University as in the town. . . . It affords amusement and exercise and the attendant social activities for the multitude of folk who either despise or are despised by their rowing brethren, who cannot afford or have not the wish to hunt, and who require more violent and exciting recreation than the afternoon's walk of the reading man or loafer.[17]

The author praised football because it brought together 'people who hail from different schools' and thus 'tended to break down the walls of public school caste'. The whole of the chapter in Wells contrasts sharply with an article in an early number of the *Badminton Magazine* by R. K. Mainwaring, who had been up at Christ Church during the 1860s. When he matriculated in 1866, Mainwaring wrote, he could already have taken a 'very fair examination in the *Racing Calendar*', and while he was an undergraduate he had joined a pack of harriers, owned horses and competed in steeplechase meetings or 'grinds'.[18]

Wells extolled 'team games'. He also praised Oxford for its part in the battle against professionalism. Football, already the sport of the crowds, had not completely succumbed to professionalism even in industrial cities. By the late 1880s university football teams could no longer hold their own against professionals from the industrial North (the last appearance of Oxford in the Football Association Cup Final was in 1880, and by 1886 there were only four amateur sides left in the fifth round), yet it remained true, as Wells put it, that 'the powerful influence of the English Universities' was still doing much 'to overcome that tendency to professionalisation' which in his view was 'the bane of all athletics as well as of football'.[19] The Amateur Athletics Association had been founded in 1880, but it was by no means self-evident that athletics would not succumb, as it seemed to be doing in the United States, to professional pressures. It is interesting to note that in the Badminton series football and athletics shared the same single volume, with Watson observing that both seemed to be living in a state of 'considerable uncertainty'.[20] Whatever the larger and larger crowds might be seeming to say, Watson himself doubted whether football had 'the steady vitality of cricket'. Cricket was, after all, dependent on amateur leadership. As one of the authors of the Badminton volume on cricket, A. G. Steel, wrote with unruffled confidence, 'amateurs have always made and always will make the best captains, and this is only natural. An educated mind, with a logical power of reasoning, will always treat every subject better than one comparatively untaught'.[21]

'*The Critics*' Cricket, *p.* 324. (*Bodleian Library*)

Although the main object of the Badminton series was not to explore what would now be called the sociology of sport but rather 'to point the way to success to those who are ignorant of the sports they aspire to master, and who have no friend or help to coach them', it was not easy in practice to separate the two. Watson himself usually preferred not to identify trends but to collect opinions. What he said about football was exceptional. For the most part he wrote like an amateur anthropologist. The 'rise and fall of favourite sports and pastimes' seemed to him 'curious'. What had happened, for instance, to roller skating in 1896?

Does anybody rink now? On an asphalted street, one may at times find a belated little boy, probably with one skate, making little straight runs with a growing confidence that ends in a fall. He has found the skate among some old lot of discarded rubbish, to which it was consigned to keep company, perhaps, with the battered croquet balls, hoops and mallets – though, by the way, croquet, in a new and more difficult shape, has recently had something of a revival.[22]

Watson, like most anthropologists, was deeply concerned with 'origins' – the volumes he commissioned on *Tennis* had a chapter on its 'palaeontology' and included an unforgettable picture of 'a ball game of olden times' complete with very Victorian-looking Greek nymphs[23] – yet he could not explain why one game 'rose' as another one 'fell'. 'Fashion changes' seemed to be all that could be adduced by way of explanation, and a study of fashion changes, as we shall see, led him not towards economics and sociology but towards art and literature.

Some of Watson's authors drew a contrast between 'new tendencies' and 'old customs', often lingering somewhat nostalgically in the past. The Duke of Beaufort himself, like the early Dickens, was at his best in describing English scenes which were already beginning to be just out-of-date:

Avoid squaring your elbows and swagger of any sort when driving. Hold your whip in your right hand – not at the end, but where it will balance nicely either for carrying or using. . . . Remember that your comfort depends on keeping on good terms with your horse. . . . Many people will be apt to say, 'How do you know at what pace you are going?' And it must be admitted that the speed of horses is very deceptive to the eye: it will often seem to the observer that a big team of sixteen-hand horses are apparently going along very slowly, but with their long stride they will in reality be going a good ten miles an hour when they look as if they were travelling not more than eight miles. . . . In these luxurious days when everybody has two grooms with a team of four horses, it may seem scarcely necessary to say where the place of the groom ought to be when the horses are standing; but in the event of a gentleman having only one man with him, let him remember above all things that that man must not go to the leaders' heads.[24]

Perhaps it was appropriate that in this detailed volume on *Riding* (1890), which should be compared at every point with the volume on *Motors and Motor Driving* (1902), Beaufort's introduction was followed immediately by a chapter on carriages by Watson. Between the dates of the two volumes there is a fascinating intermediate literature.[25] The motor car was thought of most naturally during this decade as a 'horseless carriage' (compare the negative term 'wireless' of the same period), and much attention was paid to the comparative costs of maintaining cars and horses, complete with mechanics and grooms. One of the

'*Our National Game*' Cricket, *p. 372. (Bodleian Library)*

real pioneers of the future, Henry Sturmey, who contributed to the Badminton volumes both on cycling and motoring, devoted many pages of *The Autocar* (first published in 1895) to explaining why 'in these luxurious days' both economics and sociology favoured the motor car over even the best of carriages.*

Another interesting comparison can be made between two volumes on the same subject, *Cricket,* which appeared at very different dates, 1888 and 1920. Steel's account of the 'national game', first drafted in 1888 and completely revised by him in 1893, was obviously so out-of-date by the end of the First World War that Longmans took the unprecedented step of commissioning a new Badminton volume long after the series had been brought to a close. Pelham Warner, the new author, was at pains to insist that whatever else had changed, the 'chief essential' of cricket had not – the fact that it was a synonym for 'all that is true

---

* At the first annual meeting of the Daimler Company, reported in *The Autocar*, II (1897), p. 683, the Chairman ended with a lengthy description of the advantages of keeping a car rather than a horse. 'Looking after a motor car is child's play compared to attending to a horse. If you do not use your carriage for a month it does not cost you anything – there is no horse eating off its head in the stable. If you compare the price of even a single carriage and a horse and the cost of keeping it – (A VOICE: And keeping the coachman too) you will find at the end of the year that there will not be much difference between that and the first cost of a Daimler carriage. Of course, you will want a coachman in either case. . . . Most people who own a car will want someone to do the rubbing down and the cleaning up.'

and straight'.[26] The expression 'not cricket' had survived the
great holocaust of 1914–18, although the tactics of the game had
changed considerably and professional players were more and more
involved in the big county matches. Steel and his co-author
R. H. Lyttelton, had been very sure of their judgments on social
as well as cricketing matters. 'The more cricket gets into the
hands of professional players,' they stated bluntly, 'the worse it
will be for the game and its reputation.'[27] Pelham Warner, still
with Lyttelton as co-author of the chapter, was more guarded.

At first sight it appears impossible that amateurs – men who play when they
chance to find it convenient – should be able to hold their own against
professional cricketers who make the game the business of their lives.
Cricket, however, is the one game where the two classes contend more or less
on an equality.[28]

'*The Demon Bowler*' Cricket, *p.* 96.   '*A hot return*' Cricket, *p.* 131.
(*Bodleian Library*)   (*Bodleian Library*)

Yet Steel in his well written volume of 1888 tried more than
any other writer in the Badminton series to explain as well as to
describe. He not only gave a graphic account of the vicissitudes
of the cricket professional's life – idolised in summer, unem-
ployed in winter – but sought to map a kind of social geography
of the game (something which could have been done for rugby or
football but was not). 'The sporting tendencies of the people of
Lancashire, Yorkshire and Nottingham' were 'developed to a
much greater extent than in the more southern shires'.[29] These
three counties – and especially Nottinghamshire – 'turned out
large quantities of professionals yearly'. Steel was not unkind to

the cricket professional: indeed, he summed him up in this way:

The first-class professional cricketer is usually a well-made, strong-looking man, ranging from two or three and twenty to thirty-five, with agreeable, quiet manners. He is a great favourite with the crowd, and when his side is in may be seen walking round the ground surrounded by a body of admirers, any of whom is ready and willing at any moment to treat his ideal hero to a glass of anything he may wish for. It is greatly to the player's credit that in face of this temptation to insobriety he is such a sober, temperate man. . . . I believe that, as a class, and considering the thirsty nature of their occupation and the opportunities that offer themselves for drinking, there is no more sober body of men than cricket professionals.[30]

The main social problem involved in professionalisation, Steel believed, was not drink but betting. If the game were professionalised, it would become a huge money-spinning activity with a vast betting business on the side. 'At present cricket is perhaps the most popular of our national recreations. . . . It is rightly considered to be the manliest [note how Steel returned to this concept] and the freshest from all mischievous influences.' 'The sullying influence has spread to the running path, and even, if the report says true, to the river.'[31]

There is a hint in Steel's analysis that cricket is 'the national game' not only because it expresses through its rules and through its conduct on the field the national sense of what is fair or not fair, but because it has nothing to do either with money-making or betting. The hint is broadened in all sections of the Badminton volumes (and *Magazine*) which touch briefly on the organisation of sport in the United States – the power of the market; the offering of financial incentives to players, including athletes; and the spread of advertising. This was not the way England should move. Yet the authors of the volume on racing obviously could not treat betting in the same way as the volume on cricket. 'Betting may or may not be intrinsically immoral,' they stated, 'but if it is, then undoubtedly the English character leaves much to be desired on the score of morality, for the love of betting, and more particularly of betting on horse races, is thoroughly ingrained in the average Briton. In racing, as in "all human affairs", "evil and good" are "blended".'[32] A social historian of Victorian England would not dare to qualify this judgment. However great the pressures to reform morals and however well-organised and vociferous the pressure groups, betting was never curbed. As in the case of 'drink', which Steel rightly brought into the picture also, the public was divided into the total abstainers, the temperate, the regulars and the addicts.[33]

'The sport of kings' always had its own sociology, and the authors of the volume on racing and steeple-chasing, who included Arthur Coventry, made many sociological points. The phrase 'community of backers' was misleading: 'The backers are not split into sections as is said to be the case with the Liberal party, they are divided into units.'[34] Aristocratic turf debts were deemed to be more interesting to read about than the evil effects of betting on the working classes. The Education Act of 1870 had removed young children from the racing stable: to go on employing lads at school would mean that 'they would inevitably be marked down in their goings to and fro and perse-cuted for information by all the touts of the neighbourhood'. The change from the private trainer to the public trainer had become inevitable 'as wealth largely increased and became more widely diffused': 'as the sharp distinctions of class became gradually obliterated, the turf year by year attracted more votaries.' The new trainer was called 'the boss'. 'It is impossible that jockeys can be kept in their proper position when successful members of the riding fraternity are enabled to realise fortunes of £100,000 and more within a dozen years of their first appearance in the saddle.' 'It would be tedious here to enumerate all the old-fashioned country meetings which have suffered from, or suc-cumbed to, the new limited liability undertakings.'[35]

We are back to the contrast between past and present, a main theme in the sporting life of the late-nineteenth century, even in relation to techniques and styles. Shearman noted how the development of 'passing' was transforming rugby football. Since the Oxford XV had led the way in the early 1880s 'passing has

'*A fast-forward game*' Athletics and Football, p. 303. (*Bodleian Library*)

been all the rage, no player apparently being ever satisfied now to run half a dozen yards without passing the ball'.[36] Steel, who scored 148 against Australia during the period when he was engaged on the writing of his book on cricket, was disturbed that he had recently seen 'a cautious player receive four consecutive balls and not make an attempt to hit one'. Surprisingly, perhaps, he added realistically, 'let such players please think of the un-happy spectators and of the coffers of the county club'.[37] Yet he drew the general conclusion that such lamentable performance had much to do with the rise of professionalism and its impact on the tactics both of batsmen and bowlers. Against the view from Badminton he briefly set the non-view from Bramall Lane. 'Nothing in cricket can be more dull or dismal than bowling to Louis Hall of Yorkshire on a sodden wicket at Bramall Lane in a real Sheffield fog.'[38] R. H. Lyttelton, who wrote the chapter on fielding, lingered on the same scene, but drew from it a practical moral:

Let us also assure the young practitioner that an intelligent audience, though a somewhat rough one, such as you may see at places like Bramall Lane, Sheffield, will jeer in audible and not too polite tones at the bad field long before it will do the like at bad batsmen or bowlers.[39]

We are already a long way from a Cornwall cricket ground described by W. G. Grace in his book on cricket published in 1891: 'It is told of Clarke's Eleven that on one occasion when it visited Cornwall a man fielding at long-on flushed a covey of partridges, and that a patch 40 yards by 10 was the only part of the ground that was ever cut or rolled.'[40]

If some of the Badminton volumes recall the past, the future is always uncertain. Cycling is thought to be assured, but there is a problem in that 'the roads seem in many parts of Britain to be getting worse and worse'.[41] Motoring appears likely to attain 'prodigious proportions', but it will be through a 'motoring movement' rather than through the development of a generalised means of private transport. Football, dealt with somewhat briefly in the Badminton series, is the subject of an interesting article by C. B. Fry, the cricketer, in an early issue of the *Bad-minton Magazine*. Fry recognises that towards the end of the summer in Yorkshire, Lancashire and the Midlands 'the interest in cricket palls visibly before that in football', but he still thinks that cricket will survive as 'the national game':

Football, it is claimed, has now the first place in the popular heart, and therefore has every right to be honoured with the title so long enjoyed by the other and older game. At first sight there seems to be some justice in this claim. These, we are told, are the days of democracy and radicalism. The nation, we are told, is a democracy, and the game of the people must be accepted as the game of the nation. Certainly football is a more democratic game than cricket. . . . It is much easier to play, far more readily organised, requires infinitely less elaborate preparations or equipment, and, finally, it is not only much cheaper, but brings in more money. . . . In a sense, then, football is the game of the busy classes and consequently of the people. But that does not make it the national game. The fact is that there is an essential difference between the two games. The interest in football is more or less local. . . . The interest of the average man in cricket is wider and much more free from partisan spirit. . . . The bare result of a football match is enough for most people, but nearly everyone likes to know how a cricket match is won and all about it. . . . Football, then has not yet proved its right to dethrone cricket from its position as the typical British game.[42]

'*The association game*' Athletics and Football, *p.* 334. (*Bodleian Library*)

This extraordinarily interesting passage, less tendentious than much other writing on football,* is percipient as far as it goes, and includes in the last sentence quoted the critical word 'yet'. Few other Badminton authors were as sensitive. The volume on dancing, for example, has no hints about the twentieth century. There had been considerable doubt as to whether to publish a volume on dancing in the series, and the doubts had been resolved only when a suitable woman author could be found, Mrs Lilly

* Football professionalism, whether in soccer or rugby, seemed to most of the writers in the *Badminton Magazine* to be likely to lead inexorably to 'corruptibility, disrepute and sometimes absolute decay'. 'The old gladiator system,' wrote Captain Philip Trevor in 1897, 'lacked the completeness of the recognised procedure under which prominent football players are now bought, sold and manipulated, but the balance of sportsmanship probably lies with the Romans.'

Grove FRGS, the only woman to write a Badminton volume. She began with the dances of Egypt 'in honour of the gods', included a chapter on 'the dances of savages' and ended with a note on 'balls, hostesses and guests' by the Countess of Ancaster.

'*Graceful movements, no. 1*' and '*Graceful movements, no. 2*' Dancing, *pp* 382–3. (*Bodleian Library*)

Like Watson, Mrs Grove could not account for changes of taste:

Who changes the order of things in dancing is quite as great a mystery as who is the priestess that presides over the creation of new fancies and fashions in dress, and demands the sacrifice at her shrine of so many fond ideas of what was once the ideal in dress or custom.[43]

Her own preferences remained strictly conventional, though she recognised that a new generation preferred different dances to those she liked. 'Quiet stately dancing is the only kind suited for such an occasion as a Court Ball. The young generation care for nothing but the wildest waltz or polka.'[44] Recognition of this fact carried with it disapproval. In the best mid-Victorian vein she considered dancing in moral as well as aesthetic terms. 'A moral gain is also attainable for many by this study,' she writes.

Experienced teachers have seen instances of improvement effected in nerve
and temper, undiscoverable until the stern discipline of the dancing lesson
came to the rescue, working subtly in the guise of play . . . The disobedient
become accustomed to obey; the sulky perforce throw off their habitual
mood; ill temper is forgotten. Thus, the physical benefit of the exercise is
supplemented by other elevating influences.[45]

Even Steel was far more relaxed. 'Nervous cricketers,' he remarked, 'must remember that, after all, cricket is but a game,
and no moral disgrace will attach to them if they fail.'[46]

There is very little in the volume on dancing about relations
between the sexes or changing attitudes to the place of women in
late-Victorian society. For comments on these subjects it is
necessary to turn in particular to the volumes on cycling, tennis
and golf. It was stated explicitly in 1887 that the presence of
women in cycling clubs was an advantage. 'A cricket match in
January would be an absurdity, and besides, cricket, good game
as it is, does not include the gentler sex among its votaries.'[47]
Horace G. Hutchinson, writing on golf in 1890, went one step
further. 'We do not know that a claim for absolute equality has as

'Diagram of Major Wingfield's game of
Sphairistike' Tennis, p. 137.
(Bodleian Library)

'The dawn of Golf' Golf, p. 230.
(Bodleian Library)

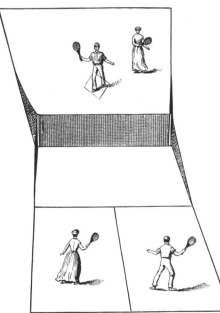

'*A Champion in Difficulties*' Golf,
p. 153. (*Bodleian Library*)

'*A caddie's duties*' Golf, p. 282.
(*Bodleian Library*)

yet been made,' he remarked, 'but the ladies are advancing in all
pursuits with such strides, or leaps and bounds, that it will, no
doubt, not be long before such a claim is formulated. ... Our
conscience is clear. We have always advocated a liberal extension
of the right of golfing to women.'[48]*

One of the chapters in the Badminton volume on golf was written by yet another member of the aristocracy, Lord Wellwood,
who sang the praises of the sport in language which points the
way forward to the 1920s rather than looks back to the 1860s:

Whether the philosopher's views of life are rose-coloured or cynical, he will
find ample material to interest him while he watches the game. We must
warn him, however, that if in the pursuit of his study he insists on accompanying matches, he may find that he proves an excuse for many a miss, and
possibly for some bad language. He must certainly be prepared for this.[49]

* The first picture of ladies playing golf appeared in *Punch* in July 1891. One of
the charges made against Mary Queen of Scots, however, had been that after the
death of Darnley she had been seen playing golf in the fields beside Seton.

We are on the edge of the world of P. G. Wodehouse:

The golfer's home bears traces of his noble infirmity. For the sake of domestic peace our advice is, that he should not be permitted to take a club home with him. But he is very sly, and has a trick of walking about with a cleek and pretending to use it as a walking stick; and whenever he finds a bit of turf he begins at once to exercise his destructive art. If he possesses a lawn he is sure to have a round of short holes upon it. If his girls have a tennis ground, he slily punches putting holes in the corners; and if he is driven from that, he practises wrist iron shots among the flower beds. Even within the house on a wet day he practises his swing in the lobby, and putts into tumblers laid upon their side upon the dining room floor. That is to say, he does all these things if his wife permits him, or if he can escape her eye. If she is a wise woman she will give in at once; the disease is incurable and ends only with life.[50]

It is clear that while a study of cricket or football could point to considerations of sociology or economics, a study of golf more easily raised basic issues of psychology. 'In some aspects,' Wellwood observed, 'golf is a selfish game in which each man fights with keenness and calculation for his own hand, grasping at every technicality and glorying in the misfortunes of his opponents.'[51] In sociological terms golf was accused during the 1890s of drawing middle-class men away from politics or religion, sometimes both, and Wellwood noted that 'there are districts of England where a person's moral character is considered of less importance than the ease of his swing'.[52]

Andrew Lang contributed the first chapter to the volume on golf, drawing deeply on Robert Chambers's *Golf, an Ancient and Royal Game* (1875). His chapter must have appealed greatly to Watson since it was packed with quotations from diaries, novels and poems, and ended with an ode by Dr Graham, written in 1848 just after the introduction of the gutta percha ball. The older balls had been expensive and unreliable. 'Hail, gutta percha, precious gum' was almost the least that the poet might have said – he did, in fact, say it – and as for the new gutta percha balls:

> Ye're keen and certain at a putt –
> Nae weet your sides e'er opens up –
> And though for years your ribs they whup,
> Ye'll never moutt a feather.[53]

'Mr Andrew Lang as seen by Mr Max Beerbohm' The Academy, 19 November 1898. (*Longman Archives*)

These verses are better than most of the verses quoted by Hedley Peek in the twenty-eighth volume of the Badminton series, which Watson expected to be the last, on *The Poetry of Sport*. Indeed, it is very disappointing after reading Peek's ambitious introduction to find virtually no poems in the anthology which deal with sport during the period when the Badminton Library was being compiled. The poets quoted included Chaucer, Spenser, Dryden, Pope, Wordsworth and even Shelley (an unlikely passage from *Oedipus Tyrannus*), but with the coming of the Victorians the Muse suddenly became silent. Of course, it may well have been reasons of copyright rather than of poetic taste which determined the absence of Victorian poems, some of which, early and middle as well as late Victorian, would make their way into a modern anthology. Yet, whatever the reason, the opportunity was missed, and to catch the poetry of the age we have to turn instead to the memorable lines of Francis Thompson:

> For the field is full of shades as I near the shadowy coast,
> And a ghostly batsman plays to the bowling of a ghost,
> And I look through my tears on a soundless clapping host,
> As the run-stealers flicker to and fro,
> To and fro.
> O my Hornby and my Barlow long ago.[54]

Many of the individual Badminton volumes include, like the volume on golf, odd quotations which are livelier and more evocative than most of the poems chosen by Peek. The volume on tennis presents as chapter headings ingeniously chosen quotations from Shakespeare, among them from *The Taming of the Shrew* — 'the poorest service is repaid with thanks'—while that on polo even quotes from an 'old classical Japanese poem'.[55] The volume on golf ends with a well-written chapter on the humour of golf by A. J. Balfour, a future prime minister.* Peek was much less playful and seems to have been somewhat daunted by his task of editing an anthology. 'There are about 1,800,000 books to be found in the British Museum,' he begins uneasily. 'How many of these contain verse in one form or another is a question that must be left for some future bibliomaniac to discover. We should roughly estimate that between a quarter and half a million, and

---

* The first golf picture in *Punch*, in 1889, was of 'The Rt. Hon. Arthur Golfour, M.P.' wearing checked knickerbockers, spats, a blazer and a tam-o'-shanter.

yet the works of at least a sixth of the older minor poets are not to be found there.' Such statistical preoccupation bodes ill, and the following sentences on the habits of poets are no more encouraging. 'It is, moreover, not safe to take for granted that it is easy to decide who is or is not likely to write on sporting subjects. The reader would hardly have expected to find a hunting song by Bishop Heber, yet one of the best in the collection was written by him. Verily the ways of poets are past understanding.'[56]

There was an even bigger inhibition. Peek found it necessary to give to his introduction the questioning subtitle 'Is sport a fitting subject for the Poet?' Was this his own or Watson's question? In either case, his own answer was a little too bluff: 'The reader who shall fail to discover in the following pages an answer in the affirmative to the question . . . must either have a mind warped by prejudice, or have never known the true passion of a sportsman.'[57]

Peek set against the 'true passion of a sportsman' the artificial passion of 'the society pet', and at this point in his argument was helped more by his ingenious illustrator than by his own eloquence. Once again the virtues of 'manliness' were extolled:

'*The Society pet*' The Poetry of Sport, *p. 4.* (*Bodleian Library*)

Want of manliness has been in many verse writers the one thing lacking to give their gift of true metrical expressiveness the power which alone can appeal to the healthy mind. A few hours daily spent in the hunting field, or in some other manly sport, would have enabled them to see how diseased and one-sided were many of their views of life.[58]

The 'healthy mind' was obviously as important to Peek as the healthy body, and 'the view of life' as important as the view from Badminton.[59]

We are reminded that *The Poetry of Sport* appeared in the year of Wilde's trial, in the middle of a decade when 'aesthetes' and 'athletes' seemed to be dividing the world between them, not only the university world, where the distinction had long been drawn, or the London society world, but the real world. *Fin de siècle* was a world-wide phenomenon. So, too, was sport. While the *Yellow Book* was drawing as much inspiration from France as from England, the 'yellow press' (as it was beginning to be called) was reporting battles for supremacy on the Manhattan Field, New York, between athletic clubs from New York and London. The Australians had captured the imagination of cricket enthusiasts, including many who never actually saw them play, since their eleven first visited England in 1878, and in 1891 Cecil Rhodes had guaranteed to cover the expenses of the first British rugby team to visit South Africa. In 1896 the first international soccer matches took place, with Germany, Austria – and Bohemia – taking part. Wilde's trial symbolised the victory of the 'manly' sportsmen over the inhabitants of international Bohemia, but already a few months earlier a writer in *Punch* had welcomed the fact that the country seemed to be receding from 'decadent excesses':

> Then here's for cricket in this year of Grace,
>   Fair-play all round, straight hitting and straight dealing
> In letters, morals, art, and commonplace,
>   Reversion unto type in deed and feeling.[60]

The *Badminton Magazine*, the successor of the Badminton Library, appeared just at this moment, appealing to exactly the same class of readers as the series of volumes on individual sports had done, and elaborating advice to readers while widening their experience.* Thus, it told women cyclists to be sensible about bicycles while always taking care:

Every new form of exercise is supposed to bring its attendant malady, and the solemn warnings as to the danger which women ran in playing lawn tennis still ring in our ears; but they never sounded its death-knell, neither will they destroy the bicycle. Yet some women cannot bicycle at all, and experience the effects immediately in great fatigue, pain in the limbs, and a general feeling of lassitude. These are warnings that should not be neglected. [61]

One feature of the *Badminton Magazine* which could not be found in the books was advertising, a booming art, if not yet an industry, in the 1890s. Here again, however, the advertisements in the *Magazine* belonged to a very special, non-vulgar world — Naldire's prize medal dog soap, which removed 'doggy smell'; Charles Lancaster's 'hammer, hammerless, ejector and reliable one trigger guns'; and Westley Richards's 'special double long range large game rifles specially adapted for South Africa'. (The author of the Badminton volume on *Big Game Shooting* (1894) had been 'a friend of Livingstone'.) The Bantam Bicycle was described as 'quite safe, easily learned, no step needed, very fast, very light, upright position, no chain'. [62] Such advertisements were a natural element in the sporting world as described in the articles. This was still the view from Badminton, with the very first article entitled 'A North Derbyshire Moor' having been written by the Marquis of Granby. There was also the first 'exotic' article — on tarpon fishing in Florida — while Hedley Peek maintained the sense of history with an article on old sporting prints which had much in common with his introduction to *The Poetry of Sport*:

When necessity drives me to London, my home may be said to be the British Museum, my haunts the auction rooms and old book or print shops. . . . My happiest hours are spent in the British Museum nursery, where they keep the national picture books. The Public knows little about this room, as the authorities, being afraid of having their pictures torn or damaged, guard the way with a policeman and a notice-board labelled 'Students only'. Fortunately, these restrictions only make it more comfortable for me. [63]

Peek's attitude to the British Museum and its 'nursery' is part of the whole pattern described in this essay, for, as Sir John Betjeman has written in *Treasures of the British Museum* (1971)

* The *Magazine* had a long life, but it soon ceased to be published by Longmans and it did not long survive the death of Watson in 1922.

the Museum is still called 'the House'. 'The hierarchical feeling
of a country house in the British Museum,' he adds, 'goes back to
the days when it *was* a country house – Montagu House – in the
flat fields of Bloomsbury, then outside London.'[64]

The *Badminton Magazine*, like the volumes in the series, was
profusely illustrated. Thomas Norton Longman was largely
responsible for the pictorial content of the volumes and while
many of the drawings were merely didactic, a number of them
had other pretensions – towards art and even, on occasion,
towards satire. The volume on *Hunting*, for example, included
illustrations by J. Sturgess and J. Charlton, with a colour-print
frontispiece called 'In the Badminton Country' (reproduced on
page 193). The frontispiece of *Riding* is a print 'after an oil
painting' of the Earl of Glamorgan – afterwards the eighth Duke
of Beaufort himself – 'at the age of ten years on a thoroughbred
filly (by Zealot-Myrtle)'. (The name of the artist is not given.)
Beaufort also figured in the frontispiece of *Driving* (reproduced
on page 192) – this time in the full dignity of age, with G. D. Giles
as the artist.

The satire, needless to say, comes in other places and, if it can
be called satire at all, is very gentle. Thus, the captions under the
G. D. Giles and F. Dadd sketches in the *Riding* volume include
'stirrup nowhere to be seen', 'decline to go quietly a dozen
yards', 'depend more or less on the horse's mouth' and (in the
Polo section of the same volume) 'A goal – "Whoo-Whoop" and
"Arcades Ambo: Ride him Off." ' It is perhaps more correct to
talk of humour rather than of satire. Thus, in *Driving* the captions
include 'left behind', 'an inextricable tangle' and 'the leaders took
fright'. A satirist could have made something of all these themes,
but his attitudes would have had to be very different from those
of the Duke of Beaufort.

Most remarkable of all the illustrations are those in the *Cycling*
volume, some of which were the work of Lord Bury himself.
'Waiting for the Pistol' and 'A Foolhardy Feat' take us far
beyond the advertisement illustrations of the Bantam Bicycle.
Watson was obviously delighted with the pictures in this volume,
and pointed out that:

When the Badminton Library was started and it was determined to have the
volumes illustrated many pictures might have been anticipated; but one
scene which nobody conceived it would ever be possible to draw was that
which now may be witnessed a dozen times in the course of a very brief

journey by road or rail – a party of men and ladies passing along a highway on bicycles, with a little concourse of golf players in the field behind them.[65]

To Watson the ladies were as surprising as the bicycles.

A large number of photographs were taken as the volumes were being prepared, but less than ten per cent were deemed suitable. It was not until the first decade of the twentieth century that instantaneous photography influenced sports illustration, ultimately to revolutionise it. Cricketers could then be shown taking brilliant catches and divers entering the water. Television was to complete the story, but that was long after the last Badminton volume had been published. The second Badminton

'*Till all at once'he saw the beast*
Come charging in his rear'
The Poetry of Sport, *p.* 350. (*Bodleian Library*)

'*A foolhardy feat*', *sketch by Bury*
Cycling, *p.* 18. (*Bodleian Library*)

'*Waiting for the pistol*', *sketch by Lord Bury* Cycling, *p.* 190. (*Bodleian Library*)

'*Then to the master him they brought*'
The Poetry of Sport, *p.* 370. (*Bodleian Library*)

volume on *Cricket* in 1920 had virtually nothing but photographs, including pictures of Ranjitsinhji scoring a four off the leg stump and Woolley taking a difficult catch in a match between Yorkshire, the champion county, and England. 'We make no claim to infallibility,' wrote Pelham Warner in his Preface, 'but in one respect, we fear no criticism, and that is in regard to the photographs.'[66] The claim was justified, for they could not be thought of simply as more refined replacements of Lucien Davis's engravings, said to be based on photographs, in the first *Cricket* volume. The only photograph then was one of A. E. Stoddart facing the camera, not even with a cricket bat in his hand.[67]

'*K. S. Ranjitsinhji*' Cricket (1920) *opp. p.* 251. (*Bodleian Library*)

'*The net is waiting ready*' The Poetry of Sport, *p.* 378. (*Bodleian Library*)

No photographs could have compensated for the admirable drawings (illustrator unidentified) in the *Mountaineering* volume of 1892, which had as its frontispiece an imposing photograph of Mont Blanc by W. F. Donkin. It also included a chapter on photography which pointed out (fairly) that while 'the tediousness of the old wet-plate process is now entirely superseded', nonetheless, 'some of the finest photographs of the Alps have been taken by this same process'.[68] The moral tone was very evident in this chapter. 'With those who carry a camera purely as a plaything,' C. T. Dent warned his readers, 'we have now no concern.'[69] Once again the *Cycling* volume was less inhibited.

Every third cyclist is a photographer. Perhaps photographer is too harsh a term to apply to these well-meaning persons; the justice of the case would be met in most instances by describing them as dabblers in photography. They are for the most part harmless, and operate chiefly on each other, and on their friends and relations.[70]

Only in the *Swimming* volume of 1893 is the absence of instantaneous photography entirely to be regretted. There are large numbers of photographs of swimmers in repose (including an alarming group of bathers under the Hoe at Plymouth on Christmas morning),[71] but the drawings by S. T. Dadd are obviously second-bests. Some of them are redeemed by their strangeness, like 'water polo – Scotch style', and one of them

'*Crack Climbers*' Mountaineering, p. 232. (*Bodleian Library*)

'*Mont Blanc*' Mountaineering: frontispiece. (*Bodleian Library*)

'Bathers under the Hoe, Plymouth – Christmas morning' Swimming, *p.* 161.
(Bodleian Library)

'Man Overboard – Rescue at Sea' is probably the most lurid in
the whole Badminton Library. Other claimants to this distinction
can be found in the *Wrestling* section of the *Fencing Boxing and
Wrestling* volume of 1889. 'The Hank' and 'The Hipe' would
hold their own in any anthology, as would 'Inside Lock or
Click, Cornwall and Devon'.[72]

'Swimming on the breast feet first'
Swimming, *p.* 134. *(Bodleian Library)*

'Inside Lock or Click, Cornwall and Devon'
Fencing *opp. p.* 200. *(Bodleian Library)*

'Recovering from the bottom of the water'
Swimming, *p.* 256. *(Bodleian Library)*

West-country style wrestling, like the illustration, pointed
back to the world of Blaine's *Encyclopaedia of Rural Sports* which
was a lively world before any of Badminton volumes were
published. 'Roguery and rowdyism' might have relegated some
ancient sports to the tavern and the fairground, yet as far as
wrestling was concerned the struggle had not yet been lost:

The Cornish man strikes with his heel or instep, using it somewhat as the
French athletes in the *savate*, endeavouring to cut away the other man's legs
from under him and thus render him an easier victim; while the Devonian
not only does this, but aims vicious blows with his toes at the shinbone of the
enemy, in the hope of inducing him through pain or faintness to yield the
day.[73]

'Lancashire wrestling' was the most 'barbarous' system of all: 'A
fair stand-up fight with the naked fists is the merest skim-milk, in
fact a perfect drawing-room entertainment in comparison.'[74] Not
surprisingly, the umpires had a rough time of it too. 'Wrestling
men are impulsive beings, and while a competition is proceeding
the judges have anything but a rosy time of it. Generally speaking,
when a close fall takes place, the two competitors crowd round
the umpires and clamour for a verdict.'[75]

Watson must have found it a fascinating editorial assignment
to combine in one volume Walter Armstrong's chapters on
wrestling – with many primitive passages of this kind – those of
E. B. Mitchell on boxing, and those of no less than three authors
on fencing, the most sophisticated of sports, including one by a
French *maître d'armes*, Camille Prévost. For good measure,
however, he appended a most learned bibliography of fencing by
Egerton Castle M.A., F.S.A.

What explanations, if any, would he have given for the changes
in sport in the twentieth century? He felt in 1895 that 'every
sport has been treated' in the Badminton Library so that no more
volumes should appear, yet he went on editing the *Badminton
Magazine* through a period of gradual transformation of the
sporting scene. The big changes were to come later during the
1920s and the biggest later still as a 'leisure industry', including
sport, began to appear in the 1960s, with increasingly massive
concentrations of power. This was not, however, the view from
Badminton, or for that matter, from Paternoster Row.

R. M. OGILVIE

Latin for yesterday

IT IS a commonplace that English education was for centuries dominated by the study of the classics,[1] in particular of Latin, but it is a commonplace whose full implications have not yet been by any means exhaustively explored. A great publishing house like Longmans can be seen to mirror some of the changing attitudes which society as a whole adopted towards this Latinate education. Few textbooks, for instance, can have had such an educational impact as Kennedy's *Latin Primer* and few were more nicely judged to suit the needs and demands of the age.

*

The Tudor grammar schools had been founded to teach Latin grammar, and thus by 1724 Latin had enjoyed two centuries of pre-eminence in schools. The methods laid down by Erasmus and by Colet still held sway. It was taught with the primary purpose of making boys fluent in speaking and writing the language, but in the process it gave them a detailed familiarity with a limited range of classical and post-classical authors. Boys began by learning the rudiments of Latin grammar. The standard textbook, authorised by Henry VIII in 1542 and confirmed by Elizabeth, had been compiled by William Lily, High Master of St Paul's with the assistance of Erasmus and Colet, then Dean of St Paul's. Colet wrote the accidence, Lily the syntax, including the rhymes 'Propria quae Maribus' and 'As in Praesenti', 'known and hated by so many generations of schoolboys'. As a grammar the textbook was written in Latin to expound the nature of Latin. As a specimen page shows, it was exceedingly thorough and gave comprehensive lists of examples and quotations. It presupposed that boys were going to master the whole intricacy of the language, as if it were a living tongue. The grammar was learnt by rote – declension by declension, conjugation by conjugation – but varied on occasion by practical sentences of a suitably improving kind. From there a boy passed to the two main branches of the subject, the study of particular books which had to be memorised by heart as well as construed, and the original composition, according to set rhetorical principles, of 'themes' on a range of appropriate topics. As tastes changed, the choice of authors might vary, but Terence, Ovid, Horace, Virgil, Seneca, Cicero and Livy would have found their places in most school curricula. The theme was a written essay, sometimes in the form of a letter, on some moralistic, but usually quite unreal, topic. It was an exercise which had survived more or less unchanged since

classical times when boys had been made to compose on such
subjects as 'why was Venus armed among the Spartans' or 'Cato
deliberates at Utica whether to commit suicide'.

As late as 1720 the system prevailed throughout the country.
The criticisms of the Puritans so far from reforming it had in
effect strengthened it, because they had concentrated their
attention on the *content* of some of the works taught rather than
on the philosophy behind the teaching. A good example of a
typical curriculum has recently been republished:[2] 'The present
method of the Congleton School', written by the Rev. Richard
Malbon, who was Headmaster of Congleton Grammar School
from 1709 to 1721. The school had ten classes, of which the top
four did some Greek and Hebrew in addition to Latin. Any boy
caught speaking English in class was beaten, prayers were said
daily between 6 a.m. and 7 a.m. in Latin, and the catechism was
learnt in Latin from an early age. In addition, every Thursday
afternoon the whole school disputed orally in Latin. Four sets of
boys were chosen to propose questions on all parts of school
learning ('but are determined by me aforehand to which part'),

A page from Lily's Grammar. (*Bodleian Library*)

and each set was primed with three questions. The opposing teams had to jot down both questions and answers and read them out. The material covered grammar, scansion, the Roman and Greek calendars, rhetoric and Roman or Greek antiquities. The victors gained an hour's play that afternoon and the losers got detention.

Friday was Repetition Day. Every boy had to repeat his set books by heart from the very beginning to the place he had now reached, and then had to ask someone else a sensible grammatical question about it. On Saturday all the learning-by-heart which had been done during each evening of the week was tested. And once a year there was a grand oral examination which determined the promotions for the following year.

Malbon lists the weekly time-table for his ten forms. A Monday (without the time devoted to Greek and Hebrew) reads as follows:

Head Class
Third lesson: they read Horace, Juvenal, Persius &c week for week.
Fourth lesson: A part out of the Latin grammar [i.e. Lily's Grammar] which this and the two next classes are employed to get by heart from the beginning without baulking any of it. And together with this they read Livy, Cicero's Orations, Sallust, Florus &c.

Second Class
Third lesson: Virgil mostly, Martial, Horace.
Fourth lesson: A part with the Head Class out of the Latin grammar and whatsoever else they read.

Third Class
The second and third classes read together the Roman historians or orators. And I generally dictate to them choice phrases which, first taken on loose papers, they afterwards transcribe into Paper Books.
Third lesson: Virgil, Martial.
Fourth lesson: Latin Grammar. These, as the first and second class, learn the whole Latin grammar, orthography, etymology &c.

Fourth Class
First lesson: Greek and Latin Grammar by heart week for week. They construe the Latin Grammar, give the meaning of each rule, parse and apply the example, make examples of their own to each rule in the syntax.
Second lesson: Read Erasmus, Phaedrus's Fables and make Latin week for week.
Fourth lesson: The Accidence, Propria, quae maribus &c., As in praesenti &c., Quae Genus &c. Sometimes syntaxis and prosodia.

Fifth Class
First lesson: Latin grammar by heart, giving the meaning of the rule, construing it and the example, and parsing and applying the example.
Second lesson: They translate Garrelson into Latin.
Third lesson: Ovid's Epistles or De Tristibus, Æsop's Fables, Tully's Epistles, week for week.
Fourth lesson: The Accidence.

Sixth Class
First lesson: Repeat Latin grammar without book, construe, parse and give the meaning of the rules.
Second lesson: They make Latin.
Third lesson: Corderius and Cato week for week.
Fourth lesson: Accidence.

Seventh Class
First lesson: Latin grammar as in the Sixth.
Second lesson: They make Latin.
Third lesson: Sententiæ Pueriles which are inconvenient. I have a project of a better if God gave me time and assistance.
Fourth lesson: Accidence by heart.

Eighth Class
First lesson: Propria, quæ maribus &c. As in præsenti &c. They first read it distinctly, then construe it and say it by heart.
Second lesson: Accidence by heart.
Third lesson: They read English.
Fourth lesson: Accidence as before.

Ninth Class
First lesson: The Accidence by heart. They also first read the lesson, then repeat it without book.
Second lesson: Read English.
Third lesson: Read English.
Fourth lesson: Accidence as before.

Lowest Class
First lesson: Read the Accidence.
Second lesson: Read English.
Third lesson: Read the Accidence.
Fourth lesson: Read English.

A very similar curriculum has newly come to light at Sir Andrew Judde's school at Tonbridge, dating from 1724.

In the scope of an essay it is possible only to select two of the consequences which followed from this singleminded pursuit of the mastery of Latin – on the development of English language itself and on the creative communication of ideas.

By the middle of the seventeenth century a need was being felt for 'ascertaining' English, that is producing a standardised, universal language which was more fitted to the capacities of the reader or the audience than to the ingenuity of the author. By 1700 such a language had been largely evolved – the language of Swift, Addison, Defoe – and it is possible to trace the process. It was largely inspired by the grammatical teaching of Latin.

Latin, as can be seen from the Congleton curriculum, was learned less from the imitation of particular authors than from phrasebooks and textbooks which tended to pick their vocabulary and their examples not just from a single author such as Cicero or Seneca but from the whole range of available and suitable Latin. The most celebrated were Lily's *Grammar* and Farnaby's *Phrases Oratoriae Elegantiores* which reached its tenth edition by 1664. As a result the Latin that was learnt in schools was a composite, amalgamated Latin, which derived its character not from a single classical author but from a single widely used schoolbook, and it was learned orally. The Latin that came to be accepted was determined by a common stock of phrases, idioms and words and by reference to certain generally acknowledged models.

When we look at the way in which English was actually taught in schools, we find that it was taught according to the same principles and on the same analogy as Latin. Indeed, it is difficult to think how else it could have been taught. One of the more famous educational programmes was that drawn up by Brinsley. Brinsley was a strict Puritan who had done first-hand research into educational problems and methods. One of his works, *A Consolation for our Grammar Schools* (1622), was designed 'more especially for all those of the inferior sort and all ruder countries and places: namely for Ireland, Wales, Virginia, with the Summer Ilands and for their more speedie attaining of our English tongue by the same labour'. It was chiefly concerned with a syllabus for Latin, and in particular for 'proprietie and puritie of speech' in Latin. It recommended two methods: phrasebooks (e.g. Farnaby) and imitation of patterns (e.g. Tullie and Erasmus). When Brinsley turned to English, of which he confessed that 'some great learned have much and long complained that there hath been little care', he advised the two same principal methods: (1) Dictionaries 'to make choice of those English words which best agree to the matter in hand'; (2) 'Adjoyne to these the books of such as have written the purest style in English in each faculty which they purpose to exercise themselves in.'

Now the application of this system was bound to mean that in the schools throughout the country a uniformity of speech and style began to be disseminated. Instead of individual and esoteric languages, largely invented by each writer, there came to be a common currency. And the more this developed, the more models there were who wrote in this currency and who could therefore be recommended for imitation. So Dryden recommends Waller, Beaumont and Fletcher as well as Bacon as worthy of study. One should certainly have, he writes, 'a conversation with those authors of our own who have written with the fewer faults in prose and verse'.

For poets and other creative writers this virtual bilingualism

Part of Brinsley's advice on compiling an English syllabus based on principles he recommended for a Latin syllabus in A Consolation for our Grammar Schools, 1622. (*British Museum*)

76   *A Consolation*

Maifter *Vdals* Grammar. Or in ſtead of *Martinius*, Maifter *Vdals* Grammar it ſelfe, which I finde to be farre more eaſie for the learner, and much ſooner gotten, for the vſe of it, and alſo may be readily deliuered and vttered in Latine, at leaſt by comparing with *Martinius*.

Lexicon Baxtorphius. For the beſt Lexicon or Dictionarie, *Baxtorphius* his Epitome for continuall vſe : and alſo his *Theſaurus* for more exquiſite knowledge : or,

For giuing the Hebrue words to the Latine; *Lexicon Latino-Hebraicum*, in the end of the Epitome of *Pagnine* by *Raphalengius*.

For helpe for conſtruing, and ſo reading priuately, and knowing the *Radices*.

The Interlineal Bible, by *Arias Montanus*.

Teſſanus. For the *Pſalmes*, *Toſſanus* may affoord ſome helpe.

Engliſh.

For our owne tongue to grow in proprietie and puritie. Concerning our owne language, whereas ſome great learned, haue much and long complained, that in moſt Schooles there hath bene litle care, to teach Scholars to expreſſe their mindes readily in proprietie and puritie of ſpeech, ſo to helpe to adorne our owne tongue; whereof wee haue continuall practiſe, to the end that they may grow herein with the Latine and other learned tongues, God hath prouided theſe helpes.

1. Grãmatical tranſlations for all the firſt beginners. 1. The vſe of the grammaticall tranſlations (hauing to that end, both proprietie and alſo varietie of words and phraſe to expreſſe the minde) may be a good entrance for the yonger ſort.

2. Other tranſlations. 2. After them, all the other tranſlations, vſed onely in ſuch ſort, as hath bene and ſhall be further ſhewed in the Grammar ſchoole; ſo to aſcend to thoſe who haue written moſt exquiſitely in that kinde of Tranſlation.

3. Dicti.

for our Grammar Schooles.   77

3. Dictionaries, where fit words are wanting, to make choiſe of thoſe Engliſh words in them which beſt agree to the matter in hand. 3. Dictionaries.

4. Adioyne to theſe, for them who would grow to more exquiſite perfection, the bookes of ſuch as haue written the pureſt ſtyle in Engliſh in each faculty, which they purpoſe to exerciſe themſelues in. 4. Beſt authors in each kinde for Engliſh.

For ſtrangers, who vnderſtand the Latine tongue, at leaſt in ſome ſort, and would learne our tongue themſelues, or would teach it vnto others publiquely or priuately, beſides the former helpes for reading Engliſh. For ſtrangers.

1. The Engliſh Grammar, called *Grammatica Anglicana*, a little Epitome written according to the rules of Art, by *P. Gr.* printed at *Cambridge Anno* 1594. The Engliſh Grammar.

2. *Logonomia Anglica*, by Maifter *Gill* Schoole-maiſter of *Paules*. Logonomia Anglica.

3. Tranſlations, firſt grammaticall; which leade the Scholar directly to learne our tongue; after other tranſlations, and ſo the beſt Engliſh Authors and Dictionaries as before. Tranſlations.

Rhetoricke.

For Rhetoricke, ſo farre as ſhall be neceſſary for the Grammar-ſchoole. For Tropes and Figures.

1. For Tropes and Figures of Rhetoricke, and ſo for other figures of Grammar, Maifter *Farnabees* Tropes and figures, ſo ſhortly comprized in verſe, as that they may be moſt eaſily gotten in a very little time, and ſo likewiſe kept in memorie, to ſerue for euery good vſe. Maiſter Farnabees tropes and figures.

2. For a more full vnderſtanding of that little booke, and of all other matters belonging to Rhetoricke, as for a methodicall handling, and ſhort comprizing of the whole Art, by precepts, illuſtrations by examples, and the like. For a more methodicall tractate, M. Butlers Rhetoricke.

L 3   Maiſter

had other attractive possibilities. The educated English, indeed European, world of the early eighteenth century shared a common classical culture which had been forged as a result of this rigorously Latin education at school and at the university. It was not, as Congleton shows, a very critical or wide-ranging education, but it did at least ensure that at the end of his schooldays a boy knew a limited range of poetry by heart in a way which he could never forget for the rest of his life. Nor, of course, did this study of the classics end with school or university. Latin literature, in the origin and in translation, remained favourite reading down to Victorian times. Thomas Burnet wrote to George Duckett on 1 June 1716: 'I am now at my leisure hours reading Horace with some diligence and find the world was just the same then that it continues to be now.' A modern generation cannot hope to know its classics as Burnet knew them but imaginative scholarship can explain to a twentieth-century reader something of what he is missing. It cannot, of course, supply the magic or the thrill of spontaneous recognition.

Take, for instance, the end of the *Epistle to Burlington on the Use of Riches*, published in 1731. The theme, a rather shallow one, is architectural taste, which Pope, true to his aim of writing 'a system of ethics in the Horatian way' (Pope to Swift, 28 November 1729) handles by a series of examples of bad taste which contain indirect hints about the nature of good taste.[3] Its climax is the portrait of an extravagant builder dubbed Timon, clearly a composite portrait and not a specific delineation, as was thought soon after and often since, of Lord Chandos and his mansion near Edgware called Canons. It ends with a contrasting picture of restrained, moderate and sensible man – Burlington himself. Pope handles his theme indirectly, assuming an easy informality and intimacy between himself as poet and Burlington. He relies on ironical anecdotes, told in a mixture of colloquial and parodying language. He does not flog his theme by sermonising: he allows it to emerge as from an intimate and well-informed conversation. His success lies precisely in being Horatian.

The finale of the epistle is justly famous (lines 173ff). Here Pope develops two different themes: (1) all such absurd architectural follies will soon be overgrown and forgotten; (2) the wise use of land, such as Burlington himself makes, will re-establish the proper harmony between man and nature. In this double message lies the philosophical point of the *Epistle*, such as it is.

Another age shall see the golden Ear
Imbrown the Slope, and nod on the Parterre,
Deep Harvests bury all his pride has plann'd,
And laughing Ceres re-assume the land.
    Who then shall grace, or who improve the Soil?
Who plants like Bathurst, or who builds like Boyle.
'Tis Use alone that sanctifies Expence,
And Splendour borrows all her rays from Sense.
    His Father's Acres who enjoys in peace,
Or make his Neighbours glad, if he encrease;
Whose chearful Tenants bless their yearly toil,
Yet to their Lord owe more than to the soil;
Whose ample Lawns are not asham'd to feed
The milky heifer and deserving steed;
Whose rising Forests, not for pride or show,
But future Buildings, future Navies grow:
Let his plantations stretch from down to down,
First shade a Country, and then raise a Town.
    You too proceed! make falling Arts your care,
Erect new wonders, and the old repair,
Jones and Palladio to themselves restore,
And be whate'er Vitruvius was before:
Proud to accomplish what such hands design'd,
Bid Harbors open, public Ways extend,
Bid Temples, worthier of the God, ascend;
Bid the broad Arch the dang'rous Flood contain,
The Mole projected break the roaring Main;
Back to his bounds their subject Sea command,
And roll obedient Rivers thro' the Land;
These Honours, Peace to happy Britain brings,
These are Imperial Works, and worthy Kings.

What is of interest is to see how Pope makes both these points indirectly, using classical association as his means of communication. The analysis of poetical borrowings is complex. At a primary level a poet borrows, adapts or translates isolated phrases from his predecessors because they catch his fancy in some way, conscious or unconscious. A second, more elaborate technique is to imitate a whole passage, often varying the actual language, in order that the reader may recognise the original and admire its transformation into its new dress. This is what Pope does so frequently with Virgilian echoes in the mock heroics of the *Rape of the Lock* and the *Dunciad*. Here the poet is imitating passages in such a way that the reader is expected to retain in his mind the associations of the original context.

His first point, that Timon's follies will soon be overgrown, combines a regular Latin commonplace with a further classical idea that such a moment will be indeed a Golden Age – 'another *age* shall see the *golden* Ear'. To have expatiated on the approach of such a blessed time could have been banal, if not ludicrous. Instead he takes his readers' minds back to Virgil. 'Laughing Ceres' recalls a pleasing ambiguity of Latin which uses *laetus* to mean both 'glad or joyful' and 'fertile'. The opening of Virgil's *Georgics* is 'quid faciat laetas segetes?' ('what makes the "laughing" crops?'). But it is 'imbrown', a striking and novel word, which pushes the association home. It is used to evoke the Latin *flavescere*, 'to grow golden-brown', which occurs in a celebrated passage of *Eclogue 4* where Virgil heralds the new Golden Age in which Troy and the other great cities will be obliterated and 'the plain will gradually grow brown with the soft ear' (28: *molli paulatim flavescet campus arista*). Pope does not have to detail his Golden Age: a reference to *Eclogue 4* will do it for him.

His second point, that one should use one's gifts sensibly because this is to reassert the harmony of man and nature, is a piece of characteristically homespun philosophy. Its moral (' 'Tis Use alone that sanctifies Expence,/And Splendour borrows all her rags from Sense') in fact is borrowed very closely from Horace (*Odes*, 2.2.1–4)

> Nullus argento color est avaris
> Abdito terris, inimice lamnae
> Crispe Sallusti, nisi temperato
>   Splendeat usu.

(Silver has no colour hidden in the greedy earth, until it grow bright with moderate use.)

Pope's main purpose, however, is to promote the picture of the ideal life in the country, where wealth does not prevent man from living at one with nature and with his environment. It is a timeless dream, a dream whose validity remains the same today as two thousand years ago. Pope establishes this by stressing his essential oneness with the dreams of Horace. He opens his account of the ideal life by identifying himself with Horace, his world with the Horatian world. 'His Father's Acres who enjoys in peace' is modelled on the opening of Horace's second *Epode*

> Beatus ille qui procul negotiis
> Paterna rura bobus exercet suis.

(Happy is the man who, far from troubles, works his father's fields
with his own cattle.)

But the picture itself of a satisfyingly productive countryside
owes everything to Virgil's *Georgics* in which Virgil set out to
show how the cooperation of man and nature in the different
branches of farming could result in happiness and prosperity. How
many people today reading lines 183-6 would feel the association?

> Whose cheerful tenants bless their yearly toil,
> Yet to their Lord owe more than to the soil,
> Whose ample Lawns are not asham'd to feed
> The milky heifer and deserving steed.

Why 'deserving'? Why 'milky'? These are not just poetic adjec-
tives, but are signposts to guide the reader to *Georgics* 2.513ff,
where the poet praises the blessings of the simple farmer's life.

> Agricola incurvo terram dimovit aratro:
> hic anni labor, hinc patriam parvosque penates
> sustinet, hinc armenta boum meritosque iuvencos.
>
> . . .
>
> casta pudicitiam servat domus, ubera vaccae
> lactea demittunt, pinguesque in gramine laeto
> inter se adversis luctantur cornibus haedi.

(The farmer cleaved the ground with his curved plough. Here is his
year's toil: from here he sustains his country and his humble home, the
herds of cattle and the deserving steers. . . . His home remains chaste
and innocent; *milky* udders hang from his cows and in the rich grass his
fat goats butt each other with their horns.)

Once again, Virgil has enabled Pope to convey much more than
he could ever have brought himself actually to say.

✳

This was the moment when Thomas Longman established
himself as a publisher. Significantly one of his first ventures was
Ainsworth's *Latin Dictionary* (1736).[4] Another, in collaboration
with S. Buckley, was to acquire by purchase from the patentees
the Royal grant and privilege of printing Lily's *Latin Grammar*.
In 1736 they issued a new edition of Lily's *Rules*, bearing the
imprint 'S. Buckley and T. Longman, Printers to the King's most
Excellent Majesty in Latin, Greek and Hebrew'. They stated in

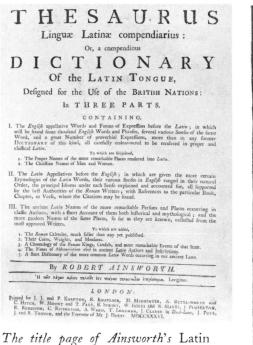

The title page of Ainsworth's Latin Dictionary, 1736. (*Longman Archives*)

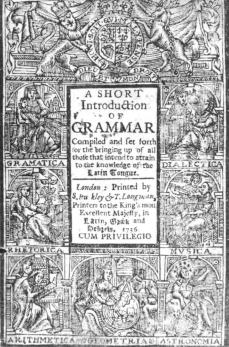

The title page of Lily's Latin Grammar, 1736 edition. (*Longman Archives*)

The title page of Lily's Rules, 1736 edition. (*Longman Archives*)

The Advertisement for an improved edition of Lily's Grammar, 1736. (*Longman Archives*)

Advertisement.

S. Buckley and T. Longman having purchased of the Family of the Nortons, the old Patentees, the Royal Grant and Privilege of printing Lily's Grammar, which, from the Time it was compiled, has by our several Kings and Queens successively been ordered *generally to be used in Schools*; have thought it their Duty and Interest to print an Edition of it, that has been revised and improved by a skilful Hand as much as the Nature of the Work would well admit: Hoping it will have the Approbation and Encouragement of those Gentlemen, who have the Care and Instruction of Youth.

At the same Time they have not the least Intention to suppress this *Common Lily's Grammar*, in the Form it now stands, and to substitute or impose the *improved Edition* in the Room of it; but will still keep this, as well as the other in Sale, leaving it to every Gentleman of the Profession to make use of either of them, as he shall think fit.

their 'Advertisement' to that edition that they 'thought it their Duty and Interest to print an Edition of it, that has been revised and improved by a skilful Hand as much as the Nature of the Work would well admit: Hoping it will have the Approbation and Encouragement of those Gentlemen, who have the Care and Instruction of Youth.'

It is interesting that Longman should have been both so quick to see the commercial value of such educational publishing and also to have recognised that, even with Latin, time does not stay still. Another of the earliest Longman books was the *Treatise of the Figures, at the end of the Rules of Construction in Latin Grammar ... for the help of the weaker sort in the Grammar Schools* (S. Buckley and T. Longman, 1738), written, significantly by John Stockwood, some time School-Master of Tonbridge. The old Renaissance ideal of Latin as a living, spoken language was being undermined. Latin no longer had a peculiar monopoly of the truth; it was long the only sure channel 'through which all useful becoming learning did and should run'.

The change can be seen most clearly in the controversy between Thomas Ruddiman, the great Scottish grammarian and publisher, and John Clarke, the schoolmaster of Hull, who was deeply influenced by Locke's ideas.[5] In 1714 Ruddiman had published a short *Rudiments of the Latin Tongue* which he expanded into the systematic *Grammaticae Latinae Institutiones* (2 vols, 1725, II, 1731). Ruddiman, of course, used Lily's *Rules*, but his work is distinguished by its original and exhaustive scholarship. Ruddiman had read and excerpted almost all classical and post-classical literature and he set down every rule and every abnormality that his acutely critical mind detected. It was a grammar in the old-fashioned sense and, in the Preface to the *Rudiments*, he explicitly states his conviction that the thorough study of Latin grammar will also help children to speak and write English better. But the *Institutiones* was a huge work and even the *Rudiments* was very far from rudimentary or brief.

The excellence and reliability of his work ensured it a long life in Scottish education, but it was quickly challenged by Clarke, who argued that the purpose of a classical education was to enable people to read rather than to speak Latin and that therefore the formal learning of grammar should be simplified to the bare minimum necessary to enable boys to read classical texts for themselves. In his *New Grammar of the Latin Tongue* (1733)

Clarke argued that many of the finer points of grammar and syntax could be picked up incidentally in the course of reading. Ruddiman felt, and argued, passionately that this was to dilute the classics. In two essays, *A Dissertation upon the Way of Teaching the Latin Tongue* (1733) and *Audi Alteram Partem* (1756), he endeavoured to uphold the traditional, rigorous training, but he was swimming against the tide. Latin had already become an accomplishment for gentlemen rather than a practical necessity. As Burnet wrote in the *History of his Own Time* (1734), 'Those who are bred to the Profession in Literature, must have the Latin correctly; and for that the Rules of Grammar are necessary: but these are not at all requisite to those who need only so much Latin, as thoroughly to understand and delight in the Roman Authors and Poets' (p. 651). The Latin language and the study of Roman antiquity have become a sign of politeness, the veneer of culture. The Grand Tour is as characteristic of the age as the rash of Horatian quotations in Parliament. Sir Robert Walpole, defending himself in February 1741 on the preliminary notice of a Motion for addressing the King for his removal, urged that he be allowed a fair hearing and concluded by laying his hand on his breast and declaring *nil conscire sibi nulli pallescere culpae*: whereupon Pulteney cried out 'your Latin is as bad as your logic: *Nulla pallescere culpa*'. Old Carteron, it will be recalled, had inscribed a line of Horace above the doorway of Fullcircle.

Three quotations, spread over a century, sufficiently illustrate this changed situation. Chesterfield wrote in 1748: 'Upon the whole, remember that learning (I mean Greek and Roman learning) is a most useful and necessary ornament, which it's shameful not to be master of. . . . Wear your learning, like your watch, in a private pocket: and do not pull it out and strike it, merely to show that you have one.' Jane Austen, writing in 1815 to the Rev. J. S. Clarke, librarian to the Prince Regent, who had invited her 'to delineate in some future work the habits of life . . . of a clergyman', replied 'I am quite honoured by your thinking me capable of drawing such a clergyman as you gave me the sketch of . . . But I assure you I am *not*. Such a man's conversation must . . . be abundant in quotation and allusions which a woman . . . like me . . . would be totally without the power of giving. A classical education . . . appears to me quite indispensable.' Leslie Stephen quotes an Eton Master of the 1840s: 'If you do not take more pains, how can you ever expect to write

good longs and shorts [Latin elegiac verse]? If you do not write
good longs and shorts, how can you ever be a man of taste? If you
are not a man of taste, how can you ever be of use in the world?'

Latin verse composition had always had a place in a classical
education and many of the finest poets, such as George Buchanan
and Abraham Cowley, chose to write in Latin in preference to the
vernacular. The eighteenth century, however, esteemed the
facility for composing in Latin verse as an elegant accomplishment. *Musae Etonenses*, an anthology of some of the finer pieces
composed in a variety of Greek and Latin metres by Etonians,
was published in 1755. Since boys in the sixth form were
expected to write twenty-six lines of elegiac verse and at least six
Horatian stanzas on original themes (not translation) every week,
it is not surprising that the quality of much of the volume is
excellent. Quite apart from verbal dexterity, there is much wit and
much sensitivity in the writing. For the composition of Latin
verse, like the writing of French sonnets, demands clarity and
concision. Some eighteenth-century Latin poems, such as John
Jortin's 'Qualis per nemorum' or Vincent Bourne's 'Qua iuxta
Alberi' have originality and merit of a high order.[6] Other schools
followed the same pattern. M. L. Clarke quotes impressive
evidence for verse composition at Harrow, Winchester and
Westminster, but the same was true at smaller grammar schools.[7]
At Tonbridge, for instance, where Jane Austen's father was
assistant master, boys were expected to compose thirty elegiacs
each week on a 'topical' subject (for example, 'The defeat of the
Notorious Pretender') chosen by the Headmaster, who defended
the practice by claiming that it taught boys to express themselves
with grace and fluency. Longman took over the publication of
Musarum Anglicarum Analecta, edited by M. Maittaire (it appears
as early as the catalogue of 1726).[8]

These educational changes did not only mean that knowledge
of Latin became less exact and less universal: they also had wider,
critical effects on English itself. Ruddiman, writing in 1714, had
defended standards of criticism which were based on 'correct-
ness'. His literary judgments were founded on rigorous verbal
criteria derived ultimately from Aristotle. He could assert with
authority whether a word was appropriate or not, whether an
imitation was successful or not. For such things admitted of
demonstrative proof. But Ruddiman's younger contemporaries
were abandoning a *decorum* of Rules in favour of a *decorum* of

Taste (to use Professor Douglas Duncan's phrase) and approached literature from a much more aesthetic and intuitive angle. Professor Duncan has detailed how this difference was highlighted by the controversy (1741–45) between Ruddiman and William Benson, Auditor of the Exchequer, over the relative merits of Buchanan's and Johnston's Latin versions of the *Psalms*. Benson's criticism was based entirely on feeling – 'What a strength of Language! What a Harmony of Numbers! ... What a Pathos!' – Ruddiman's on minute, grammatical analysis. For writers and critics of Ruddiman's generation there were acceptable canons based on classical certainties. How did one judge what was the appropriate language and style for a heroic (or mock heroic poem)? It had clearly to be elevated, to recall, by implication, the tone of Virgil and Lucan. A more Latinate vocabulary and a more Latinate syntax (involving, amongst other things, the use of inversion, which is unnatural in English that does not distinguish subjects and objects by case) are obviously suitable. So then:

> Not with more glories, in the ethereal plain
> The sun first rises o'er the purpled main
> Than, issuing forth, the rival of his beams
> Launch'd on the bosom of the silver Thames.
> (Pope, *Rape of the Lock*, Canto II, 1–4)

With the overthrow of the authority of Rules, Taste took the place of Rules as the critical tool for appreciating poetry and literature but, if Taste is to be any more than subjective, self-indulgent impression, there needs to be some means of knowing what makes good or bad taste.[9] Benson's protestations were as unfounded and naïve as Boswell's judgment of Young's *Night Thoughts*.

There is a power of the Pathetick beyond almost any example that I have seen. He who does not feel his nerves shaken, and his heart pierced by many passages in this extraordinary work, particularly by that most affecting one which describes the gradual torment suffered by the contemplation of an object of affectionate attachment visibly and certainly decaying into dissolution, must be of a hard and obstinate frame.

To avoid naïvety, some measure of Johnsonian substance and common sense was needed, and the relatively closed society and closed education of the late eighteenth century ensured that there was an adequate 'common use' of language and ideas to which appeal could be made. It derived its currency partly from formal conversation and partly from the proliferation of letter writing, but it was sufficiently consistent and evident for critics to resort to its aid. Thus Goldsmith, seeking to explain how to avoid bad writing, that 'deviation from propriety owing to the erroneous judgment of the writer', stressed the need to cultivate taste by observation and comparison. Taste is a 'natural talent', but through careful and persistent education it can be trained up into a mature and dependable organ. In other words, the taste of a single person can be taught to conform with the prevailing taste of society; in literary as well as in moral and other matters. No time was spent in arguing why the taste of society should be good: it was merely stated that it is. As Chesterfield so self-confidently asserted, 'a man of fashion takes great care to speak very correctly and to pronounce properly, that is, according to the usage of the best companies'.

In Boswell's *Life* Johnson is recorded as giving his view in 1778 on the quality of English preaching. 'All the latter preachers have a good style. Indeed, nobody now talks much of style: everybody composes pretty well. There are no such inharmonious periods as there were a hundred years ago.' Taste was an understood thing. Morals, literature, social behaviour, were all of a piece with the composition of Latin verse. There was a recognised technique and there were generally approved models of good taste. 'If you do not write good longs and shorts, how can you ever be a man of taste?'

Yet such an appeal to social taste, replacing the appeal of classical authority, was valid only as long as society was relatively uniform and cohesive, and by the beginning of the nineteenth century these conditions no longer held. The industrial revolution introduced a disturbing mobility of class and culture which destroyed the singularity of taste. It is no accident that Wordsworth utterly repudiated it.

The profound and the exquisite in feeling, the lofty and universal in thought and imagination: or, in ordinary language, the pathetic and sublime, are neither of them, accurately speaking, objects of a faculty which could ever without a sinking in the spirit of Nations have been designated by the metaphor – *Taste*.

✳

Many pressures conspired to produce further changes in the character of classical education. Not least of them was the reawakened interest in Greece and Greek studies, encouraged by the increasing accessibility of the eastern Mediterranean and by the popular enthusiasm symbolised by Byron's involvement in the War of Independence. The great classical teachers of the nineteenth century, Arnold of Rugby, Samuel Butler and B. H. Kennedy, successive headmasters of Shrewsbury, were all predominantly Greek rather than Latin scholars. As a result, Greek flourished. Plato, Thucydides, Homer and the tragedians, instead of Horace and Virgil, became the authors who had the greatest influence on the imagination and thought of schoolboys.

But there were far-reaching changes also in Latin. The impetus was given by the widespread feeling that education should be more relevant and more practical. Britain could no longer afford to breed gentlemen whose chief pursuit throughout their schooldays had been the sophisticated manufacture of Latin verse. The most articulate critic was Sydney Smith, who claimed that he had written more than ten thousand verses at Winchester. Smith was, of course, along with Lord Jeffrey and Francis Horner, one of the instigators of the *Edinburgh Review* which Longmans were later to publish,[*] and it is of note that Longmans were also to be the publishers of some of the most successful books, such as Kennedy's grammar, to meet the challenge which Smith posed.

Sydney Smith's essay was in the form of a review of R. L. Edgeworth's *Essays on Professional Education* (1809). Edgeworth argued that 'our great schools . . . devote too large a portion of time to Latin and Greek'. In particular he attacked verse composition:

It is not requisite that every man should make Latin or Greek verses; therefore a knowledge of prosody beyond the structure of hexameter and pentameter verses is as worthless an acquisition as any which folly or fashion has introduced among the higher classes of mankind. It must indeed be acknowledged that there are some rare exceptions; but even party prejudice would allow that the persons alluded to must have risen to eminence though they had never written sapphics or iambics.

Sydney Smith diversified the case. Too much attention was paid to learned minutiae, to the difficulties of the languages rather than the difficulties of the subject matter. He elaborated the attack on the place which verse composition had in the syllabus.

It would be of use that we should go on till fifty years of age making Latin verses, if the price of a whole life were not too much to pay for it.

[*] John Clive, '*The Edinburgh Review:* the life and death of a periodical' pp. 113 ff.

The prodigious honour in which Latin verses are held is surely the most absurd of all absurd distinctions. You rest all reputation upon doing that which is a natural gift and which no labour can attain.

The bias given to men's minds is so strong that it is no uncommon thing to meet with Englishmen, whom, but for their grey hairs and wrinkles, we might easily mistake for school-boys. Their talk is of Latin verses; and it is quite clear, if men's ages are to be dated from the state of their mental progress, that such men are eighteen years of age, and not a day older.

Smith's summary is concise and damning:

The present state of classical education cultivates the imagination a great deal too much, and other habits of mind a great deal too little; and trains up many young men in a style of elegant imbecility, utterly unworthy of the talents with which nature has endowed them.

These contributions should be taken into account in assessing the significance of the changes during the first half of the nineteenth century: they also pointed the way to the future. Apart from the revival of Greek, the main emphasis was to be put on the study of the classics as a 'discipline' to make boys think. Latin was no longer so much a medium of communication as it had been in 1700, nor a pleasing sign of breeding, taste and education, as it had been in 1770. It became the means of training the mind. Thomas Arnold, who shared all Sydney Smith's suspicions of verse compositions and was not particularly good at them himself, came increasingly, according to Dean Stanley, to the 'conviction of their use as a mental discipline'. 'Latin and Greek,' Sydney Smith wrote 'are useful as they inure children to intellectual difficulties, and make the life of a young student what it ought to be, a life of considerable labour.' Kennedy praised his predecessor at Shrewsbury, Dr Butler, for having established 'an emulative system in whose talent and industry always gained their just recognition and reward in good examinations'. In 1843 J. Conington, a schoolboy at Rugby, said of Cambridge classics that they 'impart a system of education valuable not so much for itself as for the excellent discipline which prepares the mind'. The whole attitude was pithily put by Matthew Arnold in *Friendship's Garland* (1871): 'But you surely don't need me to tell you, Arminius, that it is rather in training and bracing the mind for future acquisition – a course of mental gymnastics we call it – than in teaching any set thing, that the classical curriculum is so valuable.'

New approaches to composition and to grammar mark the path of the reformers. In the past composition had been almost entirely original, on set themes such as 'Virtue is a Good Thing', which Arnold so much derided. When, however, the classical tripos was established at Cambridge in 1822, translation into Greek and Latin prose and verse was prescribed. Butler introduced translation of specified passages of English into Latin or Greek at Shrewsbury and Arnold did the same at Rugby, selecting them not 'at random from the *Spectator* or other such works [but] ... extracts, remarkable in themselves from such English and foreign authors as he most admired so as indelibly to impress on the minds of his pupils some of the most striking names and passages in modern literature'. Arnold maintained that for a boy to have to express an idea in an alien language was the most effective way of clarifying for himself what he really did think. Original composition enables one to avoid facing that difficulty: it is always possible to shirk hard thought by an elegantly superficial epigram. Translation admits of no escape or circumvention.

Arnold's philosophy was very soundly grounded in psychology, and although original composition still kept its hold on many schools in the face of the challenge of set translation, a fashion had been set. Evidence presented to the Public Schools Commission of 1861 shows the pull of old methods, and even at Rugby and Shrewsbury there was a surprising amount of 'theme' work; yet at Tonbridge in 1858, for example, boys were being set passages from Macaulay's *History of England* for translation into Latin week by week. In 1855 B. H. Kennedy published his *Curriculum Stili Latini*, material for translating into Latin prose, which was revised and republished in 1862.

If Latin was to be taught for its therapeutic value and not as a language with all the ramifications and idiosyncrasies of a highly complex living organism, it was more than ever necessary to follow Samuel Clarke's example of reducing it to the bare essentials and presenting it in the most easily assimilable form. Many of its unique abnormalities had to be overlooked and the main structure set out through the medium of English (and not, as hitherto, in Latin). There was an added incentive to the simplification of Latin grammar. Scholars both in Britain and on the Continent were interesting themselves increasingly in philology and comparative grammar. In particular, great strides were made in the investigation of Greek by Porson, Dobree and other Cambridge scholars in Britain, while in Germany the work of Hermann and his pupils set the pattern for the exhaustive and meticulous research into linguistics which for good and ill was to characterise German scholarship for the rest of the century. The study of other languages, stimulated from time to time by spectacular successes such as Champollion's decipherment of Egyptian hieroglyphs or the Rosetta stone, tended to encourage speculation about the first principles of grammar.

Latin, it was generally agreed, afforded the best foundation.

To go through the grammar of one language thoroughly is of great use for the mastery of every other grammar; because there obtains, through all languages, a certain analogy to each other in their grammatical construction. Latin and Greek have now mixed themselves etymologically with all the languages of modern Europe – and with none more than our own. . . . The two ancient languages are as mere inventions – as pieces of mechanism incomparably more beautiful than any of the modern languages of Europe; their mode of signifying time and case, by terminations, instead of auxiliary verbs and particles, would of itself stamp their superiority. . . . Compared to them, merely as vehicles of thought and passion, all modern languages are dull, ill-contrived and barbarous.

So Sydney Smith. And it was to meet this need that B. H. Kennedy, wrote his many books. Before *Curriculum Stili Latini* and shortly after he became Headmaster of Shrewsbury, he compiled, first of all, a *Latin Syntax* (1838) and then a *Progressive Latin Grammar* (1844). These were the forerunners of his *Public School Latin Primer*, which, after a further full-scale revision, became – and still remains – the standard Latin grammar in English education. His *Revised* and the *Shorter Latin Primers* followed in 1888. A specimen page of Kennedy, when compared with a corresponding passage of Lily, reveals the merits of the new approach – clear presentation, simple rules, intelligible explanations in English, and a lack of superfluous examples.

Curiously enough, Kennedy's approach to the classics was far more direct and vital than Lily's.[10] After all, grammar and syntax were things which he expected to be thoroughly assimilated in the lower forms. In the Upper School his concern was that the classics should live again for the boys. The impression that he made on his pupils was much the same as Dr Arnold's. One of them, later to be a distinguished scholar in his own right (Professor Heitland), describes a lesson taken by Kennedy: 'He is not merely translating Demosthenes: he is Demosthenes speaking extempore in English.' 'Think in Latin, think in Greek' was Kennedy's constant cry. As another of his pupils, James Fraser, wrote: 'I learned how to read an ancient author.' The foundations of this advanced skill depended, Kennedy realised, on the logical understanding of the language, and it was this that he set out to simplify and inculcate. His success can be shown by the fact that the *Primer*, one of Longman's great successes, still sells 4,000 copies a year.

Left: the title-page of the eighth edition of Kennedy's Revised Latin Primer, 1909. *It subsequently has gone into numerous editions.*

Right: a page from Kennedy's Public School Latin Primer, *first published in* 1866. *Compare the treatment with that of a similar passage from* Lily's Grammar *on p.* 222.

The Revised

LATIN PRIMER

BY

BENJAMIN HALL KENNEDY, D.D.

FORMERLY FELLOW OF ST. JOHN'S COLLEGE, CAMBRIDGE
REGIUS PROFESSOR OF GREEK
AND CANON OF ELY

EIGHTH EDITION

LONGMANS, GREEN, AND CO.
39 PATERNOSTER ROW, LONDON
NEW YORK, BOMBAY, AND CALCUTTA
1909

All rights reserved

The businesslike and practical approach to Latin cannot be divorced from one other phenomenon of the early nineteenth century – competitive written examinations. These had been instituted at Oxford by the Statutes of 1800 and were popularised at Cambridge with the new Tripos of 1824. They were subsequently accepted as the best form of selection for every level of life, from schools (oral examinations were replaced by written ones at Tonbridge in the 1830s, apparently in imitation of Butler's innovations at Shrewsbury) to the Civil Service. Their attraction was that they not only minimised the unfair advantages of rank, birth or wealth, but also uncovered those desirable qualities of hard work, intelligence and stamina. Latin was an ideal subject for examination. Translation (whether into or from Latin) can be easily and accurately measured. Equally, however, there is little doubt that the need to study a subject for an examination, unless it is very sympathetically taught, tends to kill a boy's interest in it for its own sake. It becomes a chore, which only the prudential motives of securing a high class or grade induce a student to keep up.

This, at least, was part of the reason why the Victorians emphasised the therapeutic value of Latin, the less popular study of the language became and the less Latin literature inspired creative responses in its readers. But it was only part of the reason. Greek was, in any case, the language associated with the high culture of the Victorian age. A. H. Clough, on his arrival at Balliol from Rugby, commented on the almost total absence of Latin at the University. Others noted the same emphasis. Four comments serve to epitomise the general attitude to the subject among educated Victorians.

We admire [Gladstone wrote] the impressive memorials of Roman might – the roads, the bridges, the palaces – and we are affected by the Roman contribution to the art of government through their legal and administrative institutions, but we are not moved by their poetry or by their writing. They were too shallow, too derivative from the Greeks. One must go to the fountain-head of Hellas to seek refreshment.

Tennyson once confessed that he read Virgil for pleasure, but for the sound rather than the sense. 'I sometimes listen to the music of the lines without reflecting on their meaning.' Alexander Beith, minister of Glenelg and forebear of the novelist Ian Hay, used to while away the Highland evenings with a strange mixture of classical literature and contemporary novels. He had had a

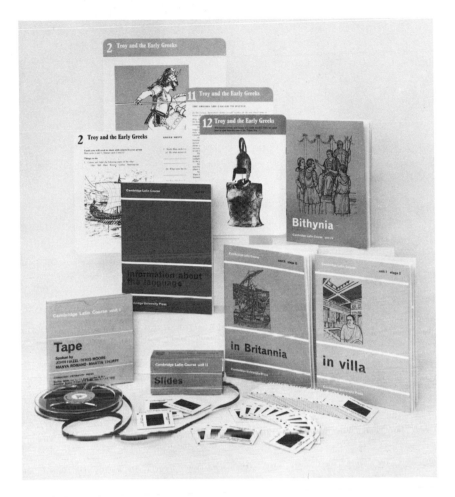

A selection of materials from the Cambridge Latin Course, published by the Cambridge University Press for the Schools Council, 1971. The old-style grammar has now been replaced by a wealth of different types of material. The language itself is taught through a series of carefully graded booklets; much of the material previously termed 'grammar and vocabulary' has now become 'information about the language'; and the emphasis has changed from this productive use of the language to comprehension. In addition, workcards, tapes and slides are all used and material provided on the history and culture. The child-centred approach to learning and the changes in curriculum development have affected the teaching of Latin, no less than other more major subjects which have now taken its once dominant place in the curriculum. Developments in the teaching of modern languages also have had a rejuvenating effect on the teaching of Latin.

sound Scottish education, culminating in a degree from Glasgow. He wrote in his diary in 1873 that

whilst I still read the Attic poets with reverence and appreciation, I have lost the fervour which I once felt for Horace and Virgil. Their world seems to me very old and empty, whereas the Stream of Ilissus [the setting of Plato's *Phaedrus*] still sparkles with life and the plain of Scamander [the scene of the *Iliad*] is warm with heroic action.

As for Thomas Arnold, 'the falsehood and emptiness of the Latin historians were for ever suggesting the contrast of their Grecian rivals'.

*

Latin of yesterday. The familiar mode of communication, the prestigious accomplishment of the gentleman, the slow training of the mind – Longmans had reflected each stage in the transition. Indeed, it would be true to say that Longmans had been in the vanguard of the change. With the close of the Edwardian age, Latin and Greek had lost their monopoly. Science, history, modern languages and English had begun to take their rightful places in the spectrum of education. It was no longer to be the case, as Cobden complained, that youths in the universities who knew nothing about the Mississippi, should know all about the little Athenian stream called the Ilissus. But not everything was lost in the process. To a late twentieth-century scholar the residual importance of Latin is the quality of experience which its literature conveys. Little, if anything, of this can be imparted by translation. For Ronald Knox the *Aeneid* of Virgil was the prototype and inspiration of a *Spiritual Aeneid*. For myself there is much comfort to be derived from the pragmatic optimism of a late Roman writer such as Lactantius (*c.* AD 320), who lived in a world whose problems were uncomfortably similar and alarmingly different. As he comments on the sexually permissive society of his day, on the violence stimulated by the gladiatorial games, on the insoluble problems of mass immigration, on the callous anonymity of a bureaucratic civil service that feared redundancy more than any other evil, on the vicious circles of inflation and high taxation, on the desperate escapism which found refuge in pseudomysticism and drugs, I find that I can gain a deeper insight into contemporary society and, perhaps, a greater sense of proportion. Latin for tomorrow will be such a subject. The views of highly articulate and cultured men in a society, which resembles but which is not our own, are always going to be prized.

BRIAN ALDERSON

Tracts, rewards and fairies

THE VICTORIAN CONTRIBUTION
TO CHILDREN'S LITERATURE

'*Elf and Owls*', *an illustration by Richard Doyle from* In Fairy Land, *text by William Allingham, Longmans,* 1870. *Actual size.* (*Bodleian Library*)

One of four vignetted scenes that were grouped on a single page and printed from wood blocks by Edmund Evans.

FOR THE Christmas season of 1869, Messrs Longmans, Green, Reader & Dyer offered their customers 'a series of pictures from the Elf-world' with a poem by William Allingham. It was a slim folio album called *In Fairy Land*, priced at a guinea and a half and bearing the date 1870 – a ploy frequently adopted by the publishers of children's books, enabling their offering to appear as a new book for two successive Christmases.

Nobody would claim much distinction for Mr Allingham's poetical effusion (after writing 'Up the airy mountain, down the rushy glen' he was probably regarded by the Victorians as a fairy bard), but the 'series of pictures' in the album was altogether different. Drawn by *Punch's* famous Dicky Doyle, they had lightness, gaiety and wit, and their printing in anything from eight to twelve colours by Edmund Evans, the country's foremost engraver and woodblock printer, was a triumph of graphic craftsmanship. Consorting in Longmans' catalogue with such volumes as Kennedy's *Latin Primer* and the improving tales of Elizabeth Missing Sewell, *In Fairy Land* has an unwonted air of levity about its magnificent pages, by which characteristic it stands as a portent of its times.

Contemporary commentators on books published for children at the end of the 1860s tended towards the fulsome in their praise for what had clearly become a very active division of the trade. The Christmas books of 1871, for instance, drew from the reviewer in *The Times* the remark that 'we cannot take leave of them without expressing our opinion that as a whole they do honour to the enterprise of English publishing'; and the year before, in the same paper, it had been suggested that children 'suffer from a multitude of books' and had of necessity grown 'somewhat blasé and critical', and very skilful at skipping away from dullness and bypassing 'the moral'.

To the reviewers (and readers) of *The Times* in those days, the stock of children's books in the major bookshops must surely have evoked some wistful comparisons with the goods that had been set before them in their own childhood. An enthusiasm for novelty and experiment was in the air, far different from the restrained attentiveness of a generation earlier – when dullness and 'the moral' were less easily evaded – and it says much for the liberality of the critics that they acclaimed this new movement so wholeheartedly.

For the world of children's reading has always been governed by a distinctly conservative regimen, in part due to an unthinking inertia – the laziness of adults who will not trouble to look beyond the books that they themselves read when young – and in part due to a submerged envy – the rejection by an older generation of enjoyments which it had itself been denied. But in the 1860s, for the first time since the early years of the century, the defences of such literary conservatism were down, overrun by the energy and exuberance of the publishers. The works of Kennedy and Miss Sewell were no longer sufficient unto a changing pattern of trade.

This is not to say that the fashions of former times had been completely abandoned. When John Ruskin recalled in *Praeterita* the books on which he had been nurtured in the 1820s, he was not talking about ephemera: 'the noble imaginative teaching of Defoe and Bunyan' on Sundays; a course of Bible work 'as soon as I was able to read'; Maria Edgeworth's *Lazy Lawrence* and (with Joyce's *Scientific Dialogues*) her little book of knowledge, *Harry and Lucy*. For history there was Scott's *Tales of a Grandfather*, and later, for the young adolescent, Mrs Sherwood's series of novels *The Lady of the Manor* and *Henry Milner*. All these earnest works were still to be found in the 1860s, together with many other refurbishings of eighteenth-century 'moral and instructive entertainments for young people'. Thomas Day's famous compendium of fictionalised Rousseau for youth, *Sandford and Merton* (1783–89), was still flourishing in a dozen editions, from Messrs Longmans' ninepenny abridgement to Messrs Routledge's 'corrected and revised edition', embellished with coloured engravings, and Messrs Cassell's astonishing nursery version, reduced by Mary Godolphin to words of one syllable (except, 'to maintain the identity of the book', the family names of the title!). Edmund Evans, even while he was working on *In Fairy Land*, was also preparing colour blocks for a new edition of Mrs Trimmer's moral fable *The Story of the Robins* (first published in 1786 as *Fabulous Histories, designed for the Instruction of Children respecting their Treatment of Animals*), which was to join Christoph von Schmid's maudlin *The Basket of Flowers* in Warne's series of Lansdowne Gift Books.

The serious cast of such traditional children's fare was certainly approved by many book-buyers in 1869, but it was now having to contend against a fresh tradition founded on the unorthodox notion that children's books should please before

55 (53)

HYMN IX.

Every painted flower hath a lesson written on its leaves.

———

COME, let us walk abroad;
let us talk of the works of
God.

Take up a handful of the
sand; number the grains of

HYMN IX.

COME, let us walk abroad;
let us talk of the works of God.
Take up a handful of sand;
number the grains of it; tell them
one by one into your lap.
Try if you can count the
blades of grass in the field,
or the leaves on the trees.
You cannot count them, they are innumerable;
much more the things which God has made.

Hymn IX from Hymns in Prose for Children *by Anna Laetitia Barbauld.
A contrast in styles. (Victoria and Albert Museum)
Left: an anonymous woodcut from the twenty-third edition published in* 1820 *by
Baldwin, Cradock & Joy.* 97 × 161 *mm.
Right: a wood-engraving by James Cooper, after a drawing by R. Barnes from
a popular Victorian edition first published by John Murray in* 1864. 145 ×
192 *mm.
The book was first published in* 1781 *and was designed 'to impress devotional
feelings as early as possible on the infant mind'.*

ever they begin to inculcate precepts. Indeed, John Ruskin's
own contribution to this new movement was not a negligible one:
the publication in 1851 of *The King of the Golden River*, one of
the first great 'original' fairy tales in English (also, incidentally,
illustrated by Dicky Doyle) and the sponsoring in 1868 of a
re-issue of the Grimm brothers' *German Popular Stories*, with
reproductions of the 'sterling and admirable art' of Cruikshank's
etchings. In later years he was also to champion Kate Greenaway,
not without much kindly criticism, and to praise Edward Lear.
'Surely,' he said in a letter on 'The Choice of Books' to the *Pall
Mall Magazine* in 1886, 'the most beneficent and innocent of all

books yet produced is the Book of Nonsense, with its corollary carols – inimitable and refreshing and perfect in rhythm. I really don't know any author to whom I am half so grateful for my idle self, as Edward Lear. I shall put him first of my hundred authors.' And the *Book of Nonsense* had first appeared in 1846, one of the first signs of unencumbered entertainment in Victorian children's books, while some of the 'corollary carols' arrived in the *Nonsense Songs* of 1871.

At this time, therefore, the publishing enterprise of which *In Fairy Land* was symbolic was but one pole of an extraordinarily varied spectrum. It would be difficult now, in the 1970s, to make much of a case for *Harry and Lucy* or *Sandford and Merton* as enduring classics of childhood, but many of the other books that were being published for children in the mid-nineteenth century still continue to be regarded as an almost mandatory element in

Decorated cloth cover for the Nonsense Botany and Nonsense Alphabets *by Edward Lear, fourth Edition, Warne, 1888. 218 × 173 mm. (Bodleian Library)*
The volume includes much material from the first edition of Nonsense Songs *published by John Bush in 1871.*

our reading experience. Apart from Lear and Ruskin themselves
(and, of course, the 'favourite old stories' that the latter so
enthusiastically recommended), authors of distinction and originality were seeing in children's literature a territory rich in
possibilities. There was, for instance, the exploration of folk
tradition by such scholars as James Orchard Halliwell, with his
collections of nursery rhymes and tales (first published in 1842
and 1849), and Sir George Webbe Dasent with his translations
of Asbjörnsen, and Moe's *Popular Tales from the Norse* (1859).
Alexander and Daniel Macmillan, who figure among the
century's most enterprising publishers of children's books,
issued Kingsley's *The Heroes* in 1856 and Annie and Eliza
Keary's *Heroes of Asgard* a year later – two books which changed
mythology from a subject for school primers into the substance

A wood-engraving by C. J. Thompson after a drawing by Richard Doyle for
the frontispiece of The King of the Golden River, *Smith Elder, 1851.*
178 × 135 mm. (Victoria and Albert Museum)

ANDROCLES AND THE LION.—p. 22

'*Androcles and the Lion*', *an illustration engraved and printed from coloured wood blocks, by the Dalziel brothers, for* The History of Sandford and Merton *by Thomas Day, in Warne's National Books Series' n.d. [c.* 1879]. 125 × 90 *mm.* (*The binding of another Victorian edition of* Sandford and Merton *is reproduced on p.* 281.)

of selfconscious art. And a few years later in 1865 the Macmillans were to undertake that most significant of all publishing ventures for children, Lewis Carroll's *Alice*, the book that for many people uniquely represents the newfound freedom of children's literature.

Jack gets the Golden Hen, away from the Giant.

Two approaches to fairy-tale by George Cruikshank.
Left: an etching for 'Rumpelstiltskin' from the first edition of German Popular
Stories *by Jacob and Wilhelm Grimm, C. Baldwyn, 1823. 76 × 69 mm.*
(British Museum)
Right: an etching from 'Jack and the Beanstalk' in 'Cruikshank's Fairy Library'
n.d. [? 1860]. *174 × 131 mm. (John Johnson Collection)*
The giant who had 'evidently drunk himself stupid' is now no longer a figure
from folk-tale, but from the temperance movement.

It was a freedom that also manifested itself in the less spectacular traditions of the children's novel: the adventure story
booming along under the compulsive influence of those men of
affairs R. M. Ballantyne and W. H. G. Kingston; the school
story, brought to classic status with Thomas Hughes's *Tom
Brown's Schooldays* (Macmillan – again, 1857), and, a year later,
brought to the edge of the ludicrous with Dean Farrar's *Eric, or
Little by Little*; and, as a final example, the story of family life,
easing itself out of the restrictive demands of severe morality with
books like Charlotte Yonge's *The Daisy Chain* (1856) and the

'Tis the voice of the lobster', an engraving by the Dalziels after a drawing by Sir John Tenniel, from the sheets of the first printing of Alice's Adventures in Wonderland, *issued in America by D. Appleton & Co., New York, 1866. 90 × 50 mm. (Bodleian Library)*
A Victorian view of the sluggard who was the lobster's original is shown on p. 259.

Two contrasting magazine covers for the year 1871, from
(a) Good Words for the Young, *234 × 158 mm.*
(b) The Boys of England, *184 × 177 mm. (British Museum)*

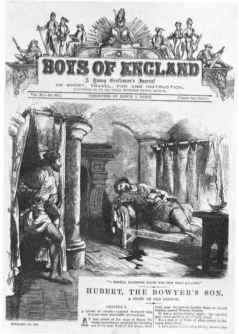

tales of Mrs Ewing, and finding an exhilarating life in those unexpected volumes from America, the chronicles of the March family. *Little Women* was first published in England by Sampson, Low in 1868 (one of the first reversals of a literary current that had hitherto flowed predominantly from east to west) and it has remained close to the top of the bestseller lists ever since.

Perhaps the most sensitive index to the Victorians' changing ideas about the nature of childhood reading is in the diversification of periodical publishing. For so long the preserve of Instruction and Piety, this area was now being encroached upon by those with less austere notions of child entertainment, whether at the very respectable level of Charlotte M. Yonge, whose *Monthly Packet* (a title which 'now sounds unfortunate' says John Rowe Townsend[1]) began publication in 1851, or with the rather dingy flamboyancy of robust Mr Beeton, whose *Boys Own Journal* of 1855 is perhaps the most notable pioneer in what was to become the flourishing trade in 'boys' papers'. It quickly attracted one rival in Routledge's *Every Boy's Magazine* (1862, later to be incorporated in *The Boy's Own Paper*), and it may well have encouraged the altogether different ebulliency of *The Boys of England* – the first of the children's 'penny dreadfuls', which began publication in 1866, and in whose lurid pages Jack Harkaway was to commence his exploits in 1871.*

Eighteen-sixty-six was also a year which saw reaction to the trade in 'blood and thunder' romances – so called by J. Erskine Clarke, who sought to combat them with the genteel variety of *Chatterbox* – and the emergence of that peer of Victorian literary periodicals for children: *Aunt Judy's Magazine*, a miscellany whose closest parallel today might be the television programme 'Blue Peter', edited first by Mrs Gatty and later by her daughter

---

* In an essay concerned chiefly with the publishing of children's books it is impossible to unravel the complex details of popular magazine fiction, much of which was aimed equally at the adult reader and the child. The pleasure derived from reading 'boys' papers' is discussed with nostalgic relish by E. S. Turner in his *Boys will be Boys*, and the corrupting influence of their 'snob-appeal' and their 'gutter patriotism' was the subject of an article by George Orwell in the March 1940 issue of *Horizon*. Whatever the truth in Orwell's accusations, there is no doubt that these magazines enjoyed an almost universal popularity, and, for present purposes, it should be noted that they fostered a cognate range of patriotic novels and fantasy adventures. The stereotyped plots and reach-me-down prose of these fictions help to explain the esteem felt by critics with a concern for style for the highly professional work of such diligent novelists as G. A. Henty and Jules Verne.

'Diamond took her hand', an actual size reproduction of one of the wood-engravings after a drawing by Arthur Hughes from At the Back of the North Wind *in* Good Words for the Young, *vol. i, 1 September 1869. 80 × 60 mm. (Bodleian Library)*

'Cramming them in', four engravings by Dalziel from drawings by Arthur Hughes for At the Back of the North Wind *by George MacDonald, as they first appeared in* Good Words for the Young, *vol. i, 1 September 1869. 232 × 165 mm. (Bodleian Library)*
The exigencies of magazine production led publishers to effect economies of this kind to the detriment of the artists' individual drawings.

Mrs Ewing (the original of Aunt Judy), many of whose stories were first serialised in the magazine. Like its sadly shortlived competitor *Good Words for the Young* (1868–72), which was edited for a while by George MacDonald and which published his *Ranald Bannerman's Boyhood* and *At the Back of the North Wind*, it represented a dignified balance between the pi and the rumbustious, a balance typical of Victorian children's literature at its best.

The diversity in the content of literature for young readers at this time is paralleled by the inventiveness which went into its presentation. Where, in the past, children's books had tended to be of modest appearance, issued in sizes ranging downwards from small or square octavo, the Victorian publishers vied with each other in exploiting a variety of larger formats and experimenting with many new materials. Pages – especially in those books for younger children that came to be classed under the generic title 'toy-books' – might be thickened up to become near-indestructible boards, or might be backed with linen, or, indeed, might be wholly linen, the first of the rag-books that are with us still.

Bindings, which had often figured as salient points of attraction to lure the young purchaser, developed with a profusion of luxury and pseudo-luxury. At one end of the scale the traditional paper or paper board cover might be toughened or glazed, the better to preserve its increasingly ornate printed decorations; while at the other end of the scale there was the panoply of heavily stamped cloth bindings, decorated with gilt, or inlaid with coloured pictures or, in many cases, both.

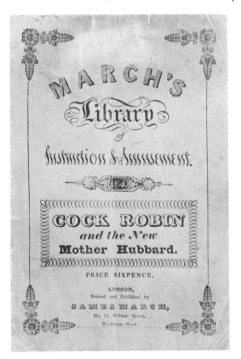

The front cover of Cock Robin and the New Mother Hubbard, *No. 4 in March's 'Library of Instruction and Amusement',* n.d. *[c. 1858]. 238 × 148 mm.* (Victoria and Albert Museum) *An example of a Victorian publisher losing his head over his wealth of typographic resources.*

The Victorians' flair for technology was certainly responsible for many of the new opportunities that came to publishers to design children's books of colourful or dramatic (and, hence, eminently vendible) appearance, and nowhere was this more obvious than in the continuous experimentation that was directed towards the process of printing itself — especially the mechanical reproduction of monochrome or colour illustrations. The old-time and comparatively simple woodcuts or copper engravings done for children's books, hand-coloured either direct or by stencil, were gradually being superseded by more sophisticated methods or combinations of methods.

The stylish wood-engraving techniques pioneered by Thomas Bewick and his school at the turn of the century were adapted to mass production methods under pressure from the magazine publishers, while at the same time the development of new approaches to colour printing, through lithography or through the harnessing of photography, enabled colour-books to be produced in a quantity and with a cheapness that had not been possible before. Companies like Dean & Son, or Routledge, or Warne, produced a host of toy-book series retailing at sixpence or a shilling, which offered the juvenile public not simply a range of illustrative style from the static 'realism' of the hack artists to the elaborate designs of Walter Crane or the fluent gaiety of Randolph Caldecott, but also 'stand-up' books, 'cut-out' books and 'movables' of great ingenuity.

One of the first of the new-style picture books for children was Heinrich Hoffmann's *Struwwelpeter*, first published in Leipzig in 1845. An English edition was printed there and issued in this country in 1848, an event which stimulated the production of many home-bred competitors, but which also symbolized the strong influence which Germany was to have on the toy-book industry throughout the century. During the 1890s the Nuremberg firm of Nister, who worked closely with their London office, had a colossal output of finely lithographed, but utterly banal, 'gift' books and ephemera circulating in England — an early example of the now common phenomenon of characterless 'international publishing'.

The imagination and energy of so much of this publishing in the middle decades of the nineteenth century should not obscure the fact that in point of quantity those volumes designed for the child's entertainment or friendly instruction were probably far

'The Sluggard': a 'graphotype' by H. Fitzcook from the edition of Isaac Watts's
Divine Songs, published by Nisbet in 1866. 165 × 111 mm. (Victoria and
Albert Museum)
(Compare illustration on p. 254.)

outstripped by those prepared for his moral and spiritual edification. Such books had long been staple fare in any publisher's
catalogue, for they derive from one of the earliest traditions of
writing for children. If one leaves aside school-books or books
devised to teach the child manners, then it is among the Puritan
writers of the seventeenth century that 'children's literature' finds
its origins. The homiletic tales and verses they produced were
rather short in liveliness of imagination, but their concern for the
child's spiritual welfare caused them to take at least the first step
towards creating books that should speak directly and naturally
to children rather than to anyone else.

Like instruction, evangelism was a tradition that died hard. In
the liberal 1970s it seems scarcely credible that the child of a
hundred years before should still be offered James Janeway's
Token for Children ('being an account of the conversion, holy and
exemplary lives and joyful deaths of several young children'
originally published in 1669), but the Religious Tract Society
had the volume in print, illustrated with Victorian woodcuts and
with changes made to 'such words and expressions as would not
be generally understood' – but with 'the sense strictly adhered to'.
And that valuable manual for the English Protestant Reform-
ation, John Foxe's sixteenth-century *Book of Martyrs*, the 'dismal
horrors' of whose pictures so edified David Copperfield, was not
only available in a quantity of restyled editions, but had even been
issued by Frederick Warne in condensed form for a shilling,
'illustrated in colours'.

Nor is it possible for children of modern times to recognise the
point of the satire implicit in *Alice*, when Lewis Carroll allows his
heroine to bungle her recitations of 'How doth the little croco-
dile' and ''Tis the voice of the lobster'. These are not the nonsense verses that they have since become, but Lewis Carroll's
gloss on 'How doth the little busy bee' and ''Tis the voice of the
sluggard', two poems which had first appeared as early as 1715
in Isaac Watts's *Divine Songs attempted in easy Language for the
Use of Children*.* Despite the fact that it was one hundred and fifty
years old, this collection had enormous popularity as a Victorian
Sunday book and all manner of editions were produced, varying
in style from barely legible penny chapbooks to the imposing
'graphotype' table-book which Nisbet's published in 1866.

The popularity of revealed religion as staple fare in children's
* For Watts and Longman, see 'Introduction', p. 7.

Three stages in the development of a toy-book series:
Story of Reynard the Fox *in 'Aunt Mavor's Picture Books for Little Readers', George Routledge & Co., n.d. [c. 1836]. 243 × 170 mm.*
A simple wood-cut design on the front cover, printed black on drab blue.
Old King Cole *in 'Aunt Mavor's Toy Books', George Routledge & Sons, n.d. [c. 1865]. 246 × 185 mm.*
The simple cover has now been converted into a gaudy lithographed yellow-back for children.
Jack and the Beanstalk *in 'Routledge's Toy Books', George Routledge & Sons, n.d. [c. 1866]. 246 × 188 mm. One of Walter Crane's ornate and carefully detailed designs.*

(Victoria and Albert Museum)

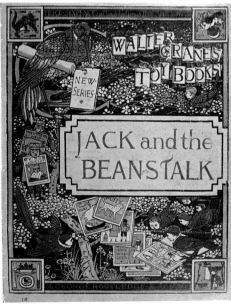

The change in colour work.
A hand-coloured illustration
of 'The Drummer' from The
Young Rifleman, *one of*
Dean's 'Untearable Cloth
Children's Coloured Toy
Books', n.d. [c. 1855?].
249 × 169 mm.

THE DRUMMER.

The DRUMMER looks grand as he walks with the band.
    The Drum and the Cymbals he beats.
The good people praise the rolls that he plays,
    As we march along through the streets.

    He strikes the Drum with conscious pride,
    And struts along with pompous stride.

Edmund Evans's colour
printing of Walter Crane's
The Absurd ABC *in*
Routledge's 'Shilling Toy
Book Series', n.d. [c. 1870].
246 × 188 mm.

(Victoria and Albert Museum)

Front cover of The Town and Country
Toy Book, *Religious Tract Society, n.d.*
[c. 1878]. 249 × 190 mm.
(Victoria and Albert Museum)
An elaborate binding in green cloth, with
gilt and pictorial decoration, used to bind
up a collection of four RTS 'toy books'
also sold separately in paper covers.

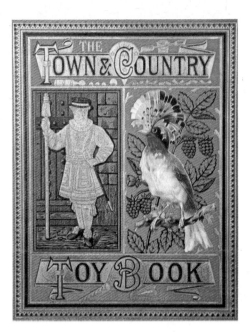

Below; left: 'The house we live in; sitting-room', the original page from
Warne's Picture Puzzle Toy Book, *n.d. [c. 1869]. 228 × 207 mm. (John*
Johnson Collection)
The blank spaces were filled in by shapes cut out from another page.

Right: 'Admiral Stork' from The Pleasant Surprises for Chicks of all Sizes,
printed in Nuremburg and published in London by Nister, n.d. [c. 1890].
172 × 123 mm. (John Johnson Collection)
An example of one of Nister's 'dissolving picture books'. When a tab at the
bottom of the page is pulled 'Admiral Stork' changes into 'Captain Puffin'.

reading made great demands on the publishers, whose hands were kept well clear of idleness and Satan by more than the reissuing of the past adjurations of Janeway and Watts. It may well be that the committees who governed those two influential houses, the Society for Promoting Christian Knowledge and the Religious Tract Society, concurred with Isaac Watts in thinking that children should know that:

> There is a dreadful hell,
>   And everlasting pains;
> There sinners must with devils dwell
>   In darkness fire and chains

but they also recognised that further sentiments in the good Doctor's book continued to have currency:

> How many children in the street

he had said in his *Praise for Mercies Spiritual and Temporal*

> Half naked I behold;
> While I am clothed from head to feet
> And covered from the cold.

Cover of Old Fashioned Fairy Tales, *SPCK, 1886. 215 × 170 mm.*
One of the best known authors to be published by the SPCK was Juliana Horatia Ewing, many of whose stories first appeared in Aunt Judy's Magazine, which was founded by her mother Mrs Gatty, and which she edited from 1874 to 1876.

Cloth binding for Hannah More's The Shepherd of Salisbury Plain, *issued as a prize by the Religious Tract Society in 1886. 185 × 120 mm.*

The desperate plight of the poor in Victorian cities sheds an almost ironic light on the popularity of *Divine Songs* in Victorian Sunday parlours.

For if one considers the pricing and the distribution of books during the 1860s and 1870s it quickly becomes clear that the exciting developments in children's literature were initially available to only a small proportion of the child population. At a time when the average weekly wage of workmen was considerably less than a pound a week, the potential market for *Alice's Adventures in Wonderland* at six shillings a copy was scarcely universal, let alone the market for folios on fairy land at thirty-one and sixpence. Given also that the movement towards 'free public libraries' was still in its infancy, that school libraries (for those children who actually attended day school, or night school or Sunday school) were often of the most rudimentary kind, and that the widespread publishing of cheap editions was still in the future, it is not surprising to find that the only people with a conscience about the reading of 'the labouring poor' were the charitable organisations.

High among the aims of the Cheap Repository for Moral and Religious Publications (which later became the Religious Tract Society) was 'to furnish the People at large with useful Reading, at so low a price as to be within reach of the poorest purchaser', and what, in 1796, when these words were written, was a campaign directed at a depressed rural populace, became seventy years later an effort to bring at least some form of 'literature' to the massed urban poor.

The Religious Tract Society and the Society for Promoting Christian Knowledge, an earlier foundation whose aims were more diverse, had developed publishing programmes with such zealous endeavour that by mid-century they had become very substantial contributors indeed to the nation's total production of books and pamphlets. Furthermore, both Societies came to recognise that they had a role to play outside their special areas of religious publishing. As early as 1832, the Standing Committee of the SPCK had realised that a publishing policy confined to the issuing of purely doctrinal literature was proving inadequate to meet the needs of an expanding readership. 'The press has been rapidly advancing its influence over the minds and conduct of the great Mass of the population,' they reported, and: 'the Boys and Girls from National Schools who form a large part of the reading

Men and Women of the present day' were rapidly becoming prey to those publications 'openly addressed to the passions and prejudices of the Multitude ... and encouraging ribaldry, sedition and hostility to the established church'.

To combat this danger, the Committee recommended forming a new General Publications Committee, financed initially with £2,000, to institute a wider publishing programme of works 'not strictly within the meaning of "Christian Knowledge" ' but extended to 'any branch of literature'. As a result of this change, by 1869 the Society sported among its theological books a considerable range of children's story-books and classroom works and competed very successfully with commercial publishers through its network of agencies.

Similarly, the Religious Tract Society was adapting itself with pragmatic flexibility to its evangelical labours, although its major resources still consisted of a great hoard of little books, priced at anything from a farthing to ninepence. They were closely aligned with the original Hannah More ideal of a social system beautiful

Left: a variety of picture books and toy books 'the largest and cheapest ever issued', listed in Dean & Sons' reference catalogue for 1875. 208 × 125 mm.
Right: a page from the General Catalogue of the Religious Tract Society, *dated August 1875, including notes on variant bindings and a recommendation of Penny Coloured Toy Books 'specially useful for Sunday School Rewards'. Later pages included long lists of books at a halfpenny and a farthing each. 208 × 125 mm. (Library Association)*

in its order 'when each according to his place pays willing
honour to his superiors'[2]; and, indeed, Hannah More's tract of
1795, *The Shepherd of Salisbury Plain* and similar productions
continued in print for the benefit not just of children, but also of
working-men, domestic servants and cottagers. The RTS even
published a maudlin little pamphlet about *The Little Tract Girl*
going her Sunday rounds among the poor, distributing 'sweet
tracts' free to the children at street corners. But as Charlotte
Yonge said of *Eric*, 'the sure reward of virtue is a fatal accident'[3],
and after half a dozen pages the little tract girl has taken a mortal
fever and that is that.

The tract at the street corner was not to be the only contribution of the RTS towards bridging the gap between the 'Two
Nations' of the rich and the poor, and in 1867, the year of the
Second Reform Bill, they published a little volume that was to
have a profound influence not simply on children's books, but to
some extent upon children's lives: 'Hesba Stretton's' *Jessica's
First Prayer*.

'Hesba Stretton', who manufactured the pseudonym as a

Left: wood engraving taken from a modern reprint of The Little Tract
Girl, *Religious Tract Society, n.d., where the illustration is enlarged. The
original page size is cited as* 91 × 62 *mm.*

Right: wood-engraved frontispiece to Jessica's First Prayer *by 'Hesba
Stretton', 1886.* 150 × 120 *mm.*

rather more colourful alternative to her own name of Sarah Smith,* had more or less been born into evangelical publishing. Her father, Benjamin Smith, had formerly been printer to the Wellington firm of Houlston's, who specialised in such work and had issued many of Mrs Sherwood's books, and he subsequently became a bookseller and small time publisher in his own right, as well as a sturdy pillar of Shropshire nonconformity. Sarah herself received early encouragement as a writer from Dickens, who published several of her stories in *Household Words* and *All the Year Round*, and by the time that *Jessica's First Prayer* was published in the July 1866 issue of the magazine *Sunday at Home* she had already learned to control and shape her stories to achieve sharpness of impact.

This was particularly necessary in writing for the Religious Tract Society, whose authors were expected to conform to a carefully devised set of rules for the composition of tract fiction, and *Jessica* has a more natural air about it than many of the contrived tales which this method fostered. It is a simple story of the 'saving' of a street-waif, daughter of a dissolute mother, and the awakening of a spirit of kindliness in a narrowly religious coffee-stall keeper, and it spoke directly to an emergent Victorian social conscience. Certainly there had been tracts enough before about the trials and vices of the poor, but no children's book – not even that quaint fantasy of Christian Socialism, *The Water Babies* – produced such repercussions as *Jessica*. From the outset, it sold by the thousand. It was translated into almost every European language; and the Tsar Alexander II ordered a copy to be placed in every Russian school, a decree rescinded by his successor, who seems to have feared that it might lead to social disruption. An estimate has been made that, by the end of the century, at least a million and a half copies had been sold – nearly ten times as many as *Alice in Wonderland*.†

* The Hesba part was made up from the initials of herself, her three sisters and her brother; Stretton from the township of Church Stretton near her birthplace, Wellington, in Shropshire.

† Apart from losses through an incalculable number of pirated editions, it would seem that the Religious Tract Society were the chief financial beneficiaries from *Jessica* since they had purchased the copyright. 'Truly all men are cheats, especially publishers,' said Sarah Smith darkly and set about arranging far more lucrative royalty terms on her subsequent books. Her *Little Meg's Children* (1868) and *Alone in London* (1869) sold together at least 750,000 copies.

Alongside the individual success of *Jessica's First Prayer* as a bestseller must also be reckoned its influence in creating a far more forceful 'literature of poverty' than had hitherto existed in the annals of the tract publishers. Soon after finishing it, 'Hesba Stretton' herself was working on such stirring companion volumes as *Pilgrim Street; a Story of Manchester Life* (1867), and – perhaps her best book – *Little Meg's Children* (1868), a plea for the small, spare, stunted East End children, 'of London growth', fending for themselves, and inarticulately 'crying for everything'. Such books encouraged not only a new tradition of 'street Arab' literature, but also a movement for social as well as political reform. It comes as no surprise to find Sarah Smith (with Angela Burdett-Coutts) foremost among those responsible for the founding of the National Society for the Prevention of Cruelty to Children in 1886.

It is clear from the tone of much street Arab literature – and indeed from statements by authors often incorporated in the text – that the expected readership of these books was the respectable and charitably inclined, rather than the Arabs themselves. Mrs Castle-Smith, for instance, who wrote under the pen-name 'Brenda', concludes her tale of *Froggy's Little Brother* (1875) with the lengthy peroration: 'Parents and little children, you especially who are rich, remember it is the Froggys and Bennys of London for whom your clergyman is pleading, when he asks you to send money and relief to the poor East End', and this was a sentiment lost neither upon Mrs Ewing, who reviewed the book in *Aunt Judy's Magazine*, where she called it 'wholesome reading for the wealthy and well cared-for', nor upon little Flora Thompson and her friends in the village Sunday School at Candleford who 'wished they could have brought those poor neglected slum

Meg teaches Robin out of the Testament. A wood engraving from Little Meg's Children, *Religious Tract Society, n.d.* [1868]. (*Bodleian Library*)

children there and shared with them the best they had of everything'.

The poor slum children themselves though, in so far as any of
them like Little Meg, might have 'learned to read a little' at night
school, would hardly have turned to the books of 'Hesba Stretton'
or 'Brenda' for their entertainment (nor yet, one imagines, to the
tracts so diligently speaking to their condition, nor even to 'the
Testament'). As the sage Mrs Ewing further remarked on one
occasion when in *Aunt Judy's Magazine* she was criticising a
volume of hymns about children, 'It is like giving poor people
nothing but books about poverty and the wash-tub and the
public-house, which (to say nothing of the readers having often
a much more real knowledge of the subject than the writer) are
by no means the most popular part of a village library.' There
is every likelihood that while the child of 1869, beside his
nursery fire, was enjoying *In Fairy Land*, or the child in a
respectable Sunday School was weeping over *Froggy*, the slum
child was making out as best he could on the traditional fare
of the disenfranchised reader: sensational papers and penny
fictions. The mass circulation paper, of which *The Boys of England*
was so eminent a precursor, had not yet entirely ousted the street
ballads and chapbooks of older times – the 'corrupt and vicious
little books' which the Cheap Repository Tracts were designed
to combat. Catnach's warehouse at Seven Dials was still in
business, and, for the avid reader in mean streets, there were still
farthing Cock Robins to be had, or lurid execution literature
('Shocking Murder of a Wife and Six Children') – superan-
nuated remnants of the tales of Jack Sheppard.

Benevolent ladies and the men from Seven Dials were not the
only visitors to the East End. Also there, 'whither my avocations

The cover for the ABC *of Pretty Tales,
n.d.* 248 × 159 *mm. (John Johnson
Collection)*
*A cheap popular book incorporating
advertisements.*

often lead me', as he put it, was Matthew Arnold, late professor of poetry at Oxford, Inspector of Schools, and author of the essays on *Culture and Anarchy*, whose publication in book form represents yet another publishing event in the clearly momentous year of 1869. In the last of these essays, 'Our Liberal Practitioners', and at the clinching point of his argument, Arnold had dwelt on 'the festering masses, without help, without home, without hope' in London's East End, and he had sought to put forward a case for principles of education based on reason and justice beyond the narrow scope of contemporary middle and upper-class sectarian arguments.

But, as he knew better than most, the right approach was not something that could easily be discovered in the tangled disputes over money and politics and religion. Wherever children of 'the Populace' were managing to attend school during the 1860s, they were being educated under a system that, as Arnold reported, 'fostered teaching by rote', a system buttressed by a government Code according to which the reward of the teacher was determined by the performance of his pupils at annual inspections. 'Payment by results' was formulated by Robert Lowe – who although a classical scholar as well as a politician was one of the leading 'Philistines' to suffer the ironic thrusts of *Culture and Anarchy* – and it was defended by him with words that have remained a perpetual theme among parliamentary educationists: 'I cannot promise the House that this system will be an economical one, and I cannot promise that it will be an efficient one, but I can promise that it shall be one or the other. If it is not cheap, it shall be efficient; if it is not efficient it shall be cheap.'

By any Arnoldian principle of culture the system possessed neither of these practical virtues, although Arnold's interpretation of Lowe's motives was challenged at the time, as it has been since. His reports as an Inspector return again and again to the destructive narrowness engendered by 'payment by results'. It was a narrowness, moreover, which long remained a characteristic of popular education in England, long after the passing of the Education Act of 1870, the first major step towards establishing a national programme of education for all children. Indeed, the manner in which most schools were conducted – ensuring that the effects of education were cramping rather than liberating – was criticised as sharply by Edmond Holmes in his *What is and what might be* (1911), just after he had retired from the Chief Inspectorship, as it had been by Arnold in mid-Victorian Britain.

The cramping effects are nowhere better seen than in the reading standards set by the Code, by which the children's progress might be judged – standards encouraging the rote learning of set pieces, to the complete neglect of even the most elementary response to literature. As Arnold reported within the first year of the passing of the Act: 'The reading books and the absence of plan being what they are, the whole use that the Government . . . makes of the mighty engine of literature in the education of the working classes, amounts to little more, even when most successful, than giving them power to read the newspapers.'

Nevertheless, despite the limited vision of many politicians, and even educationists, where the teaching of reading was concerned, and despite a very gradual attainment of competence among the readers themselves, there can be no doubt that the arrival of the 1870 Act provided a marked stimulus to activity

'Battle of the rats' an illustration by Shields, engraved by Edmund Evans for an edition of Gulliver's Travels *in Longmans' 'Shilling Entertainment Library',* 1863. 133 × 85 mm. (*John Johnson Collection*)
The Library represented an early attempt 'to provide the young, and, generally speaking, the less educated sections of the community with a set of readable books'. Retailing at one shilling per volume, cloth bound, the library was intended to be 'within reach of the poorest families and the smallest elementary schools'.

among the writers and publishers of books for children. Earlier movements in popular education, especially the proliferation of voluntary schools in the first half of the nineteenth century, had shown that, however primitive the methods employed, schooling brought about at least some increase in the book-buying public, and the combined influence of a rising standard of living, a rapidly growing literate middle class and a somewhat more systematically schooled working class caused an almost continuous boom in all forms of publishing throughout the final decades of the century. Furthermore, the rise in real wages (whose previous depression had been one of the major impediments to the widespread access to literature) was matched by an increasingly free circulation of books, not just through the agency of the expanding public library service, but through the proliferation of cheap editions and mass-produced series. The six shilling *Alice*, for example, was joined by a two-and-sixpenny 'People's Edition' in 1887, issued without profit to the author, who was anxious that 'the little ones for whom it was written' should not go without it, and by a sixpenny edition in Macmillan's Popular Series in 1898. Similar treatment was accorded to many other, less distinguished 'classics' and the boom in book production was backed up by the massive extension of the popular press. The appearance of such ventures as *Tit-Bits* and *Answers*, *Comic Cuts* and *The Halfpenny Wonder*, and their runaway success, gives a wry piquancy to Matthew Arnold's comment on giving the working class 'power to read the newspapers'.

If no engines of literature, mighty or otherwise, were used in the prosecution of education during these last years of the nineteenth century, it is a fault that can scarcely be laid at the door of the publishers. Simon Nowell-Smith says that Thomas Dixon Galpin — whose company of Cassell, Petter & Galpin had, well before 1870, built up a very substantial business in popular magazines and part-issue fiction — 'used to quote the current official figure of elementary school children as the Cassell constituency'.[4] The prospect of mass sales to the newly literate was too enticing for the book trade's entrepreneurs to be put off by the gloom of government inspectors, and one sees in the advertisements and book catalogues of the time a growing sense of the 'board school' market — the forging of a link between publishing and education that has been a permanent influence on the style and character of many books produced for children.

READING TO MY LITTLE FOLKS.

No. 10.

Wood-engraved cover illustration for Little Folks, *No.* 10 (1871), *one of the children's magazines in the 'Cassell Constituency'.* 210 × 145 *mm.*

Leaving aside the 'educational' books, those stultifying readers concocted for the little victims in Standards I to VII, the dominating feature in children's book production during the years after 1870 was probably the presence of the 'reward'. There was certainly nothing new in the notion of a book forming the ideal prize for either rectitude, punctuality or even academic achievement – John Newbery, the foremost publisher for children in the eighteenth century, had made great play in his advertisements and on his title-pages, with the slightly ironic sentiment that his books were only for good boys and girls, and 'those who are naughty to have none'.[5] Such libraries as the old national schools possessed tended to operate on the principle of lending only to the meritorious. But this not altogether logical means of disseminating literature was developed with vastly greater energy by later publishers. Many of the 'popular' houses such as Cassell, Routledge, Ward Lock, Nelson and Nisbet established category upon category of reward series. With names like 'The Laurel' and 'The Royal', and in a multitude of binding styles at a multitude of prices, the serried ranks grew; the sub-trades of gilt-blocking and label-printing flourished; and year by year such representatives of English literature as *Robinson Crusoe* and *Sandford and Merton* found homes for themselves as the involuntary foundation of a child's personal library.

Alongside the 'classics' in these prize series there were also the factitious productions of the specialist 'reward authors', turning out their modest tales for modest recompense from the religious societies and the Sunday School Unions. The possibilities are neatly summed up by the egregious Jasper Milvain in Gissing's *New Grub Street* advising his sister on how to become a professional author:

It's obvious what an immense field there is for anyone who can just hit the taste of the new generation of Board School children. Mustn't be too goody-goody; that kind of thing is falling out of date. But you'd have to cultivate a particular kind of vulgarity.

The demise of the 'goody-goody' was *de verbo* rather than *de facto*. Plenty of publishers continued to maintain a steady list of moral, hortatory or just plain instructive volumes, and plenty of parents and teachers, whether of the school or the Sunday School variety, must have felt that the aptest reward for goodness was a tract about goodness. It is, indeed, a tradition that has never entirely vanished, and catalogues issued by Ward Lock and the Lutterworth Press — residuary legatee of the Religious Tract Society — show that children of the 1970s may still benefit from the offerings of Amy Le Feuvre and that impossibly lachrymose successor to 'Hesba Stretton', Mrs O. F. Walton. Even the devil was able to call a tune of sorts when we find the redoubtable Annie Besant freeing boys and girls 'from the superstition which spoils' much of their literature.[6] She issued in 1885 from the Freethought Publishing Company a 'Young Folks' Library', possessed of all the characteristics of the tract series except for its determined effort to do down the Christians for once instead of the heathen.

Nevertheless, the naturalness and ease which were salient characteristics of emergent Victorian children's literature at its best, had their own influence, and the publishing programmes of such leading propagandists as the SPCK and RTS were constantly being modified to meet an evolving spirit of freedom quite different from Annie Besant's. There was, indeed, warrant for flexibility in Hannah More's original concept of tract literature as a means 'to encounter with their own weapons' the promoters of 'the alluring vehicles of novels, stories and songs'; even so, there was a difference in kind between her adoption of a chapbook format for morality and the frankly secularist tendency of some of the RTS colour books (borrowing Kronheim and Edmund Evans from the toy-book publishers), or the heterogeneous pages of *The Boy's Own Paper*, which was the Society's great contribution to children's reading from 1879 onwards.

Left: School Board of London prize label in the 'prize edition' of Rosamund and Godfrey *shown on p.* 281. 75 × 120 *mm.*
Right: a sobering example of the widespread fashion for prize-giving. The label appears in a bound copy of The National Temperance Mirror *for* 1887. 145 × 110 *mm.*

There is evidence of a good deal of dissension within the Society's committee, whose job it was to 'assist' the editor of *The Boy's Own Paper* – a touchiness over how far the paper could appear to adopt the devil's best tunes (in this case the roistering epics of Jack Harkaway) without adopting his practices as well. Consciousness of the ubiquitous penny-dreadfuls had perhaps compelled the editor to include an 'excessive' proportion of fiction and to give insufficient prominence to 'Christian truth and influence';[7] but circulation figures, to say nothing of competition from rival papers like Henty's *Union Jack*, spoke louder than principle and the *The Boy's Own Paper* continued to maintain its largely secular style.

Whatever the evangelicals might have to say, the magazine certainly appealed to Charlotte M. Yonge who, both as a writer for children and as a commentator on children's literature still deserves a tempered respect. Harking back once more to 1869, one finds *Macmillan's Magazine* publishing a group of articles by her on the background to contemporary children's books which for its time is remarkably balanced and free from extra-literary prejudice, while her *What Books to Lend and What to Give* of 1887 typifies exactly the mixture of informed criticism and bridled enthusiasm which might be expected of a responsible guardian of children's reading at this period.

What Books to Lend was intended to be a handlist for the guidance of Anglican teachers in voluntary schools and Sunday Schools and it is necessarily preoccupied from time to time with such matters as Catechisms, Confirmations and Mothers' Meetings. Despite this, however, and despite the primness and condescension of some of Charlotte Yonge's annotations, it shows how a feeling for 'able and interesting literature' can be reconciled with didactic and religious purpose. Miss Yonge's comment on *The Boy's Own Paper*, for instance – 'Capital, and full of adventurous tales – may have been inspired in part by her desire to find a suitable alternative to 'Jack Sheppard' literature, but one also feels that she could see what the children of the 1880s relished in it. And her pragmatic note on the *Alice* books and *The Water Babies* might have borne more repetition in subsequent years: 'It takes some cultivation to enjoy these wondrously droll compositions' and 'These are literature, though we are not sure whether ordinary school children would care for them.'

Yet for a world beyond that of Miss Yonge's 'ordinary school children', and in nurseries a long way from the contemporaneous Jago of Arthur Morrison, with its 'trotting of sorrow-laden little feet along the grim street to the grim Board School three grim streets off',[8] the expansive literature of childhood was flourishing as it had never flourished before. Almost every year from 1870 to the outbreak of the First World War brought the publication of at least one children's book still recognised today as possessing that essential gaiety or imaginative vigour without which children's books are seen by their readers simply as adjuncts of the schoolroom or the parish hall.

The growing number of critics, who followed Charlotte Yonge as commentators on children's reading, almost seem to be working in concert to publicise the manifold pleasures of this comparatively new branch of literature. Mrs E. M. Field, an early historian of children's books, whose *The Child and his Book* appeared in 1891, celebrates the universal delight that was occasioned by the picture-books of Randolph Caldecott and Kate Greenaway, whom Edmund Evans encouraged Routledge to publish alongside Walter Crane. And within two years of her regretting the recession of fairy tales before the popularity of the child's story of real life, she was able equally to celebrate a sudden resurgence of enthusiasm following the publication of the first of Joseph Jacobs's great collections, *English Fairy Tales* (1890) and the start of the series of 'Colour Fairy Books' which Andrew Lang edited for Longmans between 1889 and 1910.*

Similarly, Edward Salmon in *Juvenile Literature As It Is* (1888) and Walter Greenwood in his *Sunday School and Village Libraries* (1892) tended towards a forthright acceptance of the new spirit in children's books, where Charlotte Yonge, or

* The role of Longmans as publishers of children's literature during this period is somewhat indeterminate. Besides the Lang series they were also responsible for publishing such diverse volumes as Knatchbull-Hugesson's *Higgledy-Piggledy* (1875), Florence Upton's *Dutch Doll* series (which began in 1895), Stevenson's *A Child's Garden of Verse* (published unillustrated in 1885 and subsequently relinquished to The Bodley Head) and Walter De La Mare's first book, *Songs of Childhood* (1902). As happened both before and after this period, they were doubtless preoccupied chiefly with school-book publishing, but it is worth recording that they brought to this gloomy function, on at least one occasion, the mastery of Edmund Evans, who printed for them the colour illustrations to their 'Ship Literary Readers' and that they showed sufficient awareness of the value of fairy tales to convert the *Blue Fairy Book* (1889) into a series of school class-readers.

Advertisement tipped in behind the frontispiece of Cinderella and other Stories, *a school reader based on the tales in the* Blue Fairy Book *by Andrew Lang, Longmans* 1890. 179 × 123 *mm.* (*Bodleian Library*)
The infants of Standard I benefit from the renewed popularity of fairy tale collections.

Christabel Coleridge (who succeeded her as editor of *The Monthly Packet*) allowed themselves to be inhibited by doctrinal or social considerations – the need to be correct and the need to be respectable.

Much the most entertaining contemporary comments on the nature of Victorian children's literature do not come directly from the adult arbiters of taste, however, but from a company of children who are a part of that literature (just), and whose remarks are intended not for the records of historians but for children themselves: the comments of that buoyant company of critics: Oswald, Dora, Dicky, Alice, Noel and H. O. Bastable. Throughout such tales of family life as *The Treasure Seekers* and *The Wouldbegoods* E. Nesbit provides an incidental commentary on the way a group of alert, lively children might see the work of the writers and artists of their time – whether they be the luckless anonymous hacks whose 'books they give you for a prize at a girls' school' (and whose style is parodied until the exasperated

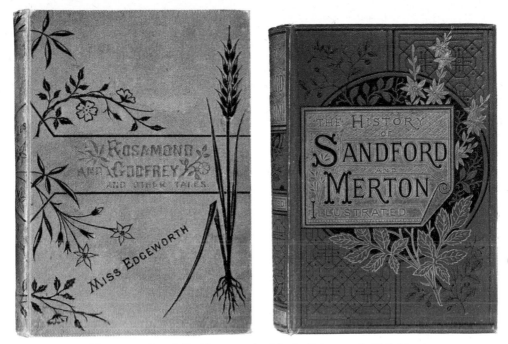

Front cover of Rosamund and Godfrey . . . *by Maria Edgeworth, Edinburgh,*
E. & S. Livingstone, n.d. [c. 1884]. 173 × 117 mm.
A famous pre-Victorian author still being issued as a school prize.

Cloth gilt binding for an edition of Thomas Day's Sandford and Merton *in*
Ward Lock's 'Good Worth Library of Popular Volumes for Presents and
Rewards', n.d. [c. 1879]. 180 × 120 mm.

An all-purpose prize label printed for the SPCK by E. Kaufmann of Lahr,
Baden [c. 1890?]. 119 × 85 mm. (John Johnson Collection)

The book which figured as the prize for the 'Essay on Total Abstinence' was
The National Temperance Mirror, *an illustrated Magazine for the Home*
Circle, National Temperance Publication Depot, *1887. 215 × 165 mm.*

Oswald says 'It's no use. I can't write like those books. I wonder how the books' authors can keep it up'), or whether they be named heroes like Rudyard Kipling, who could do nothing wrong, or killjoys like Maria Charlesworth whose *Ministering Children* receives strictures of such severity that it becomes almost a symbol of the literature of anti-child.

No one would wish to claim that Edith Nesbit was attempting any systematic critique of children's literature from behind the sheltering masks of her characters, but a consistent point of view is clearly discernible: a respect for vitality (even if it is only in a book of *Naval Heroes*), a delight in the imaginative, the exotic and the funny, a scorn for the false, the goody and the namby-pamby. A conclusion may be hazarded from the free and easy way in which the Bastables incorporate ideas drawn from children's books into their play ('So then we were the Children of the New Forest, and the mutton tasted much better. No one in the New Forest minds venison being tough and the gravy pale'); a clear distinction noted between the way in which Lewis Carroll, say, parodies Isaac Watts in *Alice* and the naturalness of the intro-duction of 'Mr Caldecott's pictures' or S. R. Crockett's 'piffle' in *The Wouldbegoods*. Reading has passed right out of reach of those who would see it primarily as a means for moral improvement or spiritual regeneration; it has become a lively, integral part of the experience of childhood.

The writers, illustrators and publishers of books for children in the reigns of Victoria and Edward VII have not been immune from criticism, founded often upon a dislike of the comfortable world which they so often portrayed and a conviction of the basic Philistinism of their assumptions. The cloying sentimentality of their view of family life, the unreality of their boarding schools, the jingoism of their imperialist adventures can indeed be shown in instances without number, but, at their best, they transcended these limitations and the touchstones for excellence chosen by E. Nesbit can still be acknowledged today. A tradition which began with The *Book of Nonsense* and *The King of the Golden River* and which culminated in such books of absolute distinction as *The Three Mulla-Mulgars*, *The Wind in the Willows* and *The Tale of Mr Tod* was more than a mere movement for emancipation; in Arnold's language it was a permanent foundation for the culture which he saw as our only defence against an all-pervasive anarchy.

HANS SCHMOLLER

The paperback
revolution

IT COULD be argued that the invention of printing from movable type in the mid-fifteenth century was inevitable and that it was merely a response to social change which had created a greater demand for books than could be satisfied by the scribes. Similarly, perhaps, the phenomenal growth of the paperback since the mid-1930s is not so much the result of a good idea (which was by no means new) being brilliantly put into practice by one person, and subsequently spreading to many parts of the world, as a development which *had* to happen as a reflection of, and a stimulus to, the great changes in society which we have seen since the end of the Second World War.

It is often difficult to determine the exact point at which a major new idea becomes tangible. As to the paperback, people with much expert knowledge have argued forward and backward in an attempt to name its 'inventor', but no general agreement has been reached. It is not in dispute, however, that the publication by Allen Lane of the first ten Penguins in 1935 was the event to which virtually all paperback developments in the western world during the past forty years can be traced.

There is no shortage of forerunners, particularly if we do not restrict our attention to books which possess all the physical properties of the modern paperback. If relative cheapness and pocketability are taken as the main criteria, then we find such forerunners about half a century after Gutenberg's invention. The great innovator was Aldus Manutius in Venice at the very

Mint proofs of 'Yellowbacks' (see p. 289). *Size of printed area (excluding spine) varies from* 165 × 100 *mm to* 172 × 109 *mm. (John Johnson Collection)*

Cheap editions stimulated by the growth of rail travel, 1846–c.1856. Sizes vary from 161 × 102 *mm to* 188 × 119 *mm. (John Johnson Collection and John Carter Collection)*

One of Routledge's 'Books for the Country', [c. 1860], (see p. 291). 168 × 117 mm.

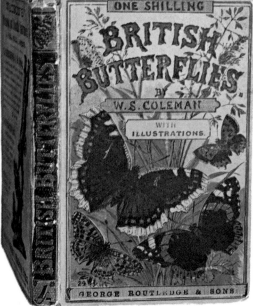

beginning of the sixteenth century. Soon he was imitated by Gryphius in Lyon, Colines and Estienne in Paris, and Plantin in Antwerp. In the seventeenth century we have the striking example of the Elzevirs in the Low Countries, whose classical texts were issued in such profusion that even today they are relatively inexpensive. If careful editing and textual accuracy had helped to establish the reputation of such houses, there were others that put out any number of inferior reprints of classical authors and pirated editions of modern ones. Though a printer may have needed the royal 'privilege', no copyright in our sense existed, and piracy was therefore a great deal easier than it would be today. Cervantes allows us to catch a glimpse of this printing and publishing chaos, when, toward the end of his book, he makes Don Quixote visit a printing office in Barcelona where, on a stroll about the city, he

happened to raise his eyes, and saw written over a door in very large letters: '*Books printed here*', which greatly pleased him, for he had never before seen any printing and longed to know how it was done.

After entering the place and seeing various well-known works on the presses

he went on farther and saw them . . . correcting another book; and when he asked its title they replied that it was the *Second Part of the Ingenious Gentleman Don Quixote de la Mancha*, composed by someone or other, native of Tordesillas.

'I have heard of this book already,' said Don Quixote, 'but truly, on my conscience, I thought it had been burnt by now and reduced to ashes for its presumption.'[1]

Such early reprints were not issued in series as nowadays; nor were they numbered and announced to the public in regular monthly lists or suchlike. Yet the reputable ones were famed among the small privileged class who could read.

In England, the beginnings of reprint series reach back into the seventeenth century. John Carter has established that a collection of some fifty 'Modern Novels' was published in 1692 by a Richard Bentley (not to be confused with the famous publisher who, between 1831 and 1855, brought out the Standard Novels).[2] The Modern Novels were issued separately and were meant for binding up in twelve volumes, each with a collective title page.

In the eighteenth century there were the two competing collections of Johnson and John Bell, both called 'British Poets', but with Bell's achieving much greater typographic distinction. Their size was about 135 by 90 mm, squarer therefore than the Aldines which measured about 160 by 90 mm, and so had almost the same slim proportions of modern paperbacks, though they were slightly smaller.

The price of such books was six or seven shillings, later five shillings, three shillings and sixpence, or even less. If that still sounds quite a lot, it must be remembered that until the 1880s the price of a *new* novel remained about one and a half guineas.

An important innovation was publishers' cloth, first used by Pickering on his Diamond Classics in 1822 or 1823; it gradually replaced leather for all but the most expensive books. Not only was cloth cheap but it could easily take print and so be used for advertising:

Specimen of beautiful typography. Jones' edition of Translations of the Classics. Decidedly the CHEAPEST and BEST ever printed, being only ONE-SIXTH the price of other editions in Octavo, and about ONE-THIRD that of inferior small editions, as may be PROVED BY COMPARISON, presenting also VAST SAVING in Expense of BINDING. A comparison of this with any other Edition now publishing will at once decide which is the cheapest and best.

Thus we read on the light brown calico binding of Jones's edition of *Herodotus*, 1830, 504 pages, price seven shillings.

Bentley's Standard Novels were launched in 1831. Twenty-four years later the collection had grown to 126 volumes. Originally bound in maroon glazed linen with two gold-blocked dark green paper labels on the spine, they underwent various changes, including a plum-coloured ribbed-morocco cloth, blind-stamped with a scroll design on sides and spine and gold-lettered on the spine only, and a brown cloth with an elaborate gold-blocked design on the spine, which also carried 'Bentley's Standard Novels', the price, and the title, but oddly not the name of the author. Among other variants there was also a morocco-grained cloth with a simpler spine design.

Thomas Hodgson's successful Parlour Library was launched in 1847 and ran for about sixteen years. It included a fair sprinkling of original titles and was the first to use lithographic paper boards, the equivalent of our modern pictorial covers.

*Three types of binding of Bentley's Standard Novels: 1836, 1848, 1859.
All 171 × 103 mm. (John Johnson Collection and Bodleian Library)*

The books cost one shilling to begin with, later eighteen pence.

Very soon there were competitors. The emergence of a
leisured and literate middle class helped to create a demand for
plenty of cheap light reading, and the vigorous growth of
Britain's network of railways caused an enormous increase in
travelling. With it came the wish to while away the tedious hours
of a journey. The first railway bookstall was opened at Euston by
W. H. Smith in 1848; and soon there they all were: Routledge's
Railway Library, the Travellers' Library, the Run and Read
Library, in bright reds, yellows, and black — as gaudy and ebul-
lient as so much in that period of rapid industrialisation. By now
it was mostly fiction, and the price of most of these books was a
shilling. Often there was also a cloth-bound edition at one
shilling and sixpence. Even this was not the bottom limit: in the
1880s there were John Dicks's illustrated series of novels by
Dickens, Bulwer Lytton, Poe, Harrison Ainsworth (and many
now forgotten authors) at sixpence a volume, his Celebrated Works
series at threepence or twopence each, and *A Christmas Carol*,
thirty-two pages demy octavo, first at twopence but soon at a
penny. Dicks proudly claimed that 'no expense is spared in
producing these novels as marvels of cheapness and elegance'.

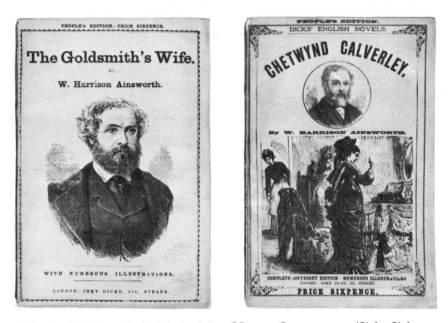

John Dicks's 'People's Edition' of the 1880s. 218 × 140 mm. (John Johnson Collection)

W. H. Smith's Railway Bookstall at Blackpool North, 1896. (W. H. Smith & Son Ltd)

During the 1850s and 1860s Routledge's had a flourishing series of Books for the Country, neat foolscap octavos in colour-printed paper boards. For one shilling one got 128 well-documented pages on *British Butterflies* by W. S. Coleman, a member of the Entomological Society of London, plus 16 black and white lithographic plates with over 200 elegantly drawn figures. The most prolific author was the Rev. J. G. Wood, who in 1860 had ten volumes in the series, among them *Our Garden Friends and Foes*, *The Fresh and Salt-Water Aquarium*, and *Bees: their habits, management, &c.*

There were other ventures aimed at offering the means for self-improvement, notable among them the Standard Library (from 1846) and the Classics (from 1853) published at a shilling a volume by H. G. Bohn. Some thirty years later there was Cassell's National Library under the remarkable editorship of Professor Henry Morley. Week by week from 1886 a new volume appeared. The format was a rather squat sixteenmo and the price threepence in paper or sixpence in cloth. Each volume had a short introduction by Morley. The average sale per volume was 30,000 copies, and the series grew to some two hundred

Choosing your blood-and-thunder before a journey in the 1870s. (Mary Evans Picture Library)

titles with a total circulation of close on seven million. It included the standard works of English literature, as well as lots of Plutarch, and a handful of other classics.

Long before that – in fact, so early that it deserves to be described as one of the major pioneering pieces of nineteenth-century publishing – the great 'Collection of British [later: and American] Authors' had been launched by the young Christian Bernard Tauchnitz in Leipzig. By 1937, when the firm celebrated its centenary (though the Tauchnitz collection itself did not really get under way until 1842), well over 5,000 volumes had been brought out, i.e. on average one volume a week for a hundred years, with a total circulation of between 50 and 60 million copies. Tauchnitz Editions had all the characteristics we associate with paperbacks. S. H. Steinberg called them

the cherished companion of English-speaking travellers in central Europe and the royal road for foreign students to the treasures of English and American literature. Tauchnitz secured the good-will of the English writers and publishers by an unprecedented step. Although not obliged to do so under the then conditions of international copyright he asked for the 'authority and sanction' of the authors and voluntarily paid them royalties on his reprints; at the same time he pledged himself not to sell these reprints in England and the Empire, while raising no objections to the sale of the original editions in Germany. Macaulay and Thackeray were among the largest beneficiaries of Tauchnitz's liberalism.[3]

When Tauchnitz once apologised to Thackeray for his poor command of English, Thackeray told him not to be afraid – 'a letter containing 50£ is always in a pretty style'. Dickens, too, was content to leave the question of remuneration to Tauchnitz:

A title in Cassell's National Library, which appeared at weekly intervals between 1886 and 1890 under Henry Morley's editorship. 141 × 93 mm.

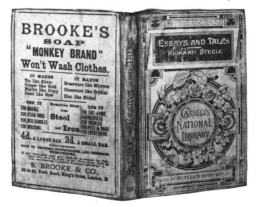

'I cannot consent to name the sum you shall pay for *Great Expectations*. I have too great a regard for you and too high a sense of your honourable dealing to wish to depart from the customs we have always observed. Whatever price you put upon it will satisfy me.'[4]

Up to the 1930s, however admirable the editorial choice, it was hardly matched typographically. The great improvement in book design since Victorian times seemed to have by-passed Tauchnitz. The books were squat, rather too wide for modern coat pockets, and set in small type with too many words per line for easy reading. The covers were white and almost identical with the title-pages. In the manner of the French *livre broché*, the pages were unopened.

When after more than ninety years a major change was at last made in the design of Tauchnitz books, it was probably because in 1932 another continental series in English entered into competition and from the outset paid the most careful attention to the way it looked. This was the Albatross Library, conceived by an international publisher of great flair, John Holroyd-Reece. For the first time different colours were used on the covers to signify major subject categories. The slim and elegant format was that adopted a few years later for Penguins and subsequently with slight variation for paperbacks everywhere.

Albatross books were promoted throughout Europe with energy and skill and, compared with the slightly fading image of Tauchnitz, had a thoroughly twentieth-century look. They quickly became famous. Allen Lane frequently stated in conversation that when he launched Penguin Books in 1935 he was

Tauchnitz editions effectively ended with the century marked by the outbreak of the Second World War. 165 × 118 mm.

trying to emulate the Albatross collection. Not only did he make
Penguins copy the same format, but he also adopted a similar system of colours for different subjects: orange for fiction, green for
crime and mystery, magenta for travel and adventure, etc. As to
the name of the series, who knows whether the Penguin was not
subconsciously hatched from an Albatross egg? After the Second
World War there was, metaphorically speaking, parricide. With
the arrival – and soon the unlimited imports – of British and
American paperbacks in Europe, several attempts failed to revive
Tauchnitz and Albatross (in 1936 the subjects of a merger, but
since 1945 in a tangle of international ramifications and legal
arguments).

One other collection, also German in origin, must be mentioned, particularly as it succeeded, like no other contemporary
venture, in meeting the demand for books of a self-improving
nature at the price of a few small coins. This is Reclam's Universal-Bibliothek, which, with so much other German publishing,
had its headquarters in Leipzig. This vast series, which is now
published from Stuttgart and is still going strong, was based on
the sudden success of a cheap twelve-volume edition of 'Shakspere' in translation. This appeared in 1858. An even greater hit
were twenty-five little volumes in pink paper covers, with one of
Shakespeare's plays each, that could be bought for the equivalent
of about one decimal penny – a sensationally low price even then.
The year 1867 (which also saw the appearance of the first volume

*Reclam's Universal-Bibliothek, launched in 1867 with Goethe's Faust,
continues to this day, unchanged in format. 147 × 95 mm.*

In format and the use of colour to denote subjects Albatross editions were prototypes of the modern paperback. 180 × 111 *mm*

of *Das Kapital*) was remarkable in German publishing annals in that under a new law the works of all German writers who had been dead for thirty years came into the public domain. Previously they had enjoyed indefinite copyright in the form of privileges or letters patent granted to their original publishers. It may have been pre ordained that Nos. 1 and 2 in Reclam's Universal-Bibliothek should be Goethe's *Faust*, Parts One and Two, but the appearance of Gogol and Pushkin, Bjornson and Ibsen, Plato and Kant during the first ten years shows that imagination went hand in hand with seriousness of purpose.

For a full fifty years the price and cover design of the little volumes remained unaltered. Since then, both have from time to time been changed. When the series was a hundred years old, some 8,000 titles – among them many original works – had been published, with a total circulation of about 400 million copies.

Of interest to the English reader is the order of precedence accorded by the German public to British and American writers . . . : Shakespeare (6.4 million copies), Dickens (1.5 million), Mark Twain (776,000), . . . Oscar Wilde (401,000), Byron (312,000), with Darwin and Faraday as close runners-up. The postwar series includes translations of *Beowulf, Gulliver, Robinson Crusoe,* nineteen Shakespeare plays, and writings by Pearl S. Buck, Joseph Conrad, Dickens, Theodore Dreiser, Faraday, William Faulkner, E. M. Forster, Galsworthy, Graham Greene, Hemingway, Aldous Huxley, Kipling, T. E. Lawrence, Jack London, Somerset Maugham, Herman Melville, E. A. Poe, J. B. Priestley, Shaw (*Pygmalion*), R. L. Stevenson, Oscar Wilde, and Thomas Wolfe. Students of literary taste and of national psychology may find food for thought in these lists.[5]

To which one can add, from the current catalogue, Samuel Beckett, Carson McCullers, Emily Dickinson, Frank O'Connor, Liam O'Flaherty, John Steinbeck, Dylan Thomas – a haphazard assembly that is probably of no deep significance as such.

It is now time to turn briefly to American paperback antecedents. Here, in 1841,

a shrewd tactician named Benjamin Park, editor of the New York literary newspaper *New World,* . . . began stuffing unbound volumes into his paper to beat the postal rates for books. . . . He didn't have the field to himself for long. In short order he was pursued by the *New York Sun* and *Mirror,* the *Boston Nation,* the *Philadelphia Public Ledger,* and his chief rival among literary newspapers, *Brother Jonathan* . . . . Each new competitor cut the price until the Post Office Department in 1843 cut all their throats collectively by charging them book rates to mail their products. They expired quietly together, and the first paperback revolution was over.[6]

Stranger things were to come some thirty years later. A drop in the price of paper prompted the *New York Tribune* to start publishing Tribune Extras and Tribune Novels at 10 and 20 cents. Soon others began to compete, most important among them Donnelley, Gasette & Lloyd of Chicago, with their Lakeside Library of paperback novels.

In 1885 you could choose from 5,000 paperback books in print and 1,500 new titles each year, mostly fiction but also including poetry, biography, science, and travel . . . . The fire was too bright, too hot, too ravenous to last. It had fed, in the first place, on an unlimited supply of British authors, who received no royalties. The international copyright law of 1891 put an end to that. Competition, price-cutting, soaring costs, heavy returns of unsold books, and a dwindling supply of new writers, even from overseas –

all these combined to cheapen the product and eventually destroy it. In 1893 *Publishers' Weekly* celebrated the 'almost entire cessation of the cheap and undesirable fiction – French and English – appropriated by piratical publishers and printed in villainous typography on worse paper in the 10-, 15-, and 25-cent "libraries" '. By 1900 the paperback business was dead again.[7]

Despite various attempts, such as Charles Boni's Paper Books from 1929 to 1931, it did not really come to life anew until just before the war.

Nobody could have foreseen during the early 1930s the immense repercussions that would be caused by an event that took place on 30 July 1935. On this day the first ten Penguins were published. If something that has been going on ever since, now for almost forty years, can be called a revolution, then this was the day on which it broke out. Unlike most revolutions, however, it had no manifesto, nor were there any far-reaching and clearly formulated plans for future action.

Allen Lane's decision to try his luck with paperback reprints of successful novels and biographies was little more than a rather desperate last throw to save the fortunes of a small publishing house, The Bodley Head, which had become famous in the 1890s, had run into financial difficulties during the 1920s (a widespread affliction in those years, when the publishing climate was very different from what it is now), and was on the verge of bankruptcy after the slump of 1929 and the great depression that followed.

In May 1935 *The Bookseller* reported that

The Bodley Head is to produce next month [in reality it was two months later] the first ten titles of a new series of cheap reprints, entitled 'The Penguin Books'. The books are bound in strong paper covers and will sell at 6d per volume. Many booksellers, it is known, do not regard very cheap reprints with great favour, and the arguments brought forward against such books are familiar. Mr Allen Lane, however, forestalls any likely critics by contributing an article to this issue in which he explains the origin of the project and his reasons for carrying it through. Booksellers' opinions will be welcomed.

Such scepticism was by no means isolated, and Allen Lane's article did little to remove it. He concluded:

One of the greatest arguments against this series is that it is unduly cheapening books and that it is bound to affect the sales of more highly priced editions. My answer to this is that in every case these books have been available in editions from 6d upwards for at least ten years, and I feel sure that any sales we may effect now will be extra sales and not at the expense of existing editions .... In choosing these first ten titles, the test which I applied to each book was to ask myself: Is this a book which, had I not read it and should I have seen it on sale at 6d, would make me say: 'That is a book I have always meant to read. I will get it now'?

I would be the first to admit that there is no fortune in this series for anyone concerned, but if my premises are correct and these Penguins are the means of converting book-borrowers into book-buyers, I shall feel that I have perhaps added some small quota to the sum of those who during the last few years have worked for the popularization of the book shop and the increased sale of books.

And what were the books for which these truly modest claims were made? They were on the whole a safe, even a conservative, choice. Detective fiction was represented by *The Mysterious Affair at Styles* by Agatha Christie and *The Unpleasantness at the Bellona Club* by Dorothy L. Sayers. There were six novels: *Gone to Earth* by Mary Webb (one of Baldwin's favourite novelists), *William* by E. H. Young, *Carnival* by Compton Mackenzie, *Poet's Pub* by Eric Linklater, *Madame Claire* by Susan Ertz, and, easily the

Nine of the ten Penguins published in July 1935. 181 × 111 *mm.* (*Penguin Books*)

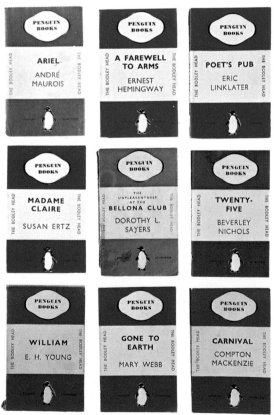

most influential, *A Farewell to Arms* by Ernest Hemingway. The group was completed by Beverley Nichols's autobiographical *Twenty-five* and André Maurois's life of Shelley, *Ariel*.

Six of these books came from the list of Jonathan Cape, whom Allen Lane in retrospect described as one of the publishers of the moment in 1935:

> He had the list of the nineteen-twenties. . . . I went to see Jonathan, and said, 'I want ten to start and ten to follow, and I want ten of them from yours.' I told him which. I was offering then twenty-five pounds advance on account of a royalty of a farthing a copy [i.e. just over four per cent], payable on publication. He wrote back after a while, saying, 'You can have them for an advance of forty pounds, all payable on signature, on account of a royalty of three-eighths of a penny.' So I got them.
>
> Years later . . . I was talking to Jonathan and he said, 'You're the b . . . that has ruined this trade with your ruddy Penguins.' I replied, 'Well, I wouldn't have got off to such a good start if you hadn't helped me.' He said, 'I know damn well you wouldn't, but like everybody else in the trade I thought you were bound to go bust, and I thought I'd take four hundred quid off you before you did.'[8]

Allen Lane had worked out that in order to break even he had to print 20,000 copies and reach sales of 17,500 soon after publication. But after a sales trip round Britain all he had collected was subscriptions of not quite 7,000 each. Disappointed but undeterred, he went to Woolworth's.

> Mr Clifford Prescott, buyer for Woolworth's, listened to Allen Lane with sympathy and attention, but explained that these books were of a kind that had hitherto been outside the Woolworth range. At that point of the conversation . . . Mrs Prescott called to see her husband. She was asked to consider herself, for the moment, the corporate British public, with sixpence to spend. . . . The books were looked at, the opinion quickly arrived at and warmly given, the sixpences were as good as already in the till. Mr Prescott gave an order. By comparison with the orders then on the new Penguin ledgers it was magnificent, but it was nothing like so good as the repeat order that came from Woolworth's a day or two later. The corporate British public had been most accurately represented by Mrs Prescott.[9]

And booksellers had been proved wrong, though it was they, not Woolworth's, who soon began to gain from the success and rapid expansion of Penguins. The second batch, again of ten, appeared in October 1935, among them *South Wind* by Norman Douglas and Samuel Butler's *Erewhon*. The January 1936 clutch included George Moore's *Esther Waters*, the first of a long row of stories by P. G. Wodehouse, and Margot Asquith's autobiography in two volumes. Reviewing all these in the *New English Weekly* George Orwell made this strange prophecy:

The Penguin Books are splendid value for sixpence, so splendid that if the other publishers had any sense they would combine against them and suppress them. It is, of course, a great mistake to imagine that cheap books are good for the book trade. Actually it is just the other way about. If you have, for instance, five shillings to spend and the normal price of a book is half-a-crown, you are quite likely to spend your whole five shillings on two books. But if books are sixpence each you are not going to buy ten of them, because you don't want as many as ten; your saturation-point will have been reached long before that. . . . Hence the cheaper books become, the less money is spent on books. This is an advantage from the reader's point of view and doesn't hurt trade as a whole, but for the publisher, the compositor, the author and the bookseller it is a disaster. . . .

In my capacity as reader I applaud the Penguin Books; in my capacity as writer I pronounce them anathema. Hutchinson are now bringing out a very similar edition, though only of their own books, and if the other publishers follow suit the result may be a flood of cheap reprints which will cripple the lending libraries (the novelist's foster-mother) and check the output of new novels. This would be a fine thing for literature, but it would be a very bad thing for trade, and when you have to choose between art and money – well, finish it for yourself.[10]

Perhaps it was not so surprising that the pundits failed to recognise the changes in social climate and conditions which were afoot and which favoured the paperback experiment; but it is astonishing that so perceptive a critic as Orwell did not recognise paperbacks as being also, in the long run, the author's and bookseller's friend. What would he have said if somebody had predicted the vast annual paperback sales of his own books – two-thirds of a million volumes in 1971 in Britain and the Commonwealth alone, achieving by all reasonable standards a splendid balance between 'art and money'?

As late as the autumn of 1938, when nearly two hundred Penguins had been issued along with forty Pelicans, about a dozen Penguin Specials, and half the Penguin Shakespeare, Stanley Unwin stated that

it is economically practicable to issue a comparatively few books in any given category at exceptionally low prices provided a mass demand is focused upon those titles. . . . But the public would be deceiving itself if it thought that such prices would be practicable were the demand not thus focused on a limited range of books. If the public wants the benefit of mass production it must be satisfied with a limited selection.[11]

Earlier in the article he had defined 'the minimum number of a sixpenny reprint that it is economically practicable to produce' as 50,000, and had gone on to demonstrate that in order to achieve this minimum and allow readers to choose from a thousand titles, a total of over 100 million copies would be needed. The reason was that 'the demand will not be spread evenly over the thousand titles; some will sell two, three or four times as many as others'.

Whether or not the revival of sixpenny reprints is a good or a bad thing for the book trade as a whole (including, of course, authors) is much disputed. A strong case can be made out by both sides. Anything which encourages the wider distribution of books is in itself good. If it could be proved – and it is much less certain than is usually supposed – that sixpenny reprints created or fostered a new reading public, the case for them would be overwhelming, but if the evidence shows that their effect is primarily a transference of demand by regular book buyers from 2s 6d and 3s 6d cloth bound reprints, there is not the same cause for rejoicing.[12]

A week later Margaret Cole took Stanley Unwin to task:

That the modern publishers . . . have found and fostered a new *book-buying* public, I do not think anybody can possibly doubt. . . . When a technical book on the ballet, which cannot be called a subject of immediate political topicality, can sell close on a hundred thousand copies in five months; when a reprint of a political book on Germany, after little more than a year's run, is approximating to the quarter of a million mark; and when of forty Pelican serious books not one has so far been withdrawn, . . . it is impossible to believe that even a tithe of this spate has been purchased by the comparative[ly] few who used to be reckoned as 'the book-buying public'.[13]

And with Fabian ardour she concluded:

No doubt some adjustment of prices may be needed, and it may be difficult in such a chaotic trade, in which no one can say that either the prices of books or the remuneration of authors is at present particularly rational. But the clue is throughout respect for the market, realization that it is high time that book-owning should cease to be the preserve of a small class and that it can only be brought to the others by giving them the best you possibly can, not either by playing down to them or by lecturing them on their 'duty' to uphold literature by doing this or that.

In retrospect, we see that Margaret Cole had here erected a signpost that clearly showed the direction which serious paperback publishing would take. And though her article was meant as a rejoinder to Stanley Unwin's, time has proved that he, too, was in at least one respect right. The growth of overall readership has not kept pace with the increasing choice that has been offered to the public; consequently, average printing numbers of individual titles are lower today than twenty or thirty years ago and prices are higher – not only in proportion to the enormous rise in the cost of materials and manufacture, but also because shorter runs have an adverse effect on the unit cost and because it costs money to hold stocks of, and promote, thousands of titles, many of which move relatively slowly.

How did young people with an appetite for books react to what took place in 1935? Richard Hoggart recalls that

I bought my first Penguin twenty-five years ago, during a week's hiking between Youth Hostels. I was sixteen, a working-class youth at a grammar-school; the book was *A Farewell to Arms*, one of the first batch. I can't claim to be a *typical* reader and don't suppose anyone can. . . . But I believe I was roughly typical of one large group of early Penguin customers. The volumes we knew best still tend to come into our mind's eye looking slightly tattered, from being pushed into the pockets of Montague Burton sports-coats or into cycle-panniers or rucksacks or kitbags. I still have some Pelicans which I bought at the Leeds University bookshop before the war and which went through North Africa and Italy. They call up, sharply, particular settings and a sense of unusual interest.

Just why Penguins were able to enlist this degree of enthusiasm – and command a kind of loyalty – is worth teasing out. They were very cheap of course and attractively presented – they looked neither meretriciously glossy nor ponderously dull. They gave us the chance to own, say, some good contemporary novels and essays . . . whereas before we had been almost confined to second-hand copies of older writers. But obviously the main foundation was a brilliant timeliness. The generation which became intellectually active in the mid-thirties was too young to have direct memories of the First World War but was greatly concerned with the movement towards the next. It was . . . larger and more mixed in its social origins. . . . Penguins, in common with several other agencies, spoke to their needs. I have mentioned the value of Penguin novels: soon Pelicans began to cater for more direct intellectual aspirations . . . ; and the Specials . . . gave background and point to their readers' efforts at making sense of that 'time of crisis and dismay'.[14]

In this passage Hoggart mentions several important ingredients of success, one of which can hardly be over-emphasised. The bright-as-a-new-pin look of the early Penguins, with their orange-white-orange panels on the covers of novels, green-white-green on crime and mystery stories, and so on through a whole palette of colours, quickly became associated with different subjects. Their impact in bookshop display must have been as great as that of Gollancz's yellow book-jackets with their startling typography in black and violet. They were immediately recognisable and acted like magnets. Carried about by their purchasers, they performed the function of countless thousands of advertisements.

After the first twelve or fifteen years there were signs that in the face of mounting competition for display space in the bookshops the simple original cover formula was losing its magic. But it was not until the 1960s that paperbacks were drawn into, and sometimes carried along rudderless by, the visual deluge that, these days, threatens to drown us with its constantly changing swirls of graphic fashion and the unscrupulous plundering of past styles, with its fondness for pastiche and all the other appurtenances and clichés of pop and camp art.

Hoggart's other important allusion is to the Penguin Specials, launched in November 1937 with an updated reprint of Edgar Mowrer's *Germany Puts the Clock Back* and followed in February 1938 by the first two of many books especially written for the series: G. T. Garratt's *Mussolini's Roman Empire* and Geneviève Tabouis's *Blackmail or War*. When war broke out less than two years later, there were more than thirty Specials, and this number had grown to about 150 by the time of Germany's collapse. Perhaps the substantial part which the Penguin Specials played in changing public attitudes towards the need to fight Hitler and in stimulating the debate about postwar Britain and the postwar world has not yet been sufficiently recognised.

For some strange reason it took another four years before the curtain rose once more, and this time permanently, on paperback publishing in the United States. In July 1939 Penguins opened their first office in New York, headed by a young American, Ian Ballantine. He had been a student, at the London School of Economics, of H. L. Beales who, together with W. E. (now Sir William Emrys) Williams and Krishna Menon, was one of the founder-editors of Pelican Books. Simultaneously Robert de Graaf, backed by Simon & Schuster, an American hardback publishing house at the height of its fame, presented a kangaroo named Gertrude who pulled from her pouch the first ten Pocket

Books: James Hilton's *Lost Horizon*, and Dorothea Brande's *Wake Up and Live!*, *Five Great Tragedies* by Shakespeare, Thorne Smith's *Topper*, Agatha Christie's *The Murder of Roger Ackroyd*, Dorothy Parker's *Enough Rope*, Emily Brontë's *Wuthering Heights*, Samuel Butler's *The Way of All Flesh*, Thornton Wilder's *The Bridge of San Luis Rey*, Felix Salten's *Bambi*. It was a more catholic choice than Allen Lane's, and it was meant to answer definitively the question why Americans would not buy paperbacks.

It had almost become an axiom in publishing that they wouldn't because there had been so many failures in the last thirty or forty years. Possibly it was my persistent nature that urged me to prove once and for all that it really wouldn't work that tempted me to try it. . . . I felt that if a first-class book, editorially and physically, could be made, the turnover would be sufficiently rapid that the wholesaler and retailer would not require the usual large margin.[15]

Before long the American Penguin enterprise and Pocket Books operated differently. Where Penguin used commission salesmen to get their books into the bookshops, Pocket Books in 1941 'added the concept of marketing . . . through independent magazine wholesalers, who had access . . . to newsstands and to railroad stations as well. Pocket Books swept the country, and the name became synonymous with paperbacks, to the distress of later competitors.'[16]

Such competition was not slow to develop. By 1945 serious differences of opinion had emerged between Allen Lane and his American director Ian Ballantine, who left in order to form a consortium whose paperback imprint became Bantam Books. The rift particularly showed in the policy to be adopted for cover designs (already pictorial in America but to remain almost entirely typographic in England for at least another ten years) and the methods to be used in marketing and distribution. Pressure in America was towards a system, borrowed from the magazine field, of using wholesalers and of saturating the market. After a fairly short time unsold books were returnable for credit. In this way huge quantities could be sold of some titles, but there were also vast numbers of returned books which in the end had to be destroyed by pulping. There were some years in the 1950s when up to 40 per cent of the entire American paperback output remained unsold and many tens of millions were pulped.

In Britain, so much smaller and more tightly knit a country, there was not quite the same need for the wholesaler as an additional middleman. He does exist and is an important link in bringing paperback front runners into many outlets that are not orthodox bookshops, but he is not as dominant as in the United States; and though returns of unsold overstocks are recognised as part of the system, and are more readily tolerated by some paperback houses than others, they have never run at anything like the American level.

Yet another major American paperback company developed directly out of Penguin's transatlantic outpost: the New American Library with its Signet and Mentor Books. This breakaway in 1947, too, was the outcome of a clash between British conservatism and caution and the more aggressive and expansionist attitude of the two chief executives in New York: Kurt Enoch, a refugee from Germany, who had been with the subsidiary since 1941 (having played a leading part in setting up Albatross in the 1930s); and Victor Weybright, a young American, who had become a friend of Lane's while attached to the US Embassy in London during the war and joined the New York office at the end of 1945. Between them, Weybright and Enoch built up Signet and Mentor lists of much distinction.

America's contribution to the paperback story is only incompletely described by putting all the emphasis on mass-marketing techniques. An equally significant development was that of 'egghead' paperbacks in the mid-1950s. Meridian, Vintage, and Anchor Books were the pioneers in publishing cheap reprints of more scholarly works that were needed by students and other sizeable minority groups. Altogether, it is difficult to over-estimate the role paperbacks now play in secondary and tertiary education. In Britain, a glance at any list of recommended or required reading for 'o' level or 'a' level GCE examinations, and for a university degree or any other post-secondary qualification, will show the extent to which paperbacks have become an integral part of education.

In 1937 it was adventurous to reprint in paperback a slim introductory outline such as Sir Leonard Woolley's *Digging Up the Past*. Its phenomenal success encouraged the publisher to spread his net, appoint an advisory editor from the academic world, and draw up long-term plans for a systematic list of specially commissioned and reprinted works on archaeology.

Outline volumes in other fields similarly heralded the publication of groups of paperbacks treating each subject in greater depth. All this was a triumph for the belief in the reader's seriousness of purpose and in his willingness to submit to quite rigorous and tough treatment. Many of the best and most successful original paperbacks make no concessions to a supposed need for 'popularity' or 'simplicity'.

Over the years there has been a spectacular rise in the number of paperback titles in print. Accurate statistics for the early days are difficult to come by, but it is unlikely that in 1948, when with the end of paper rationing there had been a return to a more or less normal balance between supply and demand, British paperback publishers could offer as many as one thousand titles. The 1972 edition of *Paperbacks in Print* lists 34,556 titles. In the United States the growth has been similar: in 1973 over 114,000 paperback titles were in print. Similar developments have taken place in Western Europe.

That the rise in the number of available titles has been greater even than the remarkable growth in the market has already been mentioned. This has brought economic problems in its wake. Investment in stock must keep some balance with turnover, especially in inflationary times, because once a price is printed on the cover of a paperback it cannot be increased: books long held in stock would therefore be sold at considerably less than is needed to provide the money for their replacement. The only ways out of this dilemma are shorter print runs and increased prices. Within reason, the public seems willing to accept this, though almost unlimited choice as one of the causes of higher prices may not be fully understood, if one is to judge by what sometimes comes out of the paperback publisher's postbag.

Another aspect of keeping thousands of titles on factual subjects in print is the need for revision – frequent in books such as *The New States of West Africa* or a *Dictionary of Politics*, less so perhaps in others. But the wish to maintain the freshness of his list will often cause a publisher to produce revised and expanded editions, even where new insights or changes in scholarly attitudes are few.

A classic example is Sir Nikolaus Pevsner's *Outline of European Architecture* which appeared in 1943 as an original Pelican of 168 pages with 107 small illustrations on 32 separate plates. It had all the shortcomings forced on its publisher by wartime stringencies.

Tentative beginnings of pictorial paperback covers in America, 1946. Sizes vary from 180 × 106 to 181 × 109 mm.

By 1963 it had reached its seventh edition (and twelfth printing). In the process it had grown to 496 enlarged pages with nearly 300 illustrations closely integrated with the text. (Even the dedication to the author's three young children had, twenty years later, been revised to include children-in-law and a large number of grandchildren!)

How is this vast mass of titles kept in reasonable order particularly in the academic bookshop which prides itself on having a wide range in stock? The original Albatross–Penguin system of

The paperback department of the Harvard Co-op in 1972. (Harvard Co-operative Society)

colour-coding has long ceased to be able to cope with the multi-
plicity of subjects. America, whose campus book-stores such as
the Co-ops at Harvard or Yale are models of organisation in large
paperback departments, gave the lead. One of the twenty-six
categories in the subject classification approved by the American
Booksellers' Association and the National Association of College
Stores can be found on the back cover of most American paperbacks, and these categories are prominently displayed above the
shelves filled with them. The categories, too, form the headings
in publishers' lists and in the collective bibliography, *Paperback
Books in Print*.

A similar system with some forty categories has for some time
been in use on everything published under the Penguin imprint.
The self-service principle in bookshops, and particularly in
paperback departments, makes it desirable that such a system is
adopted all round. This is all the more important in view of the
deep penetration paperbacks have achieved in the educational
market. Tapes, film loops, wall charts, and other audio-visual
aids as an extension of the conventional printed page add further
to the complexity of this huge field.

In contrast with the rapid growth in the scope for paperbacks
giving instruction or information, the leisure market has developed more slowly. Fiction in the past twenty years has remained
largely a matter of reprinting under licence from hardcover
publishers, despite frequent predictions that original novel publishing in paperback is just round the corner and despite occasional attempts to turn this corner. It is possible that such 1973
ventures as Hutchinson's Midway Books and the relatively
high-priced novels issued simultaneously with the corresponding
hardbacks by Wildwood House will be seen in retrospect to have
heralded a fundamental change in fiction publishing.

Individual fiction bestsellers there will surely always be, but
taking the long view the habit of novel-reading may be in a slow
decline. To make a success of paperback fiction publishing, professionalism must go far beyond merely the prudent and skilful
choice of authors and titles. Resourcefulness in promotion and
marketing, a highly efficient distribution network, and the fullest
exploitation of all possible links with film and television are
equally necessary. So is the ability to calculate the financial risks
inherent in the large advances that often have to be paid in competition with other paperback publishers bidding for the same

rights. Almost invariably such decisions have to be taken well before the hardback is published and therefore before it is known whether the book will become a critical or popular success.

In this toughly commercial field, the paperback publisher's responsibility is perhaps less apparent than elsewhere. It remains true all the same that many novels which are now acknowledged modern classics would not have become paperbacks early on if commercial caution had not been overruled by literary judgment, and that others of lasting importance and influence might not have found a publisher at all if the hardback publisher's risk had not been shared by a paperback house.

An area of spectacular growth in Britain since the early 1960s has been paperbacks for children. The singleminded dedication of Kaye Webb in her task as Puffin editor and promoter-extra-ordinary has had a lot to do with this genuine break-through. Once again, it proves what can be achieved by a blend of editorial integrity, plenty of imagination, and the enthusiastic espousal of a cause. It took many years before one publisher's predominance in this field was seriously challenged. The competition that now exists is entirely beneficial for the children: it has greatly expanded their choice and has encouraged publishers to explore wider and lesser-known territories.

The 1970s are seeing a spectacular growth of paperback publishing for children, to which Kaye Webb has made the most significant contribution.

The development of the modern vernacular paperback outside Britain and America belongs almost entirely to the postwar period. In Germany there was an extraordinary forerunner which grew out of the total collapse of the country after twelve years of literary censorship and biblioclasm. In 1947 the once famous, then banned, and now re-born publishing firm of Rowohlt began

In Germany the acute shortage of book production facilities after the war led to a short-lived experiment with publishing novels in newspaper formats of up to 380 × 270 mm.

to issue a series of novels printed on newsprint in tabloid news-paper format. At first once every two months, later at monthly intervals, during more than three years, a complete novel would appear in an edition of 100,000 copies. Though this happened less than thirty years ago, it is difficult to believe – within reach as we are of a plethora of paperbacks – just how starved were the Germans for good literature, how totally inadequate were the conventional technical means for stilling this hunger, and what a feat of imagination it was to print and distribute Hemingway, Alain-Fournier, Tucholsky, Joseph Conrad, Gide, Graham Greene, and Faulkner in newspaper format and almost at newspaper prices.

In 1950 economic and productive recovery made it possible to adopt for these 'Rowohlt-Rotations-Romane' a format similar to that which had become accepted as the international standard. As 'rororo' books they soon turned into one of the major German paperback enterprises. Another is the Fischer Bücherei, launched in 1952 by Gottfried Bermann Fischer and his wife who, as émigrés in America, had seen the growth of the American

paperback industry and on their return grafted this new branch
to an imprint which under its founder Samuel Fischer had
epitomised the best in twentieth-century German publishing. A
third, and certainly the most remarkable, is 'dtv', the Deutscher
Taschenbuch-Verlag. It was not formed until 1961, when the
supply of German paperbacks already seemed to exceed the
demand. The general prognosis was one of inevitable and rapid
failure, particularly when it became known that the covers of the
series were a pristine white, with the name of author and title in
simple black typography and a brightly coloured vignette as sole
graphic element.

Once more the prophets of doom were proved wrong. Exceptionally high standards in editorial policy and an uncompromising
adherence to, and development of, the original image served to
demonstrate that it was possible, even so late in the day, not only
to create a new style of paperback, but also to attract and hold a
large readership who acquired a special kind of imprint loyalty.
Abroad, too, 'dtv' made a considerable impact. It has become if
not yet the largest then certainly the most prestigious German
paperback publisher.

Quantitatively, France is dominated by the Livres de Poche,
published by Hachette and distributed through its nationwide
network, though other paperback publishers have done more of
the editorial pioneering. The Editions du Seuil, in the 1950s,
were first in the field with a series of original documentary
biographies in which text and illustrations were closely inter-
linked. These were prototypes of what are now often described as
'integrated' paperbacks. Other notable French enterprises are
'J'ai lu' and '10 × 18', the latter name being taken from the size
in centimetres of this particular series. More recently the house
of Gallimard, whose vastly important literary list had so far been
channelled into the Livres de Poche, has broken away and begun to
develop its own paperbacks under the name 'Collection Folio'.
Because traditionally the French book was *broché* (i.e. in the form
of sewn signatures with a simple paper cover), there has never been
quite the same polarisation between hardbacks and paperbacks
as in countries with a tradition of cased books.

None of the rest of Europe has made significant innovatory
contributions to paperback publishing. At the same time one
admires the vigour with which several countries, whose popu-
lations are so small that one might doubt the existence of an

IV   *Post Comic Weekly, September 19, 1971*

BOOKSELLERS SCOFFED—BUT HIS PAPERBACKS SWEPT THE WORLD BRINGING PLEASURE TO MILLIONS OF READERS

ONE day in 1935 stacks of brightly-coloured, pocket-size b o o k s in paper covers bearing a picture of a penguin were displayed in two big London stores.

They were priced at 6d. Customers besieged the counters all day.

By closing time the books were sold out.

The next day the stores' bosses were telephoning urgently to 32-year-old Allen Lane, head of the Penguin venture 'Send us fresh supplies; we can't cope'.

Such was the first blossoming of a modern publishing romance. Penguin books were to sell in millions.

The enterprising, energetic Lane beamed with delight.

Then, calling his secretary, he issued instructions to his printers to set their machines going again and to rush out more of the little books that captured the public's fancy — and in due course made his fortune.

Soon the books were streaming off the machines, a stream which goes on flowing today, 35 years later, when about 100,000 Penguins are despatched daily and annual sales exceed 30,000,000.

Half of these go for export, a feat which has won a Queen's Award for Industry.

ALLEN Lane (later Sir Allen) had started in publishing at the age of 16 when he was given a job in the famous Bodley Head business of his uncle John in London.

He started at the bottom, his first job being to carry books to the packers. He became clerk and book-keeper.

Learning the trade step by step, he then went 'on the road,' travelling from town to town offering Bodley Head publications to the booksellers.

He was promoted to advertising manager, then moved to the editorial side of the business.

By the age of 21 he was a director.

All the time the great idea that became Penguin Books burned in his restless brain.

He preached his vision of books by the million at prices which millions c o u l d pay to his colleagues at the office and to friends across the luncheon tables.

He set about his enterprise with the help of two brothers. He toured the country with a dummy copy of a Penguin.

But he collected few orders. Fellow publishers warned that paperback books never paid.

Wholesalers shook their heads said 'Forget it'.

BUT Lane would not be deterred. Finally he persuaded the two London stores to give the little sixpennies a trial. the trial that turned into a triumph.

Vindicated, he resigned from Bodley Head and with a capital of only £100, plunged into his adventure.

The Lanes looked for an office and warehouse. But they could find nothing which they could afford and eventually had to settle down in the crypt of a disused London church.

Here they worked frantically among ever-growing stacks of books to meet demands.

Their success was phenomenal. Within two years they sold 2,000,000 books.

Now came a series of non-fiction works called Pelicans.

The first was George Bernard Shaw's 'Intelligent W o m a n's Guide'. Shaw added new material, making it a first edition — for 6d.!

Penguins grew to embrace an astonishing range, from science and philosophy to thrillers and children's picture books.

Everyone bought Penguins, schoolchildren and students to aid their studies, adults for leisure reading and to acquire new learning.

ALLEN Lane travelled the world with his books. His brother Richard who had given up life on a New South Wales sheep station to help launch Penguins in London, went back to Australia to develop operations there from offices in Melbourne, Victoria.

During the second world war Penguins helped to pass many a weary or anxious hour for Servicemen on the fighting fronts.

The little books slipped easily into uniform pockets or packs.

Penguins of all kinds were sent by the thousand to prisoner-of-war camps.

And it was a wartime meeting that gave Penguins one of their distinguished editors, Dr E. V. Rieu, the scholar. Lane met him when they were members of a civil defence party on firewatch duty in London.

Dr Rieu invented the famous library of Penguin Classics.

Headquarters of the firm born in a church crypt is now a modern building, with a staff of 500, at Harmondsworth, near London. Sir Allen, died at the age of 67.

In 1969 he was created a Companion of Honour "for conspicuous service of national importance".

Strip-cartoon from a West African weekly, September 1971. (Penguin Books)

adequate market, have established paperbacks in the vernacular —
all the more as in Holland, for instance, and Denmark, English is
read so widely that paperbacks from Britain and America are in
direct and sharp competition with the local product.

In the emergent countries of Africa and Asia there is still too
much poverty to allow the importation of paperbacks in numbers
that bear anything like the right relation to population figures.
Yet it is these countries, in many of which English is the *lingua
franca*, that most need cheap books of instruction and information
as well as reliably edited and annotated texts of English literature,
the twentieth century included. The proper observance of
international copyright laws is thereby put under great strain, all
the more because the development of national printing and
publishing industries is naturally encouraged. Unless much
sympathy is shown by those who *have*, the have-nots may well be
driven towards taking matters into their own hands by printing
and publishing without licences, in other words by joining the
pirates who have been notorious for their activities in South-East
Asia for some years. An example of such a pirated paperback,
probably from Taiwan, is what by the cover is ostensibly a
Penguin edition of Hemingway's *The Old Men* [*sic*] *and the Sea*
but inside turns out to be an inferior photo-offset reprint of the
Jonathan Cape edition of 1957, right down to the names of the
English printer and binder transferred from the title verso to
the last page of this remarkable hybrid. On the back cover once
more we see 'Penguin Books', but there also appears the name of
another publisher, the 'Nobel Publishing Co., Ltd.,' (final comma

*Pirated edition, probably from Taiwan, symbolic of the threat to the observance
of international copyright, n.d. (after 1967) 176 × 113 mm.*

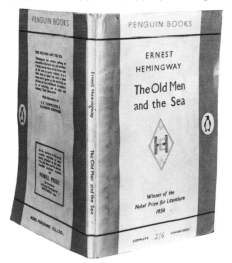

and all). If we believe an article in *The Times*[17], in which it is suggested that unless checked the pirate book industry will become a multi-million-pound business, such freaks are also a danger signal.

Until fairly recently paperbacks in Eastern Europe remained strangely underdeveloped. In a paradoxical reversal of bourgeois attitudes, the book-as-something-to-be-treasured-and-carefully-guarded was slow to give way to the book-as-an-article-for-consumption. Goethe's maxim that lack of reverence for the binding inevitably results in lack of reverence for the contents still seems to be valid in East Germany, for instance. It is neither an accident that the major international exhibition of books as objects of artistic merit (how else translate the word *Buchkunst?*) is held once every six years in Leipzig, nor that the first time an award was given to paperbacks, in 1971, it went to a group of art-historical volumes from Britain. This minor event symbolises two quite different attitudes towards the concept 'book'. It also suggests that change is in the air and that, though this particular revolution may have reached the people's republics rather late, it will make a deep impact once it gains a secure foothold and provided it is not too severely held back by ideological restraints. (At this point another paradox is worth mentioning: though in the West paperbacks have become big business, this has not prevented their publishers from giving free rein to expressing ideas strongly opposed to established political and economic systems and indeed advocating their overthrow.)

If an age of social change provides the soil in which paperbacks can flourish and cover more and more fields formerly closed to them, technical advances in printing, binding, and paper-making have to provide the means for mass-producing books at moderate cost. Not long after the war rotary presses, specially designed for the printing of paperbacks in a standard size, and using flexible rubber or plastic plates as a printing surface, came into use. At about the same time sewing as a means of holding together the signatures of a book was largely superseded by 'perfect' binding, a euphemism for removing the folded backs of every signature, thus causing each book to consist of so many single leaves which are held together by a synthetic adhesive applied to the spine. It took years before the interaction between different adhesives and papers was properly understood, with the result that one of the most frequent, perhaps *the* most frequent, complaint about paperbacks has been their tendency to fall apart in the reader's hands. A general return to thread would be quite impossible; much progress with controlling the quality of unsewn binding has been made; but further advances with adhesive techniques are needed before the critics of this particular vulnerability will become silent. The problem is increased by the climatic extremes in which paperbacks are expected to function.

While the normal rotary press prints and folds individual signatures which have to be brought together in a gathering machine before they can go to the automatic binder, the most recent development in America is a press in which the plates for all the pages of a book are mounted on two wide, endless belts. Their length is variable according to the number of pages, which can exceed a thousand. Linked with automatic binding and trimming equipment, this press, the Cameron, for the first time in the history of printing makes it possible within a minute or two to convert a reel of paper into a bound book in one continuous operation.

The highly sophisticated technology that has just been very briefly described does not add to what can adequately be reproduced in a book, if we compare it with the more conventional equipment used for the production of hardbacks and, in the early

Diagram of the Cameron belt press which has revolutionised methods of book production by converting a reel of paper into a complete book in an uninterrupted sequence of operations (Cameron Machine Company)

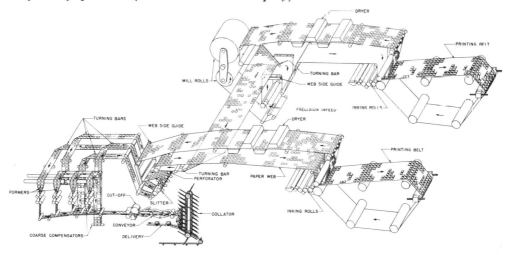

years, also for paperbacks. On the contrary, the method, though
cheap and quick, imposes severe limitations: it is strictly a
black-and-white process, and only line illustrations or rather
coarse-screened half-tones can be included. Reproductions
demanding subtler details or colour, therefore, have to be treated
as separate insets, printed on different paper by the gravure or
offset process.

Advances in the technology of offset printing are changing all
that, because in this planographic (as distinct from relief) process
illustrations as well as text can be well reproduced at high speeds
and on relatively cheap paper. Moreover, at some additional cost,
mass-produced offset printing can also include colour, either to
heighten the impact of maps and diagrams, or for the reproduction of colour photographs and paintings. Greatest advantage
of all, pictures and text can be closely married. Authors have
hardly begun to realise that in terms of production technique
there are now few limits to what can be done. Designers are aware
of it. That some of them are making the new freedoms an
excuse for totally discarding the fundamental principles and
conventions of book design is understandable; that so few are
doing it is cause for gratitude. Books, whatever their nature, will
always need the ordering hand, and mass-produced books most
of all.

In its early stage of development, offset printing from reels
(far faster than from sheets) was beset by problems: inks did not
dry quickly enough, paper wastage was disproportionately high,
and printing quality was greatly inferior to that on sheet-fed
presses. Most of these difficulties have been overcome, and
gradually the minimum length of run at which it becomes
economical to print from reels has come down. As yet, in Britain
at any rate, there is a lack of machines specifically constructed for
printing paperbacks by the offset method. It is a reasonable
assumption that this will not remain so for long. Editorially, the
pressure is on from various quarters for more and more illustrations and 'graphics'. Technically, the whole trend of typesetting is away from 'hot metal' towards film, whether produced
from alphabets on master negatives or by cathode ray tubes with
the aid of computers. Both these methods lead more readily to
the offset than the letterpress machine, though the perfection of a
process for making cheap relief plates by means of photo-
polymerisation may give a new lease of life to the letterpress

process first applied by Gutenberg but in its latest form no longer recognisable to him.

The new technologies also open the door to elaborately illustrated paperbacks being simultaneously produced in several languages and perhaps in different countries – thus spreading heavy prime costs over a number of copies several times larger than any one publisher could absorb. For years this has been the basis of international art-book publishing, and it has begun to make an impact on paperbacks too. There is a danger that books of this kind, in need of a very broad international, even intercontinental, market will tend to lack individuality and be edited, indeed over-edited, with a view to conformity and general acceptability. Already such series, spectacular but curiously devitalised in character, exist.

Few subjects in a paperback house generate so much heated discussion as cover designs. Generalisations in this field are particularly risky, yet everybody is eager to express opinions meant to help the art director in his task, or critical of what he submits. His problem is this: a cover design should reflect, or be relevant to, the contents and character of the book; it should appeal to, or intrigue, the potential buyer; it should be recognisable as a member of a family (a group of volumes by the same author, for instance, or a series of books on related subjects); it should be easily identified as coming from a publisher proud of his imprint; in a world of rapidly changing graphic fashions it should stand out from, or at least stand up to, what is displayed to its left and right, above and below; the author should like it or at any rate not violently object to it; it should be easy to reproduce and not be exorbitantly expensive to print; and if possible it should be beautiful or original or witty as an image in its own right.

It may well be that too much is made 'in the house' of the importance of the 'only right' design. It is, to say the least, unlikely that any book has ever become a bestseller on the strength of its cover design, or that a masterpiece failed to reach its public because it had a manifestly bad cover. But between these extremes there is a wide band within which covers can act as an attraction or deterrent, as something that makes us covet or put down again with indifference what we have casually picked up in a shop.

Montaigne, in his *Essays*, writes:

I never travel without books either in peace or in war. Yet many days or months will go by without my using them. Very soon, I say to myself, or tomorrow, or when I feel like it. . . . They are the best provision I have found for this human journey, and I am extremely sorry for any intelligent man who is without them. . . . When at home . . . I turn the pages now of one book, now of another, without order and without plan, reading by snatches.[18]

How near Montaigne comes to the heart of what the paperback revolution has been all about! There is no grand design, no firmly mapped-out path along which to walk. Nothing as clear as this underlies the list of any one publisher of consequence, much less the multifarious display in a general bookshop. The wish for entertainment and amusement has always existed and continues today. The earlier need for instruction and guidance has been joined by an appetite, now sharp, now a little more relaxed, for information which we pluck out of the uncoordinated yet somehow benevolent chaos of paperbacks in an age of mass culture.

SUSAN HOLMES and TIM RIX

Beyond
the book

BOOKS IN our century have had to face serious competition for the first time in their long history. The cinema, radio and television have immeasurably extended the range of options open to us for the transmission of information and entertainment, and some would say not merely extended but realigned it so that the printed word will soon become obsolete. Such visions of the future have excited the imagination of both pessimist and optimist. Ray Bradbury's *Fahrenheit 451* plays on our worst fears, depicting a society where the facility for free 'private' access to ideas and knowledge, symbolised by the printed book, constitutes the single greatest danger to a totalitarian state whose citizens are subdued and pacified by ruthless manipulation of the 'public' media. At the other extreme, Marshall McLuhan, with visionary intensity, heralds the coming of the age of the 'global village', a modern version of the primitive paradise, where harmony and understanding are made possible through the all-embracing miracle of electronic technology.

But what is the factual basis for these kinds of prophecies? In a book devoted to aspects of the publishing industry it seems appropriate to review the available evidence in order to try and achieve a balanced picture of the actual position of books in our society today. Much has been written, particularly in the last twenty years, about the new media, and new ways of looking at how the communications media work have emerged; probably the most significant of these are derived from the concept of 'mass communication' and from the belief that *techniques* of communication have an enormous influence on the impact of *what* is being communicated. Obviously, those who are concerned with the writing, production and selling of books have been influenced by these attitudes, and the expectations and needs of some of those who read books have been altered by familiarity with the new media — particularly television. Yet it is not easy to gauge to what extent the traditional functions of the book have been, or will be, taken over by its newer rivals, the latest of which, video-cassettes, are seen by some as 'visual books', the next logical step towards the audio-visual future envisaged by McLuhan, in which printed books would have little place.

In considering in limited compass the impact on the book of four of the new media in turn — cinema, gramophone, radio and television — we have chosen to look at each from two points of

view – first, popular expectations concerning their development
when they were introduced, and, second, their actual effects on
the book, so far as they can be traced, where the new medium
was well established.

There are three points of interaction between the traditional
and newer media which are particularly worth consideration –
social (broadly divided into education and entertainment), commercial, and aesthetic (where it is relevant). We have tried to look
at the situation as it developed both in England and America
since, although the book obviously has a far longer history in
England, developments in the new media in America have played
a significant and often leading role.

✳

At the time when the motion picture first appeared, the book's
position was central as a medium both of entertainment and
education in England and America; book publishing flourished
in both countries, although perhaps in America there was a
greater emphasis on less permanent forms of printed material.
It is perhaps worth stressing an important but obvious fact: the
physical form of the book had not changed significantly since the
early days of printing. Despite advances in printing techniques,
the design and concept of the book had altered little. The reasons
presumably were, first, that the traditional form had proved
adequate for and well-suited to those functions which books
were intended to serve, and, second, because the absence of even
the *idea* of an alternative means of fulfilling these functions had
resulted in a unique dependence on that form. It was against this
background that the cinema grew up, carrying within it the seeds
of a minor revolution, the expansion from verbal to visual
communication.

'The world was not consciously waiting for the motion picture'[1]
is an obvious but pertinent truth. During the last few years of the
nineteenth century, when the first 'films' were being tried out as
peepshows and minor items at vaudeville theatres, educated
public reaction was lukewarm, if not totally indifferent. Early
audiences for these spectacles, drawn mainly from a poorly
educated working-class population, displayed attitudes 'of
amazement at the remarkable new scientific marvel. Having seen
it, however, many felt no particular desire to see it again.'[2] This
public quickly recovered from its initial amazement and by about

1905, in the nickelodeons of America and the picture halls of England, were beginning to display a positive addiction to this new, romantic and popular entertainment.

Meanwhile, that other public, 'respectable' society, continued to ignore or criticise in terms which suggested that its greatest hopes for the cinema were that it would die an early death. In America it was described as 'the plaything for children of all ages', the 'cheap show for cheap people' and 'the flimsy amusement for the mob';[3] in England the reaction was similarly unsympathetic. The reason lay in the fact that the only social need which the cinema could be seen to fill was that for ephemeral entertainment. It is not surprising that little cause was found for regarding the cinema as a serious alternative to reading, or indeed any other activity, except the equally despised music hall theatre; there were the usual gloomy prognostications from pessimists who had traditionally regarded each new invention which extended the scope of social activity (the bicycle and the motor car included) as the harbinger of death to established habits, but the actual potential of the cinema was largely unperceived, except in the most exaggerated form by a few early enthusiasts:

To the final development of the kinetographic stage, than which no more powerful factor for good exists, no limitation can possibly be affixed. . . . Not only our own resources but those of the entire world will be at our command, nay, we may even anticipate the time when sociable relations will be established between ourselves and the planetary system, and when the latest doings in Mars, Saturn and Venus will be recorded by enterprising kinetographic reporters.[4]

While cinema-going and reading habits were not directly compared there was, at least in England, a growing tendency amongst the educated public to deride popular fiction and the intellectual and cultural debasement which it seemed to represent. Typical of these criticisms perhaps is the opinion of Florence B. Low writing in 1906:

. . . the habit of desultory, miscellaneous reading has, alas! taken firm root in our midst, and flourishes exceedingly amongst those who are likely to be most harmed by it . . . it would be interesting to discover what the causes are that have brought about this changed taste in reading – a change, let it be emphasized once more, not towards the vicious, but towards a lower level of literary art, the standard novel being neglected in favour of stories by tenth-rate writers, and magazines of all kinds.[5]

These criticisms began to be voiced more strongly in the early twentieth century and arose largely as a result of two widely held beliefs about book-reading. The first was to see the chief value of the book (the textbook and non-fiction work particularly) as being that of a powerful agent for the emancipation of the working classes from poverty and ignorance. This particular view had gathered momentum during the latter half of the nineteenth century, as moves were gradually made towards providing a minimum education for the working class (culminating in the 1870 Education Act). The second belief was that the reading public had mainly demanded 'good' literature until the late nineteenth century.

Neither belief was mistaken, although both were in varying degrees misleading: the first erroneously extended a concept of 'virtue' with which certain books had come to be identified, as a criterion for all other kinds of books, regardless of their function or their readers. The second ignored the large body of cheap literature, which had existed since the early nineteenth century, and included weekly periodicals with serialised fiction, as well as books. It testified to a need for popular entertainment as well as a fair degree of literacy among the working classes.

That this critical attitude arose during this period is undoubtedly the result of several different social factors, but it is reasonable to think, although it cannot be proved, that the motion picture, appealing strongly as it did to the same audience which consumed popular fiction, may have acted as a catalyst, even at this early stage. In America the situation was not quite the same, for several reasons, one being that a large part of the audience for the nickelodeons and early cinemas was drawn from the new immigrant population, many of whom at that time could not easily read English and were therefore not 'readers'; however, even after twenty or thirty years of the cinema, the intellectuals in both countries were still bemoaning the vulgarity and decadence of popular fiction, in terms which left no doubt that they held the cinema, in part at least, responsible.

In fact after its first decade, the cinema grew to astonishing proportions in a very short space of time. Around 1910 the American film industry began to predominate, overtaking the infant British industry (which until then had produced more features than its transatlantic rival). Devoted and regular filmgoers were fed a diet of romantic and epic feature films, comedies and newsreel; the star system evolved, with its accompanying glamour; and large and luxurious picture houses began to be built to cater for the rapidly expanding audiences. By the 1920s the newspaper and magazine press were acknowledging the cinema's existence, and by listing and reviewing current films, were helping both to widen its public and to establish it as a respectable entertainment. There were also small signs that its impact was beginning to make itself felt in a more subtle way. As early as 1914, the editor of the *Tribune* in New York pinned on the noticeboard the following exhortation to his writers: 'Remember you are in competition with the movies now', encouraging them to use a 'graphic' style.[6]

During this period, the production and consumption of books had steadily increased. In England the First World War had stimulated a demand for books and films, even though a paper shortage and economic restrictions temporarily slowed up book production; in America, the prodigious book production of the turn of the century was steadily maintained, even though the exceptionally high proportion of good fiction which characterised that early period of new home-grown writing, decreased towards the 1920s. The number of public libraries were expanding fast in both countries, particularly in England, after the statutory restriction of the library rate was removed in 1919, and there was a still flourishing trade for the rental and subscription circulating library. By the mid-twenties, at the height of the 'Jazz Age', the demand for entertainment of all kinds had surpassed more reasonable expectation. At the same time, in the special highly charged social climate of this period, a controversy was raging in America, centred on the products of Hollywood (which by now were the staple diet for the cinema on both sides of the Atlantic) about the dubious, and even dangerous, moral standards of contemporary entertainment – a controversy which, in due course, not only led to the establishment of the Hays Office in Hollywood, and subsequently to the formulation of the famous Production Code, but also, indirectly, focused public attention on the question of the moral censorship of literature.

At the height of this controversy the talking picture was first introduced, and then overwhelmingly accepted (1927–30). The enormous boost which this gave to the cinema, in conjunction with the still rapid growth of sensational and sentimental popular fiction, encouraged commentators of the period to talk seriously

of its effects on the book-reading habits of the majority population. Their opinions were varied; the severely critical, as
exemplified by Q. D. Leavis in her study in 1932 *Fiction and the
Reading Public*,[7] lamented the rejection of traditional literary (and
by implication, moral) values, evident in much popular fiction
produced especially for the mass market, and pointed to the
debasing influence of the cinema as one of the sources of this
rejection (she quoted the example of The Reader's Library Film
Editions – 'novelised' film stories for Woolworth's counter sale).
The bemused and slightly fearful envisaged the profound and
possibly detrimental changes which might be wrought on human
social behaviour by all the inventions of the twentieth century:

A library will consist of a store of talkie-films, by which every possible
subject – the equations of Einstein, the life of Socrates, the quality of
Elizabethan poetry – can be pictorially exposed and pithily expounded in
the space of a few minutes . . . or the change may go still further, and the
mind of man itself become a self-functioning cinema projector, screen, and
loud-speaker combined. Human intercourse will then be nothing but the
shooting out and receiving of sensual impressions in an endless reel, never
repeated, nowhere conserved.[8]

The reasoned but cautious approach was displayed by O. H.
Chesney in his *Economic Survey of the Book Industry, 1930–31*[9] in
which he examined two conflicting propositions – that the cinema
encouraged reading, and its converse, that it discouraged it, concluding that, in the first instance, whilst the cinema *did* boost the
sales of books on which films were based, it did not therefore
necessarily encourage further reading; and in the second instance,
that whilst in the absolute sense time spent at the cinema was
time lost to reading, there was no evidence to suggest that those
who were cinema addicts would have been book readers if it had
not existed. In spite of the undoubted truth of some of the accusations levelled against the cinema, Chesney's point of view was
broadly representative of the main body of opinion which was to
prevail throughout the next two decades.

Other influences could be seen to have affected public reading
habits. Thus the Depression in the 1930s, by drastically altering
the social climate in America and England, stimulated a demand
for non-fiction books dealing with political and social issues. Although the cinema continued to be dominated by escapist films it
also began to develop a social conscience, and the production of

documentaries and realistic, intelligent features, expanded alongside the standard glamorous Hollywood output.

In England the Second World War stimulated a widespread
interest in all kinds of literature which was informative, propagandist or utilitarian. In America, owing to the continuing
effects of the immigration of large numbers of ill-educated and
non-English-speaking people, and to the relative shallowness of
the social habit of 'good' reading, this trend was less marked, but
other demands for books developed. The enormous success of
the Book Clubs (and *Reader's Digest*, started in 1922) during
the 1930s and '40s, testified, for example, to a growing middle-
brow market which, although not highly educated, regarded
books as status symbols. Residual fears of the corrupting effects
of the cinema continued into the 1950s, mostly centred on the
reactions of children. The statement 'that the cinema encourages
a few livelier children to crime is its least indictment: that it turns
thousands into dull-witted adenoidal gapers is its supreme con-
demnation',[10] reflects the sort of criticism levelled at it, but by
this time the issues of mass entertainment as a whole were
looming much larger than those of the cinema alone.

Contemporary expectations and effects of the cinema in the
field of education were different – especially in that the relationship of expectations to actual effects was reversed. In the case of
entertainment, it is broadly true that early predictions about the
cinema's future grossly underestimated the size of its growth,
whereas in education, when opinions actually began to be
expressed, the film's potential was described in terms which have
certainly not been fulfilled. In retrospect it is easy to see that the
two main reasons have been lack of money, and the extreme
conservatism of most teachers. However, to those who first
envisaged the scope of the film as an educational tool, and as an
educative force, it seemed that its very desirability would enable
it to fulfil their hopes. As early as 1915, Vachel Lindsay, the
American poet, wrote in a book prophesying the age of 'photoplay' in all areas of human experience:

Textbooks in geography, history, zoology, botany, physiology and other
sciences will be illustrated by standardized films. Along with these changes,
there will be available at certain centres collections of films equivalent to the
Standard Dictionary and the *Encyclopaedia Britannica*. . . . Photoplay
libraries are inevitable, as active, if not as multitudinous, as the book-
circulating libraries.[11]

This opinion was exceptional, however, at that time. The first real upsurge of interest in the film in education came in the 1930s, when a large number of studies were made in America which examined the influence of the commercial cinema on learning habits and attitude changes (The *Payne Fund Studies* were a notable example[12]), and concluded strongly in favour of the exploitation of the film for all kinds of education.

Meanwhile, in England the documentary film had been tentatively launched by John Grierson (*Drifters* was first shown in 1929), and the movement which grew up around this new socially responsible film form in England was perhaps the single most important stimulus to enthusiasm for the use of film as an enlightener. Grierson himself was completely dedicated to the idea of the power of film as social propaganda. He rigorously campaigned for large-scale government support of film production, and envisaged a day when educators and public information services would be able to draw on 'libraries' of documentary and teaching film as extensive as their book equivalents. Didactic educational films were beginning to be made in both countries during this period, as well as other visual aids: filmstrip for classroom use and microfilm for information storage in libraries, appeared as early as in the mid-1930s, though their use was extremely restricted until after the Second World War. The proponents of film saw it as a medium which would quickly become as important as, if not more important than, the book. They asked the question 'Is the way of the books – or at least the way of the books alone – outdone and outdated?'[13] and exhorted libraries to expand quickly to cope with the almost certain demand for teaching films. Others foresaw the possibilities for film as a general stimulant to education in the wider sense:

A sound projector in every home is not a more fantastic idea than the promise of wireless telegraphy in every home would have seemed thirty years ago. . . . The buying and hiring of films may grow up, just as the sale of gramophone records has grown up. . . . Films of all lengths and kinds, on all subjects, would be demanded; stories, documentaries, nature and travel films.[14]

Yet very little acceptance of these ideas was forthcoming; there was a deep suspicion of technology, and a strong faith in the 'virtue' of books among teachers and other public servants; the first educational films were filmed 'textbooks' which did not use the new medium in an interesting way, and it was not obvious where the great advantages of film lay. By the mid-1940s, in England, the British Film Institute and the Educational Foundation for Visual Aids had been set up to support the cultural and educational uses of film, but also by then the government-sponsored documentary movement was dying as support was gradually cut down, and in both countries teaching film enthusiasts, discouraged by the painfully slow progress of the previous ten years, had come to take a much more sober view of the situation. Charles Palmer, an American film writer, summed up the prevailing attitude in 1947: 'It is doubtful whether film will ever fill more than two or three hours of the whole school week. . . . Nor will there be any reduction in the use of text-books. . . . But film can teach only principles, for comprehension, and those only in essential outline; textbooks must still present the facts, in detail, for memorisation.'[15] Certainly there *was* no reduction in the use of books for education. The production of textbooks rose steadily, as did also the proportion of non-fiction general interest books. Film showed no signs of either replacing or seriously re-aligning the use of print as educational technology, and it was not until the late 1950s in America, and the 1960s in England, that any serious increase in the use of visual aids in the classroom was achieved.

One important offshoot of the general social impact of film on the book was the gradual absorption into contemporary writing style of some of the techniques of film expression. Several critics pointed out in the 1930s that the cinema was eliminating a need for detailed descriptive writing. Readers who were accustomed to viewing exotic locations and alien settings on the screen only required a brief word sketch to evoke a scene. The reinforcement of this tendency was later to be seen in the staccato style and heavy dependence on dialogue of much popular fiction over the next few years. At the same time, film itself was beginning to be accepted as an art form, and to evolve its own aesthetic standards; novelists and poets, notably James Joyce and T. S. Eliot, began to use film montage techniques and conventions of visual symbolism in their attempts to establish new literary forms. Together, these two levels of change in literary style reflected (among other things) the genuine attempts of many writers to satisfy an expanded consciousness which the cinema had undoubtedly encouraged in their readers. Although the full impact of this interaction was not evident until some time after the establishment of television, it is interesting to remember that traditional literary art began to acknowledge the importance of the new visual art at a fairly early stage in its development.

From this brief account of the impact of film on books it can be seen that publishing and bookselling did not suffer any great depression directly as a result of the growth of the new medium. In the early days, so far as there was any impact at all, it may have been giving a boost to book sales. Starting about 1920, book trade journals on both sides of the Atlantic regularly listed successful films which had been taken from books, and pointed out the advertising potential of these versions. They encouraged the fullest exploitation of the so-called 'new market' which the cinema was carving out, and eagerly reported the large sums of money purported to be available for the purchase of film rights. During the 1920s and 1930s the film industry itself was actively interested in promotion tie-ups with the book publishers, since it relied so heavily on book authors for its screenplays. A picturesque report from the *Publishers' Weekly* of 1927 captures the spirit: 'A boy with a market basket full of books stood near a movie theatre in Washington, D.C., recently as the patrons came out after the evening performance and sold 450 copies of the book from which the movie was taken. . . . Books were almost literally in the limelight.'[16]

This kind of enthusiasm waned on both sides during the 1940s (for example MGM's novel award to authors, which had been the largest cash prize available, came to an end in 1948), but there is no doubt that 'best-sellerism' was encouraged by the commercial methods of the film industry, and that in general publishers were made to feel that mass-marketing techniques would have to be applied if they were to compete successfully. The growth of paperbacks (the subject of another essay), although by no means a direct result of the impact of the cinema, showed the consciousness of a need to reach a wider market, and the new emphasis on the visual element in the design and content of books, which, from the 1930s onwards became steadily more marked, reflected the book industry's interest in brightening up its product to meet new audience demands created by the cinema.

✳

In the technical sense, the advent of sound broadcasting was as furtive as that of the cinema. Expectation as to the potential of early wireless telegraphy at the beginning of the twentieth century was limited to the idea of message transmission. ('Our ultimate ideal must be instantaneous electrical communication with every man on earth, ashore or afloat at a cost within the reach of everyone.'[17]) There was a gap of twenty years between early experiments with wireless at the end of the nineteenth century (Marconi's company was set up in England in 1897), and the establishment of broadcasting stations with regular programmes. However, during this period the idea of 'broadcasting' – the transmission of radio signals for general reception rather than for point-to-point message communication – was evolved through the experiments of amateurs and equipment manufacturers.

In America, where developments were faster and more widespread than in England (which suffered a ban on amateur broadcasting during the First World War), enthusiasts were broadcasting music and talks, in a limited way, from about 1910 onwards. Although at this time there was little public discussion of the issues involved in broadcasting, when, in the early 1920s public broadcasting began in earnest (KDKA, Pittsburgh, USA, started in 1920, and the British Broadcasting Company in 1922) several controversies, some of which centred on the social effects of broadcasting, arose almost immediately. In England, as Asa Briggs has pointed out,[18] fears and hopes as to the possible effect of radio on established activities were more or less equal; probably the most prevalent fear was that addictive radio listening would encourage social apathy and superficiality of response. In America similar feelings were expressed, although the burden of emphasis was different; public-spirited Americans also feared the consequences of monopolistic control of broadcasting stations. The newspaper press in both countries reacted violently to the prospect of unregulated competition and protective legislation was soon enacted. Book-reading was a fairly common object of lament, and certainly figured more prominently as a likely casualty of radio than it had done of the cinema. Radio, being a homebound entertainment, offered a challenge to books as entertainment on their own territory, and also, relying heavily on verbal communication, it was in one sense a direct equivalent of, and thereby possibly a substitute for, reading.

By the mid-1920s, British and American broadcasting were firmly set on different courses; the granting of the Charter for the formation of a British Broadcasting Corporation in 1926 finally confirmed radio broadcasting in England as a public service, to be financed by revenue from receiver licences; whereas in America strong commercial pressures, coupled with the traditional American distrust of state control had led to the evolution of a commercial system. This was finally ratified when the Federal Radio Commission of 1927 was empowered to issue broadcasters' licences to any applicant prepared to conform to its restrictive regulations with regard to frequency, power units, and permitted number of broadcasting hours. Thereafter the development of broadcasting in the two countries steadily diverged, and public attitudes towards it, and its relation to book-reading, were inevitably different.

The quality and flavour of British programme content were largely determined by the personality of John Reith, who had headed the British Broadcasting Company from its early days. It is interesting that he, and his disciples, while contemplating the potential of broadcasting with a degree of awe, measured its virtues by the standards and values of a soundly based book culture:

Broadcasting is in no sense to be regarded as a substitute for the reading of good books or the study of good music. It should supplement and encourage. ... I firmly believe that the activities of the broadcaster will have at least some effect on literature and music as published. It should increase the demand for publications of certain classes, but I believe that sooner or later it will be found that the demand for the publication of other orders will decrease; that the market for certain kinds of music and printed matter will become more limited as appreciation of real worth is fostered.[19]

This conviction of Reith's that radio broadcasting could and should be used for enlightenment and 'good' entertainment in the same way as books strongly influenced not only programming but also contemporary opinion. Throughout the period when radio achieved its greatest popularity (the late 1920s and 1930s), very few commentators either expressed doubts as to its worth, or predicted that it would destroy the reading habit. The very idea of the formal script reprinted in *The Listener* had overtones of *belles lettres*. On the whole, British broadcasting retained a highly responsible image, although middle-class and puritanical in bias, which was finally reinforced by the vital importance of its role during the Second World War.

The retention of the idea of the virtue of book-reading, fostered to some extent by the BBC, manifested itself in several ways besides a steady rise in book production (curbed by the restrictions of the war). In 1935 the launching of Penguin Books, aimed at a popular market for good literature, achieved a startling success; at first the titles were all reprints, but in May 1937 the introduction of Pelican Books heralded the first original paperback titles, which were soon equally in demand.* Moreover, in 1937 book clubs came to England, the first of which was Victor Gollancz's Left Book Club, again catering for a serious reading market; other similar ventures, both in the general and political field, followed. Not all of them lasted; nevertheless it is notable that so strong a taste existed in England for good reading during the heyday of radio broadcasting.

The situation in America was not parallel. The commercial values which dominated radio were formed primarily by a need to develop mass markets, and although radio programming during the 1920s and '30s displayed a great vitality, especially in the field of entertainment, there was no commitment to using radio for the propagation of the particular moral and social values which characterised a traditionally book-oriented society. American radio somewhat resembled and pandered to the same tastes as the cinema and the newspaper press, and this, alongside the fact that it was home-based entertainment, provoked considerable criticism of its probable detrimental effects on reading habits. As already noted, there was no reduction in the number of books published during this period, nor was there any significant evidence that the reading public was seriously weaned from books by the radio, in spite of the latter's universal popularity and increasing importance for the dissemination of news. But the general level and effects of radio entertainment were continually bemoaned ('Why do the American people tolerate current radio fare? Perhaps because of the popular feeling that you should not look a gift horse in the mouth'[20]) and since the impact of the cinema and radio as mass entertainment was to some extent cumulative, by the mid 1940s in America (when television was already getting under way) some critics were still blaming the radio for a deterioration in the quality and importance of reading.

In the field of education, the progress of radio in America closely resembled that of the cinema. Owing to the lack of interest

* See Hans Schmoller, 'The paperback revolution', pp. 283 ff. The first Penguin Special was published in November 1937.

of most commercial stations, very little finance or expertise was available for realising the hopes of radio education enthusiasts. There was no direct teaching at school level, although there was, by the end of the 1930s, a small body of public service and general interest broadcasting which came under the umbrella of adult education. It was easier, of course, for the BBC to experiment with educational radio; in 1927, in spite of much resistance from a conservative teaching profession, the first educational broadcasts were tried out in Kent. Subsequently a specially planned curriculum of programmes was broadcast to 5,000 schools, in 1929–30; and after this schools broadcasting came to be more or less accepted.[21] Much of the content of these broadcasts came under the heading of 'enrichment' rather than direct teaching, and it was this kind of education which remained the staple fare of classroom radio.

Overall, the effect of these developments on the position of textbooks in schools, and non-fiction books in general education, was favourable. Schools broadcasting created a need for a large number of accompanying explanatory texts, and adult 'enlightenment' programmes often recommended and encouraged the reading of related books. This was not necessarily a direct boon to the book industry, since the BBC itself started to publish school broadcast texts, and far more people undoubtedly listened to the serious programmes than actually purchased books covering the same subjects. Nevertheless, librarians frequently reported a direct correlation between radio programmes and a demand for certain titles, and there were spectacular instances of serious books being popularised by broadcasts, for example, the Reith Lectures series. (In 1948 Bertrand Russell's *Authority and the Individual* sold 30,000 copies *before* the announcement of his Nobel Prize.[22]) This type of broadcasting definitely sanctioned and encouraged serious and minority interest reading.

The relationship of the book industry itself with broadcasting interests is reasonably straightforward. Even in the early days of radio, in England and America, a certain number of programmes were devoted to book reviewing; some publishers evinced great enthusiasm for the new medium, both as an advertising outlet and as a general spur to reading:

Personally I cannot help but feel that radio is one of the greatest allies that the book business has ever had. It keeps people at home; it makes them receptive to educational thoughts; and it creates in them a desire to know more about this peculiar world in which we live. Books are the logical answer to such a prayer. . . . The radio . . . lends itself particularly well to the advertising of books.[23]

However, it quickly became obvious that straightforward radio advertising did not boost the sales of books particularly, the main reasons being, as O. H. Chesney pointed out in 1931, that many such programmes were pitched very much above the level of the general audience, and also did nothing to create special interest in the subject matter of the books concerned. By contrast, radio serialisation of novels and of documentaries based on non-fiction books clearly did encourage the public either to buy or borrow the book versions (though this did not, of course, necessarily lead to further individual reading). The English book industry was better served by the BBC, whose average book-based content was quite high, than the American industry was served by the commercial broadcasting networks. After they had recovered from the initial impact, publishers were probably more sanguine about the effects of radio on reading habits than they were about those of the cinema, in spite of the greater number of hours devoted to it. Radio dealt mainly in words, and operated to some extent in the same way as books, whereas the cinema's combined verbal and visual images set up a different type of response, not apparently so closely allied to the particular habit of mind required for book-reading.

*

The impact of sound broadcasting helped to clarify the particular importance of what was really the first of the new twentieth-century communication technologies – the gramophone. It is not necessary to consider the development of this invention in any detail here, since its early history was not characterised by any serious comment on its potential rivalry with books. Marshall McLuhan states that 'the phonograph was involved in many misconceptions. . . . It was conceived as a form of auditory writing. . . . The idea of it as a talking machine was especially popular. Edison was delayed in his approach to the solution of its problems by considering it . . . as . . . a store-house of data from the telephone.'[24] However, by the time the machines were at all widespread, in the first decade of the twentieth century, the manufacturers had their sights firmly fixed on the musical

entertainment market. Although recording quality was bad, and
choice of music limited, the gramophone achieved great popularity in Europe and America during the next ten years, and jazz
dance bands, as well as many opera stars, owed their success to it.
Some tried, at quite an early stage, to extend the uses of the
gramophone/phonograph record beyond these limits; there were
instances in America of book publishers tentatively exploiting the
record as a boost to book sales. (In 1917 Harper and Brothers
published a series of children's books accompanied by records,
called 'The Bubble Books', which sold one million copies in twelve
months. Thereafter, several other publishers launched similar
schemes, none of which created a substantial stable market.)

It was not until the advent of radio, with its superior sound
quality, ease of operation, and variety of material available at the
turn of a knob, that the position of the gramophone record was
thrown into relief. In England the already established trend
towards high quality classical music recording was confirmed and
boosted by BBC policy, and the good sound quality of radio put
pressure on the gramophone industry to develop selective
recording. In America, where the emphasis had been mainly on
popular music, radio initially came close to destroying the
gramophone industry altogether, but finally, after much wrang-
ling, commercial interests in both industries were merged, and
the gramophone industry started to flourish again. There was
little new demand for other types of material besides music on
record after the establishment of radio, and both the industry and
the public's attention were focused on achieving the highest
possible quality in recording. Two developments after the Second
World War, magnetic tape for master recording, which did not
appear as a serious rival to the record as a mass produced product
until recently, and the LP microgroove disc, greatly assisted
this aim, and thereafter the industry grew, both in classical and
popular music fields, to enormous proportions.

A number of minority markets for the spoken voice, both
educational and entertainment, also developed, and publishers
continued to introduce book and record 'packages' from time to
time. For commercial reasons, however, these diversifications
never became significant. (One of the first such ventures in
England was Methuen's 'talking books' – a series of booklets
accompanied by records which were launched in 1959, offering
children's titles and various 'teach yourself' subjects for adults.)

The chief value of the gramophone record as a mass-produced product is as high quality storage for musical performance, and it has never seriously embraced any other function.

*

Television in its present form is effectively derived from both cinema and radio broadcasting, so that opinions and theories expressed about it are often equally applicable to, and many explicitly include, the older media. Certainly, in contrast to the beginnings of cinema and radio, the world was both waiting and prepared for the coming of television. The first regular transmission was made in Britain in 1936, and during the next three years a limited number of programmes were broadcast, which conformed basically to the patterns laid down by radio. When, during the war, television broadcasting was shut down completely in England, America began to lay the foundations of its systems, starting in 1941 with broadcasts by NBC and CBS, which were largely aimed at high income groups. The systems were of course, commercial, like radio, and by 1948, when a temporary four-year freeze was imposed on the allocation of station licences, there were 109 stations in operation or authorised. In England after the war, the BBC started transmissions again in 1946. Broadcasting hours and the number of receivers increased quickly in both countries during the last years of the 1940s.

Opinion in the early stages of television broadcasting ranged from the enthusiastic to the cynical, but there was less of the exaggerated controversy relating to broad social issues which had raged around the birth of radio. The sort of reservations which were felt in America are well exemplified by the following editorial comment from the *Saturday Review*, criticising an apocalyptic vision of television's future expressed by a fellow journalist: 'The opportunity to look upon television as a menace is irresistible, and under the present circumstances one to be grateful for. Nothing provides a better escape from a real menace than an imaginary menace. . . . Unfortunately, Mr White doesn't convince us that television is going to be more than just another bad habit, like radio.'[25] England, with a happier experience of radio behind her, felt more optimistic about the new broadcasting phenomena, and both countries had prophets who looked forward to an audiovisual future. One, who in the light of present-day developments may have been remarkably accurate, was Gerald Cock, the first director of BBC television, who prophesied in the mid-1930s: 'The growth of a television service will see a revolutionary change in the gramophone record industry. "Telegram" sets will replace radiograms and long-running film records will be used instead of discs, the picture track being shown on the home television screen.'[26]

Programming in America during the early 1940s was largely dictated by accumulated experience of radio, and as had been pointed out, one of the main contributory factors to television's early success was the direct borrowing of existing successful radio programmes. Many new programme formulae were tried out, but on the whole the staple content of early television broadcasts was derivative. The BBC, following the same course in 1946, planned a television service to fulfil its traditional ideal of public service and enlightenment (as is evidenced, for example, in its choice of dramatic fare: 'Producers at Alexandra Palace are energetic folk. At present they can offer three or four full-length plays a week. Shaw, Pinero, Priestley, Bridie, Wilde – this is a high constellation, and the light has come to us unfogged.'[27]) Although at the same time it initiated a policy of greater co-operation with commercial entertainment interests, aimed at enlivening the rather stuffy atmosphere which surrounded radio, the content of the service basically conformed to familiar patterns. There was the same continuity across the Atlantic and although there were critics, especially in America, who regretfully pointed to lost opportunities, general opinion quickly expressed acceptance of these traditional criteria.

In this situation the relation of television to book-reading and other activities was, at first, regarded as undramatic. It was thought that its effects would parallel those of radio (and cinema), continuing the process of eroding the leisure time available for reading, but not profoundly changing domestic habits. Very soon, however, it became obvious that television was fast becoming the most used and the most universally accepted of the new media. Its growth was truly astonishing; it started almost immediately to eclipse both the cinema and the radio. In America in particular, many people, observing this rapid growth, began to think seriously about trying to define its real effects on social habits. By 1950 a new approach to the problem had been pioneered – statistical surveys of the preferences and habits of 'televiewers'. The first one, made in 1948 on Long Island, had a section on book-reading which appeared to prove that for many people it was being substantially reduced by their heavy use of television. Over the next four or five years a number of similar surveys, some more statistically reliable than others, reinforced this conclusion (although the degree of reduction varied widely) which was also supported by an actual decline in the demand for popular fiction.

At the same time there grew up around the new media a school of commentary which began to deal in sociological and cultural terms with the meaning and importance of 'mass communications'. Gilbert Seldes, the American critic, who had been one of the first to take the cinema and 'popular art' seriously as early as 1927, published his famous book *The Great Audience*[28] in 1950, and at about the same time many journalists and self-appointed pundits became interested in the cultural, social and aesthetic issues raised by 'Pandora's Box'.

In England these issues were thrown into relief by the controversy about commercial television started in the early 'fifties, which led to the establishment of the Independent Television Authority in 1954. There was great concern at that time, centred on this event, for the maintenance of standards in television broadcasting, and there was also an increased interest, paralleling the slightly earlier developments in America, in studying television's specific effects. By the end of the 1950s a considerable body of writing existed covering all aspects of the impact of television. Yet there was no consensus opinion. For every point of view expressed, or 'fact' proved, there was a converse. It was shown both, for example, that reading was cut back by television, and that it was encouraged; that programme content was debasing and that it opened out new horizons; that the idea of mass entertainment was false and misleading, and that it was the single most important key to understanding twentieth-century society. Examples of different approaches to the conflict between print and television are numerous; in 1953 Roger Manvell wrote:

Words, whether written or printed, remain a specialised form of communication, highly treasured like gold by people with a literary sensitivity, but tossed about like casual coin by ordinary people. . . . This is why motion pictures and television constitute the next great stage forward in human communications. We must face it that after six centuries of printing in Western civilisation, and two generations of universal education . . . few people can read *well*.[29]

And in 1955 Leo Bogart wrote as part of his conclusion to a brief
factual survey which seemed to indicate a general cut-back in
book-reading: 'Library book circulation has continued to rise in
post-war years, primarily in non-fiction. If the libraries are
flourishing, it may very well be that this is neither in spite of
television, nor because of it, but because of the great distinctness
of function between the oldest mass medium and the newest.'[30]
Many of these views differ from similar ones expressed earlier
about radio and cinema. They were based on research, however
incomplete or inaccurate, and they displayed the beginning of
intellectual concern with the place of television and the other
media in society. There was little real clarification of the issues
involved, but there was, by the 1960s, profound interest.

Partly as a result of the strength of commercial interests
governing television (wholly, in America, and partly, in Britain),
the question of the nature of the entertainment to be transmitted
through this medium had become vexed. It was pointed out that
a large proportion of the audience for television (the mass
audience) were 'uneducated' in the sense that it was not inculcated
with the traditional 'cultural' values which still informed the main
body of what was regarded as respectable entertainment. Consequently, a heated argument ensued as to whether the channels
of mass communication should transmit material which would
attempt to raise the cultural standards of this audience, or whether
they should accept the values dictated by 'ratings' (to be inter-
preted as public demand) as the legitimate values of a new
'popular culture'. The two sides of this argument were exemplified in both British and American television; the BBC in 1962
made a strong gesture towards the interest of minority and
specialised audience groups, when it inaugurated its new service –
BBC 2, and although the rivalry of commercial television was
forcing the BBC on its other channel to enter the ratings race,
it nevertheless retained a strong bias in favour of enlightenment.
American television on the other hand, while continually criticised
by intellectuals for the vulgarity and passivity of its programmes,
was motivated not only by commercial profit motives, but also by
a strong belief in the vitality of 'popular' programme policies.
These two points of view closely resemble earlier twentieth-
century attitudes to book-reading with one important difference –
at the time, the cards were heavily stacked in favour of the
maintenance of a cultural heritage through 'good' literature, in

both countries, whereas now the absolute value of certain kinds of book or programme was not automatically acknowledged.

In America, during the 1950s, much concern had been expressed about general reading habits. It was pointed out, with truth, that 'the phenomenally pyramiding number of educated citizens has not produced a corresponding increase in sales of many kinds of books',[31] and although this concern did not result from an actual decrease in book production or consumption, it did reflect an awareness of the rather tenuous position which books as entertainment held in the American mind. The evidence in England did not point at that time to the same conclusion, since the book-reading habit was more firmly established, and also still received greater support from the other media. However, during the 1960s in both countries, the power of the nineteenth-century idea of virtue intrinsic to books was being eroded by the growth of new attitudes towards television, and all the related media. A number of theories heralding a radical changeover to visual communication were propounded early in the 1950s, and their logical culmination came with the writings of Marshall McLuhan, published in the first half of the 1960s. The extremely fuzzy nature of his ideas is characteristic of this particular area of study, and there is no doubt that they contain very little of practical value. Nevertheless, the enormous popularity attending them in the mid-1960s served to focus the attention not only of sociologists, but also of a large number of people working in the communications industries, on the social relevance of the different media as well as on the techniques. During this same period also, a few comprehensive surveys of viewing habits and their effects were made. In England, W. A. Belson's study reported that in the presence of television, 'the number of books needed for pleasure or relaxation went down by 23 per cent, and even the strength of the viewers' interest in such book-reading went down somewhat (9 per cent). Moreover, this effect appears to be of a continuing kind.'[32] In America Gary Steiner summed up the results of many statistical surveys, and pointed out that reading as an activity became more popular as the level of education went up. He added, however, that 'for fast information, or for entertainment, even the intellectual élite must often say they turn to the airwaves.'[33]

In this atmosphere of serious interest, several attempts were made to correct and clarify some of the broad assumptions implicit in the writing of early 'media' pundits; Raymond Williams and Richard Hoggart[34] are but two writers — both of them specialists in English literature, not sociologists — who have pointed out that a 'mass' audience is neither an accurate nor a particularly helpful concept, and that the commercially expedient certainty of its existence, dominating the consciousness of the whole entertainment industry, can and has led to the sterility and lack of relevance of many of its products. However, there is no doubt that for large sections of the working-class and 'new' middle-class population, television entertainment has partially displaced the subculture of 'popular' literature which flourished well into the twentieth century. The demand for fiction has diminished, but at the same time a more widespread demand for non-fiction has grown up, possibly encouraged by the selectivity of television's output.

At the beginning of the 1970s, there are still many uncertainties surrounding the media. The nature of these uncertainties, amongst people closely connected with the media, is well displayed by the following report in the *Publishers' Weekly* of 26 January 1970 setting out the results of a questionnaire given to *New York Times* journalists, covering various aspects of the impact of television:

The *Times'* critics weren't too clear about the effects of television on books. Harrison Salisbury suggested that the trend of the novel toward journalism might mean it was being killed by television. Jack Gould thought that television increased 'the appetite for junk', and Walter Kerr said that television 'has affected young people, that they pick up great quantities of information not through reading but "in the McLuhanesque way"'.

Perhaps the area in which the impact of television is most easily measurable is that of education. Alongside the growth of serious interest in the general social effects of television, which obviously extended to educationists, there grew up in the 1950s and 1960s an interest among the more radical elements of the teaching profession in revolutionising teaching methods. There is no simple cause and effect relationship between these two preoccupations, but there are points of interaction. The motivation for the 'teaching revolution' was partly political, but also involved recognition that in order to cope with the stresses of modern industrial society (greatly increased leisure, plus material prosperity, plus traditional education 'for qualifications only', equals boredom and frustration), people needed a more broadly based and 'open-ended' type of education. There was a sense, too, that the feelings and opinions of modern children were being moulded by influences, television included, of which traditional education took no account. These points had been made by educational innovators at least twenty years earlier, some of whom, like John Grierson, were audio-visual enthusiasts, but political and financial support for new methods was not forth-coming until the late 1950s in America, and the 1960s in England. Attention to the potentialities of audio-visual tech-nology in education figured largely in the planning strategy of the new educationists.

Educational television in the general sense had been planned for in America as early as 1945, but it was not until after a considerable battle between commercial and government interests that the 242 strictly non-commercial educational channels were authorised in 1952. These channels were to be used for public service, cultural enrichment and school education programmes, and they testified to the growing awareness in America of the need for intelligent use to be made of the medium, even if it involved a degree of dreaded government control. At about the same time, some American educationists started to pay serious attention to the possibilities of closed circuit, direct teaching television. In 1956 Hagerstown, Maryland, was the scene of intensive experiments in the use of closed circuit television (cctv), and a number of schools in the area subsequently made use of a complete television curriculum. The educational net-works, and cctv to a lesser extent, increased in popularity during the next few years, and there was a great deal of enthusiasm for them both inside and outside schools, although there was no attempt at large-scale coordinated national teaching programmes.

Compared with the situation in England, however, America's experience of the use of television for education was advanced, partly because of the amount of money available, and partly because of the relative novelty of the possibility of educational broadcasting. The bbc in England was committed to large-scale provision of education by sound radio, but put out a small number of 'enrichment' programmes for school viewing. The general feeling about television teaching was extremely conserv-ative. In 1954 Sir Ifor Evans, for example, summed up the prevailing attitude to broadcasting as a teaching aid and came down in favour of books as being still the most significant medium: 'The printed book must still be the medium for learning, for contemplation, for research, for technical knowledge, indeed for the constructive elements upon which a civilisation is based.'[35]

After a few years of operation, the independent channels were offering some competition in educational programming, and this encouraged the BBC to refurbish the image of their own programmes in this field, but there were still no direct teaching experiments, and very little encouragement from the teaching profession. There was, however, a growing interest throughout the 1960s in the visual media in education, given impetus by the American example.

By the beginning of the decade American educationists had already become intensively involved in research into new educational technology, and commercial interest was developing. Television itself was the main target for this interest, but simpler and less costly visual technologies, for example 8 mm cassette films and filmstrips, were developed or boosted to serve complementary functions in the classroom and lecture hall, and the use of other media such as discs and tapes also developed as a further extension of the traditional book-based education. But this new enthusiasm in America for technology in education often over-reached itself. The miraculous efficacy of audio-visual media in solving educational problems was often advocated without reference to the obvious necessity for new teaching methods, and new content.

At the same time, the question of the importance of textbooks relative to the new media caused some trepidation. There was little of the old reverence for books evident in the attitudes of those involved in curriculum reform and educational technology, but they did stress that, rather than being displaced, print would fulfil many new functions complementary to the new methods and media: 'Where educational television research now is needed . . . is in the area of the learning-teaching situation – what happens at the other end of the tube. Here we are enormously interested in working with other older media, including print',[36] and 'research . . . indicates that the combination [of reading and pictorial experience] tends to result in improved ability in the use of the higher mental processes – in the ability to make and apply inferences, to handle principles viably so that they are not just abstract symbolic formulations.'[37] The possibility, implicit in several new teaching programmes, for the displacement of the textbook in certain subject areas was on the whole adequately balanced by opportunities offered by other programmes for the broadening of its scope, and also, of course, by the steadily increasing need for cheap teaching aids (i.e. books) set up by the fast rising numbers of school and university students.

In England during this period the textbook was not under attack in quite the same way. Curriculum reform research was in progress by the early 1960s, but there was no immediately accompanying audio-visual bonanza, not necessarily through lack of interest but certainly through lack of finance. Investment in education by television, however, began to advance. The BBC broadcast its first series of direct teaching programmes (mathematics for fifth and sixth forms) in 1962–63, a few experimental CCTV schemes for different educational levels were started, and after the Labour Party's election victory in 1964, practical plans for the long-discussed Open University were put into motion. (It is interesting to note the change from some of the early conceptions of this university; programmes are only 25 per cent of a course, and 75 per cent consists of the printed word.)

Extremely successful curriculum reform schemes in England, initiated by the Nuffield Foundation in several subject areas, mainly science and languages, made large-scale use of 'audio-visual aids', but these laid at least as much emphasis on the importance of re-thinking the content and social scope of teaching as on the use of new technology.* However, the slow spread of the use of cassette film, filmstrip, and allied media, did encourage some of the same fears for the future of the textbook which had earlier been expressed in America.

By the late 1960s, on both sides of the Atlantic, there was intense involvement in curriculum reform and in research into the correct use of new technology. On the one hand there was a growing widespread recognition of the inadequacy of much primary teaching which had somehow allowed thousands of children to slip through the school system without fully acquiring reading and writing skills. Although many children at secondary level had access to the wonders of audio-visual technology, it was acknowledged that an ability to read fluently was still a vital key

---

* See Tony Becher and Brian Young, 'Planning for change', pp. 389–419.

to educational progress: consequently new approaches to the teaching of reading were pioneered, leading to the implementation of expensive programmes. On the other hand, the McLuhanesque attitude towards media which characterised contemporary thinking about their broader social implications also greatly influenced specifically educational thinking. McLuhan questioned the presuppositions of 'our traditional print-orientated culture'. 'In the first place,' he wrote, 'a book suggests to children that knowledge is closed — not open-ended. It can easily become a static thing, a sacred text . . . books can become more and more a dangerously misleading link with the past . . . they suggest that knowledge is compartmented.'[38]

This implied rejection of book-based teaching is quite commonly found in the theories of present-day educational innovators. In exaggerated cases there is heavy dependence on McLuhan's idea of the electronic image and its power to transcend and replace the verbal image; an American teacher, Caleb Gattegno, in his book *Towards a Visual Culture*,[39] puts forward a theory of education based on the use of very short televised sequences explaining various basic topics (for example, the nature of light, or of sound) in purely visual terms, his contention being that children would take in this information without secondarily verbalising it, and would therefore absorb it extremely rapidly. More generally, however, there is a strong belief, based on practical experience, in the essential importance of accompanying written and spoken words. It is interesting, in fact, that one of the most controversial and apparently successful examples of the educational use of visual media, the American television series *Sesame Street*, has as its aim the teaching of reading to underprivileged pre-school-age children. Using techniques derived directly from the slickest and most lively entertainment programmes, it testifies to a faith in the equal educational importance of books and 'popular' television culture.

✻

A movement towards brief and fragmentary literary styles which, as noted earlier, was precipitated by the rise of the cinema, intensified during the late 1950s and 1960s to the extent that many critics were speaking in terms of the 'death of the novel'. George Steiner, writing in 1958, pointed out that 'to make themselves widely understood, contemporary media of mass communication have had to reduce English to a semi-literate condition' and that 'In its endeavour to excite and hold our interest, the novel now has to compete with media of dramatic presentation far more "authentic", far easier to assimilate into our increasingly lazy, inert sensibilities. To compete at all with the strident alternatives of television and film, of the photograph and the tape recording, the novel has had to find new areas of emotional shock (or, more exactly, the serious novel has had to choose topics formerly exploited by trash-fiction).'[40] The development of this trend, considered to be extremely unfortunate by many who valued literary art, was regularly noted throughout the next decade, although few critics besides Steiner tried to derive complex cultural and aesthetic theories from it.

By the end of the 1960s the notion of 'the decay of verbal communication' was familiar; a *New York Times* critic, Hilton Kramer, spoke in 1970 of 'a deep prejudice against verbal communication' and also against 'identifying different kinds of individual experiences – which militate against the whole idea of producing novels'. Detailed reasons for 'the decline of the novel as an art form' were documented by George Linden in 1970 in *Reflections on the Screen*:[41]

This expiration apparently takes four general directions; the movement towards facticity [e.g. Truman Capote – *In Cold Blood*]*, the emphasis upon the consequential [John Barth – *Giles, Goat Boy* – detailing of events only], the cataloguing of the inconsequential [Robbe-Grillet – *Nouvelle Roman* – an attempt at 'objective anonymity'] and the sketch [Gore Vidal – *Myra Breckinridge* – reads like a 'hastily dictated' film script].

Linden, of course, was specifically referring to the cinema's effect on writing, but it can be taken that many of the relevant features of cinema were also common to television. There is certainly plenty of evidence to support these arguments, even though many other novelists still successfully exploit the old forms.

A lessening in demand for fiction in general was one of the most marked presumed side effects of television noticed by the publishing industry as early as the mid-1950s, although there was no sudden decline in book production. Small general hardback publishers suffered, but the sales of many other types of book, especially paperbacks of all kinds, continued to rise. As in

* The examples in square brackets are given by the author later in the same chapter.

the earlier days of cinema and radio, there was considerable interest in the use of television for encouraging book-reading. In 1960 the *Publishers' Weekly* reported that recently published figures showed that 1959 had been a boom year for American publishing, and the American Book Publishing Council commented that 'much of the latter's [i.e. the printed word] gain can be ascribed to stimulus from TV for example in its programmes which directly or indirectly encourage good reading'. The visual element in the design and content of books became increasingly important; there was a steady rise in the production of 'coffee table' books, mainly composed of photographs, as well as an enormous improvement in the visual standard of cover design and layout.

It is perhaps in the field of educational publishing that the effect of television and related audio-visual teaching methods has been most marked. Many American publishers started to market 'software' for the various technologies at the beginning of the 1960s, and they also watched developments in educational television very carefully to see where new needs for printed textbooks might arise. English educational publishers also became, to a limited extent, involved in the audio-visual technology market when it began to develop in the mid-1960s. The importance, for them, of this extension of traditional publishing activities was not necessarily the profitability of the ventures, but the opportunity it offered for becoming familiar with the mechanics and economics of producing new kinds of 'books'. Although the application of these new technologies remains limited, the interest and involvement of educational publishers in both countries has continued. By now it can be seen fairly clearly that in the short term at least, the printed word will not be displaced as an educational tool, and that textbooks, even if in modified forms, will continue to flourish. At the same time, sole dependence on this one medium has been reduced, and certainly this is largely due to the impact of television.

*

We can now summarise from our narrative and analysis the variety of ways in which the new technological media have gone beyond the book or extended its limits. In the order in which they have been considered the new media have had the following impact on printed books:

1. *Film* (*a*) has affected written style and content of fiction, and has also slightly encroached upon the market for light literature; (*b*) in the field of education has provided effective alternative methods of illustrating certain subjects (such as geography,) both statically (filmstrip) and in motion (16 mm sound film, 8 mm cassettes) and of storing reference material (microfilm);

2. *Radio broadcasting* (*a*) has pioneered the concept of 'packaged' information and entertainment where the necessity for selection and preconceived choice can be eliminated; (*b*) in contrast, has brought audiences into contact with many more and varied topics than they might have chosen to study in books; (*c*) has provided a form of 'talking book' which can be combined with a number of other activities;

3. *Gramophone* notably has *not* become a direct 'talking book' equivalent to the printed book, but has been developed for a specialised use only;

4. *Television* (*a*) has greatly extended these features of broadcasting mentioned above and has consequently displaced to some extent the habit of reading books purely for entertainment and relaxation; (*b*) has probably affected literary style to a more intensive degree than the cinema in that its techniques of communication have become the norm for many people; (*c*) in education, has provided the impetus for the extensive development of audio-visual aids mainly to supplement textbooks, and has also either as network television or as ccrv, shown a potential for wide-scale, coordinated teaching which can genuinely transcend, in scope if not in quality, the traditional teacher/textbook based education. Combined audio-visual techniques (for example, the combination of tapes and slides) and computer-based programmed machines have been experimented with or exploited in order to place stronger controls over the learning process in the hope that the act of learning itself will be streamlined.

Yet the book still has certain specific advantages which have allowed it to retain a very important position in the complex of modern communications media. It is cheap, relatively, to produce, and compared with alternative permanent storage technologies available to date is also cheap to buy; it is extremely portable, and, given the ability to read, absolutely simple to use – there is no restriction on where or when it can be read; it can accommodate a tremendous variety of different material, and its contents are less susceptible to outside pressures (commercial) and censorship (of any kind) than that of the other media – there is probably a more diverse range of subject matter on any one bookshelf than there is in a week or more of television broadcasting; it is still the most 'private' of the media, and allows information to be absorbed at the rate of individual preference or ability. These qualities, so far, have not been equalled by any of the 'rival' media.

There is one further point to be made relating to the technology of the book itself which is important when considering the possible ways in which books might develop. During the twentieth century there have been many advances in the techniques of printing, notably web offset, colour gravure printing and tele-typesetting, which have facilitated large-scale mass production and greatly improved visual quality. Even more significant was the invention of photocopying, which, although it has so far only been a source of competition to the publishing industry, may well prove to be a new kind of 'printing'.

The present state of development of the communication media is in some ways more uncertain and turbulent than it was in the early days of the cinema, radio and television. There are many new branches of technology, either recently established or in the process of development, some of which have large impli-cations for the future of communications. The main currents of development in this field are very well expounded in an article by Leo Bogart, which though published in 1968,[42] is equally applicable today, particularly his summary covering the areas of technical change:

The technology of communication is being transformed in five areas: in assembling information, storing it, retrieving it, compressing it, and reacting to it.

1. In the graphic arts, we are getting higher quality color reproduction by a combination of graphic techniques within the same production sequences. Telecommunication makes possible decentralised production and printing at great speed and with simultaneous operations at separated places. Computer-ized typesetting and photocomposition ... will be more broadly used to expedite and reduce the effort required to transmit information from its source to its users.

2. Electronic recording instruments, in combination with the computer, make it possible to store aural or visual communications, transmitted at extremely high speed, for rediffusion or playback at the option, and to the specifications of the individual recipient. ... The familiar tape recorder, already adapted from audio to video, is but the forerunner of far more

sophisticated home recording systems that permit information to be stored and played back to suit individual specifications. . . .

3. Microphotography has given us the economical visual storage of miniaturised records which can be classified, punch-coded, retrieved through the computer, and rapidly enlarged and reproduced. This is already revolutionising librarianship. . . . New processes now make it possible to achieve microfilm quality without developing film chemically. Electrostatic reproduction, in combination with improved data recording mechanisms, provides the means for widely dispersed facsimile reproduction of the conventional forms of print media, giving substance to the old idea of a newspaper produced in the home.

4. We have vastly increased facilities for transmitting huge flows of information. Thirty million words, the equivalent of 108,000 typed pages, can be transmitted in an hour through a television scanning system. Space satellites using solar energy will make it possible for vast quantities of messages to go directly from transmitters to home receivers in any part of the world. The internationalisation of the broadcast media will proceed apace, inhibited largely by language and by localised tastes. Throughout the world, radio and television become more and more universally accessible; more homes are linked through the telephone into communication centrals which ultimately will be put to diversified uses, as has already happened in the United States with community cable antenna TV systems. Lasers permit complex messages to be transmitted along hitherto unexploited reaches of the energy spectrum; through holography they allow us to reconstruct three-dimensional images, reduced or magnified in size. The hologram may replace microfilm for information storage, and could permit the transmission of 2,000 typewritten pages a second.

5. . . . we will soon have the means to make mass communication a two-way process. Through a home or office console unit, tied to a computer, an individual can feed back questions, demands and other reactions to his communications source . . .

Some of the techniques described here have been developed in the last three or four years in slightly different directions (for example, holography, which has been used experimentally in a television cassette playback system) and others, which were still then in a very primary stage, have been put into practice (for example, computerised audio-visual media centres in some universities in the States).

There are certainly many potential sources of competition to the printed book. At the present time fears of this competition are focused mainly on electronic recording processes for visual material, which have recently been dramatically realised in the shape of several technically different television playback cassette machines, now either on the market or about to be. These have precipitated a furore in the entertainment and publishing industries; it has been predicted that the cinema, broadcast television and, to a lesser extent, printed books, will be eclipsed by these wonders. Consortiums of film-makers, publishers and broadcasters have been formed to try and exploit the new market, and conferences have been held to try and sort out some of the confusion. Reports of a 1971 Cannes conference clearly reveal that the problem of seriously marketing these systems is much complicated by the excessive enthusiasm of the manufacturers:

It has become a cliché, although at least one speaker repeated it there, that the time between the development of a new technique and the peak of its exploitation has been diminishing. But surely the first International Cartridge TV, Videocassette and Video Disc Conference held in Cannes from April 19th to 23rd was unique. Hundreds of top executives from the United States, Japan and Western Europe gathered to discuss an industry not quite born.[43]

What is the nature of the challenge to books and the publishing industry? There are basically two different kinds of system – those, using video-tape, which have a dual function, storage and recording from television broadcasts, and those, film or disc, which can only be used for storage. The only existing media with which they can be directly compared in terms of function are magnetic sound tape and gramophone records respectively, and they appear to stand in the same relationship to television broadcasting as those media did to radio broadcasting. In this case, past evidence gives little cause for believing that the impact of the video system will be as extensive as is supposed; both sound tape and discs quickly found fairly specialised roles, and certainly did not encroach on the preserves of radio, or indeed, books. Television, however, is a much more comprehensive medium, in that it appeals to both the visual and aural senses, and it is therefore possible that canned versions of its output might have wider uses than the sound counterparts.

Video cartridges or cassettes have been vaunted as a more direct rival to books than any of the earlier new media because they combine the magic appeal of television with the opportunity, so far provided only by books, for individual choice of content. Yet if the contents of the cartridges, for economic reasons, follow the television pattern, we can reasonably conclude that the danger is not acute. Television in its role as light entertainer (the area where it has most obviously displaced books) can be seen to have achieved its current popularity partly because it encourages *evasion* of choice. It is, of course, possible that people whose interest has been stimulated in a specialised topic (such as learning a skill) would buy a video cassette rather than a book, but there are still large areas of interest needing diverse and detailed treatment which are much more adequately covered by books; also, it is important to stress again that books are *cheap* (much cheaper than cassettes are likely to be for quite some time) and are completely adaptable as to how and where they can be used. The cassettes may well be adopted for educational purposes, to provide the same kind of supplementary or, in some subjects, basic, teaching material as filmloops and filmstrips do now, but here even more than in the general field, experience so far has shown that printed texts will still be required as a back-up. At present, however, there is no doubt that much progress has to be made in solving the overwhelming problems of suitable content for the new cassettes before publishers need to think seriously about including them in their catalogues. Because of intensely competitive commercial control of the new systems it is likely that the markets chosen for primary exploitation will be, if possible, 'popular' (the youth market for contemporary pop music would seem to be a suitable start) or well-tested (educational, audio-visual use). It is unlikely that the varied subject matter covered at present by books will be available on cassette for a very long time.

Overall, the likely effects of the different developments in communications technology on books and publishing are difficult to predict. Economic limitations and lack of standardised equipment will probably restrict widespread acceptance and usage of many of the new technologies in the domestic market. On the other hand, for institutional use there is every indication that such devices as microfilm or hologram and storage computer information retrieval systems with audio-visual terminals, may well become commonplace. The contents of these systems will often be generated by the institution itself, and will not need to be processed by a publisher. They also have distinct advantages over books for these specialised functions – they are incredibly economical of space, and allow information to be located with great rapidity.

But, as past experience has indicated, the future of books does not have to be regarded purely in terms of their competition with newer and more sophisticated media. There are many ways in which books themselves may be transformed into more flexible, more easily produced and more instantly attractive media. First, it is likely that new ways of putting books together may be developed, changes for instance in the layout, make-up, binding and typography. One suggestion for possible development, elements of which have already been tried out, was put forward in the late 1960s by Dr Ernst Dichter, motivational research expert: 'You will have a book where you will just jump around, in fact a lot of people read that way. You would have a layout which had boxes drawn on the pages to frame the more important points and a method of page referals on the bottom of the box so you would be going back and forth in the book depending on what you were interested in pursuing.'[44] Second, there will undoubtedly be an increase in the integration of print with other media – following the examples set by some children's books, for instance, where the text is accompanied by slides or filmstrip and pulsed tape or record; this will enable books to provide, still relatively cheaply, multi-media communication which appeals to all the senses. Third, in a slightly different area, there are definite indications that the technology of printing will change radically within the next few years; computerised typesetting added to the decentralisation of production through the use of telecommunication on the one hand, and high speed photocopying on the other, both point to possible paths of development – already in America there is serious discussion of the setting up of 'on demand' printing centres, where books of normal length could be reproduced by photocopying from an original in a matter of minutes. This could certainly go a long way towards eliminating overproduction and large-scale pre-investment. Together these three advances may well increase enormously the scope of printed books in some areas, but it is as well to note at the same time that none of them are likely, for example, to resuscitate the novel in its traditional form which many believe not only to be changing but declining. It is probable that printed books may increasingly become a medium for informative rather than imaginative communication in an age of mass education.

✳

At this point we must refer back to the prophecies quoted at the beginning of this essay. We have tried to summarise the main effects which the new media have had on the printed book; we shall now briefly consider some of the facts which have emerged in the light of these prophecies. One of their main themes is clearly presented in the following passage by Harry J. Skornia which provides a good point of reference:

Radio and television are in certain respects unique instruments, differing from anything humanity has ever encountered. Like water or fire, television has a powerful innate attraction because it moves. Substantial evidence indicates that people often hypnotically watch whatever is offered. To maintain that this watching is an endorsement of what is on the screen is to confuse the form of the medium with its content.

Learning and enjoyment derived from the printed word, as compared with those derived from the modern time-oriented media, are slow and incomplete. Print is lineal – it is read word by word. Ideas and impressions come gradually, at a relatively slow rate, largely through the eyes and intellect. Ideas emerge at a controlled rate from a succession of relatively frozen images. The reader determines the pace; he has time to stop, analyse, re-read, or challenge. He remains in charge.

Radio and television, on the other hand, are all-engulfing; they involve the whole person – kinesthetically, subliminally, and emotionally, as well as intellectually. The medium not the viewer determines the pace.[45]

The idea that the power of the new media over their audiences derives from their technology rather than from their content, is crucial to the argument about the future of books in competition with them. If it were substantially true that television is a 'total' medium in the way that Skornia suggests, capable of eliciting a spontaneous, uncritical, and complete response to whatever is transmitted, be it for entertainment or for education, then the position of the printed book as an alternative medium would be seriously threatened. However, from what we know of the comparative progress of the old and new media in this century, we can see that, although radio and television are almost universally accepted and used in our society, they have not created the kind of wholesale dependence which this definition would lead us to expect. The fact that books have survived their onslaught as successfully as they have indicates the existence of a continuing need for certain qualities possessed by books, which are presumably not satisfactorily replaced by the 'all-engulfing' method of the new media. It also suggests that our society thrives on a variety of options. Greatly increased prosperity, leisure and education have all combined to produce a wider diversity of interests and needs, and these can support more than one kind of communication medium.

This conclusion is reinforced if we look at the way in which the position of the book has changed as a result of the pressure from these new media. Contrary to what is implied by Skornia's comparison of books and the broadcast media, books have not been supplanted in those areas where their functions are distinctively different from equivalent functions of the new media – factual, informative and educative. In these areas the opportunity which a book offers for self-controlled pace, analysis and thought has made it irreplaceable, rather than the reverse. The kind of reading, however, which *was* heavily encroached upon by its equivalent on radio and television was one which closely corresponded to them in its techniques – namely light fiction. In fact, it is interesting to note that the method by which this kind of printed entertainment was thought to make its impact, in its heyday before the establishment of radio and television, is surprisingly similar in one way to the methods of television as described above; 'It has been discovered that the greatest mind opiate in the world is carrying the eye along a certain number of printed lines in succession . . .'[46] Could it be that the new media prophets are not quite so revolutionary as they seem?

It is obviously not possible to assert that the book will never disappear. Research into uses of the new media is still probably in its infancy, and the very existence of the ideas of McLuhan, Skornia and others testifies to a high degree of interest in the possibility of re-shaping the communications network. However, it *is* fairly certain that as the functions of the existing media become more precisely defined and specialised in the future, books are likely to continue to fulfil a necessary function.

ROY YGLESIAS

Education and publishing in transition

SOME HISTORIANS claim every age to be an age of transition, with no clear dates or events worthy to be noted as watersheds. In educational history there are obvious landmarks like the great Education Acts of 1870, 1902, and 1944, but the driving force behind them can be explained only in terms of the social history of the periods preceding them, and to study their implementation it is necessary to pay attention to time lags and varying, sometimes contrasting, rates of change. What was actually happening in the classroom was often far removed from what people in Westminster thought was happening or ought to happen.

In mid-Victorian Britain, when voluntary organisation was the main instrument of public education, the immensity of the effort did not ensure an adequate local or national standard. It did not even provide for adequate industrial performance as industry became more sophisticated, or for adequate social control as the country became more urbanised. Britain, economically the most advanced country in the world, was lagging behind in education, and it was with this in mind that W. E. Forster introduced the Act of 1870 by arguing that

... on the speedy provision of elementary education depends our industrial prosperity, the safe working of our constitution, and our national power. Civilized communities throughout the world are massing themselves together, each mass being measured by its force: and if we are to hold our position among men of our own race or among the nations of the world, we must make up for the smallness of our numbers by increasing the intellectual force of the individual.[1]

Forster's warning to the Commons made good sense to that powerful section of the population for whom production was an end in itself, and for whom American, German and Belgian competition was a real menace. Yet the economic argument for educational advance, often backed by comparative industrial statistics, was never the only one.

Not only were trade and progress seen to be dependent on education: there was also political necessity. Urban male workers had been enfranchised in 1867, thus it was politically expedient to educate our masters. As Robert Lowe remarked in 1869, 'it will be absolutely necessary to compel our future masters to learn their letters'.[2] Finally there were arguments about educational enrichment as an end in itself.

The visionaries of the last century, men like Kay Shuttleworth and Arnold, when they first saw state education on the horizon, saw it as a civilising agent even more than as an instructing agent. As one of Matthew Arnold's colleagues in the Inspectorate, the Reverend Henry Moseley, Fellow of the Royal Society, put it: 'Education is not a privilege to be graduated according to men's social condition, but the right of all, inasmuch as it is necessary to the growth of every man's understanding, and into whatever state of life it may please God to call him, an essential element in his moral well-being.' And he surmised, probably optimistically, that this principle was one which both the Lords of the Committee of the Privy Council on Education and the public opinion of the day endorsed.[3]

The warmth of the argument about education in 1870, like the warmth of the argument in 1902, had more to do with politics – and with the religion that still lay behind politics – than with enrichment or economics or even the 'functional' necessities of general education in an increasingly industrialised society. There were many people in the Church of England, which retained much of its power after 1870, who still felt strongly that they should continue the job they had been doing for hundreds of years. As far back as 1841 Sir James Graham had written to Brougham: 'Religion, the Keystone of education, is in this

"OBSTRUCTIVES"

Mr. Punch (to Bull A.l): "Yes, it's all very well to say 'Go to school!' How are they to go to school with those people quarrelling in the doorway? Why don't you make 'em 'move on'?"

country the bar to its progress.'[4] In effect, educational development in England had been held back by fear; fear of violent controversy between Dissenters and Established churchmen.

In 1870 the nonconformists were in the vanguard of the militants. They wanted free, compulsory, rate-supported, non-denominational elementary schools. They had a strong pressure group – the Education League in Birmingham, supported by two Chamberlains, four Kenricks, as well as a Martineau and a Nettleford. Within four months the League had £60,000 at its disposal and had organised 200 public meetings, issued a quarter of a million publications, started a monthly paper with a circulation of 20,000, and set up branches in all the major cities.[5]

Long after the passing of the 1870 Act, religious friction continued both within the School Boards and at Westminster, while in 1902, when the Unionist government introduced its new Education Bill, all the old controversies were brought to life again. No measure had ever before been met by so many amendments, and the guillotine had to be applied in order that the measure would go through the House of Commons. Even after it was passed there was passive resistance against it, involving 70,000 prosecutions for non-payment of rates. During the Second World War, when R. A. Butler broached large-scale educational reform with Churchill, the memories of the violent controversies in 1902 encouraged Churchill to try to hold back.[6]

Yet it is only in recent years that education has become as controversial an issue as it was in 1870 and 1902. The Education Act of 1944 was the product of war-time social (and on the surface, at least, political) consensus, and there had been no substantial disagreement in 1920 when the school leaving age was raised to fourteen or during the 1920s when the Hadow Committee divided the existing all-age schools into junior and senior schools. The senior school, it was thought, had to cover a span of three years, so three was subtracted from the leaving age of fourteen and the mystic age of eleven was born.

The revival of controversy started with the effects of eleven-plus and with pressure for the final abolition of selection at eleven, and gained momentum as social and educational issues merged in the demand for a general system of comprehensive schools under local authorities. So far there has been no new landmark in educational history like 1870, 1902 or 1944, and while the warmth remains and politics often set the pace and tone, another

Above: Hanover Street Board School, Islington, 1877; below: Winstanley Road School, Clapham Junction, 1877. (Mary Evans Picture Library)

set of questions is now being almost as hotly debated. These concern what should be taught, in what manner, and with what aim and purpose; what should be the relationship between pupil and teacher; what are the proper attitudes towards rewards and punishments? And what part, if any, are pupils and students the world over to take in school (and later in university) organisation?

Much was said and written during the nineteenth century about such questions and the answers to them, although it has received less general attention than the noisier public debate about the structure and scale of provision. The belief in the virtues of individual competition in education, expressed in the educational system at the same time as it was dominating economic life, gained in strength during the nineteenth century as education became an instrument of social mobility. Yet it left other aspects of educational influence deprived. Writing on the theory of teaching at the end of the century, Edward Thring, the headmaster of Uppingham wrote:

The appeal to success, Prizes, and Prize-winning, bids fair to be the watchword of the day. But what does this do for the majority, for the non-competing crowd; who nevertheless do not politely die off, and make room; and cannot through modern squeamishness, be killed off, and buried?

The weak are pushed into a corner, and neglected; their natural tendency to shrink from labour is educated into despair, by their being constantly reminded, directly or indirectly, that their labour is no good.[7]

In 1918, at the time of the discussion of Fisher's Education Bill, R. H. Tawney was complaining that 'while the nation as a whole has seen in the Education Bill the tentative beginnings of a new and more humane educational policy, there are those to whom the subordination of education to economic exigencies is still, apparently, an indisputable axiom'.[8]

Such charges were still being echoed in 1970 during the centenary celebrations of the 1870 Act by Sir Alec Clegg, then Director of Education for the West Riding, who had the 1944 Act in mind as much as that of 1870 when he was summing up a hundred years of educational progress.

As far as the main administrative intentions go we have done well. It is true that we have not established county colleges and that ever since the last war because of the increase in births our nursery schools have been filled with children of school age. But we raised the school leaving age and we are going to do it again in 1973, we abolished Part III authorities, we unified the system and we made public monies available for church school buildings. And educationally we have also made progress for which we can take credit. We have paused to ask what we are doing and why we are doing it and what we ought to be doing that is even better, and Crowther, Newsom and Plowden have given us the answers. And we have done great things for our abler pupils. We have broadened the old School Certificate examination track which now leads to 'O' and 'A' level and we shall double it again in the next ten years, and we are prepared to pay more to educate the really afflicted child than it would cost us to send him to Eton.

But what about the grand purpose of the Act, and by this I mean the intention expressed by such phrases as 'secondary education for all', 'parity of esteem', 'education according to age, ability, aptitudes', and the 'spiritual, moral, mental and physical well-being of the community', phrases which occurred sometimes in the Act, sometimes in the supporting documents. If these phrases meant anything at all they meant in simple terms that we should get the best out of every child and in so doing we should raise the whole level of our people.[9]

Emphasis on 'competition' had been associated in the nineteenth century with emphasis on 'instruction'. Science could train observation and the classics could improve memory, and in the beginning there had to be learning by rote. This approach had changed completely by the time Sir Alec Clegg pointed to continuing deficiencies not only in provision but in attitudes. Within the 'educational world' itself there had been growing concern with relationships, initiative, powers of thought and creativity as well as the acquisition of skills and knowledge, and such concern, properly directed, which could transform the whole attitude towards 'educational advance'. Yet the concern was not always shared outside 'the educational world' as Sir Alec Clegg recognised. The work of a writer like Piaget on child development, which has been a strong intellectual influence on educationists (*Language and Thought of the Child* was first published in 1923), is less well known outside educational circles than the work of many other pioneers. 'Getting the best out of every child' requires a provision of appropriate experience in the classroom as well as the provision of adequate financial and physical resources for education.

✳

The new approach to learning, which is necessary if hopes in education are to be realised, will be discussed in the last essay in this book. So, too, will the 'role' of publishers. Changes between 1870 and now have been gradual and cumulative. Yet there is a sharp contrast between the simplicities of the old learning and the new – and the contribution of publishers. A Victorian text-book, which may still be found in second-hand bookshops, offers a starting point for reflections about the old style of learning at its most extreme. Its title is an ambitious one – *The Child's Guide to Knowledge, by a Lady*. Its appearance is austere: the authoress thinks it inadvisable to introduce any woodcuts or engravings 'lest they take off the attention of children'. Its 450 pages are filled with the cut and thrust of an unrelenting cate-chism. There is no doubt here that there is an inquisitor or about who he is. Modern theory may make the child ask the questions and the father run to his encyclopaedia for the answers, but in 1876, when the fiftieth edition of *The Child's Guide* appeared, the shoe was firmly on the other foot. The first page makes it clear that knowledge has to be acquired by rote learning: with stern moral purpose and firm control, the questioner gets to work:

Question   Who made the world?
Answer   The great and good God.
Question   Are there not many things in it you would like to know about?
Answer   Yes, very much.
Question   Pray then what is bread made of?
Answer   Flour.
Question   What is flour?
Answer   Wheat ground into powder by the miller.
Question   What injury is wheat liable to?
Answer   To three kinds of diseases, called blight, mildew and smut

The next three questions, which are naturally 'What is blight?' 'What is mildew?' and 'What is smut?' make it plain that we have now leapt from the first chapters of Genesis straight into the farmer's vade-mecum and handy reference book, and from now on there is no respite.

Many of the questions are very difficult and abstruse: 'What is soy?' 'What is saloop?' 'What are capsicums?' But occasionally the authoress grows more humane, and asks a question to which there can only be one answer: 'Had not the city of Chester, in the time of the Saxons, a severe law against those who brewed bad ale?' Or again: 'Does not the shell of the sea tortoise afford a considerable article of exportation from the Seychelles Islands?' Sometimes also an anecdote is admitted, though here, as in

Playtime at a London Board School, 1895. (Mary Evans Picture Library)

Mass drill in a Board School playground in 1906. (Radio Times Hulton Picture Library)

Greek tragedy, the dialogue form is strictly preserved by the use of unnecessary questions. For example, the child, describing how aqua-fortis was discovered, says she boiled her ribbons in the porterpot and they came out a most brilliant colour.

Question Was not her lover surprised when he saw it?
Answer Exceedingly so: and, being a clever fellow, . . .

Romance occasionally breaks in thus through the mass of facts. Speaking of the Chinese feast of lanterns, the child is made to say 'Such a profusion of rich transparent lanterns are hung out of the houses that to a stranger the whole empire looks like fairyland.'
    Patriotism is naturally in evidence:

Question Is larch a very useful wood?
Answer Yes; the Russians use no other for ship building and it is well calculated for all works exposed to the weather.
Question But is it as durable as the oak of which our ships of war are built?
Answer No; then we may consequently rely as much on the superiority of our vessels as on the bravery of our gallant sailors.

After this fervent outburst the child must feel snubbed when the questioner continues directly, 'Will not larch admit of a fine polish?'
    The only thing which is out of character in this period piece is an exchange which surely cannot have survived as a misprint into the fiftieth edition and yet cannot be anti-clerical irony in such a gentle work:

Question Who were the least educated persons at the early period of our history?
Answer The ecclesiastics and monks; this was the cause of their great influence.

The prevailing impression one gains from reading this book is of a mass of solid fact. The same impression emerges from the reminiscences of H. C. Dent who was a pupil in an elementary school – one of the new Board Schools of 1870 – at the beginning of this century. (Later he was to become a headmaster, a Professor of Education, and editor of *The Times Educational Supplement*.) In his book, *Century of Growth in English Education*, he wrote:

I was a pre-adolescent pupil in an elementary school in 1904. Like millions more, I intoned my way monotonously (and uncomprehendingly) through the multiplication tables; I was bored to nausea by the one and only 'Reader' we were allowed each year – which had to serve the dual function of giving us practice in the mechanics of reading aloud (why aloud?) and of being our introduction to English life and letters. I wrote, endlessly, in 'copybooks' morally elevating maxims – 'A stitch in time saves nine', 'Too many cooks spoil the broth' – but I never composed, much less wrote, in class a single original sentence. I memorized, in rhyme, the names and idiosyncrasies of the English kings and queens

> William the Conqueror long did reign,
> William his son by an arrow was slain . . .

and I memorized (though not in rhyme) the names of the capes, bays, county towns, mountains and rivers, literally all round Britain. And once each week I painted blobs (we called them flowers), and wove wet reeds into work baskets: the school's sole concessions to 'activity'.

Not much in all that to 'form and strengthen the character', or 'develop the intelligence', or 'make the best use of the school years', or fit children, either 'practically' or 'intellectually', 'for the work of life'. And this experience of mine, I must emphasize, was not in the class of a cynical, dull or apathetic teacher, but of a lively, intelligent, warm-hearted woman, who as a person did us boys and girls a world of good. Did she know no other way to teach? Or was she bound by the school timetable? – that sacrosanct nineteenth-century visual aid, put up 'in a prominent position' (as the Code required) by the new head teacher when he arrived, and never taken down until he left, it might well be thirty years later. (Men did not move then as they do now. Nor did women, for that matter; the age of the 'dedicated spinster' was just beginning, as one LEA after another refused to employ married women.)

Such teaching as I endured went on for many years in many schools after 1904. The spirit outlived the fact of 'payment by results' in the practice of teachers who could not change their ways, even when they wanted to, which many did. But there were others, and their numbers grew with the years, who responded eagerly to the challenge thrown down, in 1905, in the first edition of the Board of Education's *Handbook of suggestions for the consideration of Teachers and others engaged in the Work of Public Elementary Schools*:

> The only uniformity of practice that the Board of Education desire to see in the teaching of Public Elementary Schools is that each teacher shall think for himself, and work out for himself such methods of teaching as may use his powers to the best advantage, and be best suited to the particular needs and conditions of the school.

Some teachers even dared to think that they and their pupils should be friends, not foes, should work with, not against, each other; and they initiated the most profoundly important transformation of the English elementary school, from a place of hatred to one of happiness.[10]

Dent's reference to memorisation of capes and bays illustrates the influence of patterns of learning by rote; geography, like history, could be made to depend almost exclusively on the acquisition of more and more facts. Textual mnemonics and the singing of rhymes became a regular catechism together with the recital of doggerel verse. Here is an example:

> We'll over a map of the isles take a glance,
> Then start from Land's End, and sail round by Penzance.
> Mounts Bay having crossed, by the Lizard then steer
> Your course to North-East and by North quickly veer.
>
> . . .
>
> Next Yorkshire this county of large towns is full
> Here's the capital York, then there is Beverley, Hull,
> Leeds, Bradford and Halifax, Huddersfield too,
> All famous for cloth as perhaps you well know.

From opposite angles, both J. R. Green, the historian, and T. H. Huxley, the scientist (the latter in his *Preface to Physiography*) severely criticised geography textbooks. Within a nineteenth-century context, their weaknesses were apparent, not least because the world was being opened up through exploration, and British trade was drawing the country into a wider and wider network of world associations. None the less, some old textbooks outlasted Dent's schooldays, and it has taken generations of classroom experience to establish new styles. In his interesting book *The Silent Revolution*, first published in 1937, G. A. N. Lowndes wrote that 'there must be thousands of people still alive who can recite the towns of France in alphabetical order: Dieppe, Dijon, Dunkirk (querque was too difficult), Havre, Lille etc.'[11]

✳

At this point it is important to note the special relationship in this country between what goes on in the classroom and the organisation and scale of educational provision. Both in the period between 1870 and 1902, when the School Board was the providing institution, and since 1902, when power has passed to the local education authority, there has been as much freedom for different places to experiment with their own curricula and to make use of their own chosen textbooks as there was in the period before 1870, when voluntary provision was the staple. This freedom has left an opening for the publishers of textbooks to compete with each other. It has also enabled publishers to make

8   *An Introduction to Reading.*

Easy Lessons of Words not exceeding Two Syllables.

LESSON I.

A GOOD name is better than precious ointment; and the day of one's death than the day of one's birth. It is better to go to the house of mourning than the house of feasting; for that is the end of all men, and the living will lay it to his heart. Sorrow is better than laughter; for by the sadness of the looks the heart is made better. The heart of the wise is in the house of mourning, but the heart of fools is in the house of mirth. It is better to hear the rebuke of the wise, than for a man to hear the songs of fools.

LESSON II.

DID youth know the pleasure that arises from an early culture of the mind, I am led to believe they would never waste in useless pursuits the many hours that are done that way, when to their sad regret they will sooner or later find their mistake in the end.

How many have I been witness to, who would have given life almost to redeem mis-spent time, when they have seen others

of

In 1808, An Introduction to Reading for Children from 6–12 *in its* 16*th edition provided the child with moral precepts that were couched in language firmly drawn from the Bible. Hardly an easy lesson and the two syllables ignore of course the difficulty of sounding out words like 'pleasure' and 'precious'. The Godliness of content is all, the child will be drawn painfully to literacy and heaven with the minimum of 'misspent time'.*

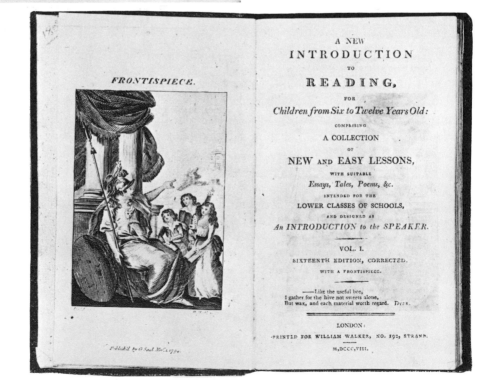

The English Alphabet.

	B b	C c
.pe	Bell	Cock
D d	E e	F f
Dog	Ea-gle	Fox
G g	H h	I i
Goose	Horse	Iun

The next example comes from Longman's eternally and enormously successful The English Spelling-Book, *in its 184th edition by 1815. It dates back to the time of Henry VII. Here the two syllables are carefully controlled, and split like an ap-ple for easier digestion. Text and illustration are concerned with objects and activities the child may be familiar with. The author is coming down to the child's level. It is a lesson not a sermon. A great deal of stress is laid on repetition, in language control. But the irresistible moral point is made as the writer admonishes 'the sil-ly little boy' who 'did not love his book much'.*

Lessons of TWO *Syllables.* 45

e-tle hums.
ck quacks.
ose cac-kles
eys chat-ter.
i hoots.

The screech-owl shrieks
The snake his-ses.
Little boys and girls
talk and read.

LESSON 2.

nt my din-ner; I want pud-ding. It is
-dy yet: it will be rea-dy soon, then
s shall have his din-ner. Lay the cloth.
are the knives, and forks, and plates?
ock strikes one; take up the din-ner.
have some meat? No: you shall have
hing ni-cer. Here is some ap-ple dump-
you; and here are some peas, and some
and car-rots, and tur-nips, and rice-pud-
nd bread.

LESSON 3.

e was a lit-tle boy; he was not a big boy,
e had been a big boy, I sup-pose he would
en wi-ser; but this was a lit-tle boy, not
than the ta-ble, and his pa-pa and mam-
him to school. It was a very pleas-ant
ng; the sun shone, and the birds sung on
es, Now this lit-tle boy did not love his
uch, for he was but a sil-ly lit-tle boy, as
efore, and he had a great mind to play in-
going to school. And he saw a bee fly-
out, first up-on one flow-er, and then up-
th-er; so he said, Pret-ty bee! will you
d play with me? But the bee said, No, I
t be i-dle, I must go and gath-er hon-ey.

LESSON 4.

the i-dle boy met a dog: and he said,
ill you play with me? But the dog said,
must not be i-dle, I am go-ing to watch
-ter's house. I must make haste for fear

98 READING WITHOUT TEARS

sun bun gun run tun

I had a bun
I had a gun
I can run
I did run

Sit on a tun
Dig in a bog

By 1857 the tone is different again. This is a fairly typical phonic first reader, written by a woman. The heavy uplift of 1808 is now Reading Without Tears, *where the content has given way to phonic regularity, repetition, the introduction of new words through a picture, and strict order if not strict sense.*

How altered the tone of The Great World War Infant's Book *published in 1920. It again is breaking the two-syllable words in two. It is almost as near prayer as the text of 1808, but trying to give its message in infant language, like a Kitchener for infants. Its propagandist buoyancy is aided by capital letters for the most powerful words, but by 1920 it must have seemed dated to the post-war child. (Museum of the History of Education, Leeds)*

10 THE GREAT WORLD WAR.

1. They carry peace and love from us to our friends a-cross the sea with whom we have so long shared the pain and sad-ness of the War.

2. So, now that the hap-py days of Peace have come, we lift our eyes to the skies and with joy and glad-ness we say, "Thank you, brave Air-men for the Peace that is with us to-day."

THE GREAT WORLD WAR. 11

1. Our brave Women! How they, too, have worked for Peace.

2. No-bly they took the place of the men who went forth to fight.

3. No work was too hard, too rough, or too heavy for them!

4. Now, they en-joy the rest and calm of Peace! We say, "Thank you! dear women of Brit-ain, for the Peace you helped to win."

John, see the aeroplanes.
One, two, three aeroplanes.
I can see three aeroplanes.

20

John said,
"See the aeroplane go up.
See the aeroplane fly.
The aeroplane can fly fast.
Fly fast, big aeroplane."

21

After the Second World War, the attitude had changed. Boys and girls were given 'Janet and John' to identify with. Language is carefully rationed, repetition constant and presented in wholesome child situations. This most famous and successful example of the 'look and say' approach to reading, imported from America in 1949, has remained immensely popular. The shape *of the words is stressed, rather than phonic regularity or the length of the word, but the language is not very natural.*

In Breakthrough to Literacy, 1970, *the approach has changed again. The stress is on using a child's natural language, and natural interests. It attempts to make a direct contact with the child, and reflects perhaps an altered attitude to children themselves, not just to their language.*

there are
lots of things
to read at school.

14

there are
lots of things
to read at home.

15

Until the first half of the nineteenth century, books were bound by hand. Leather stretched over boards sewn to the main body of the book formed the standard binding. A cheaper form was the quarter-leather binding in which paper-covered boards were strengthened by a strip of leather drawn round the spine. During the 1820s cloth replaced leather as a commercial binding material. The examples here show (above) leather and quarter-leather bindings and a re-binding in coarse cloth of The English Spelling Book *illustrated on p. 371.*

With the introduction of cloth and the increased use of paper-covered boards, new binding methods were developed. Designs were cut in brass or wood, and printed on to the flat boards before binding. The text was glued, not sewn, into the outer boards. Educational books published in the second half of the nineteenth century illustrate a practical and economic approach to binding by publishers. Some examples of books published by Longmans both for the home and overseas markets in the late nineteenth century are shown here; the simplest is the paperback – Longmans' Complete Arithmetic *has a paper cover sewn on to a single signature. The* Fairy Reader, *in contrast, has a linen-covered paper cover which is wire-stitched to the text. (Bodleian Library)*

For overseas, the covers are utilitarian in the extreme, in the interests of economy. Longmans' English Reading Books *are strengthened with a linen strip down the spine – a form of binding still in use today – but decoration has either been dispensed with or is based on that used in the home market. (Bodleian Library)*

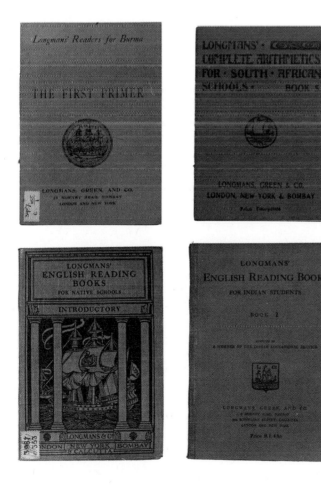

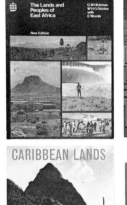

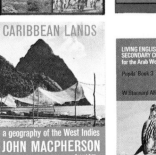

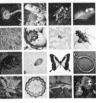

their own arrangements to commission textbooks from practising teachers. There has been a feedback, therefore, from classroom to publishing house. Of course, freedom of choice has not always meant that there was adequate money to buy books, and feedback has not always meant that writers of textbooks have been the best interpreters of changes in educational outlook and methodology. At any given moment in the history of education there is immense variety in the classroom, ranging from survival of the manifestly out-of-date, particularly obvious in a subject like geography, to experiments with media and techniques which will never have general currency.

Developments in printing help to determine what can feasibly be produced. Indeed, superficially at least, the most spectacular and noticeable aspect of the changing textbook can be seen not in content and approach but in illustrations, typography, layout and binding, and in the case of geography, cartography. The introduction of the lithographic printing process in particular, has given publishers an opportunity which they have exploited with relish. It was the impulse from children's books in America and Britain which set the stage. *The Pirate Twins* by William Nicholson was published in 1928, 'one of the first successful British children's books to be printed in colour by lithography on a matt surface paper', according to Frank Eyre in his *British Children's Books in the Twentieth Century*.[12]

The principal advantage of the lithographic process is that it allows half-tone illustrations to be printed on ordinary paper rather than on the specially coated, and expensive, 'art' paper

Today educational publishers not only have to retain this practical and economic approach but also produce books whose covers are attractive. Although a pupil today is unlikely to have a linen-covered cased book, basic principles remain much the same. Paper substitutes cloth — often with a linen texture — but the binding is still glued, or stapled, to the text. The main problem today lies in strengthening the binding, and, for some overseas markets, ensuring that they withstand heat and humidity. Perhaps the main difference lies in the change of approach towards cover design. The use of four colour is common and cover design an important consideration for an educational publisher.

Opposite are some examples of recent Longman books published for the educational market in the U.K. (above) and for overseas (below).

which was required when printing from half-tone blocks. Because of the high cost of this 'art' paper, illustrations were formerly kept apart from the text and printed as separate plates. The lithographic process makes it possible to design a much more homogeneous page or double opening and the fusion of text and illustration is a characteristic feature of both post-war picture books for children and school textbooks. The economies of the lithographic process have been seen to even more striking advantage in the growing use of full colour illustrations in school books. These were first introduced into primary school readers before the Second World War (the *Janet and John Readers*) and since the War full colour has increasingly come to be used in secondary school textbooks, including geography, as well. During the 1970s, this facility sometimes led to confusion. Artists and designers occasionally carried away publisher and author on the wings of their enthusiasm, and sometimes, in the openings they illuminated, the purpose of the text was overwhelmed by glorious colour. But on the whole this use of colour has transformed the school textbook. A transformation in approach, however, is crucial if the transformation in appearance is to be educationally significant. Coloured illustrations will enhance a textbook and attract the teacher's eye. No doubt they also contribute to the pupil's interest and taste. But in a textbook, illustrations must be an active aid to the learning process. Now if modern methods require discovery and activity on the part of the pupil, it follows that illustrations too must stimulate discovery and activity.

The change can again be exemplified from geography books. Pages of full colour pictures with descriptive captions need only a passive response, as passive a response in its way as the mid-Victorian response to the printed word. What the teacher requires, however, is a substitute for field work. The picture is used both to provoke questions and as a basis for the teacher to promote the pupils' activities. Thus the illustration is essentially part of the text, designed to stimulate the learning process.

Publishers have played a significant part in the educational process by providing both attractive textbooks and books which reflect the changing approach of modern teaching methods. Yet the economic implications of changes in the classroom can present difficulties for publishers. When sets of primary readers or, later in school life, secondary textbooks were sold to whole classes, a successful series could be printed and

Mercator's Projection, *first published in* 1569, *was much used by early explorers and navigators since all bearings are accurately represented by straight lines. It also exaggerated certain areas and because of this was widely used in nineteenth-century geography textbooks, where emphasis was put on the vast size of the Empire. The map here is taken from Longman's* Geographical Series, *Book III* (1898) (*British Museum*). *In modern books a more accurate impression is given by using, for example, a Flat Polar Equal Area Projection, such as that used in the Collins-Longman Atlas below.*

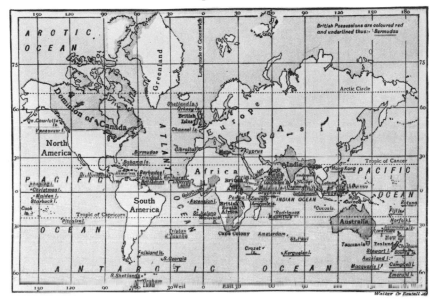

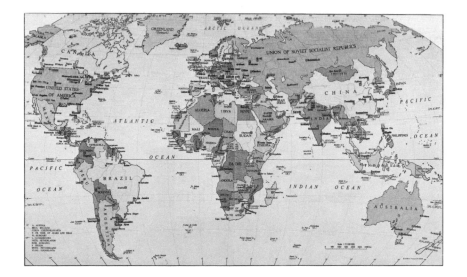

13 Contd.

extent, the *Emperor of Russia*, and the *Sultan of Turkey*. Despotic monarchs vary in the power they exercise.

A *Limited* or *Constitutional Monarch* rules after certain fixed plans, and the laws of the country are made and administered by a body of men called the *Legislature*, chosen by the people for that purpose, as in *England*.

RELIGIONS.

14

1. The **Religions** of the world are often classed under two heads—

Mono-theistic, or the worship of one God, and

Poly-theistic, or the worship of more than one God.

2. There are *three chief divisions* of Mono-theistic Religions—the Christian, Jewish, and Mahommedan.

The **Christian Religion** generally prevails in Europe and those parts of the world colonised by Europeans; such as the countries of *North* and *South America, Australia, South Africa*, and *New Zealand*.

The **Jewish Religion**, which had its origin in Palestine, is still the religion of the Jews wherever they are found.

The **Mahommedan Religion** prevails in *Turkey, Northern Africa*, and *Western Asia*, that is west of the Ganges basin.

The most prominent forms of **Poly-theistic** Religions are the various kinds of *Fetichism* prevailing among some of the natives of *Africa* and the islands of the *Pacific Ocean*.¹

QUESTIONS.

1. Of what does the surface of the Earth consist, *and in what proportions?*
2. What are the largest divisions of the Earth called?
3. How many continents are there?
4. *What is meant by the Old World and the New World?*
5. What is Oceania?
6. What are Continents divided into?
7. Explain the meaning of the terms *island, peninsula, isthmus, cape, and coast.*
8. What are volcanoes, *and what prevails in their neighbourhood?*
9. Define the terms *plain, plateau,* and *valley.*
10. What are the largest divisions of water called? Name them *and give their positions.*
11. Define the terms *sea, gulf, bay, bight, strait, channel, lake, and river.*
12. What is meant by the *basin* of a river, and the *water-shed* of a country?
13. What is the estimated population of the world?
14. How many races are there?
15. *Write out a description of each race.*
16. What is the difference between an absolute and a limited monarch?

¹ Though various idols are worshipped by the *Buddhists* of China, Further India, and Thibet, and by the *Brahmins* of India, they are regarded as emblems of Deity. The *Parsees*, too, adore the sun, as emblematic of the Deity.

THE UNITED KINGDOM.

15

1. The **United Kingdom** is situated on the *West* side of Europe, in the Atlantic Ocean, and consists of *Great Britain* and *Ireland*, with the adjacent islands.

The **area** of the United Kingdom is somewhat more than **121,000 square miles**, or nearly **one-thirtieth** part of the entire area of Europe; whilst its **population** is nearly **41½ millions**,¹ or about **one-ninth** part of that of Europe.

2. **Great Britain** is the largest *island* of Europe, and consists of *England*, in the South; *Scotland*, in the North; and *Wales*, west of England.

3. **Ireland** is an *island*, separated from England by the *Irish Sea* and *St. George's Channel*.

Ireland was conquered by England in the reign of Henry II. 1172; but Henry VIII. was the first English sovereign styled "*King of Ireland*"—his predecessors being called "*Lords of Ireland*." The Parliaments of Great Britain and Ireland were not united until the time of George III, 1801.

Wales was conquered in 1282 by Edward I., but was not incorporated with England until the time of Henry VIII., 1536.

Scotland was united to England in 1603, when James VI. of Scotland, being heir to the English throne, became James I. of England. The Parliaments of England and Scotland, however, were not united until the time of Queen Anne, 1707.

4. **England** is the *largest, wealthiest*, and *most populous* portion of Great Britain.

London, the Capital of England, is also the *Capital* of the **British Empire**, which consists of the *United Kingdom*, her *Colonies, Dependencies, Protectorates* and *British India*.

¹In 1901 the population was 41,454,621. England and Wales, 32,526,075; Scotland, 4,472,000; Ireland, 4,456,546.

Fig 31 A map of the South-West Peninsula.

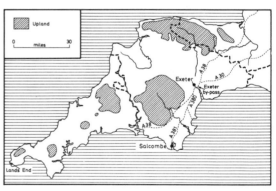

60 On Fig 31 the A381, A380 and parts of the A38 and A30 roads are marked. Find out why all these road numbers begin with '3'. Using an atlas find the names of the uplands and rivers marked on Fig 31.

61 Many visitors who go to Salcombe drive along the A38 or A30. Using an atlas suggest from which densely populated parts of Britain these visitors may have come.

62 The A.A.'s report on the traffic on the Exeter by-pass at 11 a.m. on Saturday, 20 August 1966 was:
Westbound — 1,500 vehicles per hour
a 5-mile queue;
Eastbound — 1,000 vehicles per hour
a 6-mile queue.
With the aid of a motoring map or an atlas map explain why there is such a build-up of traffic on the Exeter by-pass. Why is the traffic particularly heavy on a Saturday?

63 Using an atlas, name the sailing ports indicated by their initial letters on Fig 32.

64 Club cruises are also arranged to Ireland, Spain and the Baltic Sea. On which of these cruises would you like to be a crew member? Why?

Fig 32 Cruising grounds used by the Island Cruising Club.

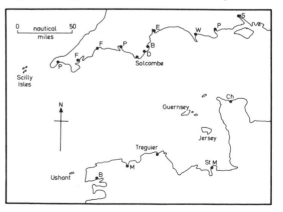

reprinted very economically in long print runs. Today, when work is done in smaller groups, teachers depend on the use of small sets of, say, half a dozen readers for classroom use. It is true that they may purchase more books and spend more money. But they spread their orders and buy for variety in small quantities. At primary level in particular, this can mean a small print run with very heavy plant cost, and a relatively high published price.

This revolution in textbook buying, which has caused considerable publishing difficulties, does not apply in the same degree to all subjects. Particularly in language courses, mathematics and the teaching of English as a second language, pupils may work in groups and individually, but the whole class will probably follow one course or series. In other subjects too there remains a demand for 'core' course-books alongside the demand for a variety of topic books, learning kits and visual aids. In a time of rapid curriculum change and educational innovation the publisher requires a balanced and experienced view of modern teaching methods to avoid expensive mistakes.

✳

In recent years response to social and educational change has been the keynote of British publishers' activities in other countries besides Britain. At first it was not so. As long ago as 1844 W. H. Hill, 'Lieutenant-Governor of Her Majesty's Forts and Settlements on the Gold Coast', wrote to the Colonial Office about the educational needs of the two hundred pupils of the school in Cape Coast Castle. After appealing for an increase in teachers' salaries, he continued: 'The books supplied for the use of the school have been much confined to Bibles, and Testaments, but I think without losing sight of religion, a more general course of instruction should be followed.'[13] He specified, among other titles, Aesop's *Fables*, Murray's *English Grammar* and an abridgement of Goldsmith's *History of England*.

Opposite: a page from the 1902 Oxford and Cambridge edition of Gill's Geography contrasted with (below) a page from the Longman's Study Geography series by J. G. Rusby and others, published in 1967. In contrast to the passive response which is demanded from Gill's Geography, the specific questions asked in the Study Geography text involve not only a different way of thinking about maps, but about the logic of the whole subject. (Museum of the History of Education, Leeds)

Governor Hill got his books, together with 1,000 quills, two gallons of black ink in bottles and a quantity of slate pencils, but not before somebody had minuted: 'The Governor makes requisitions not with reference to his means, but with reference to his wants', a succinct expression of a Colonial Office attitude that was to persist for nearly a century in an era when each colony had to finance development entirely from its own revenue. If one did have a little money, there was no doubt what books were needed in a Victorian colony. Cape Coast was typical of many: 'Beeton's *Complete Etiquette for English Gentlemen* sold at the Bookshop. English clothing and English names were postulates of the English way of life'.[14]

These Victorian attitudes contrast sharply with those of the twentieth century. Indeed, the demand for textbooks has expanded more rapidly since former colonial countries have won their independence. The annual orders for books from 7,000 primary schools in Kenya in 1973, for instance, were consolidated by computer before being passed to different publishers for supply. And almost all the books – not only in English, but in eleven African languages, specifically for Kenyan syllabuses and, increasingly, by Kenyans. Nearly all were printed in Kenya.

The concept of producing school books to suit the cultural and physical environment of particular Commonwealth countries is for the most part a growth of the last fifty years. Indeed cultural links between Britain and the old white dominions prolonged, for what now seems a remarkably long period, the use of school texts produced in and for Britain. The minorities in the colonies, the Arab world and elsewhere who in other respects felt a need to preserve their culture in the face of the imported standards of their political masters were, nevertheless, the first to press for more places for their children in the 'colonial' schools. This arose from the fact that a British academic or professional qualification was a prerequisite for personal advancement, which in turn meant passing the same examinations as were prescribed for candidates in this country. The competitive element in education was as strong as it was in nineteenth-century Britain.

The first wide-reaching agency for change was the Secretary of State's Advisory Committee on Education, set up by the Colonial Office in 1923 on the advice of Christian missions with headquarters in Britain. Apart from strengthening the hands of local educationists in their dealings with colleagues in the administration, the Committee provided a pool of more relevant knowledge and experience on which they could draw. It presided over and in many cases instigated the developments of the next thirty years, including the more rapid and active growth which followed the Second World War. It helped to produce a climate in which the first generation of locally relevant textbooks could appear. But inevitably those were the product of isolated research by individuals, as in West Africa by members of the staff of Achimota. An obstacle to large-scale progress was the lack of a body of local knowledge systematised to the extent that it could be transmitted in textbook form to the schools at large. As late as 1950 any teacher who wanted to inform his pupils of the history of the African continent, as distinct from that of European activities there, had no accessible sources to consult, let alone a pupils' text. In this field, as elsewhere, it was necessary to wait until the 1960s when the new universities, increasingly staffed by their own graduates, had developed their research and teaching to the point where a new generation of texts could be written. In the resulting work of publication Longmans took a leading part.

With the rapid dismantling of the British Empire in the twenty years following 1947 dramatic changes in the educational patterns could have been expected. In fact, the initial impact was quantitative. The new leaders saw universal education as a rapid means of uplifting their countries' economic level and the resultant massive increases in school enrolments, while greatly increasing the volume of publishing activity, created severe problems of building, staffing and administration. Thus talk of the need to preserve standards tended to divert attention from the need to consider how far the old standards were relevant. But foundations were laid, and in the publishing field those British publishers who traditionally sold in these markets, including Evans, Heinemann, Longmans, Nelson and the Oxford University Press, opened subsidiaries and branches on the spot and were soon joined by a growing number of state and local private companies. Book printers, notably in Hong Kong and the larger centres in Africa, were able to establish themselves as a result of the activities of these houses.

In the attempt to cope with the immediate problems of size, the larger questions of what the schools 'were for' and what should be taught in them tended to take second place. There were many signs, as there had been in nineteenth-century Britain – of pushing 'educational advance' without thinking of 'getting the best out of each child'. Even in the areas where local examining bodies replaced the enduring Cambridge and London syndicates, of necessity much of their time was taken up with pressing organisational tasks. Various curriculum centres, started in the wake of political independence, and financed mainly by British, United Nations and American foundations, tended in attitude, finance and staffing to ignore the educational requirements and economic situation of the countries concerned; in their apparent lack of contact with those countries' needs they often seemed an exotic rather than an indigenous growth. It is still less than a decade since the new governments and growing number of teachers' professional associations have begun effectively to influence and direct such projects, and only still more recently that fundamental enquiries into the whole basis and purpose of national education systems have begun. There are impressive achievements – the establishment of broadly based low-cost secondary education in the West Indies; a brilliantly executed modern mathematics course under the aegis of the Ghana Mathematical Association; the *Projet Baouké*, a pilot scheme for education by television; and the successful, if controversial, transfer to the medium of the Malay language in Malaysia. Yet these successes only underline the continued unrest over the creation of thousands of unemployable clerks through an essentially academic system, the marked absence from publishers' lists of the special agricultural and technical courses that due emphasis on these subjects would ensure, and the continued absence of effectively researched language material for the infant and junior schools. These are the problems of transition to be reflected in tomorrow's publishing, which will be generated and produced in the countries concerned.

✳

In many ways the greatest revolution in methods has taken place in the teaching of English as a second or foreign language and this is reflected in published materials. They are the product of a remarkable and very specialised form of educational publishing by a small group of British publishers (notably Longman, Macmillan and Oxford University Press) – remarkable because many of the textbooks and materials published are intended for use all over the world: indeed, some of them are sold into almost every country in the world. These publishing opportunities have arisen from the tremendous demand for a knowledge of the English language which has expanded steadily since the Second World War and is still expanding, a phenomenon usually referred to as 'the growth of English as a world language'. In 1965 it was estimated that 66.5 per cent of world output of writing (first publication) on scientific and technical subjects was in English, and in 1966 it was estimated that 54 per cent of the world's trading communication was in the English language. Just as French was, and to some extent still is, the language of diplomacy, so in the second half of the twentieth century English is the language of science, technology and business.

It is a phenomenon not much in the British public mind; and the work of the agencies concerned, and of the publishers, in the field of English language teaching ('ELT') is certainly not well known in this country even though it is a central activity of the British Council. The Council provides ELT skills and services in many countries, and has been very influential in fostering changes in teaching methods which have influenced the kinds of educational material published. Its officers have often acted as publishers' authors and advisers.

For a publishing activity which, at first sight, is concerned with a single subject, the markets and thus the teaching materials cover a tremendous variety of needs ranging, for example, from courses in English as a second language for primary school children to specialised manuals to teach European businessmen the English of high-level trade negotiations. It is a significant part, therefore, of British publishers' total output.

It was not until the 1930s that Sir Percy Nunn, Director of what was to become the Institute of Education in London, started arousing the interest of his colleagues and students in a new subject, the teaching of English as a foreign language. He spoke of three pioneers working in different parts of the world: Dr Harold Palmer in Japan, Dr Lawrence Faucett in China and Dr Michael West in Bengal. And these three were indeed the first of a remarkable generation of language-teaching specialists who, between the two World Wars, laid the foundations of what is now an educational discipline of major importance. Nowhere is this more evident than in the field of vocabulary selection.

West's investigations into the educational needs of Bengali children in the 1920s convinced him that the most important requirement was for a reading vocabulary of immediate use in education. In West's own words 'in order to experiment in teaching pupils to read a foreign language, it is necessary to have books for them to read. We tried material for English children, but it was no use because the vocabulary was wild, and the beginning books ("Cat sat on the mat") too babyish. So we decided to make our own.' Thus were born in 1926 the *New Method Readers*, published by Longmans, to be followed by the *New Method Course* and the *New Method Supplementary Readers*. Countless children in many parts of the world, and particularly in India and the Arab World, have become acquainted with the English language through these books.

During this period, others — notably Palmer, Faucett, C. K. Ogden, Itsu Maki and E. L. Thorndike — were actively engaged in compiling minimal English vocabularies, at the same time as Henmon and Van der Beke were editing basic word lists for French, Buchanan for Spanish and B. Q. Morgan for German. Whilst West was remarkable for the way in which he kept his eye always on the learner rather than the theoretical word-list, the remarkable open-mindedness of this generation of scholars led to the cooperation, under the auspices of the Carnegie Foundation, of Palmer, Faucett, Thorndike and West in framing a word-list published in 1936 as the *Interim Report on Vocabulary Selection*.

After the Second World War it fell to West to re-work the *Report* to include the data of Irving Lorge's *Semantic Count of English* and publish the results in 1953 as *The General Service List of English Words*, which remains the basic reference work for the selection of vocabulary in the teaching of English as a foreign language

The other great developing idea of this period was that of the 'direct method' in language teaching. The chief feature of this method was that teaching should only be in and through the language to be learnt. Naturally this meant the exclusion of the pupils' own language from the textbooks. Although the more extreme versions of this method have disappeared, it remains a fundamental feature of most contemporary language teaching that the 'target' language is the language used by the pupils.

The language teaching methodology which West pioneered was limited particularly in two ways. It was concerned exclusively with the *written* word, and the criteria for ordering the introduction of the new language to pupils were based firmly on vocabulary selection. Since 1945 and particularly during the last fifteen to twenty years the 'revolution in methods' has been concerned with developing the teaching of the *spoken* language, particularly in the initial stages, and with ordering the introduction of the language by criteria not only concerned with vocabulary but, more important, with the 'structures' of the language. These changes have come about under the influence of the developing 'science' of linguistics, especially British linguistics, and even more especially of the ideas associated with the British linguist J. R. Firth. A third major feature of the ELT revolution in methods has been the particularly Firthian idea of 'context' – that, to over-simplify, language always 'takes place' in a situation and its meaning is (or is likely to be) dependent on the situation. This has led to ideas of 'situational' language teaching which, in turn, have greatly affected the nature of ELT textbooks and other teaching materials. These are now much more highly illustrated to depict the 'situation' in which the language being taught can be 'seen' to be taking place. Increasingly, slides and filmstrips provide the visual element and discs or tapes the spoken language. Thus the term 'audio-visual' has a very special and precise significance in relation to language teaching and the whole story of inter-related change provides a remarkable example of the development of ideas in relation to the availability of technologies.

Among the growing number of writers who have expressed these developments in textbooks and other learning materials are W. Stannard Allen, author of *Living English Structure* (a book published by Longmans in 1955, and known by learners of English all over the world) and *Living English for the Arab World* (with Ralph Cooke); A. S. Hornby, author of the *Oxford Progressive English Course for Adult Learners* and of a major dictionary specially prepared for foreign learners of English, both published by Oxford University Press; and L. G. Alexander, author of *New Concept English* and many other ELT materials published by Longman.*

* The Company's imprint was changed in 1968, see p. 28.

Most of these materials were published for a 'global' market
More recently, under the further influence of developing ideas
in language teaching, there has been an increasing demand
that ELT materials should be specific to the country and language
of the learner (not, of course, necessarily the same thing) and
also to the purpose for which the language is being learnt.
Publishers have had to adapt their approach to these requirements
on the one hand, as in other 'overseas' educational publishing,
by a shift of base for publishing operations and on the other by
the greatly increased production of materials for the teaching
of English for special purposes, for example English for
engineers or English for aviation.

It is a surprising field and a very special feature of British
publishing. Not the least surprising thing about it is that ELT
methodologies and the publishing associated with them were
for many years well ahead, in their development of other modern
language teaching in Britain itself and the rest of Europe. Indeed,
to some extent they still are. 'Traditional' modern language teaching textbooks are still quite widely used in Britain based on
teaching through 'grammar' and 'translation'. This is the
reverse of the traditional (though changing) relationship between
'home' and 'overseas' educational publishing. When so much is
'transitional', the future historian of education in the developing
world, like the historian of education in Britain, will have to pay
more attention to processes than landmarks and to those varying,
sometimes contrasting, rates of change which always need to be
analysed with care.

TONY BECHER and BRIAN YOUNG

Planning for change

MANY OF the changes of style and methodology which have taken place in education have been unplanned, particularly changes within the classroom itself. For generations the emphasis lay inevitably on the acceptance of authority, on readiness for discipline (becoming self-discipline in due course, it was to be hoped), and on the ability of the pupil to subordinate immediate interests and wishes to long-term hopes and aspirations. Meanwhile, the rod was available; there was no sweetening of lessons by pictures or other means; and the child was treated as a small adult rather than as a being at his own particular stage of development with his own readiness to absorb concepts that are appropriate for him.

When teachers and administrators dip into textbooks, as all do at some time or another, they must find in these some impression of a teaching style. It is an inadequate one, probably, since the printed word is bound to be a distorted copy of the life and activity of a classroom: what is written cannot fully represent what is done and said. Yet, of all dipsticks, the quick look over the pages of a book is the one that is most satisfactory for those who are trained in the literary tradition. So it is natural that amateurs, as well as scholars and historians of education, should form their judgments on past, present, and even future, classrooms by some reference to school textbooks (which are a more convenient guide than school visits), and that their views about the changing pattern of education should interact with their impressions of the books which teachers and pupils use.

The Child's Guide, described in the last chapter, may be taken, not unfairly, to be an example of a style of teaching which has flourished more greatly than we allow during the past four hundred years – indeed for longer than that if we suppose that it had its roots in the medieval trivium (an approach to learning which was quite recently defended with vigour by Miss Dorothy Sayers, who claimed that memorising rather than understanding was the proper occupation for what she called the 'eeny-meeny-miny-mo' stage). The catechism, which appeared in 1549, is the form in which this style of learning is perhaps best known to the twentieth century. But the catechism and *The Child's Guide* are not isolated instances: other books in the intervening three centuries, like Andrew Tooke's *Pantheon* (1698), show that facts learnt by rote and delivered by set question and answer were the continuing diet of school boys.

In origin, this method looks very like dialectic, but dialectic which has become grammar. Answers which should have been given spontaneously in a viva voce examination are learnt by heart, a test which may seem to an older pupil to be an end in itself; in short, it is perhaps an old enemy – cramming for the examination. Another obvious scapegoat for this method is Latin grammar: for in this, as for the multiplication tables, there was no alternative to sheer memorising, and it must have been natural, in days when future prime ministers learnt their paradigms without seeing rhyme or reason for what they were doing, to extend so fine a system to other subjects which were less well suited by it.* Young ladies with *The Child's Guide* before them might know no Latin, but they could imbibe science and geography and history just as painfully as their brothers learnt their irregular verbs; and the effect on their characters and industry in later life was doubtless just as pleasing. To sum up, the essence of the style represented by the catechism and *The Child's Guide* and many another school primer is memory rather than understanding; the core of it is discipline rather than delight; the connection between different facts is not well established; items of information are thrown out in a most disorderly stream; and any deviation from the set text brings disaster.

Many other books – indeed, so large a majority of all textbooks ever published that it would be idle to cite names – illustrate the method of lecture rather than catechism. Throughout, the teacher's approach to the learner is clearly that of filling a pot rather than kindling a fire. The implements used by the teacher, and in particular the textbook, are of course only a part of his armoury, and it would be only fair to admit that, in all periods, the lecture and the textbook have been, as it were, the meat of the meal; what else has been allowed, through questioning and discussion and free writing, must have varied enormously from teacher to teacher, and it is important to bear in mind that the vegetables and the pudding existed, even where the traces of them are harder to find for those who look back. But, whatever cautions are needed, the overwhelming impression one gains from textbooks of the past is that the business of school education was to transfer information as forcibly as possible from the older to the younger mind.

* The development of the teaching of Latin and its place in the curriculum are discussed in Robert Ogilvie 'Latin for yesterday', pp. 219–244.

No one can deny that this old system had its successes; indeed, it was in many ways too successful, since in general it was used on a clientele that was too captive, by our way of thinking, and too well motivated. An élite that is clever at memorising and likely to move into positions of power and influence later on can all too easily perpetuate the school situation which it has to thank for its own success, and keep static a world in which school books make no concessions but shape again and again docile and capable minds. It may not be absurd to quote the words of Gaisford, which have often been ridiculed but must originally have been pronounced in seriousness: 'The chief advantages of a classical education are that it enables you to look down upon those who have not shared its benefits and also fits you for places of emolument both in this world and in that which is to come.'

Yet, despite absurdities which are all too apparent to the egalitarian, the old system also had virtues still warmly and rightly praised by élitists: for example, Lord Snow writing in *The Times Literary Supplement* (9 July 1970) expressed a feeling which is still common among those who teach the ablest pupils when he said:

But what ought they — that is, the most academically skilful — to study in depth? Here it is foolish to lay down general rules, except maybe to say this. There are some mental exercises which become effectively impossible in later life. If you don't study hard subjects before you have graduated, you never will. And without the rigour of hard subjects, and the effect of a minority devoting themselves to them, the whole mental climate will soon become altogether too relaxing. Imagination is vital, but you breathe it in your own private air. Relevance you find for yourself if you are a human being. But intellectual rigour you don't, unless you are disciplined beyond the limits of most men.

There is some truth in such an argument when what matters is the education of the top 5 per cent, but as soon as a country really cares about the education of the remaining 95 per cent, textbooks must begin to reflect a quite different tradition of education. It may well be, that in so doing, they will also provide a better training for the top 5 per cent, but that remains a matter which is fiercely disputed. There is no easy answer when the education and career of the ablest pupils form self-fulfilling prophecies of a peculiarly intractable kind.

The different tradition, of trying to work with the grain rather than against the grain, has been alive throughout the centuries, though it is perhaps more often seen in the writings of would-be reformers about education than in the books produced for children to use in the classroom. From Ascham onwards, those who have discussed education have often emphasised that children learn better when they like what they are doing, when they find it interesting, when they can slot it into their scheme of things, when they are actively involved in the process. The Chinese proverb, much recalled in recent years, which says 'I hear and I forget; I see and I remember; I do and I understand', relates an experience which must be so common that it can never be wholly dismissed. But how to provide for the seeing and the doing? Comenius in the seventeenth century stressed pictures as a means of seeing. His *Orbis Sensualium Pictus* was a famous forerunner of the modern illustrated text, illuminating every statement with a reference to an accompanying picture. Long before Marshall McLuhan, this early product of the Gutenberg age had propounded, and put into practice, the thesis that anyone who has seen a pictorial image 'can remember it more easily than if it has been described to him six hundred times'.

Pictures took a long time to reach the generality of school books and to affect those pages of close print which must often

Two pages from Comenius's Orbis Sensualium Pictus, *1746 edition.* (*Bodleian Library*)

have appalled young eyes – and indeed older eyes too. This was partly, no doubt, because pictures were for children, and a strong distinction was drawn between the amusement proper to the nursery and the instruction proper to education itself. When you became a pupil you put away childish things, and you learnt (what indeed the well-conducted nursery had already taught) that the way ahead lay not in following easy and obvious inclinations but in pursuing painfully a road that wound up hill all the way. The discipline counted for more than the delight. Yet the slow coming of pictures was not solely due to a belief that painful learning was good for the soul; it was also due to technical problems – the difficulty of reproducing good illustrations and the convenient way in which printed books made for 'hearing with the eyes' rather than for true seeing and doing. Other implements of the classroom, such as the slate and the copybook, made for imitative work than for imaginative or creative work.

Technical advance, coinciding with a kinder view of education, opened up new possibilities in the first half of the twentieth century. Pictures and diagrams and maps, with all the appeal that they could make, contributed to the 'seeing'; cheaper materials, and a readiness to use even the old pen and paper in a less rigidly

Science lesson at Rosendale School, Dulwich, 1897. (*GLC Photograph Library*)

controlled manner, helped the 'doing'. It was just in time. During the century which followed the Education Act of 1870 there was an accelerating emphasis on giving a good education to the mass of average pupils for whom the old methods could never have produced anything but despair and a sense of futility. The process is, of course, by no means completed: nevertheless, even before the Second World War, enough changes had taken place in the school textbook (often quickly and with no fuss) to make it certain that the arrival of other aids to education than the printed word would be used inventively and with an awareness of their possibilities, rather than dismissed as a tiresome distraction.

It was all a slower process than might have been expected. A careful look at twentieth-century textbooks may well breed surprise at how little school books have changed, in an era of enormous change, rather than satisfaction at the speed with which education adapted itself to new needs and new demands. The reasons for conservatism in all this are not hard to find. The most respectable reason is that, for those who have learnt to use it well and who have grown up within the tradition, the printed word remains outstandingly efficient: it enables the learner to move at his own pace, to skate quickly over what he knows already, to digest thoroughly what is new and important to him. Anyone who has chafed at the 'lockstep' pace which class teaching or a film or a programme imposes will know the feeling that a good book could do the work much more effectively in half the time or double the time as the case may be. And the opportunities which a book gives both for preliminary tasting, for seeing whether it 'speaks to your own condition', and for re-reading, savouring old experience afresh, are not matched by any other medium. Many an undergraduate has quickly found that books can in many cases give him what he needs better than lectures; so, many teachers must have found that, as they prepare themselves, nothing equals the book. It is natural enough, therefore, that they should project a preference for the most sophisticated type of communication on to children who do not yet respond to the close-packed paragraph with vigour, but rather feel inert as they read. There are of course situations, created by adults, in which pupils, too, may welcome the dry precision of the book: texts often seem much the most efficient instrument for the immediate task of passing examinations, when to learn pages 70–85 is often to make sure that at least one question will be satisfactorily dealt with. This is particularly the case when the main role of the teacher is seen as that of filling a pot rather than kindling a fire.

Another factor which makes for the retention of plain textbooks is the old instinct, 'What was good enough for me is good enough for them'. There is some rightness in this instinct, though not as much as is supposed by teachers, who are almost always those who have profited and succeeded by means of the system as it was. But there is also some laziness and timidity, since to launch into new ways of teaching which differ from those which the teacher has experienced is to risk not only extra labour but to enter an uncharted world where the adult does not know any longer what it is like to be the toad beneath the harrow. There is pride also in the attitude: everyone is familiar with people who praise the methods which made them what they are – with the implication that they could not possibly be better.

Then again there is the ingrained feeling that reforms are a matter of theory, while books and examinations are the realities of day-to-day school life. It is striking to see how often obviously sensible theories have been propounded by educational reformers and have met with general assent, only to fail in their effect because of this old division between principle and practice. It looks as though reforms must be given bodily form in the tools of the classroom before they bring about any real change. All the right things were said, sometimes for the second or third time, in the first fifty years of the present century; yet, until these ideas were reflected in the textbooks which were used, they remained simply ideas to which lip service was paid rather than ideas which were seminal, producing a real crop in the ordinary classroom.

Finally, there were the practical reasons which always militate against change. Publishers, no less than teachers, like what they have: long runs and reprints are profitable;* the temptation to hold fast to that which is good must be strongest when the conventional also proves in every way to be so acceptable.

All these considerations were buttressed by the lingering feeling that what was difficult was also best. With many a sidelong glance at the United States, with many a horror story about the terrible dilution of true learning which took place when children's enjoyment of work was given precedence, the average

*See above, pp. 381–383.

*Morden Mount Primary School, London
1971. (GLC Photograph Library)*

*Class I Infants, Batley Parish Church
School, 1937. (Museum of the History
of Education, Leeds)*

teacher between the wars continued, whatever his personal style in the classroom might be, to use textbooks which (despite better printing and better illustrations) had close affinities with those of the past.

The last few years, however, have seen remarkable changes in the classroom, changes which have been and will be reflected increasingly in the new kinds of printed materials which publishers produce, as well as in the other implements which are used in the process of education. The dawn of change was seen, naturally enough, in the primary schools. Young children are readily acknowledged to be something other than small adults as the findings of the psychologists become widely known; immediate targets, in the form of examinations, are less imminent for teachers and pupils in primary schools, especially where the 11+ (intended in any case, to be a test of aptitude rather than achievement) has been abolished; and primary teachers, being less subject-centred than those in secondary schools, can also afford to be more venturesome in their approach. So it was that, even before the era of rapid and continuous change in the early 1960s, infant teaching was gradually freed from the old tyranny of the three Rs, and emerged into the bustling, energetic and colourful primary school scene later to be portrayed in the Plowden Report. This major change has, of course, had a profound effect on the type of school books that publishers have produced. Above all, it has broken down the old division between nursery reading for pleasure and school reading for profit. Books which cater for the nursery years try to make play meaningful, and those which cater for the primary school aim to make work playful.

In the secondary modern schools, too, a new spirit was abroad in the years following 1945. Dedicated teachers saw, here and there, that relevance must precede (and sometimes preclude) drill; better visual aids led to pictures which moved, first through the film projector and later through the television screen; and activities were devised to draw pupils out of passivity into participation. A major effort to develop enlightened school leaving examinations for less academic pupils accompanied and reinforced this change. Though formless still, and barely visible to the observer, there was a growing incentive in classrooms up and down the country to add seeing and doing to hearing.

Yet the process of deliberate and planned change – with

emphasis both on the deliberation and the planning – which began in the late 1950s and early 1960s owed most to curriculum development, the main theme of this essay. This movement, starting with the work of the Physical Sciences Study Committee in the United States and travelling across the Atlantic to establish itself in the Nuffield Science Programme and the School Mathematics Project in Britain, is now familiar to most teachers. Its origins lay partly (and strangely) in the Russian Sputnik achievement; they lay also in a more general concern that young people were turning against science and mathematics in schools. There were obvious dangers if the heirs to an age dominated by technological progress should begin to dismiss these key subjects as boring and irrelevant. A scapegoat was easily found – perhaps too easily. It was the 'out-of-date' tradition of teaching and examining. Most teachers, it was argued, had learnt science in an age when biology was little more than an elaborate system of taxonomy, and when atomic physics was the esoteric pursuit of a few remote and isolated pioneers. To make matters worse, the school examination syllabuses had remained almost immutable in a context of rapid change; there was no incentive to revise the popular textbooks geared to these examinations; and without new textbooks any major syllabus reform was out of the question. Somehow the vicious circle had to be broken: and the new curriculum programmes were inserted into it with a high hopefulness and a scale of funding that enabled time to be properly bought – a rare feature of educational experiment.

Curriculum development started, then, as a move to bring the content of science and mathematics teaching up to date; but it soon became a full reappraisal of teaching method. The inspiration here was the work of a group of psychologists of 'learning', one of whose prophets was Jerome Bruner of Harvard. Bruner himself was working within the general tradition of Piaget's research on intellectual development, and so provided an indirect link with the English primary school reform movement. Earlier attempts to base science teaching on heuristic methods had made little mark, but, reinforced by the new advocates of 'learning by discovery', the curriculum reformers committed themselves to teaching science as a process of enquiry. Instead of presenting the general principles first and then showing by means of laboratory experiments that they worked, teachers were urged to stand the process on its head and lead the pupils to discover the principles for themselves. Instead of sitting passively at their desks, pupils were to be faced with problems and given only the minimum of prompting and guidance. 'Learning by doing' was promoted from a piece of conventional (but often neglected) wisdom to a psychological truth.

The discovery approach had other arguments to commend it. In particular, it could plausibly be claimed that scientific knowledge was increasing so fast that the structure of scientific thinking must inevitably be emphasised at the expense of factual information. After all, the facts could always be looked up in reference books, except in the highly artificial environment of the examination hall, and need not therefore be memorised. Children should be given the opportunity themselves to behave like scientists, rather than merely to learn at second hand what scientists already knew.

There was, therefore, a double task: to replace the more out-of-date topics by themes of contemporary interest and importance, such as the study of energy levels in the physical sciences, genetics in the biological sciences, and number theory and Boolean algebra in mathematics, and also to make a fundamental change of approach, so that 'learning' took precedence over 'being taught'. The need was not only for new topics, which are comparatively easy to bring in, but also for new tools in the classroom. The courses had to be ones in which fundamental concepts could be acquired progressively, and where techniques of investigation and methods of scientific argument were steadily built up and developed. So the old combination of blackboard and textbook, however efficiently it might pump into the pupil the knowledge of others, was to be replaced by a complex and sophisticated range of materials which would enable him to generate his own understanding. Guides to practical experiments, kits of apparatus, background readers, books of questions to trigger off new trains of thought, film-loops to illustrate laboratory techniques or to present difficult and unfamiliar ideas in a vivid way — all these had to be produced as essential elements in a carefully stage-managed sequence of discovery. And because the content and the approach embodied in the new curricula were unfamiliar to most teachers, particular attention had to be given to the teachers' handbooks which, in conjunction with special training courses, could help them to develop the novel skills they needed.

Brief extracts from one or two of the Nuffield Science publications may help to mark the emergent style of pupils' text. In contrast with Victorian materials like *The Child's Guide*, the emphasis lay in working out one's own solutions to a wealth of problems, rather than dutifully committing to memory the answers already provided by an all-knowing author. But if concessions were made to enjoyment, little scope was offered for intellectual idleness. The following three questions were directed at eleven- or twelve-year-olds during their introductory terms of secondary school science:

A gardener was asked to investigate the effect of lime on the growth of sweet peas in a certain sample of soil. He divided the soil equally between two large pots and with the soil in one pot he mixed a weighed amount of lime. He then planted an equal number of seeds in each pot and thereafter gave both groups of plants identical treatment.

Say why you think that he went to the trouble of planting seeds in soil which contained no lime.

You want to find the height of a tall aerial mast set at one side of a level sports field. You are not allowed to climb it, nor to take it down. The only 'instruments' you have are: a metre rule; a piece of thick cardboard cut into a right-angled triangle, the other angles being 45°; a drawing pin that can be pushed into the cardboard anywhere you like; a piece of thread and a small stone that can be tied to it.

How would you find the height of the mast? You may have the help of

---

292

Q. What is wainscoting?
A. The wood of the Dutch oak; it is beautifully grained, and when polished forms an elegant wooden lining for rooms.
Q. But is not the term wainscoting applied generally to all wooden linings for rooms.
A. Yes; cedar, mahogany, and even deal being often used.
Q. What kind of tree is the elm?
A. It is second only to the oak in size and beauty.
Q. What is its wood particularly used for?
A. All purposes which are to bear the extremes of wet and dry; such as waterworks, mills, pipes, pumps, and coffins.
Q. Are not frames for pictures, and other carved work, made of elm?
A. Yes, because it rarely warps.
Q. What do you mean by warp?
A. To swell, or shrivel, and bend as other wood does when it is not dry.
Q. Have not the dried leaves of the elm been used as food for cattle?

A page from The Child's Guide to Knowledge . . . *by a Lady, Simpkin Marshall, eighth edition,* 1838.

another boy or girl to hold the apparatus in any way you want, but you must tell him or her how to hold it.

If we suppose that solid substances are made up of atoms, then some very simple observations tell us quite a lot about the forces atoms exert on each other.

a. You take a piece of metal or wood or almost anything, even india-rubber, and try to pull it into two pieces. It resists your pull. What does this tell you about forces between atoms?

b. You take two pieces of metal, or india-rubber, and put them near each other. They do not fly together, and even if you touch them they do not stick. What can you now add to what you said in (a) about forces between atoms?

c. You take a piece of metal, or india-rubber, between fingers and thumb and try to squash it. It resists being squashed. What does this tell you about forces between atoms?

d. Put together the observations and your conclusions in (a), (b) and (c) in order to make a general statement about how forces between atoms vary, in a solid, with the distance apart of the atoms.

With the beginning of the curriculum development movement came two important changes in schoolbook publishing. First, a wide range of materials had to be produced and this demanded a combination of abilities which no one person was likely to possess. So the work had usually to be carried out by a team of experienced teachers. Some had a specialist knowledge of new areas of subject matter; some were adept at designing new experiments and planning the apparatus the pupils would need to carry them out; and some had a knack for devising problems for homework, class tests and examinations. The straightforward relationship between the publisher and an individual author could no longer hold good. Basic issues of design and presentation had to be settled early in the process of development – which meant, ideally, bringing in the publisher well before the team's work had been completed, or, less ideally, presenting him with a series of *faits accomplis*. Many of the editorial questions the publisher might want to raise had already been discussed and settled by the project team, who were consequently more sure of their ground and less open to suggestion than an author working on his own. Moreover, the publisher was expected to produce and market a variety of items – sound recordings, filmloops, slides and the like – which, even at that relatively recent time in history, were unfamiliar to him and had previously been the business of the specialist supplier.

A page from Introductory General
Science, *Book One, by A. Swallow,*
Longmans, 1950.

Fig. 86.

Float a short piece of lighted
candle on a piece of wood or
cork on water. Invert over the
candle a large jar. A jam jar
serves very well.

Watch what happens and
record it in your book. Perhaps
you think it would be more
accurate to say 'Record all the
things you notice in your book.'

From these experiments
would you be prepared to assert that

(*a*) a candle flame is extinguished if **heat is removed**
from it too quickly,

(*b*) a supply of **fresh air** must be maintained if a candle is
to burn?

Experiment II : To discover whether air is used up during combustion

Float a small piece of white
phosphorus in a small crucible
on water in a large trough or in
a sink.

Caution. This phosphorus
is extremely inflammable and
causes painful and nasty burns.
It is stored under water, and
must be cut under water. It is
moved with a pair of forceps,
never with the fingers.

Cover the crucible carefully
with a large bell-jar with an
open neck. Fit the neck with
an air-tight stopper.

Fig. 87.

*An opening from Nuffield Combined
Science* Activities 4. *Published by the
Longman Group Ltd., and Penguin
Books Ltd., for the Nuffield Foundation,*
1970.

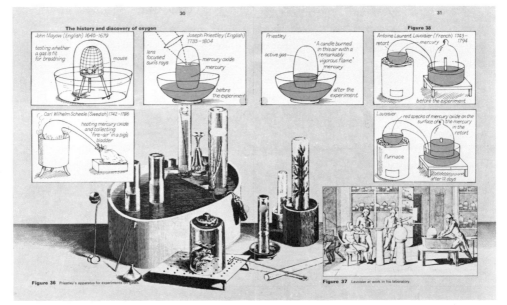

Second, the change from current teaching practice was based on ideas which had never been systematically put to the test: so the curriculum developers insisted that before their materials were published they should be used in trial schools where the teachers had undertaken to comment in detail on each aspect of the new curriculum, to identify its points of success and failure, and to suggest possible improvements. Only when revised materials could be seen to be working satisfactorily would they be handed over for large-scale production. This process of continuing trial and revision in the light of carefully analysed teachers' reports served a double purpose. It ensured that the new course actually worked in practice, and it considerably widened the circle of teachers who were involved in the development work, and hence the number of people sufficiently familiar with the materials to be able to train others in their use. But it also meant that the customary method of producing textbooks, based on the teaching experience of a single author, and published without any systematic sampling of consumer reactions, began to seem primitive by comparison. Prospective customers came to expect something more than the optimistic claims of the author's preface and the publisher's prospectus that a new schoolbook would in fact do what it was intended to do; and publishers became more conscious of the need for proofs made not on paper but in classrooms. As a result, the output of publishers required a new (and expensive) professionalism, whether it was the fruit of a curriculum development project or ancillary material written by some of the many teachers who had been involved in the work of testing. A greater emphasis on inviting teachers to try out textbooks before publication was a stimulus to both sides of an old partnership.

✳

Despite its revolutionary nature, the curriculum development movement, in the first phase of its existence, still left a great deal unchanged. Admittedly, it succeeded in making life in the classroom more active and demanding, and more interesting, for pupils; and because experiments in new examining techniques – which stressed understanding rather than memorising – were a part of every new programme, it had a major impact on the nature and style of public examinations. The whole system, however, was still geared to the conventional pattern of school organisation. The teacher remained firmly in his dominant position: he might

A group of pupils working with the Nuffield Resources for Learning materials at Peckham Girls' School, London. With the help of a wide range of materials the teacher's role has become one where she is assisting the pupils in 'discovery' rather than expounding the facts with blackboard and textbook. (Department of Education and Science)

be less of a solo instrumentalist than he used to be, but he was still unequivocally the conductor of a band playing in unison. Different courses were produced for the academically able and those with lesser intellectual gifts: pupils were still assumed to be segregated in more-or-less homogeneous batches of thirty. Despite the greater emphasis on working in small groups, or getting together to exchange ideas and hypotheses in general class discussion, competition continued to be regarded as the key motive. The assumptions were élitist, though less strongly so than before.

In the later half of the 1960s a second phase of organised curriculum change began. It proved to be based on a number of very different premises from the first. There was, of course, much in common, for the one grew from the other; but the sturdy adolescent was inevitably more confident, rebellious and venturesome than the infant of earlier years.

The emphasis in the first phase had been largely, if not entirely, on the more highly structured subjects – such as science,

mathematics and languages — where successful progress to a
later stage depended on a sufficient mastery of an earlier and more
simple stage. The subject disciplines of the earlier programmes
were, in addition, vocationally important: the national economy
needed its due share of people trained in them. Pressure groups
were ready to point out the existing deficiencies in the way they
were taught, and to argue the case for funds to improve it.

The second phase, in contrast, drew its strength not from economic but from social demands on the school. 'Equality of educational opportunity', the slogan of the earlier reformers, had
meant giving bright children the chance to shine regardless of
their social origins: the economy needed more able people, and
the hidden talents of the working classes must be tapped to
produce them. Unfortunately these talents remained, for the
most part, obstinately hidden, and slowly the realisation dawned
that social handicaps were remarkably effective barriers to
educational progress. Equal opportunities were not enough: the
underprivileged needed to be given more than their allotted share
of help. The notion of compensatory education grew from the
soil cultivated by Plowden and Newsom.

A new solution to the old dilemma of how to make the less
equal more equal began to gain currency — the creation of 'mixed
ability groupings' in which children of very diverse academic
attainments worked together. With the more able helping the
less able, cooperation was stressed and competition played down.
Because the argument was usually conducted in social rather than
in educational terms, 'unstreaming' quickly became a matter for
political controversy, but while the battle raged overhead, the
schools were left to manage as best they could. Those who
attempted to desegregate soon found that the old system of
classroom teaching, based as it had been on the assumption that
the teacher and the textbook were addressing themselves to a
roughly homogeneous audience, broke down altogether. A class
became a collection of different individuals, who might be
brought together as a group from time to time but who, for the
most part, would necessarily work at varying rates on a range of
activities which suited their diverse temperaments and interests.

A new emphasis had to be given to independent study, to
projects in which anything from two to six students worked
together, to seminars and discussions in which a teacher sat down
with a dozen or so pupils and tried to encourage even the least

articulate to have their say. Class barriers began to break down in more than a purely social sense: the timetable could no longer be neatly carved up, with one teacher working on the same textbook with thirty pupils for a fixed forty-minute period. Sometimes two or more teachers came together to manage and plan the work of larger groups over the longer time span of a whole morning or afternoon.

In this unfamiliar situation, classroom materials assumed a position of central importance. They were no longer merely aids to the teacher, which he could call on from time to time to provide illustrations or examples with which to illuminate his exposition of a theme. They provided the essential resources for learning. To a markedly greater extent than before, pupils were required to learn from things as well as from people: from 'study kits' comprising a miscellany of explanatory notes, documents, photographs, problems and practical assignments; from reference books in the school library; or – especially if they found reading difficult – from illustrated booklets, tape recordings, film loops and slides. Some teachers began to develop a tutorial style, guiding students through their courses and giving individual help where it was needed. They soon recognised the need to become efficient at organising a much more complex pattern of activities, in which pupils were no longer arranged in tidy groups all carrying out the same tasks at the same time in the same place.

A shift in emphasis from economic goals (producing highly trained manpower) to social goals (producing citizens for the 'good society') had its effect on the content of the curriculum as well as on the way the school was run. Where earlier the demand for relevance had focused attention on scientific and technological problems and on training for vocational needs, it now took the form of a greater concern with contemporary social themes: there was a new vogue for interdisciplinary studies, largely within the humanities and human sciences. Changes in method and subject matter tended to reinforce one another. It was in the 'non-linear' subjects, such as English, history, geography and the arts, that pupils of different academic ability could most readily work independently on themes which caught their interest and come together to make their individual contributions to group discussion. In considering racial discrimination, for example, no special prior knowledge was demanded in the way that it would be for learning calculus or understanding genetic theory: only a generalised experience of life, channelled through the study of relevant 'evidence' in historical and contemporary documents, illuminated by novels, poems, films, music and art. Moreover, because themes based on current social concerns cut across the subject specialisms of teachers, staff from different departments inevitably found themselves working together as members of a team. The isolation of the teacher in his classroom was eroded by the need for academic collaboration as well as by greater variety in the size of pupil groups.

In this much more loosely structured curriculum, materials had to be devised which prevented the situation from degenerating into chaos. Courses based on 'packages' for individual and group use, containing a sufficiently wide range of resource material to enable pupils to work systematically and purposefully on any given theme, demanded at least as much careful preparation as the earlier curriculum programmes had done. The formula was a similar one, of full-time teams working over a period of years to develop and try out and modify their products before publication, but because the themes they were dealing with were less clearcut, and because the aims they were expecting to achieve were less easy to specify, they could no longer aspire to the same degree of completeness and precision as their predecessors. The materials were more open-ended than they had been before. Where the earlier teams had set out to supply the teacher with most, if not all, of what he needed to introduce a new curriculum, it was now no longer possible to offer more than a basic framework, to be supplemented as far as time and opportunity allowed by the teacher's and pupils' own contributions. The first-generation projects had tended to impose a fairly firm and uniform pattern, with a clear sense of progression dictated by the subject matter, and only marginal scope for local variation. Those in the second generation deliberately laid down as few constraints as possible on the ways in which their different parts could be assembled, built up and used.

One result was to promote the teacher training programmes associated with new curriculum schemes into a position of greater importance. Teachers were now expected not only to cope with new and unfamiliar subject matter, but also to make an even more radical break with established practice than the shift to discovery methods had demanded. They had to become adept at adjusting the materials to suit the varied needs of their pupils; and at the same time they were expected to step aside from a position of authority to one in which the students largely determined their own pattern of work.

Because the materials were to be used in so many different ways and in so many different circumstances, testing them could no longer remain a systematic and rigorous process. The elements which in practice were obviously unsuitable for most users could be weeded out, and the interesting new ideas which had been developed in trial schools could be incorporated. But where in the earlier projects, after a carefully controlled feedback process, the end product could be guaranteed suitable for the majority of its intended clientèle, the new schemes offered no such certainties.

It was not only the materials which were difficult to assess: it was equally hard to evaluate student performance. It was scarcely surprising, therefore, that while the first generation of project teams had changed the nature of examinations but not questioned the necessity for their existence, the second generation were inclined to place their faith largely on 'continuous assessment'. Examinations which depended on an ability to reproduce correct answers to set questions in a fixed interval of time did not easily fit a curriculum which tried to cater for individual differences, and which dealt with complex and open-ended issues. The need was to judge each individual's progress in terms of his own capabilities rather than in comparison with some absolute or average standard: and this could only be done by systematic observation of his work over a sustained period of time.

For publishers the second generation of materials offered new possibilities. Because the centrally produced materials were deliberately designed to enable new elements to be added, producing supplementary items was easier and more attractive than before. Any publisher with a new idea and a group of writers capable of carrying it out could produce a package to add to those already prepared by a project team, or a series of individual items to add to an existing package — so taking advantage of a sizeable market which had already been created. There were also fresh problems. The range of materials was even wider; and, in particular, folders for the use of pupils, incorporating looseleaf documents of various sizes, photographs, tapes and the like, were far more troublesome to produce, assemble, package and store, than the relatively simple collections of guidebooks,

readers, workbooks and visual materials of earlier years. Because
the new courses were built up out of separate units or packages
which could be used in any desired combination, the market for
each unit was no longer assured by the demand for others in the
same series: some units were inevitably more popular than the
rest. In the case of 'linear' courses in mathematics, science and
languages, it had been difficult for a school, once it embarked on a
new curriculum, to avoid buying the whole set of basic materials,
since each element was closely linked with those which had gone
before. Now a school could buy as few or as many units as suited
its fancy. Moreover, because many packages were anthologies of
existing materials, rather than new items created specially for
the purpose, the producer often found himself involved in
tedious and protracted negotiations over copyright permission.

The second generation of curriculum materials did not in any
straightforward sense supersede those produced in the first. The
differences, as has been suggested, were considerable – but the
change was only partial. While considerable attention was given,
in the later part of the 1960s, to curricular changes in the humanities and the human sciences, the teaching of science, mathematics and languages was not, of course, abandoned; nor did the
curriculum developers in these subjects regard their task as
completed. Their continuing work was much influenced by the
new ideas which had now become current. There was, for example,
more emphasis than before on integration between the different
sciences, and a keener interest in individual and small group work
in the teaching of mathematics and languages.

Even in schools dedicated to new methods of organisation,
many elements of class teaching still survived. Teachers were
understandably reluctant to abandon altogether the familiar
pattern of 'chalk and talk', or to deny that it had its proper place.
In the linear subjects some control had to be exercised over
the pupils' rate of progress; to let each pupil proceed entirely
at his own pace would be to invite unmanageable complications.
Even in the more loosely structured curricula characteristic
of the second generation, groups had to be brought together from
time to time to round off one topic and embark upon the next
in sequence, or to enable the teacher to supplement the available
materials with his own explanations of difficult points. The
emphasis on pupils learning rather than on teachers teaching
reflected a gradual rather than an abrupt shift in direction.

*

In the early 1970s most schools are still assimilating the results of the first two waves of curriculum development. But a third generation is already in its infancy, again drawing its characteristics from a subtly different environment. It is possible to make a number of projections into the future, recognising that there are important choices to be made. In the United States there is growing interest in experiments which pursue the idea of individualised learning to an extreme where the school no longer exists as the institution we know today. Its role is more like that of a health clinic: pupils report there periodically for check-ups on their progress and for prescriptions geared to their current needs, but spend a major part of their time studying at home, or in the local library, or even in the adult working community. While the ideas behind this movement may seem to many bizarre and far-fetched, it has at least a respectable tradition to draw on. This time, however, the tradition has not filtered up from the primary schools but down from adult education.

The provision of continuing educational opportunities for those who have left the formal system of schools, colleges and universities has always been determined by consumer demand. Courses are only offered where a sufficient call for them exists. Adults are expected to learn only what they want to learn and not what someone else has decided to teach them. Some courses may be refresher courses and others exploratory and enriching, but both varieties can be described as 'post-experience' courses in which the experience itself is an important factor. The familiar traditions of adult evening classes are now beginning to change. Given that opportunities have to be created on a massive scale for people to bring their existing professional skills up to date, or to acquire entirely new ones, as well as to develop worthwhile pursuits to occupy an increasing amount of leisure, it no longer seems feasible to increase the number of experienced tutors or of adult institutes. Much learning can take place in the normal working environment or in the home, with the help of television and correspondence tuition, as well as a number of more recently developed techniques. Courses for adults have to develop a new style of their own, where personal contact with teachers and fellow students is interleaved with prolonged periods of study drawing on carefully designed self-instructional materials. Learning sequences need to be planned in relatively small units (representing perhaps ten hours or so of work), at the end of which the student can assess his own progress by means of an appropriate test, and decide for himself the areas in which he needs to do some further work.

This perhaps amounts to little more than what has been a traditional pattern of study in universities: but the elements in each learning sequence have to be systematically planned, and a great deal more material must be provided on which the student can draw. Units must be smaller than the conventional course of lectures, so that the student can himself choose the point at which he wants to stop pursuing one theme and take up a new one. The methods of 'learning at a distance' exemplified by the Open University and other bodies concerned with further education are already proving effective with older students; those, therefore, who argue that there are virtues in adopting a similar approach at the secondary school level may have a stronger case than has yet been acknowledged. The more extreme American progressives are unlikely to achieve their goal of complete 'de-schooling' for pupils of any age, but the demand for broader curricula in the sixth form has already led some schools to experiment with the cafeteria principle at the upper levels, and the day may not be far off when it is tried with younger age groups.

If this trend does indeed gather strength in the third generation of curriculum programmes, it will have far-reaching implications for teachers, for curriculum development agencies, and for educational publishers. Resting as it does on the demand

An Open University student, following a science-based course, conducts his own experiment at home. (Open University)

for freedom of consumer choice, it will be less dominated by the requirements of the skilled labour market than the first phase of development, and less dominated by considerations of society's needs than the second. It is more likely to be allied to a cult of individuality: it may vindicate the long defended (but also much ignored) thesis that the purpose of education is to foster the growth of individual personality and to provide better opportunities for self-expression. In a society with a larger ration of leisure, there will be a greater emphasis than before on developing creativity in thought and action: the old demand for 'relevance' will reappear, this time, in the guise of relevance to the learner's personal interests and needs. Pupils will no longer travel along the tramlines of a first generation curriculum, or even in the trolley-bus of a second generation one, but be free to explore in their private cars whatever route they choose to map out for themselves.

A curriculum programme of such a kind would demand a still greater exercise of responsibility by the teacher, but would allow him less direct control. He would have to develop the skills to guide and advise each of his students, to motivate them to learn, to diagnose their problems, and to judge which of any given set of self-study materials would be likely to be most helpful to them. He would also have to know at what points such materials should be supplemented by personal tuition (either by himself or a colleague), or by group or seminar work (which he would be expected to lead). All this would mean that he would have to become sensitive to different learning styles, and familiar with the whole range of available learning materials in his field. But he would have none of the satisfaction of exerting authority over others, of deciding what is best for them, and of shaping their destinies in the direct way which is open to him at present. He would be even less like a military commander and even more like a medical consultant. How many teachers in any society would be prepared to adopt this very different role is uncertain, but if the majority of those who teach adults and those who teach very young children have already succeeded in adjusting themselves to it, the change is not unthinkable.

The main sponsors of curriculum development in Britain, as in the United States, have included both privately endowed foundations and publicly funded agencies and they have managed adequately to adjust operations from the first phase of tightly de-signed teaching packages to the second phase of loosely structured learning materials. It remains an open question whether they can similarly accommodate themselves to the more complex demands of developing suitable resources for independent study. Certainly the Schools Council, which has now assumed the main sponsorship of curriculum innovation in England and Wales, has so far shown little sympathy with the advocates of more far-reaching educational change. This is perhaps understandable in a representative body which, because it has to be accountable for public funds, tends to reflect the views and the attitudes of the educational and political establishment. But there are those (and not only self-confessed radicals) who see some dangers in its present educational stance. Professor John Nisbet, in a thorough and impartial appraisal of the Council's work (prepared as one of a series of case studies of innovative institutions for the OECD Centre for Educational Research and Innovation) draws tactful attention to a number of such concerns. He points out in particular that the National Union of Teachers has a special responsibility and that if it wished, it could exert a powerful influence: 'the health of the Schools Council', he goes on, 'is linked with the vitality of democracy in the teachers' associations.' Yet even if one sets aside those considerations of educational politics which are apt to dominate many of the Council's decisions, the fundamental problem of defining the boundaries of curriculum development remains. As long as this is seen in terms of producing packages of materials, rather than of helping teachers to create a new educational tradition (in which materials would undeniably play an important part), the sponsoring agencies will find it difficult to match the new mode of innovative thinking of the 1970s.

Publishers, too, would be likely to find themselves in a challenging situation. In one respect their influence would be enhanced: the provision of study material would play a crucial part, since so much of the student's learning would be dependent on it. A new factor has, however, to be taken into account. The first generation programmes took it for granted that most pupils for whom they were designed were capable of learning in roughly the same way, through roughly the same set of experiences; and even the second generation programmes, though more adaptable to individual needs, assumed a common framework for learning. But once it were fully accepted that different people must learn in different ways, several quite distinct methods of approaching and presenting any theme would be required. Some learners think in analytic and abstract terms, others with concrete and practical examples, others again through visual information: and publishers would be expected to produce a far greater variety of materials than now exists. Because study units would be designed to cover a shorter span than a whole term or year of the curriculum, the costs of developing and testing an individual unit would be easier for an independent firm to meet. There will be less need to underwrite every curriculum pro-gramme with substantial grant funds, since the monolithic structure of the earlier schemes would have broken down into a network of more compact and self-contained items.

At the same time the total market for any given item would be reduced. It would no longer be possible to publish a text which, if it caught on, might be used by tens of thousands of students and thousands of teachers in hundreds of schools: the more detailed the specification, the fewer the people for whom it caters. More-over, methods of disseminating materials are likely to be in-creasingly sophisticated. The old methods of manufacturing and storing many copies of a particular item, and packing them up and posting them to a multitude of different destinations, will seem crude and uneconomic in an age where all kinds of infor-mation can be transmitted electronically from one point to another, and then converted into physical form for cheap and rapid reproduction as the need arises. The profit would lie in creating new materials and arranging for convenient access to them, rather than in the operation of printing and despatching them in massive quantities. Selling books, it has often been claimed, is different from selling soap: but selling opportunities to learn may eventually become more like running a computer service than either of these.

✻

Even if this is a reasonable assessment of what the new gener-ation of curriculum materials may be like, and of the fresh set of problems it may bring in its wake, its effect will inevitably be tempered by the survival of its predecessors. A triangle of forces between the demands of the national economy, of society, and of the individual, has always existed in education, and the three phases of curriculum development described above can be seen as reflecting each in turn. Each new emphasis has been the necessary reassertion of a neglected value: each phase in the process of recent change has had its predecessors in the long history of education. The early curriculum development programmes can be seen as a systematic attempt to capture the most enlightened aspects of traditional teaching; their successors owed considerable debts to late nineteenth- and early twentieth-century pioneers (the Dalton Plan, the Parents' National Education Union and the like); the current experiments with individualised learning hark back to the ideals of the 'Age of Enlightenment', in attempting to give to the many the opportunities which once existed for the few to shape their own education when they were armed with a private tutor and an extensive personal library.

The problem remains (as it has always been) of how to weld the three traditions effectively together. This requires some overall plan for the curriculum, based on a consideration of students' individual and collective needs. To allow them an informed basis of choice, some attempt must be made to offer at least an initial introduction to the main areas of human thought and action. There are obviously certain basic skills – linguistic, numerical, intellectual, social and practical – which must form part of the common equipment which the educational system aims to provide. Most of these skills will need to be developed in the primary school, though continuing practice in them must also be part of the secondary school curriculum. The more simple skills can sometimes be acquired as a result of direct training (it is here that programming techniques can most usefully be exploited); others have to be learned less directly, through a suitably rich environment in which the right experiences are built up.

These basic skills – viewed in less restrictive terms than the old reading, writing and arithmetic grind – will surely continue to form one element in the secondary curriculum. So too will the teaching of subject disciplines – although the emphasis here is likely to be on strategies for solving problems rather than on specialist knowledge as an end in itself. In any case, however the curricular cake is sliced (and it is to some extent a matter of personal taste where the cuts are made), the total number of slices will in all probability be smaller than now. Different subjects will be grouped together in much larger units, so that, for example, mathematics and science may comprise one group of activities, social and humane studies another, and communicative and expressive arts a third. The development of creative abilities through painting, sculpture, drama and music, is likely to receive greater emphasis than in the past. Whereas it was peripheral to a highly competitive system in which academic work was most prized, it is clearly central to a curriculum which seeks to develop individual talents, and attempts to provide for an age of increasing leisure.

Many of the pressing issues of contemporary society do not fit neatly into the pigeon-holes of existing disciplines, even when these are deliberately grouped together in broader categories than at present. It is not enough, for example, to consider environmental pollution only from a scientific standpoint when its social aspects are equally important; and population control needs to be illuminated by genetics and human biology as well as by the social sciences. So, if an understanding of such complex problems is agreed to be educationally important, room must also be found for interdisciplinary work in which the different basic skills and different intellectual strategies, which are characteristic of the natural sciences, the social sciences and the arts, can be brought together in exploring possible solutions. Such problem-centred enquiry would help to unify hitherto unconnected parts of the curriculum. Project work involving invention and design would similarly make for a closer link between academic and practical activities.

These different elements – the learning of skills and disciplines, the development of creative talents, interdisciplinary enquiry and project work – should provide a common basis of experience for pupils. However, the 'core curriculum' should occupy perhaps no more than two-thirds of the total available time, hard though it will be for teachers to confine it so, leaving the remaining third free for the exercise of individual options. The opportunity for specialist study along traditional lines is likely to be reduced, but optional time should enable some to explore academic subjects in depth. Others may decide to use this time mainly to develop vocational interests, particularly in their later years at school; others again may wish to exploit an artistic or creative talent, or to pursue some leisure activity which they particularly enjoy.

Within such a curricular pattern, each of the three broadly different types of curriculum material will have its place; and all three will have to be brought together to meet the varying needs of the individual, the society in which he lives and the economy in which he will work. Publishers, in helping to produce this material and to provide it where it is wanted, will continue to be important partners in the educational enterprise – perhaps more important than ever before. Their work will become more difficult, not easier, as the appetite for education grows and the demands for improvements in quality strive to keep pace with those for increases in quantity. Every phase of educational change has made its impression on publishers no less than on teachers and pupils, and will surely continue to do so in the more complex classroom of the future. Where in earlier times the transcribed lecture or the written *viva voce* was enough, it is now becoming essential to reflect in material form all the aspects of developing educational techniques. The change will be regretted by few: for though the world of *The Child's Guide* may have been, on occasions, a more comfortable one for the adult, who can doubt that it was less enjoyable and more restrictive for the great majority of children?

References

Introduction: at the sign of the ship (pp. 1–28)

1. H. Curwen *A History of Booksellers, the Old and the New*, Chatto & Windus, 1873, p. v.

2. R. D. Altick, *The English Common Reader*, Chicago University Press, 1957, p. 8.

3. Quoted in the *Critic*, 24 March 1860. The *Critic* of 1860 had a number of useful histories of publishing houses, of which that of Longman was the second. It remains a valuable source.

4. B. Little, *The City and Council of Bristol*, Werner Laurie, 1954, pp. 152–4. Little also points out the link between this voyage and the poem 'The Ancient Mariner'.

5. For the changing fortunes of the Bristol soap trade, see Bristol Records Society, vol. x. There was to be concentration in the eighteenth-century industry: the Bristol Poll Books name sixty-three soapboilers in 1722 and only twenty-three in 1784.

6. A phrase of Thomas Carlyle in a letter to John Chapman, 3 May 1852, quoted in Curwen, *op. cit.*, p. 64.

7. J. Lackington, *Memoirs of the Forty-Five First Years of the Life of James Lackington*, 1791, p. 257.

8. See below, pp. 37ff.: A. S. Collins, 'Some aspects of copyright from 1700 to 1780', *Library*, ser. 4, VII (1926).

9. The *Critic*, 24 March 1860; see also C. Blagden, 'Booksellers' trade sales, 1718–1768', *Library*, ser. 5, V (1951).

10. The *Critic*, 24 March 1860.

11. Curwen, *op. cit.*, pp. 83–84.

12. *Gentleman's Magazine*, Sept. 1758.

13. *Notes and Queries*, 26 March 1904.

14. The *Critic*, 7 April 1860. 'Thomas Longman, it is said, was one of the chief exporters of English books to the English speaking Americas. We owe the fact, or the tradition of the fact, to William West, once well known in the bookselling circles of London, and almost the only recent man who has contributed valuably, though scantily, to the literature of his trade.' For once there is a little more direct evidence. The correspondence between Henry Knox, a New England bookseller and Longman, is referred to by H. Cox in 'The House of Longman, 1724–1924' in the *Edinburgh Review*, Oct. 1924, reprinted in H. Cox and J. E. Chandler, *The House of Longman*, Longmans Green, 1925.

15. The *British and Colonial Printer and Stationer*, 24 Dec. 1884, which has an interesting article on 'The House of Longman'.

16. *Ibid.*

17. Lord Lytton, *England and the English*, Chapman, 1874, p. 228.

18. Quoted in C. Blagden, 'Fire More than Water', Longmans, 1949 (private circulation), p. 6.

19. J. J. Barnes compiled these figures and printed them in *Free Trade*

in Books, Oxford University Press, 1964, p. 46. They were derived from the *Publishers' Circular*, which had been started by William Longman in 1837, and S. Low, *The British Catalogue of Books, 1837–1852*, London, 1853.

20. *The Times*, 18 May, 29 May 1852.

21. *Parliamentary Papers*, Commons, vol. ix, 1818, pp. 15, 62, quoted in Barnes, *op. cit.*, p. 5.

22. Quoted in Altick, *op. cit.*, p. 310.

23. Curwen, *op. cit.*, p. 106.

24. Quoted in Barnes, *op. cit.*, p. 83.

25. M. St. J. Packe, *Life of John Stuart Mill*, Secker & Warburg, 1954, p. 448.

26. C. Knight, *The Old Printer and the Modern Press*, Knight, 1854, p. 267.

27. Quoted in Curwen, *op. cit.*, pp. 108–109.

28. The *British Colonial Printer and Stationer*, 24 Dec. 1884.

29. The *Illustrated London News*, 6 June 1863.

30. Cox and Chandler, *op. cit.*, p. 48, where great stress is laid on 'hereditary vigour'.

31. E. W. Parker (unpublished) 'Memoirs of the House of Longmans', 1972, a most interesting and useful account of his own experiences in the House and his contribution to it.

32. *Ibid.*

33. There is an excellent account of Lang in J. Gross, *The Rise and Fall of the Man of Letters*, Weidenfeld & Nicolson, 1969, pp. 132–139.

34. Cox and Chandler, *op. cit.*, p. 65.

35. *Ibid.*, p. 54.

36. *Ibid.*, p. 70.

37. Blagden, *Fire More than Water*, p. 29.

Copyright and Society (pp. 29–60)

1. Cyprian Blagden, *The Stationers' Company*, Allen & Unwin, 1960, p. 33.
2. James Hepburn, *The Author's Empty Purse*, Oxford University Press, 1968, p. 8.
3. *Ibid.*, p. 9.
4. See Paul Fussell, *Samuel Johnson and the Life of Writing*, Chatto & Windus, 1972.
5. *The Oxford Companion to English Literature*, 4th edn., Oxford University Press, 1967, Appendix II, p. 926.
6. W. M. Copinger and F. E. Skone James, *The Law of Copyright*, 9th edn, Sweet & Maxwell, 1958, p. 308.
7. *Quarterly Review* vol. XXI, no. xli, Jan. 1819, 211–13.
8. William Wordsworth to J. Forbes Mitchell, 21 April 1819, *The Letters of William and Dorothy Wordsworth: the middle years*, ed. E. de Selincourt, Oxford, Clarendon Press, 1937, II, 844.
9. Copyright Act 1911, Section 5 (2).
10. *Quarterly Review* vol. XXI, no. xli, Jan. 1819, 210.
11. For a detailed account of the whole affair see T. C. D. Eaves and B. D. Kimpel, *Samuel Richardson: a biography*, Oxford, Clarendon Press, 1971, pp. 378–83.
12. See Una Pope-Hennessy, *Charles Dickens*, Chatto & Windus, 1945, pp. 160ff.
13. I am indebted to Mr Montgomery Hyde for kindly showing me this letter and for allowing me to quote from it.
14. Copyright Act 1956, Section 6.
15. *Ibid.*, Section 41.
16. *Photocopying and the Law*, The Society of Authors and the Publishers' Association, 1970.
17. P. Carter Ruck and Skone James, *Copyright*, Faber 1965, p. 105.
18. Ralph Harris, 'Some issues in political economy', in Ralph Harris and A. P. Herbert, *Libraries: Free-for-All?* Hobart Paper No. 19, Institute of Economic Affairs, 1962, p. 10.
19. *The Author*, Winter, 1932, p. 32.
20. Harris, p. 11.
21. The Government has already appointed a Departmental Committee under Mr Justice Whitford to inquire into the law of copyright, with special reference to photo-copying and tape-recording.

Presenting Shakespeare (pp. 61–112)

1. D. Nichol Smith, *Shakespeare in the Eighteenth Century*, Oxford University Press, 1928. Other references to Nichol Smith are also to this book.
2. Thomas Bowdler, *A Letter to the Editor of the British Critic*, 1823, p. 17.
3. The *British Critic*, April 1822, p. 372.
4. The *Edinburgh Review* XXXVI (1821), 54.
5. The *Christian Observer* VII (1808), 326–34.
6. Quoted by M. J. Quinlan in *Victorian Prelude: a history of English manners* 1700–1830, Columbia University Press, 1941, p. 226.
7. Edmund Gosse, *Father and Son*, Heinemann, 1928, p. 290.
8. Report of the Commission to Inquire into Education: (Taunton Commission) 1868–70, Questions 13, 973–6.
9. John Churton Collins, 'Can English literature be taught?' *Nineteenth Century* XXII (1887), 644.
10. Richard D. Altick, 'From Aldine to Everyman: cheap reprint series of the English classics 1830–1906', *Studies in Bibliography* XI (1958), 3–24.
11. Charles Dickens, *Collected Papers*, (The Nonesuch Dickens, ed. A. Waugh, H. Walpole and others), Nonesuch Press, 1937, II, p. 403.
12. Richard D. Altick, *The English Common Reader*, Chicago University Press, 1957, p. 243.
13. Quoted from Kemble's 'Recollections and Reflections' (1872) in *A Shakespeare Encyclopaedia*, ed. O. J. Campbell, Methuen 1966, p. 634, (under Planché).

The *Edinburgh Review*: the life and death of a periodical
(pp. 113–140)

1. By kind permission of the editors of *History Today*, some of the material
comprising the opening section of this chapter is quoted from the author's
'The *Edinburgh Review*', *History Today* II (1952), 844–50. For the early
years of the *Review*, see also the author's *Scotch Reviewers: The Edinburgh
Review*, 1802–1815 (1957). Ascriptions of authorship of individual reviews
are based on Walter Houghton ed., *The Wellesley Index to Victorian Periodicals* 1824–1900, University of Toronto Press, 1966.
2. *ER* I (1802), 113.
3. (Sir Alexander Boswell), *Epistle to the Edinburgh Reviewers*, 1803,
pp. 4–5.
4. For details of publication arrangements, see *ER* CXCVI (1902), 290–1.
5. For details, see the author's 'The Earl of Buchan's kick: a footnote to
the history of the *Edinburgh Review*', *Harvard Library Bulletin* V (1951),
362–70.
6. *ER* XL (1812), 280.
7. *ER* XXXVI (1811), 283.
8. John Knox Laughton ed., *Memoirs of the Life and Correspondence of
Henry Reeve, C.B., D.C.L.* 2 vols (London, 1898, hereafter cited as *Reeve
Memoirs*) I, 370.
9. *ER* CXLI (1875) 157.
10. *ER* XLI (1825), 464–88. See Jane Millgate, 'Father and son:
Macaulay's *Edinburgh* Debut', *Review of English Studies* n.s. XXI (1970),
159–67.
11. Macaulay to Macvey Napier, 5 Dec. 1833, in Macvey Napier, ed.,
Selection from the Correspondence of the late Macvey Napier, Esq. (1879)
(hereafter cited as *Napier Correspondence*), p. 140.
12. Jeffrey to Napier, 2 May 1837, in *ibid.*, p. 191.
13. Quoted by Walter E. Houghton, *The Victorian Frame of Mind, 1830–
1870*, Yale University Press, 1957, p. 226.
14. Macaulay to Napier, 25 Nov. 1830, *Napier Correspondence*, p. 77;
same to same, 20 July 1838, *ibid.*, p. 262.
15. Macaulay to Napier, 22 July 1839, *Napier Correspondence*, p. 291.
16. James Stephen to Napier, 2 Feb. 1842, *ibid.*, p. 379.
17. Macaulay to Napier, 6 Dec. 1844, *ibid.*, p. 477.
18. *ER* XLIX (1829), 442–58.
19. Carlyle to Napier, 23 Nov. 1830, *Napier Correspondence*, p. 96.
20. Mill to Napier, 22 April 1840, *ibid.*, pp. 325–6.
21. Brougham to Napier, 20 Oct. 1840, *ibid.*, p. 332.
22. *ER* LXXXI (1845), 513.
23. *ER* C (1854), 430–60.
24. Macaulay to Napier, 18 April 1842, *Napier Correspondence*, pp.
382–4.

25. Wensleydale to Reeve, 31 Jan. 1867, *Reeve Memoirs* II, 126.

26. Lewis to Head, 7 Oct. 1853, Sir Gilbert Frankland Lewis, ed., *Letters of the Rt. Hon. Sir George Cornewall Lewis, Bart. to various Friends* (London, 1870), p. 271.

27. Brougham to Napier, 26 June 1835, *Napier Correspondence*, p. 168; same to same, 27 Oct. 1839, *ibid.*, p. 308.

28. Jeffrey to Napier, 27 Dec. 1837, *ibid.*, p. 219.

29. Napier to M'Culloch, 1 Jan. 1830, *ibid.*, p. 75.

30. Jeffrey to Napier, 27 Dec. 1837, *ibid.*, p. 220; Reeve to Tocqueville, 27 April 1856, *Reeve Memoirs* I, 365.

31. *ER* CV (1857), 557–67.

32. *ER* LXIII (1836), 235–6; CXCVI (1902), 306.

33. *ER* XCVIII (1853), 273–342.

34. *ER* XCV (1852), 71; LXXXXVII (1853), 357–8.

35. *ER* CIV (1856), 525.

36. *ER* CXIII (1861), 472–97.

37. *ER* CXIX (1864), 575.

38. *ER* LI (1830), 75–80.

39. *ER* CVII (1858), 177–86.

40. *ER* CXXX (1869), 602; CLXVI (1887), 90–1, 276.

41. Sedgwick to Napier, 10 April 1845, *Napier Correspondence*, p. 491.

42. *ER* LXXXII (1845), 4.

43. *ER* CXI (1860), 487–532.

44. *ER* CXXXIV (1871), 235.

45. *ER* LXVIII (1838), 76–7.

46. P. A. W. Collins, *Dickens and Education*, Collins, 1963, p. 21.

47. *ER* CII (1855), 500.

48. See pp. 91–95.

49. *ER* CXXXVII (1873), 263; CLXXIV (1891), 151.

50. *ER* CLXV (1887), 246.

51. Tait to Reeve, 16 Aug. 1881, *Reeve Memoirs* II, 298–9.

52. *ER* CLXV (1887), p. 60.

53. R. Blake, *Disraeli*, Eyre & Spottiswoode, 1966, p. 206.

54. *ER* XCVII (1853), 461.

55. *ER* CXXVI (1867), 541–3.

56. See pp. 175, 178ff.

57. *ER* CXXXII (1870), 565–93.

58. *ER* CXXXIX (1874), 557–70.

59. *ER* CXXXIX (1874), 93–129.

60. *ER* CLI (1880), 258–76.

61. *ER* CLI (1880), 553–6.

62. *ER* CLXIII (1886), 275–83.

63. *ER* CLXIII (1886), 563–4; CLXIV (1886), 289–91.

64. *ER* CLXVI (1887), 264–74.

65. *ER* CCIV (1906), 274–305.

66. *ER* cciv (1906), 391–4.
67. *ER* ccxx (1914), 468–9.
68. *ER* ccxxxxi (1925), 187–96.
69. *ER* ccxxviii (1918), 295.

Disraeli's *Endymion:* a case study (pp. 141–186)

The Disraeli letters in the Longman Archives are listed there as the Beaconsfield Correspondence (BC) and are numbered consecutively 1–41. The letters quoted from the Hughenden Papers (HP) are contained in Boxes 94 and 235, to which reference is given with the HP catalogue number. The punctuation and spelling in the correspondence has not been altered.

1. See the *Edinburgh Review* CLIII (1881), 103–29. The reviewer was Henry Reeve (see p. 136). For Disraeli's preference for the *Edinburgh Review*, see Disraeli to Thomas Norton Longman, 21 Jan. 1881 BC 38. He always disliked the tory *Quarterly*.

2. *Fraser's Magazine*, n.s., No. 612 (1880), 705–20.

3. Thomas Norton Longman to Disraeli, 26 Oct. 1880. HP 235, E/VII/B/15 (see p. 164).

4. Thomas Longman to Disraeli, 26 Jan. 1877, HP 235, E/VII/A 87; Disraeli to Longman, 29 Jan. 1877, BC/4. Longman had already published a revised edition of Disraeli's *Revolutionary Epick* in 1864 and a volume of his speeches on parliamentary reform in 1867.

5. Thomas Longman to Disraeli, 3 Nov. 1870, HP 235, E/VII/A 105.

6. See Robert Blake, 'The dating of Endymion', *Review of English Studies* n.s. XVII, 66 (May 1966), 177–82.

7. W. F. Monypenny and G. E. Buckle, *The Life of Benjamin Disraeli*, Murray, 1920, VI, 609.

8. The following two paragraphs are derived from Simon Nowell-Smith, *International Copyright Law and the Publisher in the Reign of Queen Victoria*, Oxford, Clarendon Press, 1968, pp. 50–1.

9. Obviously there were variations within each category: for a more detailed discussion of methods of payment, see R. A. Gettman, *A Victorian Publisher*, Cambridge University Press, 1960, ch. IV.

10. Rowton to Disraeli, 17 July 1880, HP 94, B/XX/Co 141.

11. Rowton to Disraeli, 21 July 1880, HP 94, B/XX/Co 143.

12. Robert Blake, *Disraeli*, Eyre & Spottiswoode, 1966, p. 519.

13. Thomas Norton Longman to Rowton, 3 Aug. 1880, HP 94, B/XX/Co 143a.

14. Rowton to Disraeli, 4 Aug 1880, HP 94, B/XX/Co 144.

15. HP 235, E/VII/B 40.

16. Disraeli to Thomas Norton Longman, 7 Aug. 1880, BC/8.

17. Rowton to Longman, 8 Aug. 1880, BC/6.

18. Longman to Rowton, 9 Aug. 1880, HP 235 E/VII/B 3.

19. Rowton to Longman, 11 Aug. 1880, BC/7.

20. Monypenny and Buckle, VI, 552–4 where the full account is printed.

21. *Ibid.*, p. 553.

22. *The George Eliot Letters*, ed. Gordon S. Haight, Oxford University Press, 1955, IV, 17–29, 34–5.

23. *Ibid.*, p. 241.

24. Blake, *Disraeli*, p. 734.

25. Monypenny and Buckle, VI, 569.

26. Blake, *Disraeli*, p. 517.

27. *Eliot Letters* IV, 17–20, 34–5.

28. *Ibid.*, p. 17.

29. Anthony Trollope, *Autobiography*, 1883, Oxford, Worlds Classics ed., 1923, pp. 332–4.

30. Robert L. Patten, 'The fight at the top of the tree: *Vanity Fair* versus *Dombey and Son*', *Studies in English Literature* XX (1970), 759–72. I am grateful to Professor Philip Collins for this reference.

31. *Eliot Letters* VII, Appendix 1.

32. Blake, *Disraeli*, p. 519.

33. Longman to Rowton, 4 Aug. 1880, HP 235, E/VII/B 40.

34. Memorandum by Longman, 13 Aug. 1880, HP 235, E/VII/B 4.

35. Longman to Disraeli, 18 Sept. 1880, HP 235, E/VII/B 7.

36. Gettman, p. 232.

37. Longman to Disraeli, 18 Sept. 1880, HP 235, E/VII/B 7.

38. Disraeli to Longman, 21 Sept. 1880, BC/10.

39. Disraeli to Longman, 23 Sept. 1880, BC/11.

40. *Ibid.*

41. Longman to Disraeli, 24 Sept. 1880, HP 235 E/VII/B 8.

42. Disraeli to Longman, 27 Sept. 1880, BC/13.

43. Longman to Disraeli, 28 Sept. 1880, HP 235, E/VII/B 9.

44. Disraeli to Longman, 29 Sept. 1880, BC/14.

45. Longman to Disraeli, 7 Oct. 1880, HP 235, E/VII/B 10.

46. Disraeli to Longman, 7 Oct. 1880, BC/16; Longman to Disraeli, 8 Oct. 1880, HP 235, E/VII/B 11.

47. Longman to Disraeli, 7 Oct. 1880, HP 235 E/VII/B 10.

48. Disraeli to Longman, 8 Oct. 1880, BC/17.

49. Longman to Disraeli, 10 Oct. 1880, HP 235, E/VII/B 12.

50. Cutting attached to Longman's letter of 10 Oct. 1880, HP 235, E/VII/B 12.

51. Thomas Longman to Disraeli, 10 April 1870, HP 235, E/VII/A 21.

52. Disraeli to Longman 6 Oct. 1880, BC/15, *Lothair's* motto was taken from Terentius; 'Nosse omnia haec salus est adolescentulis'.

53. Longman to Disraeli, 26 Oct. 1880, HP 235, E/VII/B 15. The book is thereafter often referred to as the 'bright-coloured young gentleman' in the correspondence. In the practice of choosing a binding for its eye-catching quality, the publishing house of Bentley was perhaps the most lavish. See Guinevere L. Griest, *Mudie's Circulating Library*, David and Charles, 1972, pp. 76–7. For the techniques, see B. C. Middleton, *A History of English Craft Bookbinding Technique*, Hafner, 1963.

54. Disraeli to Longman, 7 Nov. 1880, BC/22. The Queen received her copy on 24th November and Disraeli wrote to Longman:

'I had a tel. this morning from Her Majesty on her arrival at Windsor in wh: she says "I found the kind & interesting gift, for wh: my warmest thanks."

Yours sincerely,
B.'

Disraeli to Longman, 24 Nov. 1880, BC/27.

55. Nowell-Smith, p. 18.

56. See Marjorie Plant, *The English Book Trade*, Allen & Unwin, 2nd edn, 1965, pp. 424–7.

57. Longman to Disraeli, 15 Oct. 1881, HP 235, E/VII/B 14. Longman was not the only publisher to recognise the increasing sharpness of American reprinters. George Brett, manager of Macmillan's New York branch, wrote to London in August 1888 warning the firm of the dangers of pirating if the demand for copies was not met immediately by the publisher concerned. He observed sharply that 'the Americans as a nation are extremely wide awake to their own interests and if you seek to compete with them you must be equally wide awake . . . we are in an enemy's country, and . . . the enemy is ever on the watch to discover and profit by our weaknesses no less than by our successes'. *Letters to Macmillan*, ed. Simon Nowell-Smith, Macmillan, 1967, pp. 214–15.

58. Longman to Disraeli, 26 Oct. 1880, HP 235, E/VII/B 15.

59. Longman to Disraeli, 9 Nov. 1880, HP 235, E/VII/B 19.

60. Longman to Disraeli, 14 Dec. 1880, HP 235, E/VII/B 31.

61. Nowell-Smith, p. 86.

62. Longman to Disraeli, 20 Jan. 1881, HP 235, E/VII/B 36.

63. Danson to Longman, 7 Dec. 1880; 15 Dec. 1880, HP 235, E/VII/B 36a.

64. John Blackwood recounted to George Eliot his relief at hearing there was to be an adjournment of the House when *The Times* was due to review *Felix Holt*, see the *Eliot Letters* IV, p. 280. Likewise Blackwood arranged that the first part of *Daniel Deronda* 'should be published about 15 of January so as to give the Newspapers time to speak out before the meeting of Parliament' (*ibid*. VI, p. 186).

65. Longman to Disraeli, 18 Nov. 1880, HP 235, E/VII/B 23.

66. Disraeli to Longman, 26 Nov. 1880, BC/29.

67. Longman to Disraeli, 14 Dec. 1880, HP 235, E/VII/B 31.

68. Longman to Disraeli, 15 Oct. 1880, HP 235, E/VII/B 14.

69. Longman Archives, *Longman Impression Book 21*, p. 119.

70. Gettman, pp. 112–26.

71. Longman to Disraeli, 9 Nov. 1880, HP 235, E/VII/B 19.

72. Disraeli to Longman, 10 Nov. 1880, BC/23. See also *Notes on Books* CII, 30 Nov. 1880.

73. Griest, p. 22.

74. *Ibid.*, pp. 59–60.

75. Amy Cruse, *The Victorians and Their Books*, Allen & Unwin, 1935, p. 334.

76. Griest, pp. 79, 87–8.

77. Mrs Oliphant, *Annals of a Publishing House, William Blackwood and his Sons*, 2nd edn, 1897, II, 458.

78. Longman to Disraeli, 16 Nov. 1880, HP 235, E/VII/B 22.

79. Cruse, p. 330.

80. Richard Altick, *The English Common Reader*, University of Chicago Press, 1957, p. 296.

81. *Eliot Letters*, v, pp. 264–5.

82. Longman to Disraeli, 22 Nov. 1880, HP 235, E/VII/B 24.

83. Longman to Disraeli, 24 Nov. 1880, HP 235, E/VII/B 41; see also, Longman Archives, *Longman Impression Book 21*, p. 111.

84. Longman to Disraeli, 30 Nov. 1880, HP 235, E/VII/B 27.

85. Longman to Disraeli, 3 Dec. 1880, HP 235, E/VII/B 43.

86. Longman to Disraeli, 10 Dec. 1880, HP 235, E/VII/B 30.

87. Longman to Disraeli, 22 Dec. 1880 HP 235, E/VII/B 34.

88. Longman to Rowton, 9 Feb. 1881, HP 235, E/VII/B 45.

89. Longman to Disraeli, 18 Nov. 1880, HP 235, E/VII/B 23.

90. Disraeli to Longman, 19 Nov. 1880, BC/25.

91. This is a reference to Mr Phoebus's description of the critics in *Lothair* where he declares 'You know who the critics are? The men who have failed in literature and art' (ch. 35, p. 185).

92. Longman to Disraeli, 22 Nov. 1880, HP 235, E/VII/B 24.

93. *Standard*, 23 Nov. 1880.

94. Longman to Disraeli, 23 Nov. 1880, HP 235, E/VII/B 25.

95. Disraeli to Longman, 24 Nov. 1880, BC/27. The *Morning Post* was, traditionally, nominally Tory and the *Daily News*, Liberal.

96. Longman to Disraeli, 24 Nov. 1880, HP 235, E/VII/B 41.

97. Longman to Disraeli, 26 Nov. 1880, HP 235, E/VII/B 42.

98. Disraeli to Longman, 28 Nov. 1880, BC/30.

99. See 'The Newspaper Press', *Quarterly Review* CL (1880), 498–537.

100. H. R. Fox Bourne, *English Newspapers*, 1887, II, 336–7.

101. *Annual Register*, 1916, p. 192.

102. Longman to Disraeli, 29 Nov. 1880, HP 235, E VII B 26; see the charges of Sharon G. Turner to Messrs Longman for December 1880: *The late Lord Beaconsfield's Endymion*, Longman Archives.

103. Disraeli to Longman, 30 Dec. 1880, BC/31.

104. Monypenny and Buckle, VI, p. 569.

105. Disraeli to Longman, 30 Nov. 1880, BC/31.

106. *Ibid.*; *Spectator*, 27 Nov. 1880.

107. Disraeli to Longman, 30 Nov. 1880 BC/31; *Observer*, 28 Nov. 1880, Supplement, p. 1.

108. Disraeli had earlier told Longman that ' "Lord Beaconsfield et son temps par M. Cucheval-Clarigny", a distinguished writer, seems to me a

good book; written by one, who has studied, & thoroly understands, English politics — rare in a foreigner & treating public affairs with candor & consideration. I apprehend a singular contrast to my English lives which abound. I have never read, or seen, any of them, but I collect thy are Grub St. libels — worthy of a Dunciad; but I am fortunately not so irritable as Pope —' Disraeli to Longman, 7 Nov. 1880, BC/22.

109. Disraeli to Longman, 19 Dec. 1880, BC/36: M. Cucheval-Clarigny, ' "Un Roman Politique"; *Endymion* de Lord Beaconsfield', *Revue des Deux Mondes* XLII (1880), 886–907.

110. Longman to Disraeli, 26 Oct. 1880, HP 235, E/VII/B 15.

111. Longman to Disraeli, 20 Jan. 1881, HP 235, E/VII/B 36; '*Endymion* by Lord Beaconsfield', *Edinburgh Review* CLIII (Jan. 1881), 103–29. The reviewer of the *Quarterly* 'article' was Alfred Austin (the publisher of the magazine was John Murray): 'Lord Beaconsfield's Endymion', *Quarterly Review* (Jan. 1881), pp. 115–28.

112. Disraeli to Longman, 21 Jan. 1881, BC/39.

113. *Punch*, 4 Dec. 1880, p. 258.

114. '*Endymion*', *Saturday Review*, 4 Dec. 1880, pp. 707–8.

115. 'Lord Beaconsfield's new novel', *Standard*, 24 Nov. 1880, p. 2.

116. 'Lord Beaconsfield's new novel', *Daily Telegraph*, 24 Nov. 1880, p. 5.

117. 'Lord Beaconsfield's "Endymion" ', *Daily Chronicle*, 24 Nov. 1880, p. 6.

118. Lord Houghton, 'Notes on Endymion', *Fortnightly Review* n.s. CLXIX (Jan. 1881), pp. 66–76.

119. 'The political Endymion', *St James's Gazette*, 30 Nov. 1880, pp. 11–12.

120. 'Lord Beaconsfield's Novel, Endymion', *Morning Post*, 24 Nov. 1880.

121. 'Lord Beaconsfield's Worldly Widsom', *Spectator*, 27 Nov. 1880, pp. 1511–12.

122. *Saturday Review*, loc. cit.

123. *Standard*, loc. cit.

124. *Edinburgh Review* CLIII 129.

125. *Standard*, loc. cit.

126. 'Endymion', *Athenaeum*, 27 Nov. 1880, pp. 701–2.

127. 'Endymion', *Observer*, 28 Nov. 1880, Supplement, p. 1.

128. See, for instance, Blake, *Disraeli*, pp. 37ff.

129. Longman Archives, BC/7.

130. See above, p. 169.

131. *Fortnightly Review* CLXIX, 67.

132. *Standard*, 23 Nov. 1880, p. 5.

133. Disraeli to Longman, 30 Nov. 1880, BC/31.

134. Disraeli to Longman, 24 Nov. 1880, BC/27.

135. Longman to Disraeli, 20 Dec. 1880, HP 235, E/VII/B 33.

136. 'A Key to "Endymion" ', *Notes and Queries*, 6th s. II, 18 Dec. 1880, p. 484.

137. *Endymion* (and key to the characters), *Franklin Square Library*, no. 150, 26 Nov. 1880, Harper & Brothers, New York (by arrangement with Messrs Appleton & Co.).

138. *Fraser's Magazine*, n.s. No. 612 (1880), p. 720.

139. 'Endymion', *Spectator*, 27 Nov. 1880, pp. 1518–19.

140. See Griest, pp. 156–61.

141. 'Publishers and the public', letter from James Griffin in *The Times*, 17 Dec. 1880.

142. Leader in *The Times*, 17 Dec. 1880.

143. Longman to Disraeli, 17 Dec. 1880, HP 235, E/VII/B 32.

144. Disraeli to Longman, 19 Dec. 1880, BC/36.

145. Longman to Disraeli, 20 Dec. 1880, HP 235, E/VII/B 33.

146. 'Publishers and the Public', letter in *The Times*, 20 Dec. 1880, p. 8.

147. Griest, pp. 159, 259 n.46.

148. Letter to George Bentley, 18 May 1881, quoted in Gettman, p. 258.

149. *Eliot Letters* III, 283.

150. Longman to Disraeli, 12 March 1881, HP 235, E/VII/B 38.

151. Longman to Disraeli, 24 March 1881, HP 235, E/VII/B 46.

152. Disraeli to Lady Bradford, 26 Nov. 1880, printed in Monypenny and Buckle, VI, 569.

153. *Ibid.*, VI, 569.

154. R. Blake, 'The dating of Endymion', p. 178.

The View from Badminton (pp. 187–218)

1. There is a brief history of the origins and development of the series written by Watson as an introduction to H. Peek, ed., *The Poetry of Sport* (1896), pp. xi–xxxv.

2. *Badminton Magazine* LIX (1923), 511.

3. Peek, p. xii.

4. The Duke of Beaufort and Mowbray Morris, *Hunting* (1885), ch. v.

5. The Duke of Beaufort, *Driving* (1889), ch. xiii. His account of school life in Brighton (pp. 232–6) should be compared with Churchill's account of his schooldays in Brighton.

6. *Hunting*, p. 147.

7. *Ibid.*, p. 146.

8. Peek, p. xxiv.

9. Viscount Bury and G. Lacy Hillier, *Cycling* (1887), p. 7.

10. R. Pound and G. Harmsworth, *Northcliffe*, Cassell, 1959, p. 57.

11. *Ibid.*, p. 60.

12. Peek, p. xxiv. 'Is there, one wonders,' wrote Watson, 'any new pastime in store which would make as material an addition to English manufactures?'

13. *Badminton Magazine* LIX, 511.

14. The Duke of Beaufort, *Preface* to all the Badminton volumes. Sir Philip Magnus, *King Edward VII*, Murray, 1964, p. 155, mentions a visit to Paris by the Prince of Wales in 1878 when Beaufort was one of his dinner companions.

15. For a different view of the peer group, see A. Sinclair, *The Last of the Best*, Weidenfeld & Nicolson, 1969.

16. M. Shearman, *Athletics and Football* (1888), pp. xvi, xvii. See also A. Briggs, *Victorian People*, Odhams, 1955, ch. vi; and E. C. Mack, *Public Schools and British Opinion*, Methuen, 1941.

17. J. Wells, *Oxford and Oxford Life* (2nd edn, 1899), p. 97.

18. *Badminton Magazine* I, 386ff.

19. Wells, p. 91.

20. Peek, p. xxv. Shearman, *op. cit.*, had a more 'realistic' attitude to professionalism than most of the other Badminton writers. In dealing with rugby union football he challenged the view of the spokesman of the Rugby Union, Arthur Budd (President 1888–89), that one of the main tasks of the Union was to 'throttle the hydra' of professionalism. 'Surely if the Yorkshire clubs prefer to play with or against professional teams, they should be at liberty to do so' (p. 367). 'The Houses of Lancaster and Tudor in vain tried to suppress football, and the efforts of the Rugby Union will be equally vain to suppress professionalism if once it begins to pay' (p. 368). This particular 'realism', however, was belied by the subsequent separation of professional Rugby League and exclusively amateur Rugby Union.

21. A. G. Steel and R. H. Lyttelton, *Cricket* (1893 edn), p. 192.

22. Peek, p. xiii.

23. J. M. Heathcote, *Tennis* (1890), p. 5.

24. *Driving* (1890), pp. 6ff.

25. The *Autocar* (1895ff.) is the best source, but see also the *Automotor* (1890), the *Motor Car Journal* (1899) and *Motoring Illustrated* (1902). 'Automobilists find that provided they conduct themselves properly they do not receive discourtesy from the drivers of horses who are thoroughly the masters of their animals' (J. St Loe Strachey in *Driving*, p. 386).

26. J. Shuter, 'Playing the Game', ch. x of P. Warner, *Cricket* (1920).

27. Steel and Lyttelton, ch. xii; this chapter was written by Lyttelton.

28. Warner, *Cricket*, ch. viii, p. 278. This chapter was written by Warner and R. H. Lyttelton. Lyttelton had collaborated with Steel on the first volume and had written ch. xii mentioned in note 27. Lord Lyttelton, scion of a great cricket family, played for Cambridge in 1838 and had four sons in the Cambridge XI and one grandson. The family perpetuated the great nineteenth-century amateur tradition.

29. Steel and Lyttelton, p. 101.

30. *Ibid.*, p. 105.

31. *Ibid.*

32. The Earl of Suffolk and W. G. Craven, *Racing* (1886), esp. ch. vii; this volume went through five editions by 1900.

33. See B. Harrison, *Drink and the Victorians*, Faber, 1971. This volume ends with the year 1872. There were important changes in the sociology (and design) of the Victorian public houses in the 'Badminton' period after the end of Harrison's survey.

34. Suffolk and Craven, *Racing*, p. 256.

35. *Ibid.*, pp. 249, 94.

36. Shearman, *Athletic and Football*, p. 308.

37. Steele and Lyttelton, *Cricket* (1893), p. 71.

38. *Ibid.*, p. 149.

39. *Ibid.*, p. 273.

40. W. G. Grace, *Cricket* (1891), p. 103.

41. Bury and Hillier, *Cycling*, pp. 37–40. 'No one who knows what our highways were in the coaching days can deny that roadmaking has greatly deteriorated since then.' Cf. Sir Francis Jeune in *Motors and Motor Driving* (1902), p. 369: 'This is an old country, and one of the most valuable pieces of inheritance is the ancient asset of good roads penetrating every corner of the island. New countries may have fine railways, but though, and perhaps because they have fine railways they have not, and never will have roads equal to our own.' Obviously, Jeune was not referring to road surfaces.

42. C. B. Fry, 'Football' in the *Badminton Magazine* 1, 484–6.

43. L. Grove, *Dancing* (1895), p. 405.

44. *Ibid.*, p. 416.

45. *Ibid.*, p. 383. Cf. the lawyer Richard E. Webster's Introduction to the Shearman volume on *Athletics and Football*. 'Before concluding it is right that I should say one word upon that which may be called the moral aspect

of athletics. That their practice tends to encourage self-control, self-reliance, without undue confidence, and a proper appreciation of other men's merits there can be no doubt; moreover, they promote that spirit of good-fellow-ship which enables the beaten man to go up and honestly congratulate the victor who has conquered him' (*op. cit.*, p. xxiv).

46. Steel and Lyttelton, *Cricket*, p. 90.

47. Bury and Hillier, *Cycling*, p. 49.

48. H. Hutchinson, ed., *Golf* (1890), p. 47.

49. *Ibid.*, p. 30.

50. *Ibid.*, p. 51.

51. *Ibid.*, p. 30.

52. *Ibid.*, p. 20.

53. *Ibid.*, p. 28.

54. Francis Thompson's poem has been reprinted in many anthologies.

55. J. Moray Brown, *Polo* (1891), p. 241. He also includes lines by H. C. Bentley:

> 'For the daring turn and the skilful stroke,
> The ever-quickening stride,
> The ring of the stirrup, the clash of the stick,
> And the rush of the furious ride.'   (*Ibid.*, p. 237)

56. Peek, p. 17.

57. *Ibid.*

58. *Ibid.*, p. 3.

59. Even women were not entirely kept out of this picture. 'Among young ladies, too, the tricycle is a source of enjoyment. It is better for any young creature with sound limbs and healthy spirits to speed away over heaths and downs than to pore over a novel under the trees, or even to play lawn tennis on one eternal acre of grass plot' (Bury and Hillier, *Cycling*, p. 9). The ideal of the 'womanly woman' as the proper complement of the 'manly man' was obviously being subjected to criticism.

60. *Punch*, 7 June 1896.

61. *Badminton Library* I, 413.

62. *Ibid.*, p. 234.

63. *Ibid.*, pp. 92ff.

64. *Treasures of the British Museum*, 1971, Ch. 1.

65. Peek, p. xv.

66. Warner, *Cricket*, p. ii.

67. Steel and Lyttelton, *Cricket*, p. 214.

68. C. T. Dent, *Mountaineering* (1892), pp. 402–3.

69. *Ibid.*, p. 403.

70. Bury and Hillier, *Cycling*, p. 51. 'The advertising columns of the cycling papers are full of announcements of photographic materials fitted for conveyance on tricycles. The way in which cameras fold up into impossible dimensions, and so to speak, almost annihilate space, is among the things no fellow can understand.'

71. A. Sinclair and W. Henry, *Swimming* (1893), p. 160.

72. *Fencing, Boxing and Wrestling* (1889), pp. 175, 200, 202.

73. *Ibid.*, ch. iv. 'The Devon style was formerly principally characterised by kicking and tripping, while the Cornishmen were, and still are, noted for hugging and heaving.'

74. *Ibid.*, p. 230.

75. *Ibid.*, p. 232.

Latin for Yesterday (pp. 219–244)

1. M. L. Clarke, *Classical Education in Britain*, Cambridge University Press, 1959; R. M. Ogilvie, *Latin and Greek*, Routledge, 1964; David Newsome, *Godliness and Good Learning*, Murray, 1961.
2. *Latin Teaching* XXXIII (1970), 124–9.
3. R. A. Brower, *Alexander Pope: The Poetry of Allusion*, Clarendon Press, 1959; *Unisa (University of South Africa, English Studies)* VIII (1970), 1ff.
4. C. J. Longman, *The House of Longman 1724–1800: a bibliographical history with a list of signs used by booksellers of this period*, ed. E. Chandler, Longman, 1936, p. 15.
5. Douglas Duncan, *Thomas Ruddiman*, Oliver & Boyd, 1967.
6. They are included in the *Penguin Book of Latin Verse*.
7. *Classical Education*, pp. 91ff.
8. *The House of Longman*, p. 243.
9. See, for example, Donald Davie, *Purity of English Verse*, Routledge, 1967, pp. 5ff.
10. There is a moving account of Kennedy in D. S. Colman, *Sabrinae Corolla: The Classics at Shrewsbury School under Dr Butler and Dr Kennedy*, Shrewsbury, 1950.

Tracts, Rewards and Fairies: the Victorian contribution to children's literature (pp. 245–282)

1. John Rowe Townsend, *Written for Children*, Garnet Miller, 1965, p. 68.
2. Quoted from Margaret Hodgen, 'Workers Education in England and the United States' (1925) in R. D. Altick, *The English Common Reader*, Chicago University Press, 1957.
3. From the third of her articles 'Children's Literature of the Last Century', in *Macmillan's Magazine*, Sept. 1869.
4. Simon Nowell-Smith, *The House of Cassell*, Cassell, 1958, p. 128.
5. From an advertisement in the *London Chronicle*, 29 Dec. 1765, quoted by M. F. Thwaite in *A Little Pretty Pocket Book*, Oxford University Press, 1966, p. 40.
6. From Annie Besant's Preface to *Legends and Tales*, the first volume in the 'Young Folks Library'.
7. From a report quoted in Stanley Morison, *Talbot Baines Reed*, Cambridge University Press, 1960, p. 20.
8. From Arthur Morrison's 'A Street' (1891), reprinted in *Working Class Stories of the* 1890s, ed. P. J. Keating, Routledge & Kegan Paul, 1971, p. 3.

The Paperback Revolution (pp. 283–318)

1. *Don Quixote*, trans. J. M. Cohen, Penguin Classics, 1950.
2. See John Carter, 'The typography of the cheap reprint series', *Typography* VII (Winter 1938), 37. (London, Shenval Press.)
3. S. H. Steinberg, *Five Hundred Years of Printing*, Penguin Books, 1955; rev. edn. 1966.
4. Letter of 22 Dec. 1860, reproduced (like that of Thackeray quoted above) in *The Harvest: being the record of one hundred years of publishing 1837–1937*, Leipzig, Tauchnitz, 1937.
5. Steinberg, *op. cit.*
6. Clarence Petersen, *The Bantam Story: twenty-five years of paperback publishing*, Bantam Books, 1970.
7. *Ibid.*
8. Quoted by Michael Howard in *Jonathan Cape, Publisher*, Cape, 1971.
9. 'Ten years of Penguins', *The Bookseller*, London, 23 Aug., 6 Sept., and 13 Sept. 1945.
10. *New English Weekly*, 5 March 1936, as reprinted in vol. 1 of *The Collected Essays, Journalism and Letters of George Orwell*, Secker & Warburg, 1968.
11. Stanley Unwin, 'Concerning sixpennies', *The Times Literary Supplement*, 19 Nov. 1938.
12. *Ibid.*
13. Margaret Cole, 'Books for the people', *The Times Literary Supplement*, 26 Nov. 1938.
14. Richard Hoggart, *Penguin's Progress 1935–1960*, Penguin Books, 1960.
15. Robert de Graaf, quoted by Desmond Flower in *The Paper-Back: its past, present, and future*, privately circulated, 1959.
16. Petersen, *op. cit.*
17. 'Growing menace of book piracy', *The Times*, 6 April 1967.
18. Montaigne, *Essays*, Book Three, Chapter 3, 'On Three Kinds of Relationships', trans. J. M. Cohen, Penguin Classics, 1958.

Beyond the Book (pp. 319–356)

1. Terry Ramsaye, 'The rise and place of the motion picture', in Arthur F. Mclure, ed., *The Movies: an American idiom*, Cranbury, N.J., Associated University Presses, 1971, p. 41.

2. C. A. Oakley, *Where We Came In*, Allen & Unwin, 1964, p. 39.

3. Quoted in Benjamin B. Hampton, *A History of the Movies*, Noel Douglas, 1932, p. 61.

4. W. K. L. Dickson (Edison's collaborator in the invention and development of motion pictures) 1896; quoted in Kenneth Macgowan, *Behind the Screen: the history and techniques of the motion picture*, New York, Delacorte Press Books, 1965, pp. 85–6.

5. Florence B. Low, 'The reading of the modern girl', *Nineteenth Century* LIV (Feb. 1906), 280, 282–3.

6. Ramsaye, p. 47.

7. Q. D. Leavis, *Fiction and the Reading Public*, Chatto & Windus, 1932.

8. Orlo Williams, 'On book hours', *Nineteenth Century* LV (April 1929), 569, 570.

9. O. H. Chesney, *Economic Survey of the Book Industry*, 1930–31, New York, National Association of Book Publishers, 1931.

10 Competition entry sent in by Mrs M. E. Nodder to *John O'London's Weekly*, 4 April 1947, p. 330.

11. Vachel Lindsay, *The Art of the Moving Picture*, New York, Macmillan rev. edn. 1922, pp. 225–6.

12. *Payne Fund Studies:* New York, Macmillan, from 1933. Chairman, W. W. Charters (then director of the Bureau of Educational Research, Ohio State University). The preface states: 'This series of Twelve Studies of the influence of Motion Pictures upon Children and Youth has been made by the committee on educational research of the Payne Fund at the request of the National Committee for the Study of Social Values in Motion Pictures, now the Motion Picture Research Council, 366 Madison Avenue, New York City.' The studies were designed to secure authoritative and impersonal data which would make possible a more complete evaluation of motion pictures and their social potentialities.

13. Forsyth Hardy, ed., *Grierson on Documentary*, rev. edn., Faber, 1966, p. 296.

14. Margaret Kennedy, *The Mechanised Muse*, P. E. N. Books, Allen & Unwin, 1942, pp. 50–1.

15. Charles Palmer, 'Miracles come C.O.D.', *Hollywood Quarterly* (University of California Press) II, no. 4 (July 1947), 383.

16. 'Movies and a market basket', *Publishers' Weekly* (editorial), June 1927.

17. Quoted in J. Henniker Heaton, 'Wireless telegraphy and Mr Marconi', *Nineteenth Century and After* LX (Sept. 1906), 435–6.

18. Asa Briggs, *The History of Broadcasting in the United Kingdom:* I, *The Birth of Broadcasting*, Oxford University Press, 1961, pp. 14–15.

19. John Reith, *Broadcast over Britain*, Hodder & Stoughton, 1924.

20. 'Can anything be done for American radio?', *Saturday Review*, 31 Jan. 1941.

21. Briggs, *The History of Broadcasting: ii. The Golden Age of Wireless*, 1965, pp. 190–7.

22. 'A Bookman's diary', *John O'London's Weekly*, 8 Dec. 1950, p. 674.

23. R. G. Montgomery 'Making the radio sell books for you', *Publishers' Weekly*, Jan. 1927.

24. Marshall McLuhan, *Understanding Media*, Routledge, 1964, p. 276.

25. *Saturday Review* (editorial), 1 Oct. 1938, p. 8.

26. Quoted in Briggs, *The History of Broadcasting*, ii, 601.

27. J. C. Trewin, 'Plays by television', *John O'London's Weekly*, 12 July 1946, p. 144.

28. Gilbert Seldes, *The Great Audience*, The Viking Press, 1950.

29. Roger Manvell, 'A head start in television', *The Quarterly of Film, Radio and Television* (University of California Press) vii no. 3, (1953), 249.

30. Leo Bogart, *The Age of Television: a study of viewing habits and the impact of television on American life*, rev. edn., Crosby Lockwood, 1958, p. 139.

31. Harold K. Guinzburg, 'Free press, free enterprise and diversity', in Guinzburg, Frase and Waller, *Books and the Mass Market*, Fourth Annual Windsor Lectures, University of Illinois Press, 1953, p. 18.

32. W. A. Belson, *The Impact of Television*, Crosby Lockwood, 1967, p. 282.

33. Gary A. Steiner, *The People Look at Television – a study of audience attitudes*, Knopf, 1963, p. 35.

34. Raymond Williams, *Culture and Society 1780–1950*, Chatto & Windus, 1958, pp. 299–317; Richard Hoggart, 'Mass communications in Britain', in *Speaking to Each Other*, Chatto & Windus, 1970.

35. Quoted in 'Broadcasting as the ally of reading', *The BBC Quarterly* ix, 1954, 2. (Sir Ifor Evans was at that time Provost of University College, London.)

36. Robert B. Hudson in a speech made at the A.T.P.I. Management Conference: 'New structures and new media in U.S. education', 1960; reported in *Publishers' Weekly*, April 1960, p. 25.

37. Charles F. Hoban jnr, 'Research on motion pictures and other media', in *Newer Educational Media* (State University, Pennsylvania), 1961.

38. David Tribe, 'Message ends', *Twentieth Century*, 2, clxxvii no. 1037 (1968), pp. 24, 25.

39. Caleb Cattegno, *Towards a Visual Culture*, Outerbridge & Dienstfrey, 1969.

40. George Steiner, *Language and Silence*, Faber, 1967, pp. 44, 103.

41. George Linden, *Deflections on the Screen*, California, Wadsworth Publishing, 1970, pp. 51–4.

42. Leo Bogart, 'Mass media in the year 2000', in D. Manning White and
R. Averson, eds, *Sight, Sound and Society*, Beacon Press, 1968, pp. 412–13.
43. Herbert R. Lottman, 'Report from Cannes – A. V. Conference: an
industry not quite born', *Publishers' Weekly*, 17 May 1971, p. 27.
44. Ernst Dichter in an interview with Barbara Williams, 'Dichter on
Mcluhan', *Twentieth Century*, 2, CLXXVII, no. 1037 (1968), p. 14.
45. Harry J. Skornia, *Television and Society – An Inquest and Agenda for
Improvement*, McGraw-Hill, 1965, p. 148.
46. Quoted in Leavis, *Fiction and the Reading Public*, p. 56.

Education and Publishing in Transition (pp. 357–388)

1. W. E. Forster, *Hansard*, 17 Feb. 1870, vol. 199, col. 443.
2. R. Lowe, *Speeches and Letters on Reform*, 1867.
3. Henry Moseley, Report for the year 1847, *Minutes of the Council on Education: with appendices*, 1847–48, HMSO, 1848, i, 24.
4. Quoted in C. S. Parker, *Sir James Graham*, 1907, vol. 1.
5. See F. A. Adams, *History of the Elementary School Contest in England* (1882); new edition, with introduction by Asa Briggs, Harvester Press, 1972.
6. R. A. Butler, *Memoirs: the Art of the Possible*, Hamish Hamilton, 1971, p. 100.
7. Edward Thring, *Theory and Practice of Teaching*, Cambridge University Press, 1894, pp. 80, 81.
8. R. H. Tawney, 'Keep the workers' children in their places', reprinted in *The Radical Tradition*, Allen & Unwin, 1964.
9. Alec Clegg, 1870 *Education Act Commemorative Lecture*, HMSO, 1970.
10. H. C. Dent, 1870–1970: *Century of growth in English education*, Longman, 1970, pp. 69–70.
11. G. A. N. Lowndes, *The Silent Revolution*, Oxford University Press, 1937, p. 13.
12. Frank Eyre, *British Children's Books in the Twentieth Century*, Longman, 1971, p. 41.
13. Public Record Office C.O. 96/4. Letter from W. H. Hill to the Colonial Office, 20 March 1844.
14. E. W. Smith, *Aggrey of Africa*, SCM Press, 1929, p. 43.

Contributors

Asa Briggs is Professor of History at, and Vice-Chancellor of, the University of Sussex.

Ian Parsons is Chairman of Chatto & Windus and Chairman of the Publishers Association Copyright Committee. He was President of the Publishers Association 1957–1959.

David Daiches is Professor of English at the University of Sussex.

John Clive is Professor of History and Literature at Harvard University.

Annabel Jones is the history publisher in the Longman Group U.K. Schools Division.

Robert Ogilvie is the Headmaster of Tonbridge School, formerly Fellow and Senior Tutor of Balliol College, Oxford.

Brian Alderson is lecturer in Children's Literature at the Polytechnic of North London School of Librarianship, and Children's books editor of *The Times*.

Hans Schmoller is Director of Production, Penguin Books.

Susan Holmes is a social worker and formerly an audio-visual production controller with the Longman Group.

Tim Rix is joint managing director of the Longman Group.

Roy Yglesias is joint managing director of the Longman Group and Chairman (1972–1974) of the Educational Publishers Council, a division of the Publishers Association.

Tony Becher is Assistant Director of the Nuffield Foundation.

Brian Young is Director General of the Independent Broadcasting Authority and was formerly Director of the Nuffield Foundation 1964–1970.

Index

Location of Longman premises throughout the world

- ■ subsidiary company
- ▲ associated company
- △ company
- • office